THE 2018-19 NBA PREVIEW ALMANAC

by

Richard Lu

Credits:

Additional Scouting and Editing:
Alan Lu

Stats and Information:
Basketball-Reference.com
Spotrac
RealGM
probasketballtransactions.com/basketball
NBA.com/stats
82games.com
nbawowy.com

Cover:
Hayley Faye, fayefayedesigns on fiverr.com
Cover photo based on a photo by Melissa Majchrzak, NBAE via Getty Images

Back cover photo by:
Josh Springer
Josh Springer Photography, joshspringerphotography.com

For all comments, questions and requests, the author can be reached at lurv82@gmail.com. The author also can be found on Twitter as @rvlhoops.

For all of the author's work go to:
www.amazon.com/author/rvlhoops

TABLE OF CONTENTS

Welcome to The 2018-19 NBA Preview Almanac

For the last two summers, including this one, I released an annual edition of my basketball almanac that provides in-depth analysis on draft prospects, analyzes the state of each NBA team heading into the offseason, and includes original research on various team-building topics. After the release of the 2018 Edition of The NBA Summer Almanac, I received some requests to do a preview book. However, I was hesitant at first because I felt the turn-around time was going to be too quick to produce a book that was up to my own quality standards. After some internal deliberation, I decided to do this preview almanac as a companion to the annual summer almanac to offer NBA fans a handy guide into the upcoming season filled with valuable information based on years of intensive research. With this in mind, here are the answers to the two most common questions that you may have at this point.

1.   *This is my first time reading any of your work. Who are you and what is your background?*

I have been conducting thorough, in-depth research on the NBA for more than a decade and I have provided analytic consulting services to help the Phoenix Suns and Chicago Bulls. My main area of expertise in the NBA Draft, which explains why draft analysis covers a significant portion of my annual summer almanac. With the Similarity Based Projection Model that I currently use to analyze and evaluate draft prospects, I made a recommendation for the Bulls to use one of their first-round picks in 2011 to take Jimmy Butler, who has gone on to become a four-time All-Star that has made an appearance on one of the league's All-NBA teams in each of the last two seasons. Prior to that, I provided the Suns with advanced statistical analysis to help them in their Western Conference Finals run in 2010. My primary contribution was that I identified a critical defensive switch in the team's first round series against Portland that allowed the Suns to win the series. Specifically, I sifted through lineup analytics to suggest that the team's defense would improve if Grant Hill was tasked to guard Andre Miller instead of Jason Richardson. With this switch, Hill's on-ball defense neutralized the effectiveness of Miller. Then, Richardson went on to average over 25 points per game for the remainder of the series because he was freed from primary defensive responsibilities. In my writing, I draw from my background and past experiences to deliver the same high-quality analysis that I used to help NBA front office personnel to enrich my readers' knowledge of the NBA.

2.   *How is this book different from your annual almanac?*

Because of the quick turn-around time, this season forecast book is much less writing intensive and a little more straight-forward than the summer draft almanac. After all, I had roughly two months to put this book together whereas the summer one usually takes a solid eight months to produce. Like the almanac, I use a projection model for my analysis, but it is different from my draft analysis system. The system used in this book is called RAFER, which will be explained in detail in the next section, to analyze and project the future performance of NBA players and teams. In this book, I will discuss the results of my analysis to provide you with a guide of what to expect from each of the 30 teams, as well as insights into the individual performance of any given NBA player. Because this book is dealing with mostly well-known, established NBA players rather than relatively unknown draft prospects, I have chosen to explain their resulting projections with simple bullet-pointed notes instead of detailed prose.

As a quick disclaimer, I'm not going to make the claim that every forecast in this book is absolutely going to be correct because even the best projection algorithms can be wrong. What I can guarantee is that, with the information contained in this book, you will get a better sense of what to expect in the NBA this upcoming season than you would have had otherwise. After all, my RAFER projection system applies years of meticulous research to analyze every piece of relevant statistical data to provide you with the best and worst scenarios for each team as well as a comprehensive guideline into every current NBA player's potential performance for this coming season. If you are looking for an interesting, fun read to enhance your knowledge of the NBA for this upcoming 2018-19 season with high-quality, well-researched analysis, please turn the page and enjoy The 2018-19 NBA Preview Almanac.

Introducing RAFER

After finding some initial success with my draft projection system, I wanted to see if I could apply a similar methodology to project the performance of NBA players. Fortunately, due to the work of many different analytics experts over the years, I had much more data to work with than I did when I first created my draft system. This made it easier to develop this forecasting system called RAFER, which stands for **R**ichard's **A**lgorithmic **F**orecast of **E**mpirical **R**esearch. If you are wondering, the way I came up with the name was that I listed various words until I landed on a group that created a plausible sounding acronym that also coincided with the name of a past or current NBA player. In this case, the namesake of this projection system is former journeyman guard, Rafer Alston, also to known to streetball aficionados as Skip to My Lou. Anyway, RAFER is a similarity-based projection model that compares any given NBA player's stats against every individual player season from the 1979-80 season to the present. To be specific, the stats used for any given player are from the last three seasons with more weight placed on his most recently completed season. Then, the system projects a player's future performance based on a set of comparable players.

Like my draft system, RAFER calculates Similarity Scores to generate an appropriate list of comparable players. However, the categories involved in this specific Similarity Score calculation are different because there were better metrics available to work with. The following lists the 16 categories that are used in producing the Similarity Scores.

1. Height
2. Weight
3. Age as of February 1
4. Percentage of Team Minutes Played
5. Usage Percentage
6. Three-Point Attempts per Field Goal Attempt
7. Free Throw Attempts per Field Goal Attempt
8. Effective Field Goal Percentage
9. Free Throw Percentage
10. Assist Percentage
11. Turnover Percentage
12. Offensive Rebound Percentage
13. Defensive Rebound Percentage
14. Steal Percentage
15. Block Percentage
16. Per-Minute Personal Fouls

If you are unfamiliar with any of these metrics, you can find an explanation of them in the next section. With this being said, I chose these metrics because they allowed me to work with the largest possible sample size. Even though there are other valuable advanced stats available like the various plus-minus numbers or the situational Synergy metrics, I omitted them because they simply don't go back very far, and it would limit the pool of comparables to predominantly current players. This wouldn't have helped me accomplish the goals of this system because I wanted to not just be able to project future performance, but also to detect patterns detailing how different types of players aged over time.

After calculating the Similarity Scores, RAFER uses a composite of the most comparable players to generate a baseline projection for any given NBA player. The forecasted metrics that are produced by the system are mostly rate statistics because raw counting statistics are often dependent on the subjective decisions of coaches, which haven't always been rational and are thus difficult to appropriately quantify. For the various newcomers entering the league, I do the following. I use the most appropriate projection of an incoming college players using the forecasted metrics generated by my draft system. I didn't post those numbers in either of the two summer almanacs because they were published before their respective drafts and I didn't have a solid estimation of their expected playing time. Then for players that played in a professional league outside of the NBA, I translate their stats based on calculated league strength values and run them through RAFER. These translations aren't perfect, but they can provide insight into how a player from overseas could perform in the NBA. To forecast the performance of teams, I weight the individual projections based on my best estimate of any given team's playing time distribution, assuming the roster is going to be at full strength. My projections do incorporate injury history to an extent, but I don't try to predict future injuries because they can be a bit random. After all, historically durable players can be injured and players with significant injury history can stay healthy in a given year. Therefore, I only account for injuries if it's widely reported that a player is going to miss significant time coming into the season. From here, I take the projected individual metrics that are most relevant to team success and weight them based on that player's expected role in the rotation to get a base rating for a team's potential win total. Then, I adjust that rating based on the matchups from the actual NBA schedule to get a projected win total that's not so much a definitive prediction of the actual win total, but rather an insight into any given team's expected talent level.

This is generally how the system works. In summary, this projection system called RAFER takes a weighted average of a player's stats up to a three-year period and compares them against all player seasons in the NBA's modern three-point era, the 1979-80 season to the present. From there, the system produces a projected forecast of any given player's future performance based on a set of statistical comparables. Then, a weighted combination of the individual projections is used to gain insight into the potential win totals or talent level of any given team. The system isn't perfect by any means, but it can be an incredibly helpful tool that can give you a better idea of what to expect in the NBA this coming season by analyzing present information against the past to project the most likely future outcome.

The Projections Pages Explained

This section will briefly explain the various metrics and abbreviations that you will see on any given NBA player's projection page. To provide you with a visual, here is a sample projection and I will walk you through everything that you will see on the page.

Player A [1]		Height 6'4"	Weight 170	Cap # $$$$	Years Left #

		Similar at Age	24		
		[2]	Season	SIMsc	
	1	Tyler Johnson	2016-17	856.5	
	2	Cuttino Mobley	1999-00	856.5	
	3	Sleepy Floyd	1984-85	856.3	
	4	Michael Dickerson	1999-00	851.2	
	5	Leandro Barbosa	2006-07	847.7	
	6	Monta Ellis	2009-10	846.2	
	7	Ray Allen*	1999-00	845.5	
	8	Darrell Griffith	1982-83	845.0	
	9	Ronald Murray	2003-04	842.9	
	10	Latrell Sprewell	1994-95	842.4	

Baseline Basic Stats   [3]

MPG	PTS	AST	REB	BLK	STL
35.3	18.9	4.0	4.0	0.4	1.4

Advanced Metrics   [4]

USG%	3PTA/FGA	FTA/FGA	TS%	eFG%	3PT%
25.8	0.299	0.320	0.595	0.546	0.397

AST%	TOV%	OREB%	DREB%	STL%	BLK%
18.6	10.8	3.4	18.0	2.1	2.1

PER	ORTG	DRTG	WS/48	VOL	
23.74	116.6	102.9	0.253	0.354	

[1] – This part is pretty self-explanatory, as this top row provides basic information like the player's name, listed height and weight, current cap number and the years left on the player's current contract after this upcoming season.

[2] – This specific list is the set of the ten most statistically similar players at a given age. The number on the right of the list, abbreviated as SIMsc, is the Similarity Score that tells you how similar the comparable season was to any given player. The Similarity Scores are out of 1000, so a score of 850 would represent an 85% level of similarity. I used 1000 instead of 100 to make the differences between players more distinct. An asterisk next to a comparable's name denotes that the player is in the Hall of Fame.

[3] – This row is a weighted average of projected basic per-game stats based on a composite of the comparables used by the system. The composite consists of more data points than the ten players listed on the projection page.

[4] – This set of three rows are the player's projected advanced stats. Here is a breakdown of what each abbreviation and metric means.

USG%, Usage Percentage – An estimate of the percentage of team plays used by the player while he's on the floor

3PTA/FGA, Three-Point Attempts per Field Goal Attempt

FTA/FGA, Free Throw Attempts per Field Goal Attempt

TS%, True Shooting Percentage – A measure of shooting efficiency that accounts for field goals, threes and free throws

eFG%, Effective Field Goal Percentage – A measure of field goal shooting efficiency that accounts for the additional point value of a three-pointer

3PT%, Three-Point Percentage

AST%, Assist Percentage – An estimate of the percentage of teammate field goals a player assisted on while he was on the floor

TOV%, Turnover Percentage – An estimate of turnovers per 100 plays

OREB%, Offensive Rebound Percentage – An estimate of the percentage of offensive rebounds a player grabs while he's on the floor

DREB%, Defensive Rebound Percentage – An estimate of the percentage of defensive rebounds a player grabs while he's on the floor

STL%, Steal Percentage – An estimate of the percentage of opponent possessions that end in a steal by the player while he's on the floor

BLK%, Block Percentage – An estimate of the percentage of opponent two-point field goal attempts blocked by the player while he's on the floor

PER, Player Efficiency Rating – A linear weights rating developed by John Hollinger that sums up all of a player's positive box score accomplishments, subtracts the negative ones, and returns a per-minute rating of a player's performance. The built-in average is 15.

ORTG, Offensive Rating – An estimation of points produced per 100 possessions

DRTG, Defensive Rating – An estimation of points allowed per 100 possessions

WS/48, Win Shares per 48 Minutes – An estimate of the number of wins contributed by the player per 48 minutes. League average is approximately 0.100.

VOL, Volatility Rating – My personal metric to measure the level of variability within a given projection. A lower number means that the performances of the comparables are within a reasonable range of the projected metrics. A higher number means that the performances of the comparables vary considerably and are either significantly higher or lower than the projected metrics. A value above 0.400 would be considered volatile.

Below the metrics are a series of bullet points to provide a quick scouting report of the player, so you can get a greater understanding of who the player is and what you could expect from him next season. As a side note, the sample projection of Player A does correspond to an actual person that plays in a basketball league outside of the NBA. If you want to guess who this is, send your guess to me using the contact information provided in the credits section after the first page. Anyway, this is how the projection pages work and we can move on to previewing the upcoming NBA season.

PREVIEWING THE EASTERN CONFERENCE

RAFER Rankings

1. Toronto Raptors
2. Boston Celtics
3. Philadelphia 76ers
4. Washington Wizards
5. Milwaukee Bucks
6. Miami Heat
7. Charlotte Hornets
8. Detroit Pistons
9. Indiana Pacers
10. Cleveland Cavaliers
11. Brooklyn Nets
12. New York Knicks
13. Orlando Magic
14. Atlanta Hawks
15. Chicago Bulls

Rosters are accurate as of September 10, 2018

TORONTO RAPTORS

Last Season: 59 – 23, Lost 2nd Round to Cleveland (0 – 4)

Offensive Rating: 113.8, 2nd in NBA   Defensive Rating: 105.9, 5th in NBA

Primary Executive: Masai Ujiri, Team President   Head Coach: Nick Nurse

Key Roster Changes

Subtractions   **Additions**
DeMar DeRozan, trade   Kawhi Leonard, trade
Jakob Poeltl, trade   Danny Green, trade
Lucas Nogueira, free agency   Greg Monroe, free agency
Alfonzo McKinnie, waived

RAFER Projected Win Total: 49.1

Projected Best Five Man Unit   **Other Rotation Players**
  1. Kyle Lowry   Pascal Siakam
  2. Delon Wright   Serge Ibaka
  3. OG Anunoby   C.J. Miles
  4. Kawhi Leonard   Fred VanVleet
  5. Jonas Valanciunas   Danny Green
                                                        Norman Powell
                                                        Greg Monroe

Remaining Roster

- Malachi Richardson
- Lorenzo Brown
- Kay Felder (partially guaranteed)
- Kyle Collinsworth (partially guaranteed) – not profiled, signed right before the book was finalized
- Deng Adel (partially guaranteed) – not profiled, signed right before the book was finalized
- Jordan Loyd, 25, 6'4", 210, Indianapolis (Two-Way)
- Chris Boucher, 26, 6'10", 182, Oregon (Exhibit 10)

Season Forecast

The Raptors decided to push their chips into the middle by making the deal to send multiple years of DeMar DeRozan to San Antonio for one year of Kawhi Leonard, as a way to potentially improve their playoff fortunes. If Leonard shows that he's fully recovered from his quad injury and his play resembles his performance in the 2016-17 season, then Toronto could possibly reach the Finals because they could rely on one of the league's best two-way players to go along with a rotation that goes about eleven-deep. However, the source of the team's greatest strength is also the source of its greatest weakness, as they haven't been able to find a reliable crunch-time unit to close out tight playoff games.

By playing mostly Eastern Conference teams, Toronto can get away with using a lot of sub-optimal lineups because most of the other teams in the East can't consistently put five positive contributors on the floor for a full 48 minutes. Therefore, managing the rotation in the regular season isn't going to be much of an issue because their depth will allow them to handle all of the issues that come with the 82-game schedule. The biggest challenge for new head coach, Nick Nurse is to find a closeout lineup to beat other contending teams in higher leverage situations. As the projected best five-man unit above suggests, Nurse will have to make some tough decisions. On the plus side, he mainly played lineups with only one big guy in his years in the G-League with Rio Grande Valley, so there's a good chance that Leonard could be used in his best position on this roster as a four in crunch-time. However, it opens up the possibility that the team could be using a lineup with two sub-optimal players. Danny Green and Serge Ibaka are still quality players and they would be crunch-time players on most teams, but this roster presents better alternatives. Delon Wright provides more playmaking and efficient overall shooting than Green while Jonas Valanciunas is a more effective scorer and a better rebounder than Ibaka. If the team is concerned with Valanciunas' lack of mobility, then Pascal Siakam is projected to be the next best option. Last season, the Raptors were better on a per-possession basis with Siakam on the floor and Ibaka off the floor by about 2.7 points per 100 possessions, according to nbawowy.com. This is mainly because Siakam is a bit better than Ibaka as a perimeter defender and playmaker.

Therefore, the lineup above with either Valanciunas or Siakam at the five would give them the best chance to change their playoff fortunes because they could complement their two All-Stars, Leonard and Kyle Lowry with consistent outside shooting to space the floor, additional playmaking to improve their offensive flow as well as an interior presence to protect the rim and finish possessions with a defensive rebound. Overall, it's a make or break year for Toronto because it's uncertain Kawhi Leonard will stay with the team past this season, as he's set to be a free agent this summer. If the Raptors can make it out of the regular season fully healthy and they can make the necessary rotational tweaks to play a dynamic, versatile lineup, then they could reach their franchise's first NBA Finals. On the other hand, if they utilize their roster in the same way that they did last season, the results will probably be pretty similar to what they have been historically with a disappointing playoff defeat, but the Raptors could be left in a much worse long-term position with a capped out roster that may be unable to replace a major piece like Leonard, leaving them no choice but to start over and rebuild.

Veterans

Kyle Lowry

	Height	Weight	Cap #	Years Left
	6'0"	175	$31.000M	1

Similar at Age **31**

		Season	SIMsc
1	Chris Paul	2016-17	915.9
2	Tim Hardaway	1997-98	903.3
3	Darrell Armstrong	1999-00	902.5
4	Damon Stoudamire	2004-05	898.1
5	J.J. Barea	2015-16	897.4
6	Jameer Nelson	2013-14	894.7
7	Rafer Alston	2007-08	893.8
8	Jason Terry	2008-09	890.6
9	Mookie Blaylock	1998-99	888.0
10	John Starks	1996-97	884.9

Baseline Basic Stats

MPG	PTS	AST	REB	BLK	STL
32.5	15.9	6.4	4.0	0.2	1.5

Advanced Metrics

USG%	3PTA/FGA	FTA/FGA	TS%	eFG%	3PT%
22.7	0.532	0.306	0.581	0.530	0.392

AST%	TOV%	OREB%	DREB%	STL%	BLK%
30.9	14.7	2.4	13.2	2.1	0.6

PER	ORTG	DRTG	WS/48	VOL	
19.67	116.8	106.6	0.164	0.320	

- In his early 30s, may be heading into a decline phase, still projects to be an All-Star level point guard
- Fairly durable over the last three years, except for a wrist injury that required surgery in 2016-17
- Great with the ball in his hands, good on isolations, excels as a pick-and-roll ball handler, very good playmaker
- Good outside shooter that makes spot-up jumpers and can run off screens
- Going to rim less, more of a jump shooter now, made almost 40% of his threes last season
- Solid on-ball defender, Steal Percentage was at a career low last season, good defensive rebounding point guard

Kawhi Leonard

	Height	Weight	Cap #	Years Left
	6'7"	225	$23.114M	Player Option

Similar at Age 26

		Season	SIMsc
1	Danny Granger	2009-10	881.2
2	Kevin Durant	2014-15	880.2
3	Vince Carter	2002-03	868.9
4	Gary Forbes	2011-12	859.3
5	Jimmy Butler	2015-16	859.2
6	Stephen Jackson	2004-05	858.1
7	Glenn Robinson	1998-99	856.8
8	Paul George	2016-17	852.7
9	Tracy McGrady*	2005-06	848.3
10	Gordon Hayward	2016-17	847.7

Baseline Basic Stats

MPG	PTS	AST	REB	BLK	STL
35.3	21.2	3.5	5.8	0.6	1.4

Advanced Metrics

USG%	3PTA/FGA	FTA/FGA	TS%	eFG%	3PT%
29.0	0.305	0.351	0.573	0.513	0.356

AST%	TOV%	OREB%	DREB%	STL%	BLK%
18.7	11.0	3.5	16.3	2.7	2.1

PER	ORTG	DRTG	WS/48	VOL	
23.17	112.1	102.2	0.179	0.510	

- Elite two-way wing in his prime, one of the best all-around players in the NBA when healthy
- Coming off a quad injury that cost him most of last season
- Volatility in his projection because of the games missed due to injury and his high level of performance in his two healthy seasons
- Excellent one-on-one player that can score on post-ups or isolations
- Solid playmaking skills allow him to be a very good pick-and-roll ball handler
- Excellent spot-up shooter that has made almost 39% of his threes for his career
- One of the best on-ball wing defenders in the league
- Active as a help defender, gets steals, blocks and defensive rebounds at a high rate

Serge Ibaka

	Height	Weight	Cap #	Years Left
	6'10"	220	$21.667M	1

Similar at Age **28**

		Season	SIMsc
1	Raef LaFrentz	2004-05	911.7
2	Rasheed Wallace	2002-03	907.5
3	Brad Lohaus	1992-93	900.1
4	Chris Bosh	2012-13	898.3
5	Channing Frye	2011-12	894.7
6	Joe Smith	2003-04	893.3
7	Andrea Bargnani	2013-14	892.8
8	Keith Van Horn	2003-04	887.6
9	Wayne Cooper	1984-85	886.2
10	Peja Stojakovic	2005-06	884.9

Baseline Basic Stats

MPG	PTS	AST	REB	BLK	STL
29.1	12.5	1.4	6.2	1.4	0.6

Advanced Metrics

USG%	3PTA/FGA	FTA/FGA	TS%	eFG%	3PT%
19.6	0.374	0.151	0.541	0.520	0.361

AST%	TOV%	OREB%	DREB%	STL%	BLK%
6.6	9.9	4.8	19.7	0.9	3.8

PER	ORTG	DRTG	WS/48	VOL	
14.46	105.9	104.5	0.105	0.576	

- Highly volatile projection, not many shooting big men in the database
- Primarily a spot-up shooter at this stage, slightly above league average three-point shooter for his career
- Can still be effective as a rim runner, but is straying further away from the hoop in recent years
- Still a solid rim protector, shot blocking rate projects to be about the same as last year
- Decent position defender, good defensive rebounder

Jonas Valanciunas

	Height	Weight	Cap #	Years Left
	6'11"	231	$16.539M	Player Option

Similar at Age 25

		Season	SIMsc
1	Kris Humphries	2010-11	916.2
2	Roy Tarpley	1989-90	914.6
3	Rony Seikaly	1990-91	914.4
4	Lorenzen Wright	2000-01	912.8
5	Melvin Turpin	1985-86	910.2
6	Joakim Noah	2010-11	904.8
7	James Edwards	1980-81	899.9
8	Jerome Whitehead	1981-82	898.9
9	Cherokee Parks	1997-98	898.7
10	Mehmet Okur	2004-05	898.6

Baseline Basic Stats

MPG	PTS	AST	REB	BLK	STL
27.7	12.8	1.3	8.9	1.1	0.6

Advanced Metrics

USG%	3PTA/FGA	FTA/FGA	TS%	eFG%	3PT%
21.5	0.046	0.358	0.587	0.539	0.344

AST%	TOV%	OREB%	DREB%	STL%	BLK%
7.5	12.5	11.8	26.8	0.9	2.8

PER	ORTG	DRTG	WS/48	VOL	
20.51	116.4	104.0	0.175	0.317	

- Big man in his prime that provides scoring efficiency and rebounding
- Excellent post-up player, ranked by the NBA in the 92nd percentile on post-ups on a per-possession basis
- Developing his three-point shot, shot 40.5% on threes on 74 attempts
- Great rebounder on both ends, blocks shots at a decent rate
- Limited as an on-ball defender due to his plodding foot speed

Danny Green

	Height	Weight	Cap #	Years Left
	6'6"	210	$10.000M	0

Similar at Age 30

		Season	SIMsc
1	Jud Buechler	1998-99	924.1
2	DeMarre Carroll	2016-17	920.1
3	Kyle Korver	2011-12	919.1
4	Brandon Rush	2015-16	909.5
5	Ime Udoka	2007-08	909.4
6	Morris Peterson	2007-08	908.1
7	Francisco Garcia	2011-12	907.7
8	Dan Majerle	1995-96	907.0
9	Garrett Temple	2016-17	900.8
10	J.R. Smith	2015-16	900.5

Baseline Basic Stats

MPG	PTS	AST	REB	BLK	STL
24.0	7.9	1.6	3.3	0.4	0.8

Advanced Metrics

USG%	3PTA/FGA	FTA/FGA	TS%	eFG%	3PT%
15.3	0.605	0.121	0.522	0.502	0.361

AST%	TOV%	OREB%	DREB%	STL%	BLK%
10.0	12.0	2.4	13.2	1.7	2.3

PER	ORTG	DRTG	WS/48	VOL
10.80	102.6	105.0	0.079	0.274

- In his early 30s, his performance in the last three seasons has been down from his career averages
- Low volume, three-and-D wing, three-point percentages have fluctuated over the last three years
- Now just a stationary spot-up shooter, Three-Point Percentage over the last three seasons hovers around league average
- Good on-ball wing defender that actively contests shots
- Posted the highest Block Percentages of his career, solid defensive rebounder

OG Anunoby

	Height	Weight	Cap #	Years Left
	6'8"	232	$1.953M	2 Team Options

Similar at Age **20**

		Season	SIMsc
1	Danilo Gallinari	2008-09	899.5
2	Mario Hezonja	2015-16	888.8
3	Jaylen Brown	2016-17	887.3
4	Mike Miller	2000-01	886.9
5	Nicolas Batum	2008-09	886.3
6	Stanley Johnson	2016-17	885.8
7	Joe Johnson	2001-02	885.6
8	Martell Webster	2006-07	883.9
9	Trey Lyles	2015-16	874.4
10	Shawne Williams	2006-07	870.8

Baseline Basic Stats

MPG	PTS	AST	REB	BLK	STL
22.6	8.3	1.2	3.3	0.3	0.7

Advanced Metrics

USG%	3PTA/FGA	FTA/FGA	TS%	eFG%	3PT%
16.2	0.520	0.214	0.560	0.538	0.367

AST%	TOV%	OREB%	DREB%	STL%	BLK%
6.9	9.8	3.3	11.2	1.5	0.9

PER	ORTG	DRTG	WS/48	VOL	
11.49	109.5	108.3	0.099	0.404	

- Somewhat volatile projection, not many 20-year old wing players in the database
- Better suited for a lower usage role, lacks the ability to create his own shot
- Used mainly as a spot-up shooter, made 37.1% of his threes overall, shot 45.2% on corner threes
- Effective as a cutter in a small sample of possessions
- Emerged as Toronto's best on-ball wing defender last season, very good defender overall
- Can defend both forward spots, much better against perimeter players
- More of a stay-at-home defender, solid defensive rebounder

Fred VanVleet

	Height	Weight	Cap #	Years Left
	6'0"	195	$8.654M	1

Similar at Age 23

		Season	SIMsc
1	Yogi Ferrell	2016-17	932.7
2	Shawn Respert	1995-96	931.8
3	Langston Galloway	2014-15	926.2
4	Tony Delk	1996-97	918.9
5	Toney Douglas	2009-10	917.1
6	Trey Burke	2015-16	916.4
7	Isaiah Canaan	2014-15	913.3
8	Ronnie Price	2006-07	908.9
9	Earl Watson	2002-03	907.3
10	Mo Williams	2005-06	904.1

Baseline Basic Stats

MPG	PTS	AST	REB	BLK	STL
22.5	9.1	3.0	2.4	0.1	0.9

Advanced Metrics

USG%	3PTA/FGA	FTA/FGA	TS%	eFG%	3PT%
20.2	0.408	0.184	0.516	0.482	0.384

AST%	TOV%	OREB%	DREB%	STL%	BLK%
22.6	12.2	1.8	11.6	2.1	0.6

PER	ORTG	DRTG	WS/48	VOL
14.30	107.1	107.9	0.095	0.431

- Some volatility in his projection due to playing only one year as full-time rotational player
- Good on-ball defender, defense was 4.4 points per 100 possessions better with him on the floor
- Can defend both guard spots, active off the ball
- Gets steals at a solid rate, good defensive rebounder for his size
- Effective as a pass-first, pick-and-roll ball handler and spot-up shooter
- Assist Percentage improved, made 41.4% of his threes, shot a much higher percentage inside of three feet
- Struggles to create his own shot, below average in isolation situations

Delon Wright

	Height	Weight	Cap #	Years Left
	6'5"	190	$2.537M	0

Similar at Age **25**

		Season	SIMsc
1	Lucious Harris	1995-96	926.4
2	Brent Barry	1996-97	921.7
3	Nando De Colo	2012-13	916.4
4	Alexey Shved	2013-14	915.4
5	Courtney Lee	2010-11	906.5
6	Alvin Williams	1999-00	906.4
7	Rex Walters	1995-96	902.7
8	Doug Christie	1995-96	901.5
9	Kerry Kittles	1999-00	901.4
10	Pace Mannion	1985-86	900.5

Baseline Basic Stats

MPG	PTS	AST	REB	BLK	STL
22.7	8.9	2.6	2.6	0.3	1.0

Advanced Metrics

USG%	3PTA/FGA	FTA/FGA	TS%	eFG%	3PT%
18.2	0.355	0.307	0.550	0.501	0.371

AST%	TOV%	OREB%	DREB%	STL%	BLK%
19.0	13.0	3.0	10.9	2.4	1.3

PER	ORTG	DRTG	WS/48	VOL
15.82	112.5	106.0	0.119	0.434

- Didn't play much in his first two seasons, has been effective when he's played, role has expanded every year
- Missed games in 2016-17 due to a torn labrum and a dislocated right shoulder
- Big playmaking guard that excels as a pick-and-roll ball handler
- Uses his slashing abilities in isolation situations to finish shots at the rim or draw fouls
- Good cutter, struggles a little in spot-up situations
- Three-point shot has been a little inconsistent, career percentage is just over league average
- Solid on-ball defender that can guard multiple positions
- Active help defender that gets steals and defensive rebounds at a fairly high rate, occasionally blocks shots

Pascal Siakam

	Height	Weight	Cap #	Years Left
	6'9"	230	$1.545M	Team Option

Similar at Age 23

		Season	SIMsc
1	Larry Nance Jr.	2015-16	938.8
2	Dante Cunningham	2010-11	924.5
3	Lavoy Allen	2012-13	919.6
4	Josh McRoberts	2010-11	916.6
5	Brian Cook	2003-04	916.4
6	Chris Singleton	2012-13	911.6
7	Cherokee Parks	1995-96	911.0
8	Kyle Anderson	2016-17	910.8
9	Richaun Holmes	2016-17	910.6
10	Terry Mills	1990-91	910.6

Baseline Basic Stats

MPG	PTS	AST	REB	BLK	STL
20.1	7.1	1.1	4.5	0.6	0.7

Advanced Metrics

USG%	3PTA/FGA	FTA/FGA	TS%	eFG%	3PT%
16.1	0.214	0.218	0.546	0.524	0.275

AST%	TOV%	OREB%	DREB%	STL%	BLK%
9.2	11.4	7.3	17.1	1.7	2.5

PER	ORTG	DRTG	WS/48	VOL
14.68	112.0	105.2	0.130	0.303

- Still developing, heading into his mid-20s
- Modern energy big, can defend on the perimeter and provide some rim protection
- Improved as a position defender, cut his fouls rate
- Not sacrificing position to go blocks like he did the season before, Defensive Rebound Percentage has improved
- Greatly improved as a passer, but his outside shot is still a work-in-progress
- Good mid-range shooter, trying to extend his range, only made 22% of his threes last season
- May be better utilized as a rim runner, shot over 68% on shots inside of three feet over his career

C.J. Miles

	Height	Weight	Cap #	Years Left
	6'6"	210	$8.333M	Player Option

Similar at Age 30

		Season	SIMsc
1	Kyle Korver	2011-12	918.3
2	Nick Young	2015-16	915.2
3	Morris Peterson	2007-08	913.2
4	Anthony Morrow	2015-16	911.9
5	Gerald Green	2015-16	908.9
6	Andres Nocioni	2009-10	904.3
7	Carlos Delfino	2012-13	904.2
8	Gordan Giricek	2007-08	904.1
9	Alan Anderson	2012-13	903.8
10	J.R. Smith	2015-16	903.4

Baseline Basic Stats

MPG	PTS	AST	REB	BLK	STL
20.8	8.3	0.9	2.5	0.2	0.6

Advanced Metrics

USG%	3PTA/FGA	FTA/FGA	TS%	eFG%	3PT%
18.4	0.669	0.139	0.555	0.532	0.377

AST%	TOV%	OREB%	DREB%	STL%	BLK%
5.8	7.1	1.9	11.9	1.4	1.1

PER	ORTG	DRTG	WS/48	VOL	
11.98	109.5	108.1	0.089	0.251	

- In his 30s, has some decline potential but his performance so far is still consistent with his career averages
- Fairly durable over the last four seasons with exception to a right shoulder injury at the end of the 2015-16 season
- Mainly a catch-and-shoot player on offense, good at running off screens and spotting up
- League average three-point shooter for his career, has been much better in the corners with a percentage of 42%
- Good on-ball wing defender, more of a stay-at-home guy, solid defensive rebounder

Norman Powell

	Height	Weight	Cap #	Years Left
	6'4"	215	$9.367M	2 + PO

Similar at Age 24

		Season	SIMsc
1	Shannon Brown	2009-10	939.0
2	Randy Foye	2007-08	937.2
3	Rashad McCants	2008-09	931.1
4	John Jenkins	2015-16	926.5
5	Victor Oladipo	2016-17	925.8
6	Shelvin Mack	2014-15	924.5
7	Dion Waiters	2015-16	922.7
8	O.J. Mayo	2011-12	922.7
9	Shelvin Mack	2013-14	921.8
10	Eric Piatkowski	1994-95	920.3

Baseline Basic Stats

MPG	PTS	AST	REB	BLK	STL
23.8	10.0	2.2	2.7	0.2	0.8

Advanced Metrics

USG%	3PTA/FGA	FTA/FGA	TS%	eFG%	3PT%
20.3	0.427	0.205	0.528	0.492	0.346

AST%	TOV%	OREB%	DREB%	STL%	BLK%
14.6	12.7	2.1	11.0	1.8	0.9

PER	ORTG	DRTG	WS/48	VOL
12.54	103.8	108.8	0.068	0.371

- Coming off a down year, did not play much in the playoffs last season
- Three-Point Percentage has dropped in each of the last three seasons
- Struggled to adjust to more stationary lower volume role, better on the move
- Most effective at running off screens and cutting to the rim
- Solid on-ball defending wing player, decent rebounder, will actively contest shots and occasionally get a block

Greg Monroe

	Height	Weight	Cap #	Years Left
	6'11"	253	$1.513M	0

Similar at Age 27

		Season	SIMsc
1	Andray Blatche	2013-14	912.6
2	Isaac Austin	1996-97	911.6
3	Carlos Boozer	2008-09	901.4
4	Jeff Ruland	1985-86	896.3
5	Nikola Pekovic	2012-13	895.4
6	Mike Gminski	1986-87	893.0
7	LaSalle Thompson	1988-89	891.8
8	Malik Rose	2001-02	890.9
9	Brad Miller	2003-04	887.5
10	Al Horford	2013-14	887.3

Baseline Basic Stats

MPG	PTS	AST	REB	BLK	STL
29.5	14.0	2.1	8.1	0.7	0.9

Advanced Metrics

USG%	3PTA/FGA	FTA/FGA	TS%	eFG%	3PT%
22.3	0.006	0.333	0.564	0.522	0.142

AST%	TOV%	OREB%	DREB%	STL%	BLK%
15.7	15.2	9.8	23.2	1.8	1.7

PER	ORTG	DRTG	WS/48	VOL
19.27	109.6	105.2	0.137	0.423

- Still an effective big man in the prime of his career
- Playing time has been significantly reduced due to his lack of a fit in the modern NBA
- Not a great rim protector, doesn't block shots
- Struggles to defend on the ball inside, lacks the lateral mobility to defend on the perimeter
- Excellent rebounder on both ends, good post-up big man that scores efficiently on shots inside of three feet, very good passing big man

Malachi Richardson

	Height	Weight	Cap #	Years Left
	6'6"	205	$1.569M	Team Option

Similar at Age 22

		Season	SIMsc
1	Darrun Hilliard	2015-16	951.0
2	Reggie Bullock	2013-14	929.2
3	Kevin Brooks	1991-92	928.0
4	James Anderson	2011-12	927.8
5	Corey Crowder	1991-92	924.2
6	Bill Walker	2009-10	923.0
7	Chris Carr	1996-97	923.0
8	Jason Kapono	2003-04	919.9
9	Daequan Cook	2009-10	917.9
10	Tracy Jackson	1981-82	917.7

Baseline Basic Stats

MPG	PTS	AST	REB	BLK	STL
20.1	7.6	1.3	2.4	0.2	0.6

Advanced Metrics

USG%	3PTA/FGA	FTA/FGA	TS%	eFG%	3PT%
17.3	0.433	0.228	0.517	0.478	0.350

AST%	TOV%	OREB%	DREB%	STL%	BLK%
8.9	10.7	2.1	10.8	1.5	0.5

PER	ORTG	DRTG	WS/48	VOL	
9.76	101.8	112.3	0.037	0.408	

- Fringe player at this stage, has only played 522 minutes in two seasons
- Hasn't established any major strengths, performance in the G-League has been inconsistent as well
- Struggled offensively in a low volume spot-up shooting role, below 30% career three-point shooter
- Flashed some potential as an on-ball wing defender in limited minutes, decent defensive rebounder

Lorenzo Brown

	Height	Weight	Cap #	Years Left
	6'5"	189	$1.513M	0

Similar at Age 27

		Season	SIMsc
1	Delonte West	2010-11	905.3
2	Doug Overton	1996-97	903.4
3	Jimmy Oliver	1996-97	901.4
4	Steve Bardo	1995-96	901.0
5	Fred Hoiberg	1999-00	898.7
6	Andre Owens	2007-08	898.5
7	Rodney Buford	2004-05	897.6
8	Derek Anderson	2001-02	895.8
9	Keith McLeod	2006-07	892.8
10	Michael Dickerson	2002-03	892.6

Baseline Basic Stats

MPG	PTS	AST	REB	BLK	STL
19.4	6.9	2.4	2.1	0.1	0.8

Advanced Metrics

USG%	3PTA/FGA	FTA/FGA	TS%	eFG%	3PT%
17.4	0.365	0.198	0.496	0.461	0.275

AST%	TOV%	OREB%	DREB%	STL%	BLK%
20.4	14.6	1.2	11.7	2.0	0.5

PER	ORTG	DRTG	WS/48	VOL	
10.95	101.2	107.9	0.040	0.489	

- Fringe player, hasn't been able to get minutes aside from one stint in Minnesota in 2014-15
- Hasn't shot well in the NBA, was only about break-even in his G-League career
- Tall playmaking guard that mainly looks to slash to the rim to either finish shots inside or draw fouls
- Active help defender that gets steals, good defensive rebounder
- Shown potential to defend multiple positions in a small sample of minutes

Kay Felder

	Height	Weight	2018 Cap #	Years Left
	5'9"	176	$1.513M	0

Similar at Age 22

		Season	SIMsc
1	J.J. Barea	2006-07	891.2
2	Rodrigue Beaubois	2010-11	885.7
3	Eddie House	2000-01	879.0
4	Bryce Cotton	2014-15	874.8
5	Leon Wood	1984-85	871.1
6	Scott Skiles	1986-87	870.5
7	Franklin Edwards	1981-82	868.6
8	Andre Barrett	2004-05	866.5
9	Mark Price	1986-87	863.2
10	Mookie Blaylock	1989-90	860.7

Baseline Basic Stats

MPG	PTS	AST	REB	BLK	STL
19.9	8.6	3.1	1.9	0.1	0.8

Advanced Metrics

USG%	3PTA/FGA	FTA/FGA	TS%	eFG%	3PT%
23.1	0.224	0.221	0.488	0.443	0.319

AST%	TOV%	OREB%	DREB%	STL%	BLK%
24.2	15.1	2.2	9.3	1.9	0.7

PER	ORTG	DRTG	WS/48	VOL
11.91	98.5	109.8	0.017	0.504

- Contract for 2018-19 is partially guaranteed
- Split time over the last two years between the NBA and G-League for three different organizations
- Decent playmaking and ball control skills allowed him to be an above average pick-and-roll ball handler in a small sample of minutes with Cleveland in 2016-17
- Struggled to shoot efficiently in the NBA, three-point percentage is below break-even
- Shot better in the G-League, but his percentages have still been inconsistent
- Mainly has trouble finishing at the rim, below 50% for his career on shots inside of three feet
- Below average on-ball defender, constantly targeted due to his smallish size
- Decent at getting steals, good defensive rebounder for a sub-six footer

BOSTON CELTICS

Last Season: 55 – 27, Lost Conference Finals to Cleveland (3 – 4)

Offensive Rating: 107.6, 18th in NBA   Defensive Rating: 103.9, 1st in NBA

Primary Executive: Danny Ainge, GM and President of Basketball Operations

Head Coach: Brad Stevens

Key Roster Changes

Subtractions   **Additions**
Greg Monroe, free agency   Robert Williams, draft
Shane Larkin, free agency   Brad Wanamaker, free agency
Jonathan Gibson, free agency
Abdel Nader, trade
Kadeem Allen, waived

RAFER Projected Win Total: 47.6

Projected Best Five-Man Unit   **Other Rotation Players**
1. Kyrie Irving   Jaylen Brown
2. Gordon Hayward   Terry Rozier
3. Jayson Tatum   Marcus Smart
4. Marcus Morris   Aron Baynes
5. Al Horford

Remaining Roster

- Daniel Theis
- Guerschon Yabusele
- Semi Ojeleye
- Brad Wanamaker
- Robert Williams
- Jabari Bird
- P.J. Dozier, 22, 6'7", 201, South Carolina (Two-Way)
- Walt Lemon, Jr., 26, 6'3", 180, Bradley (Two-Way)

Season Forecast

The Boston Celtics didn't make any major moves this summer because they are counting on getting a significant addition to their rotation by getting both Gordon Hayward and Kyrie Irving back from injury. Because there were fewer teams with available cap space due to overspending in past seasons, they were able to re-sign Marcus Smart at a fairly reasonable price to maintain their depth and provide insurance behind Irving. Of the teams in the Eastern Conference, the Celtics are built the best for the playoffs because their optimal lineups will likely feature four All-Star level players on the court at the same time in Irving, Hayward, Al Horford and Jayson Tatum. At full strength, Boston can throw out a dangerous closing lineup that should be able to defend at a very high level and efficiently generate offense. The difference between Marcus Morris, Jaylen Brown and Terry Rozier as the fifth man was pretty minimal, but the edge went to Morris because of his rebounding skills and ability to limit turnovers. If the team wanted a potentially more dynamic unit, they easily switch out Morris for Brown to increase its athleticism or they could go to Rozier in a smaller lineup for more quickness.

With the strength of having a solid core of top-end players, the main challenge for the Celtics is managing their minutes over the course of the regular season to ensure that they are healthy for the playoffs. With this in mind, they could look to play some of their back-end players to possibly lengthen out their rotation. Fortunately, they have a player that has showed promise in limited stints. Specifically, Guerschon Yabusele flashed some potential as a rotation player in a small sample of minutes with the Celtics last season and also had a strong performance in both the G-League and this year's Summer League. There's a chance that he could improve to the point where he could factor into the team's rotation to give them some more depth. In the last of couple years, head coach, Brad Stevens has demonstrated a unique ability to consistently put teams in a position to win despite some unfavorable conditions. Even if they face some adversity this season, Boston still should be one of the best teams in the East. However, if they succeed in keeping everyone healthy for the playoffs, their combination of high-end talent, versatility and stout defense should make them the favorites to come out of the East to play in the Finals.

Veterans

Kyrie Irving

	Height	Weight	Cap #	Years Left
	6'2"	180	$20.099M	Player Option

	Similar at Age	**25**	
		Season	**SIMsc**
1	Lou Williams	2011-12	928.7
2	Jrue Holiday	2015-16	921.6
3	Damian Lillard	2015-16	914.9
4	Jeff Teague	2013-14	914.2
5	Jordan Farmar	2011-12	913.9
6	Tony Parker	2007-08	913.9
7	Mo Williams	2007-08	910.7
8	Stephon Marbury	2002-03	909.7
9	Stephen Curry	2013-14	905.5
10	Troy Hudson	2001-02	901.4

Baseline Basic Stats

MPG	PTS	AST	REB	BLK	STL
33.5	19.1	6.0	3.4	0.3	1.2

Advanced Metrics

USG%	3PTA/FGA	FTA/FGA	TS%	eFG%	3PT%
27.7	0.339	0.264	0.581	0.532	0.386

AST%	TOV%	OREB%	DREB%	STL%	BLK%
29.9	11.7	2.0	9.3	1.7	0.7

PER	ORTG	DRTG	WS/48	VOL
21.84	115.1	107.2	0.195	0.383

- Elite point guard in his prime, had the best season of his career last year
- Has missed considerable portions of the 2015-16 and 2017-18 seasons due to injuries to his left knee
- One of the best pick-and-roll ball handlers in the league, excellent playmaking skills
- Excellent isolation scorer that can score from anywhere, great all-around shooter
- Very good in spot-ups and at running off screens, made over 40% of his threes in three of the last four seasons
- Improved as an on-ball defender last season, solid overall on defense
- Took more a stay-at-home approach, solid defensive rebounding point guard

Al Horford

	Height	Weight	Cap #	Years Left
	6'10"	245	$28.929M	Player Option

Similar at Age 31

		Season	SIMsc
1	Bill Laimbeer	1988-89	901.8
2	Herb Williams	1989-90	895.1
3	Dave Corzine	1987-88	893.5
4	David West	2011-12	889.3
5	Paul Millsap	2016-17	889.2
6	Lamar Odom	2010-11	889.0
7	Marcin Gortat	2015-16	888.7
8	Rasheed Wallace	2005-06	888.3
9	Brad Miller	2007-08	887.5
10	LaMarcus Aldridge	2016-17	885.4

Baseline Basic Stats

MPG	PTS	AST	REB	BLK	STL
28.5	11.4	2.3	6.5	1.0	0.7

Advanced Metrics

USG%	3PTA/FGA	FTA/FGA	TS%	eFG%	3PT%
18.6	0.261	0.207	0.555	0.524	0.387

AST%	TOV%	OREB%	DREB%	STL%	BLK%
18.0	13.0	5.4	19.5	1.1	2.7

PER	ORTG	DRTG	WS/48	VOL
16.30	111.4	104.9	0.133	0.380

- In his early 30s, has been steadily declining over the last three seasons
- Solid complementary stretch big that is among the league's best passing big men
- Has been a better outside shooter in Boston than he was in Atlanta, shot over 39% on threes overall over the last two seasons
- Effective as a screener in pick-and-roll, not as effective as a post-up player at this stage of his career
- Great defensive big man that can rebound, adequately protect the rim and handle perimeter players on switches

Jayson Tatum

	Height	Weight	Cap #	Years Left
	6'8"	205	$6.701M	2 Team Options

Similar at Age 19

		Season	SIMsc
1	Maurice Harkless	2012-13	901.4
2	Andrew Wiggins	2014-15	901.1
3	Brandon Ingram	2016-17	898.1
4	Giannis Antetokounmpo	2013-14	887.5
5	Luol Deng	2004-05	886.2
6	Devin Booker	2015-16	882.9
7	Kevin Durant	2007-08	880.1
8	Martell Webster	2005-06	878.7
9	Justise Winslow	2015-16	875.1
10	Darius Miles	2000-01	870.3

Baseline Basic Stats

MPG	PTS	AST	REB	BLK	STL
32.1	13.9	2.5	5.1	0.6	1.1

Advanced Metrics

USG%	3PTA/FGA	FTA/FGA	TS%	eFG%	3PT%
20.9	0.264	0.308	0.588	0.543	0.416

AST%	TOV%	OREB%	DREB%	STL%	BLK%
13.6	11.9	3.3	15.6	2.0	1.5

PER	ORTG	DRTG	WS/48	VOL	
17.27	112.5	104.4	0.147	0.275	

- Extremely productive as a rookie last season, took his performance to a higher level in the playoffs
- 2nd most Win Shares ever by a rookie in his age-19 season behind Dwight Howard
- Efficiently in a complementary scoring role, not quite ready to take on a primary scoring load, below average in isolation situations
- Performed well as a post-up player and as a pick-and-roll ball handler
- Most effective as a spot-up shooter, made 43.4% of his threes overall, also was a very good cutter
- Good on-ball defender that could guard multiple positions
- Used his length to actively contest and block shots, good defensive rebounding wing

Gordon Hayward

	Height	Weight	Cap #	Years Left
	6'8"	207	$31.214M	1 + PO

Similar at Age 27

		Season	SIMsc
1	Sean Elliott	1995-96	944.4
2	Danny Granger	2010-11	936.9
3	Jalen Rose	1999-00	931.7
4	Steve Smith	1996-97	930.0
5	Joe Johnson	2008-09	923.0
6	Mike Dunleavy, Jr.	2007-08	922.0
7	Glen Rice	1994-95	918.5
8	Stephen Jackson	2005-06	918.5
9	Josh Howard	2007-08	915.7
10	J.R. Smith	2012-13	912.2

Baseline Basic Stats

MPG	PTS	AST	REB	BLK	STL
36.6	19.9	3.4	4.7	0.4	1.1

Advanced Metrics

USG%	3PTA/FGA	FTA/FGA	TS%	eFG%	3PT%
25.2	0.336	0.331	0.565	0.509	0.384

AST%	TOV%	OREB%	DREB%	STL%	BLK%
17.4	10.9	2.8	12.8	1.5	0.7

PER	ORTG	DRTG	WS/48	VOL	
18.61	112.5	107.6	0.149	0.328	

- Projection above mostly based on his previous two healthy seasons
- Only played five minutes last season due to a freak injury where he suffered a fractured tibia in his left leg and dislocated his left ankle
- Played well in a moderate usage role in his earlier years in Utah, slightly below average in isolation situations
- Very good playmaking wing that excels as a pick-and-roll ball handler
- Good higher usage outside shooter that can run off screens and make spot-up jumpers, Three-Point Percentage is above league average for his career
- Good stay-at-home on-ball wing defender, good defensive rebounder

Jaylen Brown

	Height	Weight	Cap #	Years Left
	6'7"	225	$5.170M	Team Option

Similar at Age 21

		Season	SIMsc
1	Omri Casspi	2009-10	944.5
2	Aaron Gordon	2016-17	932.8
3	Martell Webster	2007-08	927.5
4	Chase Budinger	2009-10	927.0
5	Kawhi Leonard	2012-13	924.1
6	Mike Miller	2001-02	924.0
7	Richard Jefferson	2001-02	919.5
8	Wilson Chandler	2008-09	917.3
9	Tobias Harris	2013-14	917.1
10	Quentin Richardson	2001-02	916.6

Baseline Basic Stats

MPG	PTS	AST	REB	BLK	STL
27.1	12.0	1.7	4.3	0.3	0.8

Advanced Metrics

USG%	3PTA/FGA	FTA/FGA	TS%	eFG%	3PT%
20.0	0.248	0.274	0.544	0.512	0.353

AST%	TOV%	OREB%	DREB%	STL%	BLK%
10.0	11.9	3.9	13.4	1.6	0.9

PER	ORTG	DRTG	WS/48	VOL
13.22	105.6	106.9	0.094	0.383

- Improved significantly in his second year, was much better in the playoffs last season
- Will have to adjust to a lower usage role, his improved three-point shot is a positive sign
- Good spot-up shooter that made almost 40% of his threes last season, also above average at running off screens
- Fairly good isolation scorer that can slash to the rim to either finish inside or draw fouls
- Needs to improve his free throw shooting, Free Throw Percentage dropped to 64.4% last season
- Good on-ball defending wing player, aggressive to contest shots, good defensive rebounder

Terry Rozier

	Height	Weight	Cap #	Years Left
	6'2"	190	$3.050M	0

Similar at Age 23

		Season	SIMsc
1	Langston Galloway	2014-15	948.8
2	Jordan Farmar	2009-10	936.2
3	Toney Douglas	2009-10	933.8
4	Ray McCallum	2014-15	924.9
5	E'Twaun Moore	2012-13	922.2
6	Shawn Respert	1995-96	920.7
7	Eric Washington	1997-98	912.8
8	Avery Bradley	2013-14	911.7
9	Luther Head	2005-06	910.4
10	A.J. Price	2009-10	908.8

Baseline Basic Stats

MPG	PTS	AST	REB	BLK	STL
21.4	8.1	2.3	2.1	0.1	0.7

Advanced Metrics

USG%	3PTA/FGA	FTA/FGA	TS%	eFG%	3PT%
18.8	0.476	0.172	0.506	0.476	0.360

AST%	TOV%	OREB%	DREB%	STL%	BLK%
17.5	10.8	2.8	12.4	1.8	0.6

PER	ORTG	DRTG	WS/48	VOL
12.73	105.1	106.2	0.090	0.377

- Greatly improved in his third year with increased levels of production during the playoffs last season
- Showed great potential as a scoring point guard, will have to adjust to either a bench or lower usage role if the team is at full strength
- Improved ability to make catch-and-shoot threes is a step in the right direction, shot 40.3% in this situation last season
- Decent playmaking skills, not quite as effective as a pick-and-roll ball handler
- Not getting to the rim as frequently, playing further away from the basket
- Decent on-ball defender that can defend both guard spots
- Steal and block rates have increased in each of his three seasons, good defensive rebounding guard

Marcus Smart

	Height	Weight	Cap #	Years Left
	6'4"	220	$11.661M	3

Similar at Age 23

		Season	SIMsc
1	Ron Baker	2016-17	918.8
2	Randy Foye	2006-07	916.6
3	O.J. Mayo	2010-11	913.7
4	Jerian Grant	2015-16	910.9
5	Norman Powell	2016-17	905.9
6	Thabo Sefolosha	2007-08	905.6
7	Baron Davis	2002-03	899.5
8	Iman Shumpert	2013-14	899.2
9	Aaron McKie	1995-96	899.1
10	Tyreke Evans	2012-13	898.9

Baseline Basic Stats

MPG	PTS	AST	REB	BLK	STL
26.2	9.8	3.0	3.1	0.3	1.1

Advanced Metrics

USG%	3PTA/FGA	FTA/FGA	TS%	eFG%	3PT%
19.0	0.476	0.245	0.512	0.468	0.329

AST%	TOV%	OREB%	DREB%	STL%	BLK%
20.5	15.3	2.7	10.6	2.1	1.1

PER	ORTG	DRTG	WS/48	VOL	
12.29	103.1	107.1	0.075	0.273	

- Solid defensive guard entering his prime years
- Defends multiple positions, better at defending wings than smaller guards
- Gets steals at a fairly high rate, can occasionally block shots, decent defensive rebounder
- Inefficient as a scorer, should look to drive more to draw more fouls and take advantage of his solid free throw shooting
- Struggles to make shots outside of three feet, slightly below break-even three-point shooter from the corners
- Decent playmaker, but can be wild and turnover prone

Marcus Morris

	Height	Weight	Cap #	Years Left
	6'9"	235	$5.375M	0

Similar at Age **28**

		Season	SIMsc
1	Jeff Green	2014-15	960.8
2	Ersan Ilyasova	2015-16	948.8
3	Al Harrington	2008-09	936.1
4	Peja Stojakovic	2005-06	935.6
5	Chris Crawford	2003-04	930.2
6	Terry Mills	1995-96	921.2
7	Tracy Murray	1999-00	921.2
8	Chris Copeland	2012-13	917.4
9	Wayman Tisdale	1992-93	915.6
10	Lamond Murray	2001-02	915.2

Baseline Basic Stats

MPG	PTS	AST	REB	BLK	STL
25.1	11.0	1.3	4.3	0.3	0.6

Advanced Metrics

USG%	3PTA/FGA	FTA/FGA	TS%	eFG%	3PT%
20.0	0.425	0.229	0.537	0.502	0.361

AST%	TOV%	OREB%	DREB%	STL%	BLK%
8.3	9.4	3.7	15.5	1.1	0.9

PER	ORTG	DRTG	WS/48	VOL
13.15	106.9	107.1	0.094	0.359

- Solid veteran combo forward, was ineffective in the playoffs last season
- Defends both forward spots, has historically been more effective when used as a four
- More of a stay-at-home position defender, good defensive rebounder
- Effective as the screener in pick-and-roll, can knock down spot-up jumpers
- Around a league average three-point shooter for his career
- Good at posting up smaller perimeter players, above average in isolation situations if he's got a mismatch

Aron Baynes

	Height	Weight	Cap #	Years Left
	6'10"	260	$5.194M	Player Option

Similar at Age 31

		Season	SIMsc
1	Sean Rooks	2000-01	931.6
2	Marc Jackson	2005-06	913.3
3	Dave Corzine	1987-88	911.9
4	Kent Benson	1985-86	910.6
5	Rick Mahorn	1989-90	909.6
6	Rasho Nesterovic	2007-08	906.1
7	Joe Kleine	1992-93	905.1
8	Scott Williams	1999-00	903.4
9	Kelvin Cato	2005-06	902.4
10	Fabricio Oberto	2006-07	901.5

Baseline Basic Stats

MPG	PTS	AST	REB	BLK	STL
17.0	5.4	0.8	4.3	0.5	0.4

Advanced Metrics

USG%	3PTA/FGA	FTA/FGA	TS%	eFG%	3PT%
16.0	0.026	0.248	0.512	0.473	0.135

AST%	TOV%	OREB%	DREB%	STL%	BLK%
7.6	13.7	8.8	20.8	1.0	2.5

PER	ORTG	DRTG	WS/48	VOL	
12.15	104.5	104.3	0.092	0.319	

- Older big man in his early 30s decline phase, still a solid situational, physical, big body center
- Effective rebounder that provides some rim protection
- Decent shot blocker, good defensive rebounder
- Solid position defender that can clog the lane
- Vulnerable against quicker players due to a lack of mobility
- Shooting efficiency is down because he's playing further away from the basket
- Started shooting corner threes in the playoffs, made 11 out of 23 of them (47.8%)
- If his suddenly improved three-point shot sticks, it could extend his career significantly

Daniel Theis

	Height	Weight	Cap #	Years Left
	6'9"	215	$1.378M	0

Similar at Age 25

		Season	SIMsc
1	Aaron Williams	1996-97	922.4
2	Amir Johnson	2012-13	911.1
3	Alexis Ajinca	2013-14	899.7
4	James Singleton	2006-07	899.6
5	Ben Coleman	1986-87	891.4
6	Edgar Jones	1981-82	890.2
7	Rickey Brown	1983-84	890.2
8	Kenny Gattison	1989-90	889.4
9	Carlos Rogers	1996-97	886.9
10	Terry Tyler	1981-82	886.8

Baseline Basic Stats

MPG	PTS	AST	REB	BLK	STL
20.9	7.3	1.0	5.2	0.9	0.6

Advanced Metrics

USG%	3PTA/FGA	FTA/FGA	TS%	eFG%	3PT%
15.8	0.174	0.352	0.578	0.539	0.316

AST%	TOV%	OREB%	DREB%	STL%	BLK%
8.4	16.5	9.9	20.0	1.4	3.3

PER	ORTG	DRTG	WS/48	VOL
14.79	111.9	102.3	0.152	0.403

- Solid rookie season after coming over from Germany
- Tore his meniscus towards the end of last season, return is uncertain
- When healthy, he's an energetic, slightly undersized big man with mobility that can provide solid interior defense
- Good shot blocker and overall rebounder, decent on-ball interior defender, better at handling fours
- On offense, scores efficiently inside on dives to the rim and a small sample of post-ups, draws fouls
- Flashed some stretch potential, made over half of his corner threes, but shot 31% on threes overall
- Decent passing big man, a bit turnover prone

Semi Ojeleye

	Height	Weight	Cap #	Years Left
	6'7"	241	$1.378M	2

Similar at Age 23

		Season	SIMsc
1	Jae Crowder	2013-14	900.0
2	P.J. Hairston	2015-16	895.2
3	Dorian Finney-Smith	2016-17	889.1
4	Quincy Pondexter	2011-12	886.1
5	Anthony Brown	2015-16	878.1
6	Reggie Bullock	2014-15	875.2
7	Jeff Taylor	2012-13	874.7
8	Glenn Robinson III	2016-17	873.0
9	Derrick Williams	2014-15	872.6
10	Joe Harris	2014-15	872.0

Baseline Basic Stats

MPG	PTS	AST	REB	BLK	STL
18.2	6.3	0.8	2.7	0.2	0.4

Advanced Metrics

USG%	3PTA/FGA	FTA/FGA	TS%	eFG%	3PT%
13.0	0.606	0.223	0.525	0.494	0.355

AST%	TOV%	OREB%	DREB%	STL%	BLK%
4.9	8.6	3.5	12.4	1.0	0.6

PER	ORTG	DRTG	WS/48	VOL	
9.25	107.0	107.5	0.112	0.546	

- Regular rotation player in his rookie season, was used mainly as a second unit combo forward
- Primarily a defensive specialist that showed an ability to defend wings and big men on occasion
- More of a stay-at-home position defender, decent defensive rebounder
- Very low volume offensive player that struggled to shoot efficiently
- Had trouble getting to the rim and finishing shots inside of three feet
- Has flashed an ability to make spot-up threes, made 37.1% of his corner threes last season

Guerschon Yabusele

	Height	Weight	Cap #	Years Left
	6'7"	260	$2.668M	2 Team Options

Similar at Age 22

		Season	SIMsc
1	Kenny Thomas	1999-00	880.7
2	Linas Kleiza	2006-07	869.6
3	Dontonio Wingfield	1996-97	866.7
4	Winston Crite	1987-88	861.4
5	Jae Crowder	2012-13	858.8
6	Michael Kidd-Gilchrist	2015-16	858.6
7	DaJuan Summers	2009-10	858.0
8	Wayne Selden	2016-17	856.5
9	Solomon Hill	2013-14	856.1
10	Malik Hairston	2009-10	849.9

Baseline Basic Stats

MPG	PTS	AST	REB	BLK	STL
20.8	7.4	1.1	4.0	0.4	0.6

Advanced Metrics

USG%	3PTA/FGA	FTA/FGA	TS%	eFG%	3PT%
16.7	0.426	0.329	0.551	0.511	0.302

AST%	TOV%	OREB%	DREB%	STL%	BLK%
9.5	12.6	6.8	15.2	1.2	1.7

PER	ORTG	DRTG	WS/48	VOL
13.04	110.1	107.1	0.113	0.605

- Played sparingly in his rookie year, but flashed promise in limited minutes
- Combo forward that can occasionally serve as an undersized center
- Decent position defender and solid overall rebounder
- Good playmaker for his size and shot efficiently last season
- Can finish inside, draw fouls and occasionally knock down a three, outside shot still needs improvement

Jabari Bird

	Height	Weight	Cap #	Years Left
	6'6"	197	$1.349M	1

Similar at Age **23**

		Season	SIMsc
1	Bryce Dejean-Jones	2015-16	883.4
2	David Thirdkill	1983-84	882.8
3	Garrett Temple	2009-10	878.0
4	Derrick Brown	2010-11	874.6
5	DeAndre Liggins	2011-12	874.3
6	Spencer Dinwiddie	2016-17	874.1
7	Darrin Hancock	1994-95	873.4
8	Shandon Anderson	1996-97	871.1
9	Alec Burks	2014-15	870.9
10	Danny Vranes	1981-82	870.6

Baseline Basic Stats

MPG	PTS	AST	REB	BLK	STL
18.0	6.6	1.5	2.6	0.2	0.6

Advanced Metrics

USG%	3PTA/FGA	FTA/FGA	TS%	eFG%	3PT%
17.1	0.302	0.389	0.572	0.560	0.358

AST%	TOV%	OREB%	DREB%	STL%	BLK%
12.6	15.3	5.2	11.8	1.6	0.7

PER	ORTG	DRTG	WS/48	VOL	
13.15	108.0	107.0	0.097	0.596	

- Played on a two-way contract last season and spent most of the year with the Maine Red Claws in the G-League
- Effective in limited minutes at the end of the season with Boston as a slashing wing that could finish around the basket and draw fouls at a very rate
- Outside shot is still a work-in-progress, below average three-point shooter in the G-League
- Decent defender that can potentially guard multiple positions
- Fairly active help defender that gets steals and blocks at a solid rate, good on the defensive boards
- Could miss a considerable portion of the season due to a serious domestic violence arrest

Newcomers

Brad Wanamaker

		Height	Weight	Cap #	Years Left
		6'4"	209	$0.838M	0

Baseline Basic Stats

MPG	PTS	AST	REB	BLK	STL
21.3	7.5	2.2	2.4	0.1	0.8

Advanced Metrics

USG%	3PTA/FGA	FTA/FGA	TS%	eFG%	3PT%
16.8	0.495	0.267	0.549	0.501	0.351

AST%	TOV%	OREB%	DREB%	STL%	BLK%
19.3	12.8	2.8	11.4	2.3	0.3

PER	ORTG	DRTG	WS/48	VOL	
12.00	115.8	116.3	0.085	0.800	

- Translated EuroLeague stats, played with Fenerbahce in Turkey, will be in his age-29 season this year
- Originally played in college at Pittsburgh from 2007-2011
- Combo guard with solid playmaking skills, cut his turnover rate significantly last season
- Solid three-point shooter that can slash to the rim to finish or draw fouls
- Can possibly defend both guard spots, gets steals at a high rate, solid rebounding guard
- Not overly explosive as an athlete, probably better suited for a lower volume, backup role

Robert Williams

		Height	Weight	Cap #	Years Left
		6'10"	241	$1.654M	1 + 2 TO

Baseline Basic Stats

MPG	PTS	AST	REB	BLK	STL
12.0	4.1	0.4	3.1	0.5	0.3

Advanced Metrics

USG%	3PTA/FGA	FTA/FGA	TS%	eFG%	3PT%
17.9	0.031	0.376	0.496	0.465	0.200

AST%	TOV%	OREB%	DREB%	STL%	BLK%
5.2	15.0	10.5	19.2	1.4	3.4

PER	ORTG	DRTG	WS/48	VOL	
12.48	99.4	104.8	0.066	N/A	

- Drafted by Boston in the first round with the 27th overall pick
- Suffered a left knee contusion in Summer League, but is expected to be healthy for training camp
- Raised concerns about his work ethic because he missed his introductory conference call and his flight on the first day of Summer League
- Could be useful in limited minutes as a rim running big man that predominantly scores on dunks and provides the team with additional rebounding and shot blocking
- May benefit from some additional seasoning in the G-League to become a more disciplined position defender and improve his offensive skill level

PHILADELPHIA 76ERS

Last Season: 52 – 30, Lost 2nd Round to Boston (1 – 4)

Offensive Rating: 109.5, 12th in NBA

Defensive Rating: 105.0, 4th in NBA

Primary Executive: Position Still Vacant

Head Coach: Brett Brown

Key Roster Changes

Subtractions
Marco Belinelli, free agency
Ersan Ilyasova, free agency
Richaun Holmes, trade
Timothe Luwawu-Cabarrot, trade
Justin Anderson, trade

Additions
Zhaire Smith, draft
Landry Smith, draft
Jonah Bolden, signed 2017 draft pick
Wilson Chandler, trade
Mike Muscala, trade

RAFER Projected Win Total: 46.4

Projected Best Five-Man Unit
1. Ben Simmons
2. J.J. Redick
3. Robert Covington
4. Dario Saric
5. Joel Embiid

Other Rotation Players
Wilson Chandler
T.J. McConnell
Amir Johnson
Mike Muscala

Remaining Roster

- Markelle Fultz
- Jerryd Bayless
- Furkan Korkmaz
- Jonah Bolden
- Zhaire Smith
- Landry Shamet
- Demetrius Jackson, 24, 6'1", 201, Notre Dame (Two-Way)
- Shake Milton, 22, 6'6", 205, SMU (Two-Way)
- Anthony Brown, 26, 6'7", 210, Stanford (Exhibit 10)
- Norvel Pelle, 25, 6'11", 215, Los Angeles, CA (Exhibit 10)

Season Forecast

The Philadelphia 76ers had an unusual offseason because they had to make some critical roster decisions without a formal General Manager as a result of Bryan Colangelo's resignation relating to questionable activity from his secret social media accounts. They had initially planned to take a run at LeBron James, but they never got a formal meeting. From there, they decided to bring back primary rotation players like J.J. Redick and Amir Johnson and make smaller pickups by trading for Wilson Chandler and Mike Muscala while maneuvering with their future cap space to make a push next summer. As it stands, the results for this coming season should be similar to last year and Philadelphia is probably going to be a solid top-four seed in the Eastern Conference.

The main challenge for the Sixers is managing the schedule, so the team can be at full strength in the playoffs. One reason for this is Joel Embiid's considerable injury history. Last season, Embiid went through the full season mostly unscathed, except for a concussion and a broken orbital bone in March. Even so, it was a positive sign for the franchise and if they can keep him healthy, they can eventually become contenders in the East. Managing the minutes of the other primary players is important because they are a bit top heavy at the moment and their starters had to carry a considerable workload. Therefore, the Sixers could benefit from incorporating a younger back-end player in the lineup to lengthen their rotation. At this stage, Markelle Fultz is a wild card because though he's an extremely talented former first overall pick, it's uncertain if he'll regain the confidence in his jump shot after going through either a shoulder injury or a mental anxiety issue. Furkan Korkmaz had a strong performance in the Las Vegas Summer League in July, which included a game where he scored 40 points on 18 shots. If he improves, he could give the team another outside shooter. Finally, they also signed Jonah Bolden, their second round pick from 2017, and if his performance from EuroLeague translates, he could add depth as a rotational big that can rebound and occasionally space the floor. If the team enters the playoffs at full strength, they could have a good, but still flawed closing unit. Embiid and Ben Simmons are both All-Star level players, but neither one excels at creating his own shot in a half-court set, which resulted in some struggles against Boston in their second round series. Against most of the other teams, their primary lineup listed above should be very effective as long as Simmons can consistently dictate the pace with his transition and playmaking abilities and Embiid continues to score efficiently inside to open up opportunities for their complementary shooters. Right now, Philadelphia isn't quite a contender yet, so it's likely that they will be eliminated around the second round like last season if they make no changes to their current roster. However, if they use their ample assets to swing a deal for an elite, shot creating wing player, they could take the next step and become legitimate contenders in the Eastern Conference.

Veterans

Joel Embiid

	Height	Weight	Cap #	Years Left
	7'0"	250	$25.250M	4

Similar at Age **23**

		Season	SIMsc
1	Tim Duncan	1999-00	864.7
2	Patrick Ewing*	1985-86	862.9
3	Mike Gminski	1982-83	857.0
4	Benoit Benjamin	1987-88	854.9
5	DeMarcus Cousins	2013-14	852.3
6	Alonzo Mourning*	1993-94	849.9
7	Alex Len	2016-17	848.2
8	Spencer Hawes	2011-12	846.5
9	Anthony Davis	2016-17	832.1
10	Hakeem Olajuwon*	1985-86	831.9

Baseline Basic Stats

MPG	PTS	AST	REB	BLK	STL
33.0	18.5	2.5	9.7	2.2	0.9

Advanced Metrics

USG%	3PTA/FGA	FTA/FGA	TS%	eFG%	3PT%
30.0	0.144	0.456	0.575	0.519	0.351

AST%	TOV%	OREB%	DREB%	STL%	BLK%
16.1	15.4	8.2	26.5	1.3	5.0

PER	ORTG	DRTG	WS/48	VOL	
22.74	107.3	101.1	0.154	0.424	

- Considerable injury history, played in 60 or more games for the first time in his career
- One of the best centers in the NBA when healthy, heading into his prime years
- Elite defensive center with the mobility to defend on the perimeter while providing excellent rim protection and rebounding
- Great post-up big man with good passing skills that can occasionally hit a three to stretch the defense
- Excellent as a rim runner that can finish shots inside of three feet
- Above average mid-range shooter as well

Ben Simmons

	Height	Weight	Cap #	Years Left
	6'10"	230	$6.435M	Team Option

		Similar at Age	**21**	
			Season	**SIMsc**
1	Lamar Odom		2000-01	889.9
2	Kevin Garnett		1997-98	879.0
3	Shawn Kemp		1990-91	873.2
4	Nerlens Noel		2015-16	872.8
5	James Worthy*		1982-83	870.8
6	Giannis Antetokounmpo		2015-16	869.0
7	Chris Bosh		2005-06	867.3
8	John Williams		1987-88	861.9
9	Terry Cummings		1982-83	861.8
10	Greg Monroe		2011-12	860.7

Baseline Basic Stats

MPG	PTS	AST	REB	BLK	STL
34.5	18.0	4.1	8.3	1.2	1.3

Advanced Metrics

USG%	3PTA/FGA	FTA/FGA	TS%	eFG%	3PT%
22.8	0.030	0.372	0.559	0.525	0.127

AST%	TOV%	OREB%	DREB%	STL%	BLK%
29.5	17.7	6.8	19.4	2.2	2.0

PER	ORTG	DRTG	WS/48	VOL	
19.83	111.5	102.7	0.164	0.276	

- Won Rookie of the Year last season

- Size of a big man with elite playmaking skills to create offense for others

- Efficient scorer, almost exclusively does his damage inside, rarely looks to take jump shots

- Only took three non-heave three-pointers last season, missed all three of them

- Good as a pick-and-roll ball handler and isolation scorer

- Excellent help defender that gets steals, can block shots and grab defensive rebounds

- Mainly used as a roamer, solid on-ball defender that can guard multiple positions

Robert Covington

	Height	Weight	Cap #	Years Left
	6'9"	215	$10.464M	3

Similar at Age 27

		Season	SIMsc
1	James Posey	2003-04	916.3
2	Danny Green	2014-15	914.7
3	DeMarre Carroll	2013-14	905.8
4	Trevor Ariza	2012-13	894.7
5	Wilson Chandler	2014-15	893.5
6	Marvin Williams	2013-14	893.2
7	Kyle Korver	2008-09	889.1
8	David Benoit	1995-96	888.5
9	Al Harrington	2007-08	888.0
10	Morris Peterson	2004-05	886.9

Baseline Basic Stats

MPG	PTS	AST	REB	BLK	STL
28.6	11.0	1.8	5.1	0.5	1.2

Advanced Metrics

USG%	3PTA/FGA	FTA/FGA	TS%	eFG%	3PT%
17.7	0.593	0.207	0.545	0.511	0.356

AST%	TOV%	OREB%	DREB%	STL%	BLK%
9.2	12.9	3.7	16.7	2.3	1.8

PER	ORTG	DRTG	WS/48	VOL	
12.95	104.9	104.6	0.090	0.400	

- Three-and-D wing player in his prime years
- One of the best on-ball defending wings in the league
- Defends both forward spots, better at handling threes
- Active help defender, gets steals and blocks at a high rate, good defensive rebounding wing
- Low volume, one-dimensional spot-up shooter, struggled offensively in the playoffs
- League average overall three-point shooter for his career, slightly better in the corners

Dario Saric

	Height	Weight	Cap #	Years Left
	6'10"	223	$2.527M	Team Option

Similar at Age 23

		Season	SIMsc
1	Vladimir Radmanovic	2003-04	932.8
2	Mike Dunleavy, Jr.	2003-04	932.1
3	Danilo Gallinari	2011-12	921.2
4	Lamar Odom	2002-03	919.0
5	Tim Thomas	2000-01	918.5
6	Tobias Harris	2015-16	916.0
7	Peja Stojakovic	2000-01	909.7
8	Omri Casspi	2011-12	908.7
9	Rodney Hood	2015-16	908.1
10	Rashard Lewis	2002-03	907.7

Baseline Basic Stats

MPG	PTS	AST	REB	BLK	STL
30.0	14.1	2.0	5.3	0.4	0.9

Advanced Metrics

USG%	3PTA/FGA	FTA/FGA	TS%	eFG%	3PT%
22.4	0.408	0.250	0.558	0.515	0.378

AST%	TOV%	OREB%	DREB%	STL%	BLK%
12.7	12.2	5.5	16.9	1.3	1.0

PER	ORTG	DRTG	WS/48	VOL
15.99	108.9	107.4	0.113	0.312

- Improved in his second year, production increased in the playoffs
- Good playmaking combo forward that excels as a pick-and-roll ball handler
- Effective in isolation situations if he gets a mismatch
- Improved to become a good outside shooter that can make spot-up threes and run off screens
- Shot over 39% on threes last season, much more consistent as a corner three-point shooter
- Average position defender that can guard both forward spots, middling as a defensive rebounder

J.J. Redick

	Height	Weight	Cap #	Years Left
	6'4"	190	$12.250M	0

Similar at Age 33

		Season	SIMsc
1	Ray Allen*	2008-09	923.6
2	Danny Ainge	1992-93	923.2
3	Vernon Maxwell	1998-99	918.2
4	Joe Dumars*	1996-97	917.6
5	Jamal Crawford	2013-14	903.4
6	Reggie Miller*	1998-99	902.6
7	Dell Curry	1997-98	899.6
8	Gerald Wilkins	1996-97	894.6
9	Brent Barry	2004-05	892.7
10	Latrell Sprewell	2003-04	890.2

Baseline Basic Stats

MPG	PTS	AST	REB	BLK	STL
29.0	13.9	2.4	2.4	0.2	0.8

Advanced Metrics

USG%	3PTA/FGA	FTA/FGA	TS%	eFG%	3PT%
21.2	0.485	0.228	0.584	0.543	0.408

AST%	TOV%	OREB%	DREB%	STL%	BLK%
12.2	9.5	1.0	7.9	1.2	0.4

PER	ORTG	DRTG	WS/48	VOL	
15.02	113.3	108.7	0.127	0.374	

- In his mid-30s, some decline risk, but recent performance is still consistent with his career averages
- One of the best pure shooters in the league
- Excels at making spot-up jumpers and running off screens, shot 42% on threes last season
- Effective at cutting to the rim
- Ball handling and passing has improved to allow him to be good in a small sample of possessions as a pick-and-roll ball handler
- Has become a solid position defender if given favorable matchups

Wilson Chandler

	Height	Weight	Cap #	Years Left
	6'8"	225	$12.801M	0

Similar at Age 30

		Season	SIMsc
1	Luol Deng	2015-16	959.2
2	Walt Williams	2000-01	940.8
3	Mike Dunleavy, Jr.	2010-11	932.8
4	Antawn Jamison	2006-07	932.7
5	Danny Ferry	1996-97	929.8
6	Andres Nocioni	2009-10	926.1
7	Richard Jefferson	2010-11	925.5
8	Marvin Williams	2016-17	925.2
9	Bryon Russell	2000-01	924.4
10	Tim Thomas	2007-08	922.4

Baseline Basic Stats

MPG	PTS	AST	REB	BLK	STL
25.0	9.3	1.7	3.9	0.3	0.6

Advanced Metrics

USG%	3PTA/FGA	FTA/FGA	TS%	eFG%	3PT%
16.8	0.400	0.185	0.533	0.507	0.355

AST%	TOV%	OREB%	DREB%	STL%	BLK%
9.6	11.5	4.3	15.3	1.2	1.0

PER	ORTG	DRTG	WS/48	VOL
11.84	107.3	109.4	0.078	0.327

- In his early 30s, may be starting to decline
- Effective in a low usage role last season, made threes at around a league average rate
- Good at shooting off screens and posting up smaller wing players
- Used in a small sample of pick-and-rolls, did well as both the screener and ball handler
- Fairly good stay-at-home on-ball wing defender, good defensive rebounder

T.J. McConnell

	Height	Weight	Cap #	Years Left
	6'2"	200	$1.601M	0

Similar at Age 25

		Season	SIMsc
1	Raymond Felton	2009-10	918.0
2	Haywoode Workman	1990-91	912.9
3	Sam Vincent	1988-89	900.6
4	Earl Watson	2004-05	899.5
5	Anthony Carter	2000-01	899.2
6	Mike Bratz	1980-81	897.7
7	Jay Humphries	1987-88	897.4
8	Gary Grant	1990-91	895.7
9	Rumeal Robinson	1991-92	894.3
10	Ronnie Price	2008-09	894.1

Baseline Basic Stats

MPG	PTS	AST	REB	BLK	STL
24.2	8.2	4.6	2.5	0.1	1.2

Advanced Metrics

USG%	3PTA/FGA	FTA/FGA	TS%	eFG%	3PT%
15.6	0.177	0.185	0.516	0.482	0.318

AST%	TOV%	OREB%	DREB%	STL%	BLK%
27.3	17.6	2.3	9.5	2.6	0.4

PER	ORTG	DRTG	WS/48	VOL
13.19	108.1	106.9	0.090	0.332

- Solid backup point guard in his prime years
- Low volume, game manager with very good playmaking skills
- Good as a pick-and-roll ball handler
- Steadily improving his ability to finish close range shots
- Shooting percentage on shots inside of three feet has increased each season
- Excelled in spot-up situations by making 43.5% of his threes last season, but his outside shot has historically been inconsistent
- Decent position defender that is capable of defending both guard spots
- Gets steals at a fairly good rate, solid defensive rebounder for his size

Amir Johnson

	Height	Weight	Cap #	Years Left
	6'9"	210	$1.513M	0

Similar at Age 30

		Season	SIMsc
1	Cliff Levingston	1990-91	910.1
2	Joe Meriweather	1983-84	908.9
3	Earl Cureton	1987-88	907.8
4	Derrick McKey	1996-97	903.1
5	Sam Pellom	1981-82	899.6
6	Robert Horry	2000-01	898.5
7	Aaron Williams	2001-02	898.4
8	Taj Gibson	2015-16	897.2
9	Bo Outlaw	2001-02	896.2
10	Billy Owens	1999-00	892.8

Baseline Basic Stats

MPG	PTS	AST	REB	BLK	STL
18.9	5.5	1.2	4.4	0.7	0.6

Advanced Metrics

USG%	3PTA/FGA	FTA/FGA	TS%	eFG%	3PT%
12.8	0.093	0.314	0.575	0.554	0.328

AST%	TOV%	OREB%	DREB%	STL%	BLK%
11.0	15.8	10.2	17.6	1.7	2.9

PER	ORTG	DRTG	WS/48	VOL
13.55	116.2	104.5	0.137	0.398

- Veteran entering his 14th season, performance has been slightly declining
- Primarily an interior defender at this stage of his career
- Can still block shots and is a decent rebounder
- Struggles to defend on the ball, not quite big enough to handle interior players, limited mobility to guard quicker perimeter players
- Lower volume player that can make spot-up jumpers and is effective as the screener in pick-and-rolls
- Above average mid-range shooter for his career, just above break-even on threes, percentages have fluctuated on a year-to-year basis
- Has improved as a passer in the last three seasons

Mike Muscala

	Height	Weight	Cap #	Years Left
	6'11"	239	$5.000M	0

Similar at Age 26

		Season	SIMsc
1	Justin Hamilton	2016-17	924.6
2	Channing Frye	2009-10	916.0
3	Charlie Villanueva	2010-11	911.8
4	Troy Murphy	2006-07	910.4
5	Jonas Jerebko	2013-14	905.5
6	Austin Croshere	2001-02	905.3
7	Pete Chilcutt	1994-95	901.8
8	Matt Bonner	2006-07	899.4
9	Vladimir Radmanovic	2006-07	898.3
10	Spencer Hawes	2014-15	897.6

Baseline Basic Stats

MPG	PTS	AST	REB	BLK	STL
17.2	6.3	1.1	3.7	0.4	0.5

Advanced Metrics

USG%	3PTA/FGA	FTA/FGA	TS%	eFG%	3PT%
16.1	0.456	0.174	0.570	0.541	0.381

AST%	TOV%	OREB%	DREB%	STL%	BLK%
9.1	10.9	5.7	17.9	1.3	2.1

PER	ORTG	DRTG	WS/48	VOL
13.80	112.1	107.6	0.118	0.229

- Rotational shooting big in his prime years
- More of a lower volume catch and shoot player at this stage
- Effective as a spot-up shooter and screener in the pick-and-roll
- Career 37.8% three-point shooter overall, 44.1% shooter on corner threes
- Can somewhat protect the rim, decent shot blocker, Block Percentage has been declining for the last three seasons
- Solid on the defensive boards last seasons, has trouble defending on the ball due to a lack of quickness

Markelle Fultz

	Height	Weight	Cap #	Years Left
	6'4"	195	$8.340M	2 Team Options

Similar at Age **19**

		Season	SIMsc
1	Ricky Davis	1998-99	875.6
2	Tony Wroten	2012-13	873.0
3	Marquis Teague	2012-13	863.2
4	Archie Goodwin	2013-14	863.0
5	Emmanuel Mudiay	2015-16	860.2
6	Shaun Livingston	2004-05	857.3
7	Gerald Wallace	2001-02	855.4
8	Tyus Jones	2015-16	852.1
9	Lou Williams	2005-06	846.7
10	DeShawn Stevenson	2000-01	843.7

Baseline Basic Stats

MPG	PTS	AST	REB	BLK	STL
21.5	9.7	3.0	2.7	0.3	0.9

Advanced Metrics

USG%	3PTA/FGA	FTA/FGA	TS%	eFG%	3PT%
23.6	0.052	0.277	0.482	0.451	0.121

AST%	TOV%	OREB%	DREB%	STL%	BLK%
28.8	13.2	4.2	12.2	2.3	1.0

PER	ORTG	DRTG	WS/48	VOL	
14.72	101.9	108.5	0.047	0.670	

- Missed most of last season due to a mysterious shoulder ailment or anxiety issue
- Showed promise as a playmaker that could drive hard to the rim and make explosive plays in transition
- Made almost 66% of his shots inside of three feet
- Very reluctant to take outside shots
- Missed his only three-pointer last season, shot below 50% on free throws
- If his shooting doesn't improve, fit may be a concern because his skill set would overlap with Ben Simmons
- Played solid defense against both guard spots, was better against point guards than he was against wing guys
- Active help defender that got steals at a high rate, could occasionally block a shot, good defensive rebounding guard

Furkan Korkmaz

	Height	Weight	Cap #	Years Left
	6'7"	185	$1.740M	2 Team Options

Similar at Age 20

		Season	SIMsc
1	Sasha Vujacic	2004-05	891.3
2	Sergey Karasev	2013-14	879.5
3	Rashad Vaughn	2016-17	875.4
4	Kelly Oubre	2015-16	870.7
5	Otto Porter	2013-14	859.8
6	Jeremy Lamb	2012-13	857.2
7	Adonis Thomas	2013-14	853.0
8	James Young	2015-16	851.2
9	Martell Webster	2006-07	849.4
10	Ben McLemore	2013-14	842.6

Baseline Basic Stats

MPG	PTS	AST	REB	BLK	STL
17.1	5.9	0.9	2.1	0.2	0.5

Advanced Metrics

USG%	3PTA/FGA	FTA/FGA	TS%	eFG%	3PT%
16.2	0.578	0.156	0.490	0.472	0.366

AST%	TOV%	OREB%	DREB%	STL%	BLK%
7.4	8.1	2.3	11.3	1.5	0.9

PER	ORTG	DRTG	WS/48	VOL	
8.30	100.7	106.8	0.062	0.533	

- Missed a chunk of the season due to a left foot injury
- Only played 80 minutes in the NBA and 9 games in the G-League
- Strong performance in this year's Las Vegas Summer League, posted a 22.36 PER and shot 37% on threes
- Showed decent playmaking skills while limiting his turnovers
- Played adequate on-ball defense, solid on the defensive boards, could occasionally get steals and blocks
- Could develop into a shooting specialist if his Summer League performance translates

Jerryd Bayless

	Height	Weight	Cap #	Years Left
	6'3"	200	$8.576M	0

Similar at Age 29

		Season	SIMsc
1	Keyon Dooling	2009-10	933.1
2	Eldridge Recasner	1996-97	930.7
3	Charlie Bell	2008-09	930.7
4	Marcus Thornton	2016-17	929.7
5	Erick Strickland	2002-03	925.6
6	Ben Gordon	2012-13	920.0
7	Emanual Davis	1997-98	916.6
8	Doug Overton	1998-99	916.0
9	Ricky Davis	2008-09	914.3
10	Gary Neal	2013-14	913.6

Baseline Basic Stats

MPG	PTS	AST	REB	BLK	STL
20.9	8.2	2.0	2.0	0.1	0.6

Advanced Metrics

USG%	3PTA/FGA	FTA/FGA	TS%	eFG%	3PT%
19.0	0.398	0.218	0.527	0.485	0.383

AST%	TOV%	OREB%	DREB%	STL%	BLK%
15.3	14.1	2.2	9.5	1.2	0.4

PER	ORTG	DRTG	WS/48	VOL
10.31	102.1	109.8	0.041	0.395

- Missed significant portions of the last two seasons due to a nagging left wrist injury
- Struggled to fit into a stationary low volume role last season
- Most effective in motion by running off screens and cutting to the basket
- Slightly above league average three-point shooter for his career, decent playmaking combo guard
- Middling on-ball defender at best, has to be hidden in favorable matchups
- Lateral quickness is slightly diminished, better against bigger two guards

Newcomers

Jonah Bolden

		Height	Weight	Cap #	Years Left
		6'10"	220	$0.838M	3

Baseline Basic Stats

MPG	PTS	AST	REB	BLK	STL
20.5	6.8	1.3	4.5	0.7	0.7

Advanced Metrics

USG%	3PTA/FGA	FTA/FGA	TS%	eFG%	3PT%
14.6	0.360	0.259	0.563	0.540	0.322

AST%	TOV%	OREB%	DREB%	STL%	BLK%
10.6	15.2	7.4	21.1	2.4	3.1

PER	ORTG	DRTG	WS/48	VOL	
12.82	111.5	113.0	0.090	0.407	

- Translated EuroLeague stats, Played in Israel last season for Maccabi Tel Aviv
- Drafted by Philadelphia with the 36th overall pick in 2017
- Has improved his interior defense to the point where he was a solid rebounder and shot blocker in the EuroLeague, also got steals at a high rate
- A solid big passing big man, but a little bit turnover prone
- Effectively scores inside and will draw fouls, has shot below 60% on his free throws over the last two seasons
- Some stretch potential, but his outside shot is inconsistent
- Made 40.5% of his threes in the Adriatic League in 2016-17
- Three-Point Percentage dropped to 30.7% last season with Maccabi

Zhaire Smith

	Height	Weight	Cap #	Years Left
	6'5"	195	$2.612M	1 + 2 TO

Baseline Basic Stats

MPG	PTS	AST	REB	BLK	STL
11.9	4.1	0.7	1.9	0.2	0.4

Advanced Metrics

USG%	3PTA/FGA	FTA/FGA	TS%	eFG%	3PT%
17.9	0.192	0.290	0.497	0.454	0.271

AST%	TOV%	OREB%	DREB%	STL%	BLK%
9.8	12.6	5.4	12.4	1.7	1.4

PER	ORTG	DRTG	WS/48	VOL
11.31	100.3	106.8	0.058	N/A

- Drafted by Phoenix with the 16th overall pick and later traded to Philadelphia
- Could miss most of the season due to a foot fracture suffered at a Las Vegas development camp in August
- If he plays this season, he will be in his age-19 season, but he's still a bit raw and could use additional seasoning in the G-League
- Struggled a bit in Summer League in July
- Flashed some playmaking skills and the ability to avoid turnovers
- Did not shoot well in a low volume role, made less than a third of his field goals, was 3-for-15 on threes
- Decent on the defensive end, more of a stay-at-home defender
- Could use length to aggressively contest shots, rebounded at a below average rate

Landry Shamet

	Height	Weight	Cap #	Years Left
	6'4"	180	$1.704M	1 + 2 TO

Baseline Basic Stats

MPG	PTS	AST	REB	BLK	STL
10.4	3.4	1.2	1.2	0.1	0.4

Advanced Metrics

USG%	3PTA/FGA	FTA/FGA	TS%	eFG%	3PT%
18.1	0.380	0.199	0.475	0.442	0.320

AST%	TOV%	OREB%	DREB%	STL%	BLK%
17.7	16.0	2.4	10.4	1.8	0.6

PER	ORTG	DRTG	WS/48	VOL
9.49	96.6	107.0	0.038	N/A

- Drafted by Philadelphia in the first round with the 27th overall pick
- Missed Summer League due to a sprained right ankle
- Good outside shooter in college that was most effective at running off screens and spotting up
- Decent playmaking skills, generally avoids turnovers
- Middling defender at best, will likely have to be hidden in favorable matchups in the NBA
- May need to spend most of the year in the G-League to get used to the longer NBA three-point line

WASHINGTON WIZARDS

Last Season: 43 – 39, Lost 1st Round to Toronto (2 – 4)

Offensive Rating: 109.3, 14th in NBA   Defensive Rating: 108.7, 15th in NBA

Primary Executive: Ernie Grunfeld, President of Basketball Operations

Head Coach: Scott Brooks

Key Roster Changes

Subtractions
Marcin Gortat, trade
Mike Scott, free agency
Tim Frazier, free agency
Chris McCullough, free agency
Ramon Sessions, free agency
Ty Lawson, free agency

Additions
Austin Rivers, trade
Troy Brown, draft
Thomas Bryant, claimed off waivers
Dwight Howard, free agency
Jeff Green, free agency

RAFER Projected Win Total: 45.2

Projected Best Five-Man Unit
1. John Wall
2. Bradley Beal
3. Tomas Satoransky
4. Otto Porter
5. Dwight Howard

Other Rotation Players
Kelly Oubre
Markieff Morris
Jeff Green
Austin Rivers

Remaining Roster

- Ian Mahinmi
- Jodie Meeks
- Troy Brown, Jr.
- Thomas Bryant
- Jason Smith
- Devin Robinson, 23, 6'8", 190, Florida (Two-Way)
- Chasson Randle, 25, 6'2", 185, Stanford (Exhibit 10)

Season Forecast

At the beginning of the summer, the Washington Wizards seemed like they were stuck in place, as they were basically capped out with very little room to maneuver. However, they found a way to shake things up a little by dealing Marcin Gortat to the Clippers for Austin Rivers and then they picked up Dwight Howard and Jeff Green to fill out their rotation. The signing of Howard carries some major risk because he's gained a reputation for being something of a locker room cancer due to his issues with immaturity, a lack of accountability for his faults and a stubborn insistence on getting a high volume of post touches. Teammates have had problems with Howard in stints with four different teams, so there's a significant chance that he may revert back to his ways and cause the Wizards to implode. However, if Howard gets his act together and plays his expected role as a rim runner and rim protector, Washington could be a top-four seed in the East.

After all, the Wizards feature one of the best backcourts in the league with All-Stars John Wall and Bradley Beal. Additionally, Otto Porter has turned into a very good third option and is one of the better two-way wing players in the NBA. Theoretically, Howard is an upgrade over Gortat, but he will have to adjust to a lower usage role, which has been a problem in the past to say the least. The injury to Wall last season did allow them to uncover a potentially useful fifth man for their closing unit in Tomas Satoransky because of his very efficient shooting. However, it's probably unlikely that Scott Brooks would deploy the lineup listed above because he tends to stick his familiar five-man units. Therefore, it's more likely than Kelly Oubre or Markieff Morris will be the team's primary fifth man. Either one isn't a bad option and the resulting lineup should allow them to finish games against a good chunk of the East, but they may not have enough spacing or playmaking to compete against the top teams in the league. Also, their bench is still a bit thin because Rivers and Green have had some history of inconsistency, so the Wizards will have to find a way lengthen their rotation by either internally developing a back-end player like rookie Troy Brown, Jr. or making a small pickup from the G-League. Overall, the Wizards are a high risk, moderate reward team because of Howard's presence. On average, if there are no major problems, the team should be a solid playoff team in the East, but they may only have enough talent to win one round in the playoffs. On the other hand, if Howard reverts to his toxic ways, they could find themselves in the disappointing position of being a lower seed in the East or even out of the playoffs entirely. If that worst-case scenario occurs, Washington will have to explore a major shake-up that may involve dealing one of its top players in the future.

Veterans

John Wall

	Height	Weight	Cap #	Years Left
	6'4"	195	$19.170M	3 + PO

Similar at Age **27**

		Season	SIMsc
1	Deron Williams	2011-12	907.3
2	Baron Davis	2006-07	899.3
3	Sam Cassell	1996-97	895.0
4	Russell Westbrook	2015-16	886.2
5	Eric Bledsoe	2016-17	884.9
6	Jeff Teague	2015-16	884.7
7	Devin Harris	2010-11	884.4
8	Jason Kidd*	2000-01	881.5
9	Steve Francis	2004-05	879.5
10	Kendall Gill	1995-96	875.1

Baseline Basic Stats

MPG	PTS	AST	REB	BLK	STL
33.9	18.3	7.6	4.3	0.5	1.6

Advanced Metrics

USG%	3PTA/FGA	FTA/FGA	TS%	eFG%	3PT%
27.5	0.286	0.331	0.532	0.481	0.351

AST%	TOV%	OREB%	DREB%	STL%	BLK%
41.4	16.4	2.2	11.6	2.3	1.7

PER	ORTG	DRTG	WS/48	VOL
20.05	108.0	107.5	0.125	0.448

- All-Star level point guard in his prime, missed a large chunk of the season due to a left knee injury that required surgery
- Dynamic playmaker with explosive athleticism when healthy, a little bit turnover prone
- Good scorer that uses his quickness to blow by defenders in isolation situations, draws fouls at a high rate
- Shot an above average percentage on threes last season
- Three-Point Percentage fluctuates from-year-to-year, below break-even career three-point shooter
- Decent on-ball defender that uses his length to contest shots, can be beaten off the dribble by quicker guards
- Active help defender that gets steals, blocks and defensive rebounds at a high rate when healthy

Bradley Beal

	Height	Weight	Cap #	Years Left
	6'3"	207	$25.434M	2

Similar at Age 24

		Season	SIMsc
1	C.J. McCollum	2015-16	948.3
2	Ben Gordon	2007-08	937.4
3	Damian Lillard	2014-15	937.3
4	Ray Allen*	1999-00	929.5
5	O.J. Mayo	2011-12	923.3
6	Brandon Knight	2015-16	918.9
7	Reggie Jackson	2014-15	911.5
8	Isaiah Rider	1995-96	909.7
9	Allan Houston	1995-96	909.4
10	Marcus Thornton	2011-12	908.5

Baseline Basic Stats

MPG	PTS	AST	REB	BLK	STL
32.8	18.5	3.8	3.6	0.3	1.0

Advanced Metrics

USG%	3PTA/FGA	FTA/FGA	TS%	eFG%	3PT%
26.5	0.371	0.267	0.570	0.524	0.390

AST%	TOV%	OREB%	DREB%	STL%	BLK%
20.6	11.2	2.3	10.3	1.5	0.8

PER	ORTG	DRTG	WS/48	VOL
18.74	111.3	109.6	0.120	0.350

- Entering his prime, one of the best two guards in the league
- Improved playmaking skills made him very effective as a pick-and-roll ball handler
- Above average in isolation situations
- Great overall shooter that makes spot-up jumpers and can run off screens
- Good overall three-point shooter with a career percentage of 39.3%
- Solid position defender, much better at handling bigger wing players than quicker guards
- Posted the highest Defensive Rebound Percentage of his career last season

Otto Porter

	Height	Weight	Cap #	Years Left
	6'9"	198	$26.012M	1 + PO

Similar at Age 24

		Season	SIMsc
1	Chandler Parsons	2012-13	921.6
2	Dorell Wright	2009-10	912.5
3	DerMarr Johnson	2004-05	906.9
4	Trevor Ariza	2009-10	900.4
5	Mike Dunleavy, Jr.	2004-05	895.5
6	James Posey	2000-01	895.3
7	Shane Battier	2002-03	890.1
8	Hedo Turkoglu	2003-04	889.8
9	Scott Burrell	1994-95	889.6
10	Courtney Lee	2009-10	889.4

Baseline Basic Stats

MPG	PTS	AST	REB	BLK	STL
32.8	13.7	2.4	5.2	0.5	1.2

Advanced Metrics

USG%	3PTA/FGA	FTA/FGA	TS%	eFG%	3PT%
18.4	0.410	0.183	0.591	0.563	0.418

AST%	TOV%	OREB%	DREB%	STL%	BLK%
10.8	8.2	4.0	16.2	2.1	1.4

PER	ORTG	DRTG	WS/48	VOL
17.36	118.4	107.9	0.145	0.243

- Excellent complementary, two-way combo forward in his prime
- Thrives in a lower usage role with his very efficient shooting and ability to avoid turnovers
- Has become an excellent shooter that makes spot-up jumpers and can run off screens
- Has made 43.7% of his threes over the last two seasons
- Improved playmaking skills allowed him to have success as a pick-and-roll ball handler in limited situations
- Defends multiple positions and is capable of handling the tougher assignments
- Active help defender that get steals at a solid rate
- Can use length to contest and occasionally block shots, good defensive rebounding wing player

Dwight Howard

	Height	Weight	Cap #	Years Left
	6'11"	240	$5.337M	PO + 1

Similar at Age 32

		Season	SIMsc
1	Artis Gilmore*	1981-82	895.0
2	Robert Parish*	1985-86	884.1
3	Marcin Gortat	2016-17	883.9
4	Elden Campbell	2000-01	875.0
5	Tyson Chandler	2014-15	873.8
6	Tim Duncan	2008-09	872.0
7	Will Perdue	1997-98	870.3
8	Samuel Dalembert	2013-14	867.6
9	Patrick Ewing*	1994-95	867.1
10	Rony Seikaly	1997-98	865.8

Baseline Basic Stats

MPG	PTS	AST	REB	BLK	STL
30.3	14.1	1.6	9.8	1.5	0.7

Advanced Metrics

USG%	3PTA/FGA	FTA/FGA	TS%	eFG%	3PT%
20.6	0.006	0.568	0.587	0.566	0.115

AST%	TOV%	OREB%	DREB%	STL%	BLK%
8.1	16.1	11.0	29.6	1.0	3.6

PER	ORTG	DRTG	WS/48	VOL
18.84	110.3	103.3	0.139	0.428

- Approaching his mid-30s, some decline risk, but his production has been consistent for the last six seasons
- Durable, no major injuries over the last three seasons, but he has been a notorious chemistry disruption in his stops with four different teams
- Good rim running big man and still one of the league's rebounders and shot blockers
- Inefficient post-up player, still turnover prone and his Free Throw Percentage is still below 60%
- Can protect the rim, doesn't cover his man out on the perimeter, prone to giving up open outside shots to opposing stretch bigs

Markieff Morris

	Height	Weight	Cap #	Years Left
	6'10"	245	$8.600M	0

Similar at Age 28

		Season	SIMsc
1	Mehmet Okur	2007-08	930.2
2	Herb Williams	1986-87	925.3
3	Channing Frye	2011-12	923.1
4	Nemanja Bjelica	2016-17	919.4
5	Terry Mills	1995-96	917.0
6	Rasheed Wallace	2002-03	916.5
7	Wayman Tisdale	1992-93	913.3
8	Jordan Hill	2015-16	913.2
9	Keith Van Horn	2003-04	911.7
10	Ersan Ilyasova	2015-16	910.1

Baseline Basic Stats

MPG	PTS	AST	REB	BLK	STL
26.3	11.4	1.8	5.7	0.6	0.7

Advanced Metrics

USG%	3PTA/FGA	FTA/FGA	TS%	eFG%	3PT%
19.5	0.304	0.209	0.546	0.511	0.366

AST%	TOV%	OREB%	DREB%	STL%	BLK%
10.3	13.2	4.9	18.9	1.4	1.7

PER	ORTG	DRTG	WS/48	VOL	
13.39	105.0	107.2	0.081	0.381	

- Durable, no major injury history, rotational big man in his prime years
- Lower usage player, has been an above average three-point shooter in each of the last two seasons
- Effective as a cutter, can post-up smaller players, fairly good in isolations if given a mismatch
- Average overall defender that plays physical, solid rebounder
- Has trouble moving laterally, below average at defending on the ball

Kelly Oubre

	Height	Weight	Cap #	Years Left
	6'7"	205	$3.209M	0

Similar at Age 22

		Season	SIMsc
1	Caris LeVert	2016-17	926.7
2	Rodney Carney	2006-07	924.5
3	Nicolas Batum	2010-11	923.4
4	Chase Budinger	2010-11	922.6
5	Evan Turner	2010-11	917.3
6	Khris Middleton	2013-14	916.5
7	C.J. Miles	2009-10	915.9
8	Terrence Ross	2013-14	915.1
9	Nik Stauskas	2015-16	914.4
10	Maurice Harkless	2015-16	913.1

Baseline Basic Stats

MPG	PTS	AST	REB	BLK	STL
26.3	10.4	1.6	3.6	0.4	0.8

Advanced Metrics

USG%	3PTA/FGA	FTA/FGA	TS%	eFG%	3PT%
18.1	0.437	0.234	0.546	0.507	0.362

AST%	TOV%	OREB%	DREB%	STL%	BLK%
8.1	9.7	3.1	13.5	1.7	1.2

PER	ORTG	DRTG	WS/48	VOL
12.40	107.8	108.1	0.088	0.343

- Still developing, has improved in each of his three seasons
- Great athleticism makes him a solid on-ball perimeter defender
- Good at using his length to contest shots, occasionally gets steals, solid defensive rebounder
- Lower volume catch-and-shoot player at this stage
- Good finisher in transition, but outside shot still needs improvement
- Three-Point Percentage was still slightly below the league average, but above break-even

Tomas Satoransky

	Height	Weight	Cap #	Years Left
	6'7"	210	$3.129M	0

Similar at Age 26

		Season	SIMsc
1	James Ennis	2016-17	926.1
2	Marty Byrnes	1982-83	924.7
3	John Salmons	2005-06	922.9
4	Harold Pressley	1989-90	917.5
5	Eddie Robinson	2002-03	916.0
6	Alonzo Gee	2013-14	910.5
7	Mike O'Koren	1984-85	909.3
8	Chase Budinger	2014-15	909.0
9	Shandon Anderson	1999-00	909.0
10	Jiri Welsch	2005-06	906.7

Baseline Basic Stats

MPG	PTS	AST	REB	BLK	STL
21.3	7.0	2.1	2.8	0.3	0.7

Advanced Metrics

USG%	3PTA/FGA	FTA/FGA	TS%	eFG%	3PT%
15.0	0.248	0.261	0.545	0.507	0.364

AST%	TOV%	OREB%	DREB%	STL%	BLK%
18.5	15.6	4.0	10.6	1.7	0.8

PER	ORTG	DRTG	WS/48	VOL	
12.55	110.5	109.3	0.100	0.376	

- Dramatically improved in his second season, but was ineffective in limited minutes in the playoffs
- Big playmaking guard that shot the ball very efficiently last season, shot 46.5% on threes over 101 attempts
- Was one of the best per-possession cutters in the NBA last season, ranked by the NBA in the 98th percentile
- Solid on-ball defender that can defend both guard spots
- Better at using his size to defend point guards, somewhat lacking in lateral quickness
- Decent rebounder that can occasionally play passing lanes to get steals

Jeff Green

	Height	Weight	Cap #	Years Left
	6'9"	235	$1.513M	0

Similar at Age **31**

		Season	SIMsc
1	Sam Perkins	1992-93	926.0
2	Mike Dunleavy, Jr.	2011-12	922.8
3	Chris Bosh	2015-16	921.3
4	Tim Thomas	2008-09	917.5
5	Juwan Howard	2004-05	911.2
6	Lamond Murray	2004-05	911.1
7	David West	2011-12	905.6
8	Rashard Lewis	2010-11	905.5
9	LaPhonso Ellis	2001-02	903.7
10	Dave Robisch	1980-81	903.0

Baseline Basic Stats

MPG	PTS	AST	REB	BLK	STL
23.5	9.7	1.4	4.1	0.4	0.6

Advanced Metrics

USG%	3PTA/FGA	FTA/FGA	TS%	eFG%	3PT%
18.8	0.320	0.318	0.562	0.507	0.346

AST%	TOV%	OREB%	DREB%	STL%	BLK%
8.8	10.3	4.0	13.4	1.2	1.4

PER	ORTG	DRTG	WS/48	VOL	
13.78	111.0	109.6	0.097	0.404	

- Had a resurgence last season in Cleveland after some inconsistent play with three teams in the previous two seasons
- Got more touches around the basket to improve his scoring efficiency
- May be better utilized as a roll man in pick-and-roll situations
- Historically has been a middling post-up player and a below average three-point shooter
- Decent defensively, can match up with perimeter players and big men, more of a position defender at this stage

Austin Rivers

	Height	Weight	Cap #	Years Left
	6'4"	200	$12.650M	0

Similar at Age **25**

		Season	SIMsc
1	Jerryd Bayless	2013-14	941.1
2	Antonio Daniels	2000-01	935.8
3	Anthony Peeler	1994-95	933.9
4	Smush Parker	2006-07	932.2
5	Jeremy Lin	2013-14	931.0
6	Chauncey Billups	2001-02	929.1
7	Fred Jones	2004-05	927.4
8	Wayne Ellington	2012-13	926.6
9	O.J. Mayo	2012-13	926.2
10	Jordan Crawford	2013-14	924.3

Baseline Basic Stats

MPG	PTS	AST	REB	BLK	STL
25.7	10.7	2.6	2.4	0.2	0.8

Advanced Metrics

USG%	3PTA/FGA	FTA/FGA	TS%	eFG%	3PT%
20.4	0.413	0.219	0.529	0.498	0.369

AST%	TOV%	OREB%	DREB%	STL%	BLK%
16.9	12.1	1.5	8.1	1.5	0.6

PER	ORTG	DRTG	WS/48	VOL	
12.57	104.6	110.7	0.058	0.291	

- Rotational combo guard in his prime years
- Has become an above average three-point shooter and his playmaking abilities have improved
- Effective with the ball in his hands last season, good as a pick-and-roll ball handler and could score on isolations
- Good at cutting to the rim in a small sample of possessions
- Below average defender, lacks the quickness to defend smaller guards and not long enough to handle bigger wing players
- Occasionally gets steals, below average overall rebounder

Ian Mahinmi

	Height	Weight	Cap #	Years Left
	6'11"	230	$15.944M	1

Similar at Age 31

		Season	SIMsc
1	John Salley	1995-96	934.1
2	Vin Baker	2002-03	930.6
3	Mark West	1991-92	914.8
4	Scott Williams	1999-00	896.9
5	Major Jones	1984-85	894.5
6	Ryan Hollins	2015-16	893.4
7	Ervin Johnson	1998-99	893.2
8	Joakim Noah	2016-17	893.0
9	Mikki Moore	2006-07	891.2
10	Marvin Webster	1983-84	887.4

Baseline Basic Stats

MPG	PTS	AST	REB	BLK	STL
17.1	5.0	0.7	4.5	0.7	0.5

Advanced Metrics

USG%	3PTA/FGA	FTA/FGA	TS%	eFG%	3PT%
14.5	0.007	0.501	0.565	0.528	0.198

AST%	TOV%	OREB%	DREB%	STL%	BLK%
6.6	20.1	11.0	19.0	1.8	3.0

PER	ORTG	DRTG	WS/48	VOL	
12.54	107.4	105.3	0.094	0.488	

- Situational big man, possibly in his decline phase, production lower than his career averages
- Tore the meniscus in his left knee in 2016-17
- Some ability as a rim runner that finishes shots inside of three feet
- Will draw fouls at a high rate, good offensive rebounder
- Decent rim protector, solid shot blocker, adequate defensive rebounder
- Struggles with position defense, lacks lateral mobility, highly foul prone

Jodie Meeks

	Height	Weight	Cap #	Years Left
	6'4"	208	$3.455M	0

Similar at Age **30**

		Season	SIMsc
1	Willie Green	2011-12	932.3
2	Marco Belinelli	2016-17	922.1
3	Gary Neal	2014-15	921.9
4	Anthony Peeler	1999-00	920.2
5	Gordan Giricek	2007-08	917.1
6	Nick Young	2015-16	915.2
7	Anthony Morrow	2015-16	913.1
8	Matt Carroll	2010-11	911.5
9	Voshon Lenard	2003-04	908.6
10	Kevin Grevey	1983-84	906.7

Baseline Basic Stats

MPG	PTS	AST	REB	BLK	STL
22.2	9.0	1.7	2.0	0.2	0.6

Advanced Metrics

USG%	3PTA/FGA	FTA/FGA	TS%	eFG%	3PT%
18.3	0.516	0.221	0.553	0.510	0.379

AST%	TOV%	OREB%	DREB%	STL%	BLK%
10.5	9.5	1.5	9.7	1.5	0.5

PER	ORTG	DRTG	WS/48	VOL	
12.30	109.9	110.8	0.087	0.429	

- Must serve a 25 game suspension for testing positive for two banned substances on the PED list
- In early 30s, some decline risk, situational shooting specialist at this stage in his career
- Primarily a spot-up shooter, historically has been a 37.2% three-point shooter
- Shot just above break-even on threes last season
- Decent position defender if given favorable matchups, fairly solid defensive rebounder

Thomas Bryant

	Height	Weight	Cap #	Years Left
	6'10"	248	$1.378M	0

Similar at Age 20

		Season	SIMsc
1	Brandon Bass	2005-06	869.8
2	Trey Lyles	2015-16	860.0
3	Damien Inglis	2015-16	859.3
4	Henry Ellenson	2016-17	850.9
5	Ryan Anderson	2008-09	849.8
6	Domantas Sabonis	2016-17	848.4
7	Samaki Walker	1996-97	845.5
8	Derrick Williams	2011-12	841.3
9	Noah Vonleh	2015-16	841.3
10	Jermaine O'Neal	1998-99	840.4

Baseline Basic Stats

MPG	PTS	AST	REB	BLK	STL
17.0	6.3	1.0	3.9	0.4	0.4

Advanced Metrics

USG%	3PTA/FGA	FTA/FGA	TS%	eFG%	3PT%
17.9	0.407	0.320	0.496	0.460	0.240

AST%	TOV%	OREB%	DREB%	STL%	BLK%
11.0	10.1	6.0	18.9	1.0	1.6

PER	ORTG	DRTG	WS/48	VOL
12.51	104.9	108.4	0.072	0.610

- Only played 72 minutes for the Lakers last season, spent most of the year with South Bay in the G-League
- Played very well in the G-League, 9th in PER, 10th in Win Shares, 3rd in True Shooting Percentage
- Efficient scorer overall, good at finishing plays inside
- Showed stretch potential by making 36.4% of his threes in 184 attempts
- Decent passing big man that generally doesn't turn the ball over
- Blocked shots at a high rate, may sacrifice positioning to go blocks, adequate defensive rebounder

Jason Smith

	Height	Weight	Cap #	Years Left
	7'0"	240	$5.450M	0

Similar at Age 31

		Season	SIMsc
1	Bill Wennington	1994-95	897.6
2	Greg Foster	1999-00	893.6
3	Francisco Elson	2007-08	885.7
4	Matt Geiger	2000-01	880.4
5	Rasho Nesterovic	2007-08	879.9
6	Zeljko Rebraca	2003-04	876.2
7	Joe Barry Carroll	1989-90	875.7
8	Sam Bowie	1992-93	875.0
9	Kris Humphries	2016-17	874.0
10	Mehmet Okur	2010-11	872.6

Baseline Basic Stats

MPG	PTS	AST	REB	BLK	STL
14.0	4.9	0.7	2.8	0.4	0.3

Advanced Metrics

USG%	3PTA/FGA	FTA/FGA	TS%	eFG%	3PT%
18.2	0.167	0.195	0.511	0.475	0.330

AST%	TOV%	OREB%	DREB%	STL%	BLK%
8.2	13.0	7.1	15.2	0.9	3.3

PER	ORTG	DRTG	WS/48	VOL	
10.99	102.2	108.7	0.055	0.360	

- Older player in his 30s, in the decline stage of his career
- Missed two months due to a sprained right shoulder
- Below average position defender and rebounder
- Has blocked shots at a high rate over the last three seasons
- Predominantly a good mid-range shooting big man, could keep his career alive if he extends his shooting range to the three-point line
- Almost a break-even three-point shooter for his career, shoots much better in the corners at 36% for his career

Newcomers

Troy Brown, Jr.

	Height	Weight	Cap #	Years Left
	6'7"	215	$2.749M	1 + PO

Baseline Basic Stats

MPG	PTS	AST	REB	BLK	STL
11.0	3.9	1.2	1.4	0.1	0.4

Advanced Metrics

USG%	3PTA/FGA	FTA/FGA	TS%	eFG%	3PT%
20.6	0.159	0.287	0.461	0.418	0.264

AST%	TOV%	OREB%	DREB%	STL%	BLK%
17.0	17.3	4.6	10.1	1.9	0.8

PER	ORTG	DRTG	WS/48	VOL
9.87	91.6	108.4	-0.004	N/A

- Drafted by Washington in the first round with the 15th pick
- Decent performance at Summer League
- Very good athlete, has the potential to defend multiple positions
- Got steals at a fairly high rate, good on the defensive boards
- Still not polished at this stage, could benefit by getting some additional seasoning in the G-League
- Showed some playmaking skills, but was a bit turnover prone
- Good from inside, made 50% of his two-point shots
- Outside shot needs considerable work, went 3-for-19 on threes at Summer League

MILWAUKEE BUCKS

Last Season: 44 – 38, Lost 1st Round to Boston (3 – 4)

Offensive Rating: 109.8, 9th in NBA

Defensive Rating: 110.1, 19th in NBA

Primary Executive: Jon Horst, General Manager

Head Coach: Mike Budenholzer

Key Roster Changes

Subtractions
Jabari Parker, free agency
Jason Terry, free agency

Additions
Donte DiVincenzo, draft
Ersan Ilyasova, free agency
Brook Lopez, free agency
Pat Connaughton, free agency

RAFER Projected Win Total: 42.8

Projected Best Five-Man Unit
1. Eric Bledsoe
2. Khris Middleton
3. Giannis Antetokounmpo
4. Ersan Ilyasova
5. John Henson

Other Rotation Players
Malcolm Brogdon
Tony Snell
Brook Lopez
Matthew Dellavedova

Remaining Roster

- Thon Maker
- Tyler Zeller
- Pat Connaughton
- D.J. Wilson
- Sterling Brown
- Donte DiVincenzo
- Jaylen Morris, 23, 6'5", 185, Molloy College (Two-Way)
- Trevon Duval, 20, 6'3", 186, Duke (Two-Way)
- Shabazz Muhammad, 26, 6'6", 223, UCLA (Exhibit 10)
- Christian Wood, 23, 6'11", 220, UNLV (Exhibit 10)
- Jordan Barnett, 23, 6'7", 215, Missouri (Exhibit 10)
- Brandon McCoy, 20, 7'0", 250, UNLV (Exhibit 10)
- Travis Trice, 26, 6'0", 170, Michigan State (Exhibit 10)

Season Forecast

The wheels for this season were set in motion last season when they fired their previous head coach, Jason Kidd. This summer, they quickly pounced to hire former 2014-15 Coach of the Year, Mike Budenholzer when he resigned from his job with the Atlanta Hawks. Milwaukee made some subtle tweaks to roster to add shooters by picking up Ersan Ilyasova, Brook Lopez and Pat Connaughton in free agency. If the team makes a quick adjustment to Budenholzer's system, they could be an interesting dark horse in the East because they now have the conference's best player in Giannis Antetokounmpo, now that LeBron James has gone to the West.

Under the previous regime, the Bucks struggled to effectively defend, and their offense tended to stagnate due to a lack of ball movement. If Budenholzer gets a full buy-in from his team, these issues should be corrected because when provided sufficient talent, his teams were usually among the league's best defensive teams and they typically ranked high in all of the NBA's ball movement metrics. With a new system that encourages more ball and player movement, the greatest beneficiary is likely to be Antetokounmpo because he wouldn't have to work as hard to create his own offense. Also, his teammates would be in a better position to complement him and accentuate his unique skill set.

Most likely, the Bucks will lean on their defense to win games because their best players are only about average three-point shooters at best. The lineup on the previous page represents the best way to use length to disrupt their opponents and generate enough offense to execute late in games. John Henson would give them a solid rim protector that has shown enough mobility to switch out on a guard for a few dribbles. Khris Middleton could take the primary responsibility to defend elite wing players and Ilyasova is versatile enough to defend big men and some wings, freeing Antetokounmpo to be a dynamic, roaming help defender. If they needed some more offense or extra mobility, they could pull Henson, move Antetokounmpo to the five and insert Malcolm Brogdon to give them an extra playmaker and shooter. In general, Milwaukee could be an interesting team in the Eastern Conference because they will be implementing a system that has been pretty successful in the past, especially at getting great production from unheralded sources. It initially took Budenholzer's Hawks team a full season to adjust to his system, but this Bucks roster is much more talented, so the learning curve might not be as steep. If that is the case, then Milwaukee could wind up becoming a surprise contender in the East with an outside chance to reach the Finals. In all likelihood, they will be a solid playoff team that is good enough to win a round in the playoffs.

Veterans

Giannis Antetokounmpo

	Height	Weight	Cap #	Years Left
	6'9"	210	$24.157M	2

Similar at Age **23**

		Season	SIMsc
1	Kevin Durant	2011-12	901.2
2	Anthony Davis	2016-17	895.9
3	Terry Cummings	1984-85	894.7
4	Josh Smith	2008-09	893.9
5	Kevin Garnett	1999-00	893.2
6	Larry Bird*	1979-80	890.8
7	Vince Carter	1999-00	888.0
8	Shareef Abdur-Rahim	1999-00	885.5
9	Carmelo Anthony	2007-08	884.7
10	Antonio McDyess	1997-98	880.7

Baseline Basic Stats

MPG	PTS	AST	REB	BLK	STL
37.1	22.9	4.0	9.0	1.4	1.4

Advanced Metrics

USG%	3PTA/FGA	FTA/FGA	TS%	eFG%	3PT%
29.2	0.132	0.422	0.586	0.533	0.318

AST%	TOV%	OREB%	DREB%	STL%	BLK%
22.6	11.8	6.3	22.4	2.0	3.1

PER	ORTG	DRTG	WS/48	VOL
25.85	114.8	104.3	0.211	0.201

- Entering his prime, one of the best overall players in the NBA, potential MVP candidate
- Has played all five positions in his career
- Versatile defender that can guard perimeter players and big men
- Better as a roaming help defender that can rebound, play passing lanes to get steals and block shots on the weak side
- Efficient scorer, does most of his damage inside, great playmaking skills, has cut his turnover rate every season
- Excels in pick-and-roll situations as both the screener and ball handler, above average post-up player
- Below average on isolations, inefficient shooter outside of three feet

Eric Bledsoe

	Height	Weight	Cap #	Years Left
	6'1"	190	$15.000M	0

Similar at Age **28**

		Season	SIMsc
1	Mario Chalmers	2014-15	911.2
2	John Starks	1993-94	910.0
3	Kyle Lowry	2014-15	909.4
4	David Wesley	1998-99	908.4
5	Raymond Felton	2012-13	906.6
6	Mike Bibby	2006-07	905.5
7	Mike Conley	2015-16	902.1
8	Greg Anthony	1995-96	901.7
9	Jameer Nelson	2010-11	901.4
10	Mo Williams	2010-11	899.7

Baseline Basic Stats

MPG	PTS	AST	REB	BLK	STL
32.4	16.0	5.9	3.5	0.3	1.5

Advanced Metrics

USG%	3PTA/FGA	FTA/FGA	TS%	eFG%	3PT%
24.3	0.388	0.348	0.561	0.505	0.350

AST%	TOV%	OREB%	DREB%	STL%	BLK%
28.4	15.0	2.1	11.3	2.5	1.1

PER	ORTG	DRTG	WS	VOL	
18.50	109.4	108.7	0.103	0.395	

- Good starting point guard in the prime of his career
- Has been durable over the last seasons, but missed most of the 2015-16 season with a torn meniscus in his left knee
- High volume scoring guard that relies on his ability to slash to the rim
- Solid playmaking skills, a little bit turnover prone
- Only a break-even three-point shooter, was slightly above average as a mid-range shooter last season
- Below average on-ball defender, solid help defender that gets steals and can occasionally rotate to block a shot on the weak side

Khris Middleton

	Height	Weight	Cap #	Years Left
	6'7"	215	$13.000M	Player Option

Similar at Age 26

		Season	SIMsc
1	Glen Rice	1993-94	940.9
2	Paul George	2016-17	932.5
3	Stephen Jackson	2004-05	931.5
4	Caron Butler	2006-07	928.2
5	James Posey	2002-03	925.1
6	Jimmy Butler	2015-16	924.5
7	Tracy Murray	1997-98	923.9
8	Bobby Phills	1995-96	921.7
9	Josh Howard	2006-07	921.2
10	Gordon Hayward	2016-17	920.0

Baseline Basic Stats

MPG	PTS	AST	REB	BLK	STL
34.0	16.8	3.1	4.7	0.4	1.3

Advanced Metrics

USG%	3PTA/FGA	FTA/FGA	TS%	eFG%	3PT%
23.2	0.326	0.282	0.563	0.512	0.387

AST%	TOV%	OREB%	DREB%	STL%	BLK%
16.7	12.2	2.3	13.3	2.0	0.7

PER	ORTG	DRTG	WS/48	VOL
16.46	109.5	109.3	0.115	0.355

- Two-way wing in his prime, missed the first half of the 2016-17 season with a torn left hamstring
- Very good on-ball defender that can guard multiple positions
- Gets steals at a solid rate, good defensive rebounder
- Solid offensive player, maintained his efficiency in a higher usage role
- Good at making spot-up threes, career 39.1% overall three-point shooter
- Has made almost 45% of his corner threes for his career
- Improved ball handling and playmaking skills allowed him to be effective as a pick-and-roll ball handler and isolation player last season

John Henson

	Height	Weight	Cap #	Years Left
	6'11"	220	$11.327M	1

Similar at Age 27

		Season	SIMsc
1	Keon Clark	2002-03	963.9
2	Taj Gibson	2012-13	923.5
3	Calvin Booth	2003-04	920.1
4	Elden Campbell	1995-96	914.7
5	Marcus Camby	2001-02	913.5
6	Tony Battie	2003-04	910.7
7	Olden Polynice	1991-92	910.6
8	Mark West	1987-88	909.4
9	Louis Amundson	2009-10	905.6
10	John Salley	1991-92	903.4

Baseline Basic Stats

MPG	PTS	AST	REB	BLK	STL
23.7	8.3	0.9	6.3	1.5	0.5

Advanced Metrics

USG%	3PTA/FGA	FTA/FGA	TS%	eFG%	3PT%
16.4	0.008	0.341	0.544	0.518	0.129

AST%	TOV%	OREB%	DREB%	STL%	BLK%
7.6	13.4	9.3	21.0	1.1	4.7

PER	ORTG	DRTG	WS/48	VOL
15.12	108.6	104.3	0.113	0.393

- Steady complementary big man, fairly durable with exception to missing games due to a back injury in the 2015-16 season
- Good rebounder, one of the best shot blockers in the league, can protect the rim
- Struggles with his position defense, not quite strong enough to handle interior players, somewhat foul prone
- High efficiency, low volume rim runner, primarily scores on shots inside of three feet
- Draws fouls at a high rate, struggles to make free throws, career Free Throw Percentage is below 60%

Malcolm Brogdon

	Height	Weight	Cap #	Years Left
	6'5"	215	$1.545M	0

Similar at Age 25

		Season	SIMsc
1	Courtney Lee	2010-11	936.0
2	Lance Stephenson	2015-16	932.8
3	Anthony Peeler	1994-95	928.8
4	George McCloud	1992-93	928.6
5	Fred Jones	2004-05	928.1
6	Keith Bogans	2005-06	924.9
7	DeShawn Stevenson	2006-07	924.2
8	O.J. Mayo	2012-13	922.3
9	Randy Foye	2008-09	920.8
10	Ernie Grunfeld	1980-81	920.4

Baseline Basic Stats

MPG	PTS	AST	REB	BLK	STL
26.9	11.7	2.4	2.9	0.2	0.9

Advanced Metrics

USG%	3PTA/FGA	FTA/FGA	TS%	eFG%	3PT%
20.0	0.343	0.207	0.549	0.511	0.378

AST%	TOV%	OREB%	DREB%	STL%	BLK%
17.2	11.7	2.2	10.3	1.8	0.7

PER	ORTG	DRTG	WS/48	VOL	
14.22	108.9	110.8	0.085	0.317	

- Missed two months of last season due to a torn quadriceps tendon in his left leg
- When healthy, solid two-way combo guard that can knock down spot-up threes at a rate of almost 40% in his two-year career
- Good playmaker that handles the ball well enough to be effective as a pick-and-roll ball handler
- Fairly good in isolation situations in a small sample of possessions
- Pretty good position defender that can handle quicker guards or bigger wing players, solid defensive rebounding guard

Tony Snell

	Height	Weight	Cap #	Years Left
	6'7"	200	$10.607M	1 + PO

Similar at Age 26

		Season	SIMsc
1	Dorell Wright	2011-12	926.3
2	Martell Webster	2012-13	907.9
3	Iman Shumpert	2016-17	900.3
4	Kyle Korver	2007-08	898.3
5	Courtney Lee	2011-12	897.2
6	Morris Peterson	2003-04	894.7
7	Brandon Rush	2011-12	894.1
8	Klay Thompson	2016-17	893.3
9	Kyle Singler	2014-15	893.2
10	Wesley Johnson	2013-14	892.6

Baseline Basic Stats

MPG	PTS	AST	REB	BLK	STL
24.4	8.8	1.3	3.1	0.3	0.6

Advanced Metrics

USG%	3PTA/FGA	FTA/FGA	TS%	eFG%	3PT%
14.3	0.592	0.159	0.548	0.518	0.384

AST%	TOV%	OREB%	DREB%	STL%	BLK%
7.2	8.6	1.1	11.2	1.0	1.1

PER	ORTG	DRTG	WS/48	VOL
9.58	107.7	111.2	0.067	0.442

- Rotational defensive specialist in his prime years
- Good stay-at-home position defender that uses his length to contest shots
- Limited offensively, low volume spot-up shooter at this stage
- Has shot over 40% on threes in each of the last two seasons
- Pretty much a stationary spot-up shooter, doesn't excel in any other situation

Ersan Ilyasova

	Height	Weight	Cap #	Years Left
	6'9"	235	$7.000M	2

Similar at Age 30

		Season	SIMsc
1	Al Harrington	2010-11	936.3
2	Tim Thomas	2007-08	932.9
3	Rodney Rogers	2001-02	931.7
4	Jeff Green	2016-17	928.1
5	Mirza Teletovic	2015-16	925.6
6	Kris Humphries	2015-16	924.5
7	Marvin Williams	2016-17	922.0
8	Mike Dunleavy, Jr.	2010-11	919.9
9	Sam Perkins	1991-92	917.9
10	Walt Williams	2000-01	916.1

Baseline Basic Stats

MPG	PTS	AST	REB	BLK	STL
23.9	9.8	1.3	4.5	0.4	0.7

Advanced Metrics

USG%	3PTA/FGA	FTA/FGA	TS%	eFG%	3PT%
18.7	0.404	0.231	0.540	0.505	0.353

AST%	TOV%	OREB%	DREB%	STL%	BLK%
8.3	10.2	6.0	17.4	1.5	1.2

PER	ORTG	DRTG	WS/48	VOL
13.64	108.4	107.1	0.093	0.324

- In his early 30s, some decline risk, production has been close to his career averages at this point
- Situational, low volume stretch four with a Three-Point Percentage that has hovered around average over the last three seasons
- More of a stationary shooter, doesn't move well off the ball
- Good at posting up smaller perimeter players
- Decent position defender against interior players, good defensive rebounder

Brook Lopez

	Height	Weight	Cap #	Years Left
	7'0"	260	$3.382M	0

Similar at Age **29**

		Season	SIMsc
1	Chris Kaman	2011-12	890.0
2	Marc Gasol	2013-14	872.8
3	Mehmet Okur	2008-09	869.0
4	Jason Smith	2015-16	868.5
5	James Johnson	2016-17	863.6
6	Luc Longley	1997-98	863.6
7	Rasheed Wallace	2003-04	863.4
8	Andrew Lang	1995-96	861.8
9	Benoit Benjamin	1993-94	861.1
10	Zeljko Rebraca	2001-02	860.7

Baseline Basic Stats

MPG	PTS	AST	REB	BLK	STL
27.1	12.7	1.9	6.2	1.2	0.6

Advanced Metrics

USG%	3PTA/FGA	FTA/FGA	TS%	eFG%	3PT%
23.5	0.247	0.258	0.552	0.515	0.358

AST%	TOV%	OREB%	DREB%	STL%	BLK%
12.0	12.5	5.9	16.7	0.9	3.8

PER	ORTG	DRTG	WS/48	VOL	
16.54	105.5	107.9	0.090	0.482	

- Production dipped due to a reduced role on a rebuilding Lakers team
- Good offensive center that scores efficiently inside on post-ups and rolls to the rim
- Fairly good spot-up shooter, has become a break-even three-point shooter over the last two seasons
- Solid passing big man that limits turnovers
- Below average defensively, not particularly mobile and struggles with position defense
- Blocks shots at a high rate, sacrifices some defensive position to go for blocks
- Below average defensive rebounder for the last two seasons

Matthew Dellavedova

	Height	Weight	Cap #	Years Left
	6'4"	200	$9.608M	1

Similar at Age 27

		Season	SIMsc
1	Donald Sloan	2014-15	913.9
2	Chris Childs	1994-95	912.2
3	Andre Owens	2007-08	907.9
4	Jerryd Bayless	2015-16	906.2
5	Greivis Vasquez	2013-14	905.0
6	Jon Barry	1996-97	904.8
7	Malcolm Delaney	2016-17	904.7
8	Fred Hoiberg	1999-00	899.0
9	Bob Sura	2000-01	895.4
10	Randy Foye	2010-11	894.7

Baseline Basic Stats

MPG	PTS	AST	REB	BLK	STL
22.4	7.7	3.7	2.1	0.1	0.7

Advanced Metrics

USG%	3PTA/FGA	FTA/FGA	TS%	eFG%	3PT%
16.5	0.429	0.221	0.527	0.482	0.387

AST%	TOV%	OREB%	DREB%	STL%	BLK%
27.3	19.4	2.0	8.4	1.5	0.2

PER	ORTG	DRTG	WS/48	VOL
11.62	106.1	111.5	0.070	0.443

- Missed most of last season due to tendinitis in his left knee and a sprained right ankle
- Low volume, backup point guard that is a solid playmaker
- Turnover Percentage has increased in each of the last four seasons
- Made 37.2% of his threes last season overall, was open or wide open on almost 72% of his shots
- Has a history of being an irritant on defense, but struggles to stay with quicker guards
- Mainly a stay-at-home defender, does not get steals, blocks or defensive rebounds at a high rate

Thon Maker

	Height	Weight	Cap #	Years Left
	7'1"	216	$2.800M	Team Option

Similar at Age 20

		Season	SIMsc
1	Bruno Sundov	2000-01	870.5
2	Andray Blatche	2006-07	869.4
3	Eddie Griffin	2002-03	869.3
4	Rashard Lewis	1999-00	867.6
5	Christian Wood	2015-16	866.5
6	Travis Outlaw	2004-05	861.6
7	Kevon Looney	2016-17	860.2
8	Meyers Leonard	2012-13	859.9
9	Domantas Sabonis	2016-17	859.7
10	Al-Farouq Aminu	2010-11	856.1

Baseline Basic Stats

MPG	PTS	AST	REB	BLK	STL
20.9	7.6	1.1	4.2	0.7	0.6

Advanced Metrics

USG%	3PTA/FGA	FTA/FGA	TS%	eFG%	3PT%
17.3	0.343	0.259	0.521	0.485	0.360

AST%	TOV%	OREB%	DREB%	STL%	BLK%
7.6	10.9	6.5	15.3	1.4	2.8

PER	ORTG	DRTG	WS/48	VOL
12.44	105.9	109.0	0.072	0.550

- Received more playing time in his second year, but his development regressed
- Shooting efficiency decreased dramatically
- Had trouble finishing shots inside and making outside shots, turnover rate also increased
- Below average in virtually every half-court situation last season
- Showed good shot blocking skills, but he struggled with his position defense, highly foul prone
- Flashed a lot of tools, but may need to spend some time in the G-League to establish his strengths and fine tune his skill set

Tyler Zeller

	Height	Weight	Cap #	Years Left
	7'0"	250	$1.934M	0

Similar at Age 28

		Season	SIMsc
1	Paul Mokeski	1984-85	918.3
2	Jake Voskuhl	2005-06	917.6
3	Timofey Mozgov	2014-15	917.0
4	Clemon Johnson	1984-85	913.3
5	Cherokee Parks	2000-01	912.3
6	Joe Kleine	1989-90	910.0
7	Greg Foster	1996-97	908.7
8	Jerome Jordan	2014-15	905.0
9	Dave Corzine	1984-85	904.6
10	Tim McCormick	1990-91	903.6

Baseline Basic Stats

MPG	PTS	AST	REB	BLK	STL
18.7	6.6	0.9	4.7	0.6	0.4

Advanced Metrics

USG%	3PTA/FGA	FTA/FGA	TS%	eFG%	3PT%
16.8	0.040	0.255	0.541	0.512	0.205

AST%	TOV%	OREB%	DREB%	STL%	BLK%
8.5	12.2	9.7	19.3	0.9	2.6

PER	ORTG	DRTG	WS/48	VOL	
14.10	109.7	106.9	0.102	0.441	

- Contract for 2018-19 is not guaranteed, could potentially lose his roster spot
- Low volume, rim running big man that scores efficiently from close range on rolls to the rim
- Has flashed some passing skills in years past, good offensive rebounder
- Offers little value on defense, below average rim protector
- Struggles with position defense, but is a decent rebounder

Pat Connaughton

	Height	Weight	Cap #	Years Left
	6'5"	206	$1.641M	1

Similar at Age 25

		Season	SIMsc
1	Iman Shumpert	2015-16	922.1
2	Von Wafer	2010-11	919.0
3	Rodney McGruder	2016-17	916.8
4	Martell Webster	2011-12	913.7
5	Anthony Morrow	2010-11	913.2
6	Brandon Rush	2010-11	912.2
7	Arron Afflalo	2010-11	911.9
8	Antoine Wright	2009-10	909.6
9	Walter Bond	1994-95	908.8
10	Wayne Ellington	2012-13	908.4

Baseline Basic Stats

MPG	PTS	AST	REB	BLK	STL
23.2	8.6	1.3	2.6	0.2	0.5

Advanced Metrics

USG%	3PTA/FGA	FTA/FGA	TS%	eFG%	3PT%
15.7	0.515	0.151	0.564	0.540	0.395

AST%	TOV%	OREB%	DREB%	STL%	BLK%
9.8	11.3	2.7	10.6	1.0	0.8

PER	ORTG	DRTG	WS/48	VOL
11.19	110.3	111.2	0.081	0.493

- Cracked Portland's rotation after spending his first two seasons at the end of the bench
- Filled a role as a low volume shooter that could make threes at just over a 35% rate
- Better player in motion than as a stationary spot-up shooter
- Most effective at running off screens and cutting to the rim
- Stay-at-home position defender that can hold his own if given favorable matchups

Sterling Brown

	Height	Weight	Cap #	Years Left
	6'5"	225	$1.378M	1

Similar at Age **22**

		Season	SIMsc
1	Iman Shumpert	2012-13	924.3
2	Quincy Pondexter	2010-11	919.9
3	Norman Powell	2015-16	914.3
4	Justin Anderson	2015-16	911.0
5	P.J. Hairston	2014-15	904.4
6	David Noel	2006-07	903.1
7	Kedrick Brown	2003-04	902.5
8	Arron Afflalo	2007-08	900.2
9	Paul Zipser	2016-17	897.6
10	Allen Crabbe	2014-15	895.4

Baseline Basic Stats

MPG	PTS	AST	REB	BLK	STL
20.2	6.3	1.1	2.7	0.2	0.6

Advanced Metrics

USG%	3PTA/FGA	FTA/FGA	TS%	eFG%	3PT%
14.3	0.469	0.170	0.522	0.494	0.353

AST%	TOV%	OREB%	DREB%	STL%	BLK%
6.0	11.2	3.6	13.7	1.7	1.0

PER	ORTG	DRTG	WS/48	VOL	
9.11	102.6	110.9	0.059	0.421	

- Worked his way into a steady bench role as a rookie, played 776 minutes last season
- Flashed potential on defense with decent position defense on wing players
- High rebound rate for his size and a solid ability to get steals
- Limited offensively, low volume shooter that makes threes about a 35% rate
- Better shooter when coming off screens, not as effective as a stationary spot-up shooter

D.J. Wilson

	Height	Weight	Cap #	Years Left
	6'10"	234	$2.534M	2 Team Options

<u>Similar at Age</u> **21**

		Season	SIMsc
1	Vladimir Radmanovic	2001-02	877.9
2	Jared Jeffries	2002-03	873.4
3	Damir Markota	2006-07	872.9
4	Kyle Anderson	2014-15	871.7
5	Hedo Turkoglu	2000-01	868.3
6	Juan Hernangomez	2016-17	865.6
7	Maurice Harkless	2014-15	859.3
8	Jan Vesely	2011-12	857.0
9	Qyntel Woods	2002-03	851.7
10	Donte Greene	2009-10	847.5

Baseline Basic Stats

MPG	PTS	AST	REB	BLK	STL
18.2	6.4	1.1	3.5	0.4	0.5

Advanced Metrics

USG%	3PTA/FGA	FTA/FGA	TS%	eFG%	3PT%
15.7	0.235	0.221	0.563	0.542	0.333

AST%	TOV%	OREB%	DREB%	STL%	BLK%
8.5	17.0	4.7	14.2	1.7	1.2

PER	ORTG	DRTG	WS/48	VOL
11.13	103.2	109.2	0.066	0.508

- Only played 71 minutes as a rookie, split time between Milwaukee and the Wisconsin Herd of the G-League
- Solid showing at this year's Summer League, showed improvement over last year
- Flashed potential as a stretch big that could knock down threes at a break-even rate in both the G-League and Summer League
- Decent passing big man, cut his turnovers down in Summer League
- Not really a rim protector, improved on the defensive glass and as a position defender in Summer League

Newcomers

Donte DiVincenzo

	Height	Weight	Cap #	Years Left
	6'5"	205	$2.481M	1 + 2 TO

Baseline Basic Stats

MPG	PTS	AST	REB	BLK	STL
10.9	3.5	0.9	1.4	0.1	0.4

Advanced Metrics

USG%	3PTA/FGA	FTA/FGA	TS%	eFG%	3PT%
17.4	0.334	0.223	0.472	0.439	0.291

AST%	TOV%	OREB%	DREB%	STL%	BLK%
12.4	13.4	3.4	11.0	1.8	0.8

PER	ORTG	DRTG	WS/48	VOL
9.48	96.8	107.6	0.037	N/A

- Drafted by Milwaukee in the first round with the 17th overall pick
- May not crack the rotation as a rookie due to Milwaukee's guard and wing depth
- May need additional seasoning in the G-League, struggled in a small sample of games at Summer League
- Didn't show much in two Summer League games overall
- Played with high energy on defense, got steals and blocks at a high rate
- In the long-term, projects to be a combo guard that can space the floor and provide additional playmaking
- Defensive potential is uncertain, play on defense at Summer League is a sign that he might be an improved defender

MIAMI HEAT

<u>Last Season</u>: 44 – 38, Lost 1st Round to Philadelphia (1 – 4)

<u>Offensive Rating</u>: 106.8, 22nd in NBA   <u>Defensive Rating</u>: 106.3, 7th in NBA

<u>Primary Executive</u>: Pat Riley, Team President   <u>Head Coach</u>: Erik Spoelstra

Key Roster Changes

Subtractions   **Additions**
Dwyane Wade, free agency   Briante Weber, free agency
Udonis Haslem, free agency
Luke Babbitt, free agency
Jordan Mickey, free agency

RAFER Projected Win Total: 42.5

Projected Best Five-Man Unit   **Other Rotation Players**
1. Goran Dragic   Bam Adebayo
2. Tyler Johnson   Kelly Olynyk
3. Josh Richardson   Wayne Ellington
4. James Johnson   Justise Winslow
5. Hassan Whiteside   Dion Waiters
                                              Rodney McGruder

Remaining Roster

- Derrick Jones, Jr.
- Briante Weber
- Udonis Haslem
- Dwyane Wade - not profiled, signed right before the book was finalized
- Yante Maten, 22, 6'8", 243, Georgia (Two-Way)
- Duncan Robinson, 24, 6'8", 215, Michigan (Two-Way)
- Marcus Lee, 24, 6'9", 225, California (Exhibit 10)
- Malik Newman, 21, 6'3", 190, Kansas (Exhibit 10)
- Jarnell Stokes, 25, 6'9", 263, Tennessee (Exhibit 10)

Season Forecast

The Miami Heat had a relatively quiet summer because they committed their cap dollars to their current roster and had no room to make any significant improvements. The team is likely to get a full recovery from Dion Waiters after an ankle injury cut his season short last year. However, his impact probably isn't going to dramatically improve Miami's fortunes. In all probability, the team's performance is going to fall in line with what it has been over the last two seasons, with their record being slightly above 0.500 and competing for a back-end playoff seed.

The Heat should be a very competitive team because they have been very good at utilizing their depth to consistently put a highly effective defensive unit on the floor at all times. They ranked in the top seven in Defensive Rating in each of the last two seasons. With the same rotation intact, they should be one of the league's best defensive teams again this year. Even with their great defense, Miami is stuck in place because they simply don't have enough offensive firepower to compete with the upper echelon teams in the NBA. A lot of offensive responsibility falls on the shoulders of Goran Dragic, but it's uncertain if he'll be able to sustain his current level of production because he's now an older player in his 30s and there's always a risk of age-related decline at this stage. Waiters does give them another shot creator if he's healthy, but historically, he's been inconsistent and inefficient as a shooter. They do have a lot of interchangeable wings that can defend and knock down threes as well as big men that can protect the rim, so they can consistently produce lineups that can maximize their primary shot creator. Therefore, if Dragic maintains his level of play, the Heat might be able to cobble together enough offense to win some games. Otherwise, they may have to make a drastic change to give them a better chance to succeed in the Eastern Conference. If the performance from their current roster falls in line with its recent average, the Miami Heat will be a solid playoff team in the East, but they might not have enough high-end talent to get out of the first round. However, if they get any kind of decline from any of their main players, there's a risk that they could possibly finish just outside of the playoff picture.

Veterans

Goran Dragic

	Height	Weight	Cap #	Years Left
	6'4"	180	$18.109M	Player Option

Similar at Age **31**

		Season	SIMsc
1	Derek Harper	1992-93	941.1
2	John Starks	1996-97	925.8
3	Sam Cassell	2000-01	924.7
4	Gary Payton*	1999-00	921.1
5	Joe Dumars*	1994-95	920.9
6	Danny Ainge	1990-91	918.0
7	Tony Parker	2013-14	914.7
8	Latrell Sprewell	2001-02	913.5
9	Vernon Maxwell	1996-97	913.3
10	Dennis Johnson*	1985-86	913.3

Baseline Basic Stats

MPG	PTS	AST	REB	BLK	STL
29.6	14.2	4.4	2.8	0.2	1.0

Advanced Metrics

USG%	3PTA/FGA	FTA/FGA	TS%	eFG%	3PT%
23.7	0.246	0.257	0.535	0.492	0.369

AST%	TOV%	OREB%	DREB%	STL%	BLK%
25.2	13.0	2.3	9.7	1.6	0.4

PER	ORTG	DRTG	WS/48	VOL	
16.07	107.4	108.7	0.108	0.374	

- Durable over the last three seasons, made his first All-Star team last season
- Entering his age-32 season, possible decline risk, efficiency decreased last season
- High usage scoring guard that will draw fouls and make threes at an above average rate
- Solid playmaking skills, posted the Highest Assist Percentage of his career last season
- Most effective as a pick-and-roll ball handler, isolation scorer and spot-up shooter
- Solid on-ball defending point guard, fairly good rebounder for his size

Josh Richardson

	Height	Weight	Cap #	Years Left
	6'6"	200	$9.367M	3

Similar at Age 24

		Season	SIMsc
1	Danny Green	2011-12	941.1
2	Courtney Lee	2009-10	932.9
3	Dorell Wright	2009-10	928.7
4	James Anderson	2013-14	925.6
5	Eddie Jones	1995-96	925.3
6	Rodney Carney	2008-09	917.7
7	Wesley Person	1995-96	917.3
8	Victor Oladipo	2016-17	915.0
9	Terrence Ross	2015-16	914.3
10	Shannon Brown	2009-10	913.8

Baseline Basic Stats

MPG	PTS	AST	REB	BLK	STL
27.2	11.3	2.0	3.3	0.5	1.0

Advanced Metrics

USG%	3PTA/FGA	FTA/FGA	TS%	eFG%	3PT%
18.6	0.423	0.190	0.544	0.511	0.378

AST%	TOV%	OREB%	DREB%	STL%	BLK%
13.2	11.6	2.6	10.3	2.0	1.7

PER	ORTG	DRTG	WS/48	VOL
13.56	106.9	107.6	0.092	0.246

- Improved in his third season, but struggled to efficiently make shots in the playoffs
- Solid three-and-D wing player entering his prime years
- Very active wing defender, plays good position defense
- Steals and blocks rates have increased every year
- Low volume spot-up shooter, Three-Point Percentage is above average for his career
- Three-Point percentages have fluctuated on a year-to-year basis
- Above average at cutting to the rim, isn't as effective in other offensive situations

Hassan Whiteside

	Height	Weight	Cap #	Years Left
	7'0"	235	$25.434M	Player Option

Similar at Age 28

		Season	SIMsc
1	Robert Parish*	1981-82	914.7
2	Matt Geiger	1997-98	906.3
3	JaVale McGee	2015-16	890.5
4	Samuel Dalembert	2009-10	884.7
5	Dino Radja	1995-96	884.6
6	Hakeem Olajuwon*	1990-91	883.5
7	Alton Lister	1986-87	878.4
8	Tim Duncan	2004-05	878.2
9	Marcin Gortat	2012-13	878.0
10	Patrick Ewing*	1990-91	873.0

Baseline Basic Stats

MPG	PTS	AST	REB	BLK	STL
28.9	15.2	1.5	9.2	2.1	0.7

Advanced Metrics

USG%	3PTA/FGA	FTA/FGA	TS%	eFG%	3PT%
22.9	0.003	0.342	0.564	0.532	0.456

AST%	TOV%	OREB%	DREB%	STL%	BLK%
7.2	12.9	11.5	30.6	1.2	5.2

PER	ORTG	DRTG	WS/48	VOL	
20.97	109.6	99.6	0.167	0.585	

- Missed games last season due to a bruised left knee and a sore left hip
- One of the best rebounders and shot blockers in the league, below average position defender
- Doesn't come out to guard opposing big men on the perimeter, prone to giving up a lot of open outside looks
- Good at diving to the rim on offense, will crash the offensive boards
- Solid post-up player, very low Assist Percentage for his career

James Johnson

	Height	Weight	Cap #	Years Left
	6'9"	245	$14.652M	1 + PO

Similar at Age 30

	Player	Season	SIMsc
1	Al Horford	2016-17	922.5
2	Tim Thomas	2007-08	893.8
3	Kenyon Martin	2007-08	893.2
4	Danny Manning	1996-97	891.7
5	Brad Miller	2006-07	889.8
6	Rodney Rogers	2001-02	886.5
7	Mehmet Okur	2009-10	885.0
8	LaPhonso Ellis	2000-01	883.5
9	Frank Brickowski	1989-90	881.7
10	Tom Gugliotta	1999-00	880.6

Baseline Basic Stats

MPG	PTS	AST	REB	BLK	STL
26.2	10.9	2.4	5.5	0.8	0.9

Advanced Metrics

USG%	3PTA/FGA	FTA/FGA	TS%	eFG%	3PT%
19.6	0.273	0.263	0.548	0.516	0.328

AST%	TOV%	OREB%	DREB%	STL%	BLK%
17.7	15.5	4.5	17.8	1.7	2.4

PER	ORTG	DRTG	WS/48	VOL	
15.02	106.0	104.7	0.108	0.403	

- Older player entering his age-31 season, performance over the last two seasons is higher than his career averages
- Reinvented himself as a defensive four man that can play interior defense and guard perimeter players
- Solid defensive rebounder, can occasionally get steals and blocks
- Steal and Block Percentages are down from his career averages
- Low volume offensive player with greatly improved playmaking skills
- Good spot-up mid-range shooter that was great at cutting to the rim
- Good as the screener in pick-and-roll, could post up smaller perimeter players
- Effective on isolations when he has a mismatch

Dion Waiters

	Height	Weight	Cap #	Years Left
	6'4"	210	$11.550M	2

Similar at Age 26

		Season	SIMsc
1	O.J. Mayo	2013-14	955.7
2	Voshon Lenard	1999-00	950.3
3	Randy Foye	2009-10	934.8
4	Fred Jones	2005-06	933.8
5	Willie Green	2007-08	929.3
6	Shannon Brown	2011-12	926.2
7	Shelvin Mack	2016-17	923.6
8	Reggie Jackson	2016-17	923.5
9	Ben Gordon	2009-10	919.5
10	Sean Kilpatrick	2015-16	917.9

Baseline Basic Stats

MPG	PTS	AST	REB	BLK	STL
24.9	11.0	2.5	2.5	0.2	0.8

Advanced Metrics

USG%	3PTA/FGA	FTA/FGA	TS%	eFG%	3PT%
22.9	0.373	0.202	0.506	0.473	0.351

AST%	TOV%	OREB%	DREB%	STL%	BLK%
18.5	12.7	1.6	9.3	1.5	0.7

PER	ORTG	DRTG	WS/48	VOL
12.24	99.9	110.1	0.044	0.337

- Missed most of last season due to a sprained left ankle that required surgery
- High volume scoring guard, above break-even three-point shooter for his career
- Takes a lot of long two-pointers, makes less than 40% of them
- Career True Shooting Percentage is below 50%
- Solid playmaking skills make him most effective as a pick-and-roll ball handler
- Decent stay-at-home position defender if he's hidden in favorable matchups

Tyler Johnson

	Height	Weight	Cap #	Years Left
	6'4"	186	$19.245M	1

Similar at Age 25

		Season	SIMsc
1	Kerry Kittles	1999-00	939.6
2	Luther Head	2007-08	935.3
3	Cory Joseph	2016-17	932.8
4	George Hill	2011-12	929.8
5	Delonte West	2008-09	928.7
6	Smush Parker	2006-07	925.1
7	Courtney Lee	2010-11	925.0
8	Marco Belinelli	2011-12	924.4
9	Lucious Harris	1995-96	924.3
10	Leandro Barbosa	2007-08	923.3

Baseline Basic Stats

MPG	PTS	AST	REB	BLK	STL
25.9	10.7	2.5	2.6	0.2	0.9

Advanced Metrics

USG%	3PTA/FGA	FTA/FGA	TS%	eFG%	3PT%
19.2	0.394	0.216	0.538	0.502	0.360

AST%	TOV%	OREB%	DREB%	STL%	BLK%
14.5	10.5	2.1	10.5	1.7	1.0

PER	ORTG	DRTG	WS/48	VOL
13.50	108.2	107.9	0.103	0.327

- Has been durable over the last two seasons, but missed two months of the 2015-16 season due to a left shoulder injury
- Combo guard in his prime, decent playmaker that is effective as a pick-and-roll ball handler
- Drew fouls at a high rate in previous seasons, but increased his three-point attempt rate considerably last season
- Good spot-up shooter that makes threes at an above league average rate
- Good cutter last season in a small sample of possessions
- Versatile defensively, can defend both guard spots, actively contests shots, good rebounder for his size

Wayne Ellington

	Height	Weight	Cap #	Years Left
	6'4"	200	$6.270M	0

Similar at Age **30**

		Season	SIMsc
1	Willie Green	2011-12	920.2
2	Nick Young	2015-16	913.0
3	Anthony Morrow	2015-16	909.7
4	Marco Belinelli	2016-17	907.9
5	Kyle Korver	2011-12	902.0
6	Raja Bell	2006-07	901.3
7	J.J. Redick	2014-15	899.9
8	Keith Bogans	2010-11	899.5
9	Charlie Bell	2009-10	898.1
10	Anthony Peeler	1999-00	897.5

Baseline Basic Stats

MPG	PTS	AST	REB	BLK	STL
22.2	8.4	1.2	2.2	0.2	0.6

Advanced Metrics

USG%	3PTA/FGA	FTA/FGA	TS%	eFG%	3PT%
16.5	0.691	0.108	0.559	0.540	0.381

AST%	TOV%	OREB%	DREB%	STL%	BLK%
6.6	7.3	1.3	10.1	1.3	0.5

PER	ORTG	DRTG	WS/48	VOL
11.10	109.9	110.1	0.083	0.317

- Entering his age-31 season, some decline risk
- Production in the last two seasons has been higher than his career averages
- Low volume, situational shooting specialist, career Three-Point Percentage is 38.1%
- Most effective as a spot-up shooter that could also run off screens, almost 83% of shots were threes last season
- Decent stay-at-home position defender, still fairly good on the defensive glass

Justise Winslow

	Height	Weight	Cap #	Years Left
	6'7"	225	$3.449M	0

Similar at Age **21**

		Season	SIMsc
1	Jumaine Jones	2000-01	926.6
2	Richard Jefferson	2001-02	917.7
3	Kawhi Leonard	2012-13	917.5
4	Vincent Yarbrough	2002-03	916.4
5	Dorell Wright	2006-07	914.4
6	Kedrick Brown	2002-03	913.9
7	Joe Johnson	2002-03	911.5
8	Omri Casspi	2009-10	909.8
9	Anthony Bennett	2014-15	909.6
10	Hedo Turkoglu	2000-01	905.9

Baseline Basic Stats

MPG	PTS	AST	REB	BLK	STL
24.0	9.0	1.6	4.0	0.3	0.8

Advanced Metrics

USG%	3PTA/FGA	FTA/FGA	TS%	eFG%	3PT%
17.1	0.201	0.244	0.500	0.469	0.330

AST%	TOV%	OREB%	DREB%	STL%	BLK%
12.2	12.3	4.3	15.3	1.7	1.0

PER	ORTG	DRTG	WS/48	VOL	
11.52	102.5	106.6	0.076	0.345	

- Still developing, improved in his third season
- Missed the second half of the 2016-17 season with a torn labrum in his right shoulder
- Defensive specialist at this stage, good on-ball defender that can guard multiple positions, better against perimeter wings
- Very good defensive rebounder, posted a career high Block Percentage last season
- Still inefficient, low volume offensive player, struggles in most offensive situations
- Has shown improved playmaking skills to allow him to be effective as a pick-and-roll ball handler
- He shot 38% from the three-point line in 129 attempts, was left wide open on 81.6% of his threes

Kelly Olynyk

	Height	Weight	Cap #	Years Left
	7'0"	238	$12.538M	1 + PO

Similar at Age 26

		Season	SIMsc
1	Charlie Villanueva	2010-11	913.6
2	Troy Murphy	2006-07	906.9
3	Markieff Morris	2015-16	901.8
4	Scott Padgett	2002-03	893.8
5	Vladimir Radmanovic	2006-07	893.1
6	Jon Leuer	2015-16	890.6
7	Spencer Hawes	2014-15	888.1
8	Matt Barnes	2006-07	885.6
9	Jim Petersen	1988-89	884.9
10	Austin Croshere	2001-02	884.4

Baseline Basic Stats

MPG	PTS	AST	REB	BLK	STL
21.4	8.9	1.5	4.7	0.5	0.6

Advanced Metrics

USG%	3PTA/FGA	FTA/FGA	TS%	eFG%	3PT%
19.6	0.416	0.228	0.584	0.553	0.381

AST%	TOV%	OREB%	DREB%	STL%	BLK%
13.6	13.0	5.2	20.2	1.5	1.6

PER	ORTG	DRTG	WS/48	VOL
15.89	112.2	105.8	0.131	0.245

- Career best season in his first year in Miami, maintained his level of performance in the playoffs
- Productive rotational stretch big, solid three-point shooter, good passing big man
- Excels as the screener in pick-and-roll situations
- Very good at making spot-up jumpers and cutting to the rim
- Below average interior defender, limited rim protection skills, good defensive rebounder

Bam Adebayo

	Height	Weight	Cap #	Years Left
	6'10"	243	$2.956M	2 Team Options

Similar at Age 20

		Season	SIMsc
1	Zaza Pachulia	2004-05	941.3
2	Amare Stoudemire	2002-03	920.5
3	Derrick Favors	2011-12	918.4
4	J.J. Hickson	2008-09	911.3
5	Samaki Walker	1996-97	906.2
6	Noah Vonleh	2015-16	903.8
7	Jonas Valanciunas	2012-13	903.3
8	Michael Kidd-Gilchrist	2013-14	902.5
9	Jackie Butler	2005-06	899.5
10	Yi Jianlian	2007-08	894.2

Baseline Basic Stats

MPG	PTS	AST	REB	BLK	STL
26.6	10.3	1.3	7.3	0.8	0.7

Advanced Metrics

USG%	3PTA/FGA	FTA/FGA	TS%	eFG%	3PT%
18.2	0.022	0.443	0.567	0.514	0.187

AST%	TOV%	OREB%	DREB%	STL%	BLK%
9.6	13.0	9.7	21.4	1.3	2.0

PER	ORTG	DRTG	WS/48	VOL	
16.79	114.5	105.9	0.142	0.261	

- Effective part of Miami's rotation as a rookie
- Strictly a rim running big man, scores efficiently inside on close range shots
- Draws fouls, makes free throws, showed improved passing skills
- Most effective at running the floor in transition
- Interior defender with decent rim protection skills, decent shot blocker, solid defensive rebounder
- Slightly below average position defender, struggled to interior players on the ball, had some lapses when making defensive rotations

Rodney McGruder

	Height	Weight	Cap #	Years Left
	6'4"	205	$1.545M	0

Similar at Age 26

		Season	SIMsc
1	Anthony Peeler	1995-96	908.6
2	Wayne Ellington	2013-14	906.0
3	Marcus Thornton	2013-14	905.9
4	E'Twaun Moore	2015-16	905.6
5	Rex Walters	1996-97	898.4
6	Iman Shumpert	2016-17	895.9
7	Keith Bogans	2006-07	895.5
8	Gary Neal	2010-11	892.5
9	Lance Blanks	1992-93	891.4
10	Raja Bell	2002-03	890.3

Baseline Basic Stats

MPG	PTS	AST	REB	BLK	STL
20.8	8.1	1.8	2.2	0.1	0.6

Advanced Metrics

USG%	3PTA/FGA	FTA/FGA	TS%	eFG%	3PT%
16.4	0.460	0.146	0.540	0.521	0.384

AST%	TOV%	OREB%	DREB%	STL%	BLK%
13.0	8.6	3.1	9.4	1.3	0.7

PER	ORTG	DRTG	WS/48	VOL	
12.05	111.7	110.4	0.088	0.513	

- Missed the first half of last season with a stress fracture in his lower left leg
- Good on-ball defending wing player when healthy, more of a stay-at-home defender
- Low volume spot-up shooter that only makes threes at about break-even percentage for his career
- Went 15-for-35 on threes last season when he returned from injury
- Effective at cutting to the rim if opponents overplay his shot

Derrick Jones, Jr.

	Height	Weight	Cap #	Years Left
	6'7"	190	$1.513M	1

Similar at Age 20

		Season	SIMsc
1	Pete Williams	1985-86	882.6
2	Brandan Wright	2007-08	875.1
3	Otto Porter	2013-14	859.9
4	Gordon Hayward	2010-11	854.6
5	Alec Burks	2011-12	851.5
6	Gerald Green	2005-06	846.8
7	Kevon Looney	2016-17	846.5
8	Kelly Oubre	2015-16	846.3
9	Nicolas Batum	2008-09	846.2
10	Corey Benjamin	1998-99	844.9

Baseline Basic Stats

MPG	PTS	AST	REB	BLK	STL
18.6	6.7	1.1	2.8	0.4	0.6

Advanced Metrics

USG%	3PTA/FGA	FTA/FGA	TS%	eFG%	3PT%
15.3	0.295	0.326	0.555	0.511	0.278

AST%	TOV%	OREB%	DREB%	STL%	BLK%
7.5	9.4	6.2	10.3	1.3	2.2

PER	ORTG	DRTG	WS/48	VOL	
13.22	114.8	109.5	0.109	0.535	

- Played limited minutes in his first two seasons, spent most of his career in the G-League
- Excellent raw athleticism and length gives him great potential on the defensive end
- Solid as an on-ball defender in a small sample of minutes over two seasons
- Blocks shots at a high rate in the NBA and the G-League, good defensive rebounding wing
- Primarily a slasher that drives hard to the rim to either finish above the rim with dunks or draw fouls
- Inefficient outside shooter at this stage, Three-Point Percentage is below break-even over two seasons in the G-League

Briante Weber

	Height	Weight	Cap #	Years Left
	6'2"	165	$1.513M	0

Similar at Age 25

		Season	SIMsc
1	Tom Garrick	1991-92	889.2
2	Lowes Moore	1982-83	886.6
3	Sedric Toney	1987-88	884.0
4	Jerry Sichting	1981-82	883.5
5	Ronnie Price	2008-09	882.0
6	Jorge Gutierrez	2013-14	881.0
7	Jason Hart	2003-04	876.3
8	Tim Frazier	2015-16	874.7
9	Eddie Gill	2003-04	873.6
10	Randy Brown	1993-94	873.2

Baseline Basic Stats

MPG	PTS	AST	REB	BLK	STL
18.5	5.8	2.8	1.7	0.1	0.9

Advanced Metrics

USG%	3PTA/FGA	FTA/FGA	TS%	eFG%	3PT%
14.7	0.280	0.226	0.513	0.475	0.329

AST%	TOV%	OREB%	DREB%	STL%	BLK%
18.5	17.4	2.8	9.9	2.9	0.9

PER	ORTG	DRTG	WS/48	VOL	
11.54	103.6	106.8	0.075	0.566	

- Journeyman, backup point guard, limited playing time in the NBA, has played with six teams in three seasons
- Has spent bulk of his career in the G-League
- Good playmaker at the G-League level, a little turnover prone
- Efficient scorer from two-point range, three-point shot is inconsistent
- Energetic defender, excels at applying pressure to his man, gambles a bit too much
- Active career leader in the G-League in Steals per Game and Steal Percentage, good defensive rebounding point guard

Udonis Haslem

	Height	Weight	Cap #	Years Left
	6'8"	230	$1.513M	0

Similar at Age 37

		Season	SIMsc
1	Sam Perkins	1998-99	878.7
2	Robert Horry	2007-08	877.6
3	Antawn Jamison	2013-14	876.1
4	Juwan Howard	2010-11	866.1
5	Frank Brickowski	1996-97	860.2
6	Mark West	1997-98	845.8
7	Mark Bryant	2002-03	845.4
8	Stacey Augmon	2005-06	844.1
9	A.C. Green	2000-01	839.0
10	Chris Andersen	2015-16	838.5

Baseline Basic Stats

MPG	PTS	AST	REB	BLK	STL
12.8	3.3	0.6	2.4	0.3	0.4

Advanced Metrics

USG%	3PTA/FGA	FTA/FGA	TS%	eFG%	3PT%
13.2	0.373	0.268	0.397	0.365	0.207

AST%	TOV%	OREB%	DREB%	STL%	BLK%
9.0	12.4	5.3	17.1	1.4	1.5

PER	ORTG	DRTG	WS/48	VOL
7.20	89.2	104.5	0.030	0.186

- Has not been a regular rotation player for the last five seasons
- Played only 462 minutes over the last three seasons for Miami
- Performance has heavily declined, essentially an assistant coach in uniform
- Solid on-ball position defender and rebounder when he was younger, not nearly as effective on defense now
- Low usage player that mainly relied on an above average mid-range shot and scoring on put-backs in the past
- Diminishing athleticism doesn't allow him to go to the offensive glass anymore
- Shooting has become more inconsistent with less playing time
- Trying to shoot threes with very little success

CHARLOTTE HORNETS

<u>Last Season</u>: 36 – 46, Missed the Playoffs

<u>Offensive Rating</u>: 109.4, 13th in NBA   <u>Defensive Rating</u>: 109.1, 16th in NBA

<u>Primary Executive</u>: Mitch Kupchak, President of Basketball Operations and General Manager

<u>Head Coach</u>: James Borrego

Key Roster Changes

Subtractions	**Additions**
Dwight Howard, trade	Miles Bridges, draft
Julyan Stone, trade	Devonte Graham', draft
Treveon Graham, free agency	Bismack Biyombo, trade
Michael Carter-Williams, free agency	Tony Parker, free agency

RAFER Projected Win Total: 42.5

Projected Best Five-Man Unit
1. Kemba Walker
2. Jeremy Lamb
3. Marvin Williams
4. Michael Kidd-Gilchrist
5. Cody Zeller

Other Rotation Players
Nicolas Batum
Bismack Biyombo
Tony Parker
Frank Kaminsky
Malik Monk
Miles Bridges

Remaining Roster

- Willy Hernangomez
- Dwayne Bacon
- Devonte' Graham
- J.P. Macura, 23, 6'5", 203, Xavier (Two-Way)
- Jaylen Barford, 23, 6'3", 202, Arkansas (Exhibit 10)
- Joe Chealey, 23, 6'3", 190, College of Charleston (Exhibit 10)
- Zach Smith, 23, 6'8", 220, Texas Tech (Exhibit 10)
- Isaiah Wilkins, 23, 6'8", 205, Virginia (Exhibit 10)

Season Forecast

The Charlotte Hornets started their organizational overhaul in the middle of last season when they let go of the previous GM, Rich Cho in favor of Mitch Kupchak. The team decided to make a coaching change by hiring former Spurs assistant, James Borrego as their new head coach. From there, they made a few tweaks to the roster by dumping the contract of Dwight Howard, adding Miles Bridges in the draft and picking up veteran Tony Parker to serve as their backup point guard. They have had some bad luck over the last two seasons because they have had to deal with some injuries and they had difficulties closing out tight games. With a healthy roster and a few positive breaks, the Hornets have enough talent in a weakened Eastern Conference to contend for a playoff spot. However, they may need to make some adjustments with their rotation to optimize the team's overall performance.

The main adjustment that the Hornets will have to make is to reduce Nicolas Batum's workload and give more of his minutes to a younger, more efficient offensive player like Jeremy Lamb. Batum may be feeling the aftereffects of playing a lot of minutes over the course of the previous seven seasons because he has already showed some signs of early decline. He was in and out of the lineup due to a series of injuries and his overall performance dropped significantly below his career averages last season. The team could benefit by increasing the role of Lamb because his True Shooting Percentage has been higher in each of the last two seasons and Batum's defense has diminished to the point where they may be about even as defenders. Therefore, the team's already above average offense could improve a bit by making that slight switch. Additionally, the Hornets may be getting an addition by subtraction when they traded Howard. Stylistically, their offense could feature fewer inefficient post-ups and more pick-and-rolls with their All-Star, Kemba Walker. Also, they would have more minutes available for a stretch big like Frank Kaminsky to give them more spacing and an additional three-point threat. If things break right for the Hornets, they could improve enough to land one of the lower playoff seeds in the Eastern Conference. They don't have enough talent to legitimately be a threat to upset one of the projected top seeds, so their season will likely end after the first round. However, if events play out as they have been for the last two seasons, they would probably be on the outside of the playoff picture and they possibly could be looking at a rebuild, as Walker is set to hit the free agent market this coming summer.

Veterans

Kemba Walker

	Height	Weight	Cap #	Years Left
	6'1"	172	$12.000M	0

Similar at Age 27

		Season	SIMsc
1	Mike Conley	2014-15	928.6
2	Mike Bibby	2005-06	925.8
3	Mo Williams	2009-10	919.7
4	Nick Van Exel	1998-99	911.6
5	Jeff Teague	2015-16	908.6
6	Kyle Lowry	2013-14	907.1
7	Eddie House	2005-06	905.6
8	John Starks	1992-93	903.9
9	Jannero Pargo	2006-07	898.6
10	B.J. Armstrong	1994-95	898.0

Baseline Basic Stats

MPG	PTS	AST	REB	BLK	STL
33.3	16.6	5.9	3.2	0.2	1.2

Advanced Metrics

USG%	3PTA/FGA	FTA/FGA	TS%	eFG%	3PT%
25.4	0.436	0.276	0.555	0.506	0.385

AST%	TOV%	OREB%	DREB%	STL%	BLK%
29.7	11.9	1.4	9.8	1.8	0.6

PER	ORTG	DRTG	WS/48	VOL	
19.06	112.0	109.1	0.127	0.257	

- In the midst of his prime, named an All-Star in each of the last two seasons
- Excellent playmaking and ball control skills
- One of the best pick-and-roll ball handlers in the league
- Efficient shooter that can run off screens and make spot-up jumpers
- Made 38.6% of his threes over the last three seasons
- Middling on-ball defender, rebound and steals rates have declined

Nicolas Batum

	Height	Weight	Cap #	Years Left
	6'8"	200	$24.000M	1 + PO

Similar at Age 29

		Season	SIMsc
1	Doug Christie	1999-00	929.1
2	Stephen Jackson	2007-08	903.6
3	Walt Williams	1999-00	901.9
4	Toni Kukoc	1997-98	897.2
5	Marko Jaric	2007-08	896.3
6	Dennis Scott	1997-98	895.1
7	Chris Morris	1994-95	894.1
8	Luol Deng	2014-15	893.2
9	Derek Anderson	2003-04	892.5
10	Tracy McGrady	2008-09	892.1

Baseline Basic Stats

MPG	PTS	AST	REB	BLK	STL
29.7	12.3	3.6	4.4	0.4	1.1

Advanced Metrics

USG%	3PTA/FGA	FTA/FGA	TS%	eFG%	3PT%
19.9	0.397	0.254	0.526	0.478	0.345

AST%	TOV%	OREB%	DREB%	STL%	BLK%
22.4	14.9	2.7	14.2	1.7	0.9

PER	ORTG	DRTG	WS/48	VOL
14.14	105.0	108.5	0.080	0.421

- May already be showing signs of decline, missed a few games last season due to injuries to his elbow and Achilles
- Still a solid playmaker, but has become a lower volume spot-up shooter
- Has been a slightly above break-even three-point shooter over the last three seasons
- Effective in a small sample of isolation possessions last season
- Versatile, multi-positional defender when he was younger, is a step slower right now, has some trouble with quicker players
- Steals rate is still consistent with his career average, Block Percentage is declining, solid defensive rebounder

Michael Kidd-Gilchrist

	Height	Weight	Cap #	Years Left
	6'7"	232	$13.000M	Player Option

Similar at Age 24

		Season	SIMsc
1	Derrick Brown	2011-12	936.8
2	Matt Harpring	2000-01	925.0
3	Quincy Acy	2014-15	923.9
4	Dante Cunningham	2011-12	923.7
5	Desmond Mason	2001-02	922.6
6	Joey Graham	2006-07	921.5
7	Reggie King	1981-82	920.1
8	Luc Mbah a Moute	2010-11	919.8
9	Marvin Williams	2010-11	919.6
10	Chucky Brown	1992-93	915.8

Baseline Basic Stats

MPG	PTS	AST	REB	BLK	STL
26.6	9.9	1.4	5.4	0.5	0.8

Advanced Metrics

USG%	3PTA/FGA	FTA/FGA	TS%	eFG%	3PT%
16.7	0.079	0.328	0.548	0.506	0.212

AST%	TOV%	OREB%	DREB%	STL%	BLK%
7.9	9.4	6.2	15.6	1.4	1.4

PER	ORTG	DRTG	WS/48	VOL	
14.33	112.3	107.2	0.114	0.443	

- In his athletic prime, but performance has declined in each of the last three seasons
- Pretty durable for the last two seasons, missed most of the 2015-16 season with a torn labrum in his right shoulder
- Defense has slipped a bit, now is an average defender that can adequately guard multiple positions
- More of a stay-at-home defender now, rebounding rate has dropped off to only about an adequate level
- Offensive skills don't really fit the modern NBA, has no outside shot or any real playmaking skills
- Good at cutting to the rim, can post up smaller perimeter players, scores on isolations against a mismatch

Marvin Williams

	Height	Weight	Cap #	Years Left
	6'9"	230	$14.088M	Player Option

Similar at Age 31

		Season	SIMsc
1	Peja Stojakovic	2008-09	920.6
2	Richard Jefferson	2011-12	918.1
3	Chuck Person	1995-96	913.0
4	Donyell Marshall	2004-05	909.2
5	Shane Battier	2009-10	908.3
6	Mike Dunleavy, Jr.	2011-12	908.2
7	Anthony Tolliver	2016-17	907.7
8	Rashard Lewis	2010-11	906.0
9	Luol Deng	2016-17	904.0
10	Dennis Scott	1999-00	903.8

Baseline Basic Stats

MPG	PTS	AST	REB	BLK	STL
24.4	8.3	1.5	4.1	0.4	0.7

Advanced Metrics

USG%	3PTA/FGA	FTA/FGA	TS%	eFG%	3PT%
15.2	0.521	0.209	0.562	0.528	0.381

AST%	TOV%	OREB%	DREB%	STL%	BLK%
8.1	10.1	3.8	16.0	1.4	1.6

PER	ORTG	DRTG	WS/48	VOL	
12.81	111.8	106.8	0.109	0.437	

- Has been pretty consistent over the last two seasons despite being an older player coming off his age-31 season
- Efficient in a low volume role, has become a good three-point shooter in his four years in Charlotte
- Good spot-up shooter that can also run off screens, can also post-up smaller perimeter players
- Adequate defensive player that can guard multiple positions, more of a stay-at-home defender, decent on the defensive boards

Bismack Biyombo

	Height	Weight	Cap #	Years Left
	6'9"	229	$17.000M	Player Option

Similar at Age 25

		Season	SIMsc
1	Samaki Walker	2001-02	928.1
2	Adam Keefe	1995-96	925.8
3	John Salley	1989-90	917.9
4	Taj Gibson	2010-11	916.0
5	Etan Thomas	2003-04	913.2
6	Leon Douglas	1979-80	908.4
7	Antonio Davis	1993-94	908.0
8	Marcin Gortat	2009-10	907.9
9	Ed Davis	2014-15	904.3
10	Chris Andersen	2003-04	900.1

Baseline Basic Stats

MPG	PTS	AST	REB	BLK	STL
21.0	6.9	0.8	5.8	1.0	0.4

Advanced Metrics

USG%	3PTA/FGA	FTA/FGA	TS%	eFG%	3PT%
15.0	0.003	0.500	0.552	0.523	0.062

AST%	TOV%	OREB%	DREB%	STL%	BLK%
6.1	15.8	10.2	22.3	0.9	3.8

PER	ORTG	DRTG	WS/48	VOL	
13.59	108.5	106.8	0.093	0.183	

- Durable, rotational big man in his athletic prime, only missed one game in three seasons
- Slightly undersized big man, very good shot blocker and rebounder
- Below average position defender, not quite strong enough to handle interior players, somewhat foul prone
- Limited offensively, low volume rim runner that mainly scores on dunks and other shots from close range
- Most effective at running the floor in transition, good offensive rebounder

Jeremy Lamb

	Height	Weight	Cap #	Years Left
	6'5"	180	$7.488M	1

Similar at Age 25

		Season	SIMsc
1	Will Barton	2015-16	939.3
2	Kerry Kittles	1999-00	928.3
3	Rex Chapman	1992-93	913.2
4	Lucious Harris	1995-96	911.7
5	Courtney Lee	2010-11	906.1
6	Leandro Barbosa	2007-08	905.8
7	Alec Burks	2016-17	905.0
8	Michael Dickerson	2000-01	904.2
9	George Hill	2011-12	898.5
10	Jordan McRae	2016-17	896.8

Baseline Basic Stats

MPG	PTS	AST	REB	BLK	STL
23.8	11.3	2.1	3.0	0.3	0.8

Advanced Metrics

USG%	3PTA/FGA	FTA/FGA	TS%	eFG%	3PT%
21.2	0.360	0.222	0.561	0.520	0.362

AST%	TOV%	OREB%	DREB%	STL%	BLK%
13.7	9.1	2.7	14.2	1.5	1.1

PER	ORTG	DRTG	WS/48	VOL	
16.21	112.3	109.7	0.131	0.384	

- Has shown improvement in each of his six seasons, maintained his efficiency from the season before in an increased role
- Efficient scorer, shoots a high percentage inside of 16 feet
- The best per-possession cutter in the NBA last season
- Became a slightly above average three-point shooter last season, most effective in spot-up situations
- Improved playmaking and ball handling skills allowed him to be a good in isolations and as a pick-and-roll ball handler
- Middling overall wing defender, can use length to contest shots and rebounds well for his size

Cody Zeller

	Height	Weight	Cap #	Years Left
	7'0"	240	$13.528M	2

Similar at Age 25

		Season	SIMsc
1	Zaza Pachulia	2009-10	933.5
2	Will Perdue	1990-91	931.4
3	Matt Geiger	1994-95	931.4
4	Tarik Black	2016-17	926.5
5	Duane Causwell	1993-94	924.6
6	Chris Welp	1988-89	921.4
7	Ryan Hollins	2009-10	920.9
8	Chris Hunter	2009-10	920.6
9	Cherokee Parks	1997-98	920.3
10	Jason Smith	2011-12	920.1

Baseline Basic Stats

MPG	PTS	AST	REB	BLK	STL
20.2	7.3	0.9	5.1	0.8	0.5

Advanced Metrics

USG%	3PTA/FGA	FTA/FGA	TS%	eFG%	3PT%
16.4	0.021	0.422	0.574	0.532	0.344

AST%	TOV%	OREB%	DREB%	STL%	BLK%
7.9	13.4	9.4	19.1	1.3	3.0

PER	ORTG	DRTG	WS/48	VOL
15.47	114.2	105.9	0.136	0.420

- Missed most of last season due to a torn meniscus in his left knee
- Very efficient, low volume rim running big man that's very active on the offensive boards when healthy
- Draws fouls at a high rate, 73.2% free throw shooter for his career
- Below average on-ball interior defender, provides middling rim protection, solid shot blocker and defensive rebounder

Frank Kaminsky

	Height	Weight	Cap #	Years Left
	7'0"	242	$3.628M	0

Similar at Age 24

		Season	SIMsc
1	Kelly Olynyk	2015-16	930.1
2	Danilo Gallinari	2012-13	914.5
3	Tim Thomas	2001-02	910.0
4	Marcus Morris	2013-14	905.4
5	Jeff Green	2010-11	905.0
6	Linas Kleiza	2008-09	904.8
7	Vladimir Radmanovic	2004-05	904.8
8	Ryan Anderson	2012-13	899.5
9	Marvin Williams	2010-11	896.1
10	Hedo Turkoglu	2003-04	892.8

Baseline Basic Stats

MPG	PTS	AST	REB	BLK	STL
27.2	12.7	1.9	5.5	0.6	0.7

Advanced Metrics

USG%	3PTA/FGA	FTA/FGA	TS%	eFG%	3PT%
21.1	0.409	0.273	0.558	0.515	0.378

AST%	TOV%	OREB%	DREB%	STL%	BLK%
12.2	9.2	3.6	18.0	1.1	1.4

PER	ORTG	DRTG	WS/48	VOL	
16.02	110.6	108.3	0.121	0.442	

- Has improved steadily in each of his three seasons
- Solid rotational stretch big that has become a good three-point shooter, good at coming off screens and spotting up
- Has improved at making shots around the basket every year
- Above average on post-ups last season
- Above average passing big man that rarely turns the ball over
- Liability on defense, below average position defender with few rim protection skills, rebounds at a below average rate

Tony Parker

	Height	Weight	Cap #	Years Left
	6'2"	180	$5.000M	1

Similar at Age 35

	Player	Season	SIMsc
1	Fred Brown	1983-84	920.8
2	Gerald Henderson	1990-91	910.7
3	Sam Cassell	2004-05	909.6
4	Gary Payton*	2003-04	907.7
5	Vinnie Johnson	1991-92	907.0
6	Rod Strickland	2001-02	905.3
7	Brad Davis	1990-91	902.5
8	Frank Johnson	1993-94	896.0
9	Avery Johnson	2000-01	892.1
10	Derek Harper	1996-97	890.3

Baseline Basic Stats

MPG	PTS	AST	REB	BLK	STL
23.9	9.2	4.2	2.1	0.1	0.8

Advanced Metrics

USG%	3PTA/FGA	FTA/FGA	TS%	eFG%	3PT%
18.7	0.131	0.230	0.512	0.478	0.330

AST%	TOV%	OREB%	DREB%	STL%	BLK%
25.3	14.9	1.2	8.4	1.5	0.2

PER	ORTG	DRTG	WS/48	VOL
12.67	104.7	107.4	0.082	0.569

- Declining veteran entering his age-36 season
- Still has solid playmaking skills, but scoring abilities are greatly diminished
- Above average as a pick-and-roll ball handler and cutter
- No longer has the quickness to drive by defenders in isolations
- Below break-even for his career as a three-point shooter
- Can be a passable position defender if hidden in favorable matchups

Malik Monk

	Height	Weight	Cap #	Years Left
	6'3"	200	$3.447M	2 Team Options

Similar at Age **19**

		Season	SIMsc
1	Dajuan Wagner	2002-03	910.5
2	Jamal Murray	2016-17	903.8
3	Bradley Beal	2012-13	900.2
4	Rashad Vaughn	2015-16	871.3
5	Devin Booker	2015-16	867.3
6	Martell Webster	2005-06	866.1
7	D'Angelo Russell	2015-16	859.6
8	J.R. Smith	2004-05	853.4
9	Emmanuel Mudiay	2015-16	846.9
10	Dante Exum	2014-15	842.5

Baseline Basic Stats

MPG	PTS	AST	REB	BLK	STL
23.0	10.8	2.3	2.3	0.2	0.7

Advanced Metrics

USG%	3PTA/FGA	FTA/FGA	TS%	eFG%	3PT%
23.8	0.432	0.165	0.540	0.513	0.396

AST%	TOV%	OREB%	DREB%	STL%	BLK%
18.3	10.8	1.6	8.7	1.6	0.6

PER	ORTG	DRTG	WS/48	VOL
13.85	105.8	111.5	0.056	0.432

- Received steady playing time off the bench in his rookie season, struggled with his efficiency
- Higher usage player that shot threes at a break-even rate, most effective as a spot-up shooter
- Took very few shots at the rim, settled for low percentage mid-range shots, flashed some playmaking abilities
- Had limitations defensively, couldn't contain quicker point guards and didn't have enough length to defend taller wing players

Willy Hernangomez

	Height	Weight	Cap #	Years Left
	6'11"	240	$1.497M	1

Similar at Age 23

		Season	SIMsc
1	Thomas Robinson	2014-15	928.3
2	David West	2003-04	920.6
3	Brad Miller	1999-00	918.7
4	Henry Sims	2013-14	916.0
5	Nikola Vucevic	2013-14	910.7
6	Willie Cauley-Stein	2016-17	910.7
7	Joffrey Lauvergne	2014-15	906.5
8	Alaa Abdelnaby	1991-92	905.4
9	Jonas Valanciunas	2015-16	904.8
10	Eric Riley	1993-94	904.0

Baseline Basic Stats

MPG	PTS	AST	REB	BLK	STL
22.4	9.5	1.0	6.8	0.8	0.6

Advanced Metrics

USG%	3PTA/FGA	FTA/FGA	TS%	eFG%	3PT%
20.7	0.057	0.362	0.562	0.526	0.346

AST%	TOV%	OREB%	DREB%	STL%	BLK%
9.7	13.3	11.9	25.2	1.5	2.5

PER	ORTG	DRTG	WS/48	VOL
19.07	112.1	106.4	0.143	0.391

- Minutes were significantly reduced in his second year after being a rotation player with the Knicks the previous season
- Efficient inside scorer around the basket, good rim runner that also is effective as a post-up player
- Fairly good passing big man, excellent rebounder, decent shot blocker
- Flashed some stretch potential, but inconsistent in limited three-point attempts
- A bit of liability on defense, lacks mobility, struggles with position defense

Dwayne Bacon

	Height	Weight	Cap #	Years Left
	6'6"	222	$1.378M	1

Similar at Age **22**

		Season	SIMsc
1	Quincy Pondexter	2010-11	932.3
2	James Anderson	2011-12	911.9
3	David Noel	2006-07	906.1
4	Glenn Robinson III	2015-16	906.0
5	Sergei Monia	2005-06	904.9
6	Corey Crowder	1991-92	904.1
7	Arron Afflalo	2007-08	903.6
8	Kedrick Brown	2003-04	901.8
9	Kareem Rush	2002-03	899.6
10	DeQuan Jones	2012-13	899.4

Baseline Basic Stats

MPG	PTS	AST	REB	BLK	STL
19.3	6.9	1.0	2.8	0.2	0.6

Advanced Metrics

USG%	3PTA/FGA	FTA/FGA	TS%	eFG%	3PT%
16.0	0.290	0.171	0.493	0.462	0.324

AST%	TOV%	OREB%	DREB%	STL%	BLK%
8.2	10.7	2.3	14.7	1.4	0.5

PER	ORTG	DRTG	WS/48	VOL
9.39	98.7	110.0	0.038	0.489

- Played a limited role in his rookie season, playing 713 minutes, played four games with Greensboro in the G-League
- Flashed some potential as a defensive specialist, solid on-ball defender that rebounds well for his size
- Didn't establish any offensive strengths in a low volume role in the NBA, will need to improve his outside shot significantly
- Very good playmaking wing in the G-League, did not shoot efficiently in a small sample of G-League games

Newcomers

Miles Bridges

	Height	Weight	Cap #	Years Left
	6'7"	225	$3.207M	1 + 2 TO

Baseline Basic Stats

MPG	PTS	AST	REB	BLK	STL
20.0	7.5	1.3	2.8	0.2	0.5

Advanced Metrics

USG%	3PTA/FGA	FTA/FGA	TS%	eFG%	3PT%
18.9	0.300	0.205	0.502	0.470	0.337

AST%	TOV%	OREB%	DREB%	STL%	BLK%
10.5	11.9	4.5	11.7	1.4	0.9

PER	ORTG	DRTG	WS/48	VOL
11.58	101.2	108.5	0.047	N/A

- Drafted by the Clippers with the 12th overall pick then traded to Charlotte
- Strong performance in the Las Vegas Summer League with a PER of 18.07 in 6 games
- Showed promise as an aggressive defender that can guard multiple positions
- Active in weak side help by playing passing lanes and rotating to block shots, good rebounder on both ends
- Struggled to efficiently make shots, but was effective at limiting turnovers

Devonte' Graham

	Height	Weight	Cap #	Years Left
	6'2"	185	$0.988M	2

Baseline Basic Stats

MPG	PTS	AST	REB	BLK	STL
13.4	4.9	1.9	1.3	0.1	0.5

Advanced Metrics

USG%	3PTA/FGA	FTA/FGA	TS%	eFG%	3PT%
19.4	0.311	0.247	0.484	0.445	0.343

AST%	TOV%	OREB%	DREB%	STL%	BLK%
21.5	14.9	2.4	9.0	1.8	0.6

PER	ORTG	DRTG	WS/48	VOL
11.11	98.5	110.8	0.039	N/A

- Drafted by Atlanta in the second round with the 34th overall pick then traded to Charlotte
- Up-and-down showing at the Las Vegas Summer League
- Flashed solid playmaking skills, but was a bit turnover prone
- Struggled to efficiently make shots, did not a make a three, posted a True Shooting Percentage below 45%
- Did not stand out as a defender, decent on the defensive boards
- Would be best served by spending most of this season in the G-League to get some additional seasoning

DETROIT PISTONS

<u>Last Season</u>: 39 – 43, Missed the Playoffs

<u>Offensive Rating</u>: 107.2, 19th in NBA   <u>Defensive Rating</u>: 107.3, 10th in NBA

<u>Primary Executive</u>: Ed Stefanski, Senior Advisor to the Owner

<u>Head Coach</u>: Dwane Casey

Key Roster Changes

Subtractions	**Additions**
Anthony Tolliver, free agency	Bruce Brown, Jr., draft
James Ennis, free agency	Khyri Thomas, draft
Jameer Nelson, free agency	Glenn Robinson III, free agency
Eric Moreland, waived	Jose Calderon, free agency
Dwight Buycks, waived	Zaza Pachulia, free agency

RAFER Projected Win Total: 42.4

Projected Best Five-Man Unit	**Other Rotation Players**
1. Ish Smith	Reggie Jackson
2. Reggie Bullock	Langston Galloway
3. Glenn Robinson III	Stanley Johnson
4. Blake Griffin	Luke Kennard
5. Andre Drummond	Zaza Pachulia

Remaining Roster

- Jon Leuer
- Jose Calderon
- Henry Ellenson
- Bruce Brown
- Khyri Thomas
- Keenan Evans, 22, 6'3", 190, Texas Tech (Two-Way)
- Zach Lofton, 26, 6'4", 180, New Mexico State (Exhibit 10)

Season Forecast

Last season's trade for Blake Griffin didn't quite pay off with a playoff appearance, so the Detroit Pistons decided to make a major organization shake-up by relieving Stan Van Gundy of his coaching and personnel responsibilities. In his place, they installed the most recent Coach of the Year winner, Dwane Casey as the new head coach and they hired Ed Stefanski, a former GM of three different franchises, to oversee the still yet to be completed search for a permanent new GM. From a roster standpoint, they had very little room to maneuver, so they made some minor tweaks to add role players such as Glenn Robinson III, Zaza Pachulia and Jose Calderon. These additions may only provide an incremental upgrade at best, but that might be all that is necessary for Detroit to land a spot in the playoffs in a more wide open Eastern Conference.

In essence, this year's Pistons team is looking to follow the path of last year's version of the New Orleans Pelicans, as Detroit is now in the same situation that the Pelicans were in last year. Like Detroit last season, New Orleans had acquired DeMarcus Cousins and the team's chemistry didn't click immediately, but after a full training camp, New Orleans found a way to get their two All-Star big men to coexist. The Pistons are hoping for a similar result using a different coaching staff. The acquisitions they made this summer are a step in the right direction, as they got lower volume players that could allow Griffin and Andre Drummond to get the bulk of the offensive touches. From there, Casey is probably going to have to make a few tweaks to the team's rotation. Primarily, the team would be better served by having Ish Smith play the bulk of the minutes at the point instead of Reggie Jackson. This is mainly because Smith's lower volume, pass-first tendencies are a better fit around Drummond and Griffin than Jackson's higher volume, shoot-first style because it will simply result in more touches for Drummond, the team's best player. Next, the Pistons should look to favor Robinson as their other wing player alongside Reggie Bullock because he could provide similar defensive value to Stanley Johnson, but Robinson's outside shooting would give them more floor spacing and potentially a slightly more efficient offense. If the Pistons can incrementally improve their offense, they could put themselves in a better position to win games because they were a very good defensive team last season. In fact, they ranked 10th in the league in Defensive Rating. This was mainly because Drummond provided them with an excellent rim protector and they have a lot of interchangeable players that could defend multiple positions. At worst, their defense should allow them to be competitive on a night-to-night basis. If Detroit can build a more cohesive offensive unit, they could sneak into the playoffs as long as they continue to play solid defense. Otherwise, they may need to look at making some major roster changes to improve the team's long-term future.

Veterans

Andre Drummond

	Height	Weight	Cap #	Years Left
	6'10"	270	$25.434M	1 + PO

		Similar at Age	24	
			Season	SIMsc
1	Emeka Okafor		2006-07	877.6
2	Elton Brand		2003-04	867.3
3	Greg Anderson		1988-89	866.1
4	Hakeem Olajuwon*		1986-87	865.8
5	Derrick Favors		2015-16	864.8
6	Shawn Kemp		1993-94	864.1
7	DeMarcus Cousins		2014-15	861.5
8	LaSalle Thompson		1985-86	860.8
9	Andrew Bynum		2011-12	860.0
10	Jamaal Magloire		2002-03	859.8

Baseline Basic Stats

MPG	PTS	AST	REB	BLK	STL
32.4	16.8	1.8	10.7	1.8	1.2

Advanced Metrics

USG%	3PTA/FGA	FTA/FGA	TS%	eFG%	3PT%
23.2	0.016	0.431	0.545	0.518	0.215

AST%	TOV%	OREB%	DREB%	STL%	BLK%
10.7	13.5	13.7	31.1	2.0	3.9

PER	ORTG	DRTG	WS/48	VOL	
21.89	109.9	100.6	0.163	0.183	

- Very durable, All-Star level center in the prime of his career
- Good rim protector, arguably the league's best rebounder
- Has finished first or second in Rebound Percentage in each of the last five seasons
- Primarily a rim running big man, passing skills and free throw shooting has improved dramatically
- Assist Percentage last season doubled his career average
- Shot over 60% last season at the free throw line last season, way up from his career average of 42.1%

Blake Griffin

	Height	Weight	Cap #	Years Left
	6'10"	251	$32.089M	2 + PO

Similar at Age 28

		Season	SIMsc
1	David Lee	2011-12	903.6
2	Chris Webber	2001-02	902.0
3	Kevin Love	2016-17	897.9
4	Jamal Mashburn	2000-01	897.4
5	Tom Gugliotta	1997-98	895.0
6	Rudy Gay	2014-15	884.0
7	Mehmet Okur	2007-08	882.4
8	Isaac Austin	1997-98	882.1
9	Terry Mills	1995-96	881.1
10	Dirk Nowitzki	2006-07	878.8

Baseline Basic Stats

MPG	PTS	AST	REB	BLK	STL
32.9	17.4	2.6	8.1	0.6	0.9

Advanced Metrics

USG%	3PTA/FGA	FTA/FGA	TS%	eFG%	3PT%
25.1	0.233	0.318	0.552	0.504	0.364

AST%	TOV%	OREB%	DREB%	STL%	BLK%
19.3	11.5	5.3	21.2	1.3	1.2

PER	ORTG	DRTG	WS/48	VOL
19.06	110.5	106.6	0.122	0.291

- Three seasons removed from his last All-Star appearance
- Dealt with a long list of injuries over the last three seasons
- Showing some signs of decline, production is down from his career averages
- Dynamic playmaking big man that excels as a pick-and-roll ball handler
- Efficient scorer in one-on-one situations, still a good post-up player, solid in isolation situations
- Has developed into a break-even three-point shooter over the last three seasons
- No longer the aggressive offensive rebounder he was when he was younger, drawing fouls at a much lower rate
- Above average on-ball position defender, solid on the defensive boards, not really a shot blocker

Reggie Bullock

	Height	Weight	Cap #	Years Left
	6'7"	205	$2.500M	0

Similar at Age 26

		Season	SIMsc
1	Sam Mack	1996-97	923.1
2	Dorell Wright	2011-12	920.6
3	Chase Budinger	2014-15	918.8
4	Martell Webster	2012-13	914.1
5	Kyle Korver	2007-08	911.8
6	Iman Shumpert	2016-17	910.9
7	Wesley Johnson	2013-14	904.3
8	Morris Peterson	2003-04	904.2
9	Danny Green	2013-14	903.6
10	Keith Bogans	2006-07	903.3

Baseline Basic Stats

MPG	PTS	AST	REB	BLK	STL
23.3	8.6	1.3	2.9	0.3	0.6

Advanced Metrics

USG%	3PTA/FGA	FTA/FGA	TS%	eFG%	3PT%
16.1	0.530	0.138	0.568	0.545	0.405

AST%	TOV%	OREB%	DREB%	STL%	BLK%
9.0	8.4	2.3	11.0	1.4	0.9

PER	ORTG	DRTG	WS/48	VOL	
12.65	112.7	109.6	0.107	0.449	

- Entering his age-27 season, became a regular in his fifth season after spending his first four years as a seldomly used bench player
- Low volume spot-up shooter that made 44.5% of his threes last season, rarely turns the ball over
- Also effective at coming off screens and cutting to the rim
- Very good on-ball wing defender, more of a stay-at-home position defender

Reggie Jackson

	Height	Weight	Cap #	Years Left
	6'3"	208	$17.043M	1

Similar at Age 27

		Season	SIMsc
1	Donald Sloan	2014-15	917.9
2	Derrick Rose	2015-16	916.3
3	Jarrett Jack	2010-11	916.0
4	Baron Davis	2006-07	910.2
5	Sam Cassell	1996-97	909.3
6	O.J. Mayo	2014-15	909.2
7	Carlos Arroyo	2006-07	906.8
8	Ben Gordon	2010-11	906.7
9	Sean Kilpatrick	2016-17	905.8
10	Chauncey Billups	2003-04	902.4

Baseline Basic Stats

MPG	PTS	AST	REB	BLK	STL
28.8	13.8	4.8	2.9	0.2	0.9

Advanced Metrics

USG%	3PTA/FGA	FTA/FGA	TS%	eFG%	3PT%
24.4	0.310	0.242	0.527	0.481	0.348

AST%	TOV%	OREB%	DREB%	STL%	BLK%
29.8	14.0	2.1	8.8	1.4	0.4

PER	ORTG	DRTG	WS/48	VOL
15.81	106.8	110.7	0.081	0.450

- Has missed portions of the last two seasons due to injuries to his left knee and right ankle
- Good playmaker, high usage point guard
- Middling scoring efficiency, inconsistent three-point shooter
- Most effective as a pick-and-roll ball handler and spot-up shooter
- Slightly above average mid-range shooter
- Below average overall on defense, may have lost a step of quickness due to his injuries

Glenn Robinson III

	Height	Weight	Cap #	Years Left
	6'7"	222	$4.075M	Team Option

Similar at Age 24

	Player	Season	SIMsc
1	Solomon Hill	2015-16	941.5
2	Jarvis Hayes	2005-06	925.6
3	Chase Budinger	2012-13	924.7
4	Quincy Pondexter	2012-13	923.9
5	Cartier Martin	2008-09	911.3
6	Yakhouba Diawara	2006-07	911.2
7	James Jones	2004-05	909.5
8	Martell Webster	2010-11	908.6
9	Reggie Bullock	2015-16	907.4
10	Robbie Hummel	2013-14	907.0

Baseline Basic Stats

MPG	PTS	AST	REB	BLK	STL
20.5	7.2	1.1	2.8	0.2	0.6

Advanced Metrics

USG%	3PTA/FGA	FTA/FGA	TS%	eFG%	3PT%
15.0	0.441	0.185	0.548	0.521	0.402

AST%	TOV%	OREB%	DREB%	STL%	BLK%
7.6	8.4	3.6	11.3	1.6	0.7

PER	ORTG	DRTG	WS/48	VOL
11.84	111.2	110.2	0.090	0.404

- Missed most of last season due to a left ankle injury that required surgery
- Efficient, low volume spot-up shooter that has improved his three-point in each of the last three seasons
- Made 39.3% of his threes over the last three seasons
- Very good on-ball wing defender with excellent overall athleticism when healthy
- Posted the highest Steal Percentage of his career in a small sample of minutes last season
- Won the 2017 NBA Slam Dunk Contest

Stanley Johnson

	Height	Weight	Cap #	Years Left
	6'7"	245	$3.940M	0

Similar at Age 21

		Season	SIMsc
1	Kawhi Leonard	2012-13	902.9
2	Dontonio Wingfield	1995-96	897.5
3	Kelly Oubre	2016-17	890.7
4	John Williams	1987-88	885.0
5	Mario Hezonja	2016-17	884.5
6	Lamond Murray	1994-95	882.5
7	Vladimir Radmanovic	2001-02	882.4
8	Peja Stojakovic	1998-99	881.8
9	Chase Budinger	2009-10	880.7
10	Marcus Smart	2015-16	880.1

Baseline Basic Stats

MPG	PTS	AST	REB	BLK	STL
24.9	9.8	1.6	4.2	0.4	0.9

Advanced Metrics

USG%	3PTA/FGA	FTA/FGA	TS%	eFG%	3PT%
17.1	0.271	0.265	0.506	0.465	0.309

AST%	TOV%	OREB%	DREB%	STL%	BLK%
10.0	12.6	3.4	13.5	2.1	0.9

PER	ORTG	DRTG	WS/48	VOL	
11.00	101.2	106.7	0.071	0.334	

- Had his best season in his third year, became a regular starter for the first time
- Solid wing defender with good athleticism, aggressive, steals rate has improved in every season, good on the defensive glass
- Limited offensively, inefficient in a lower volume role, struggles to make shots outside of three feet
- Below average in virtually every offensive situation last season

Ish Smith

	Height	Weight	Cap #	Years Left
	6'0"	175	$6.000M	0

Similar at Age **29**

		Season	SIMsc
1	Larry Drew	1987-88	931.3
2	Pooh Richardson	1995-96	919.5
3	Sherman Douglas	1995-96	918.6
4	Darren Collison	2016-17	918.1
5	Jameer Nelson	2011-12	913.0
6	J.J. Barea	2013-14	910.1
7	Kenny Anderson	1999-00	909.3
8	Tyronn Lue	2006-07	908.8
9	David Wesley	1999-00	906.9
10	Mike Bibby	2007-08	904.7

Baseline Basic Stats

MPG	PTS	AST	REB	BLK	STL
26.8	11.3	4.7	2.4	0.1	1.0

Advanced Metrics

USG%	3PTA/FGA	FTA/FGA	TS%	eFG%	3PT%
20.5	0.201	0.180	0.515	0.487	0.352

AST%	TOV%	OREB%	DREB%	STL%	BLK%
28.2	12.4	1.7	9.8	1.8	0.7

PER	ORTG	DRTG	WS/48	VOL
15.08	107.4	109.0	0.095	0.358

- Entering his age-30 season, coming off a career year
- Good ball control point guard with solid playmaking skills
- Effective as a pick-and-roll ball handler, can use quickness to beat his man off the dribble in isolation situations
- Posted a career high in True Shooting Percentage by making 67% of his shots inside of three feet and making threes at a break-even percentage
- Middling defender, got steals earlier in his career, more of a position defender now

Luke Kennard

	Height	Weight	Cap #	Years Left
	6'6"	206	$3.275M	2 Team Options

Similar at Age 21

		Season	SIMsc
1	C.J. Miles	2008-09	947.2
2	Timothe Luwawu-Cabarrot	2016-17	938.6
3	Chase Budinger	2009-10	927.6
4	Tim Hardaway, Jr.	2013-14	926.0
5	Nik Stauskas	2014-15	923.8
6	Klay Thompson	2011-12	922.5
7	Evan Fournier	2013-14	920.3
8	Ben McLemore	2014-15	918.1
9	Martell Webster	2007-08	917.8
10	Terrence Ross	2012-13	917.8

Baseline Basic Stats

MPG	PTS	AST	REB	BLK	STL
25.2	10.4	1.7	3.0	0.3	0.7

Advanced Metrics

USG%	3PTA/FGA	FTA/FGA	TS%	eFG%	3PT%
17.6	0.322	0.189	0.549	0.517	0.387

AST%	TOV%	OREB%	DREB%	STL%	BLK%
12.2	12.2	1.9	11.1	1.5	0.7

PER	ORTG	DRTG	WS/48	VOL
11.73	106.6	109.3	0.081	0.349

- Was a regular part of Detroit's rotation as a rookie, played 1463 minutes
- Efficient in a low usage role, made 41.5% of his threes, showed decent passing skills
- Mainly utilized as a spot-up shooter, ranked in the 96th percentile in spot-up situations according to the NBA
- Got a lot of favorable matchups, solid as a position defender in these situations, solid defensive rebounder

Zaza Pachulia

	Height	Weight	Cap #	Years Left
	6'11"	240	$1.513M	0

Similar at Age 33

		Season	SIMsc
1	Danny Schayes	1992-93	912.8
2	Christian Laettner	2002-03	903.6
3	Bob Lanier*	1981-82	903.1
4	Shawn Kemp	2002-03	898.1
5	Kenyon Martin	2010-11	897.9
6	Anderson Varejao	2015-16	894.7
7	David Lee	2016-17	894.5
8	Amar'e Stoudemire	2015-16	892.7
9	Nene Hilario	2015-16	890.2
10	Frank Brickowski	1992-93	887.0

Baseline Basic Stats

MPG	PTS	AST	REB	BLK	STL
21.0	7.5	2.0	5.3	0.4	0.8

Advanced Metrics

USG%	3PTA/FGA	FTA/FGA	TS%	eFG%	3PT%
16.6	0.013	0.347	0.584	0.540	0.073

AST%	TOV%	OREB%	DREB%	STL%	BLK%
13.8	17.3	10.6	22.0	2.0	1.6

PER	ORTG	DRTG	WS/48	VOL	
16.31	114.0	101.6	0.152	0.465	

- Started most of the last two seasons with Golden State

- Fell out of the rotation at the end of last season, rarely played in the playoffs

- Low volume, efficient inside scorer that is most effective as a roll man and cutter

- Draws fouls at a high rate, good free throw shooter, decent passing big man

- Not really a rim protector, mainly a position defender

- Older big man with limited mobility, still a very good overall rebounder

Langston Galloway

	Height	Weight	Cap #	Years Left
	6'2"	201	$7.000M	1

Similar at Age 26

		Season	SIMsc
1	Marcus Thornton	2013-14	925.8
2	Shammond Williams	2001-02	917.1
3	Daniel Gibson	2012-13	916.6
4	Charlie Bell	2005-06	914.5
5	Damon Jones	2002-03	911.1
6	Anthony Peeler	1995-96	907.0
7	A.J. Price	2012-13	906.4
8	Wayne Ellington	2013-14	905.5
9	Seth Curry	2016-17	903.8
10	Patty Mills	2014-15	899.9

Baseline Basic Stats

MPG	PTS	AST	REB	BLK	STL
22.7	8.7	2.1	2.2	0.1	0.7

Advanced Metrics

USG%	3PTA/FGA	FTA/FGA	TS%	eFG%	3PT%
18.3	0.523	0.142	0.515	0.488	0.366

AST%	TOV%	OREB%	DREB%	STL%	BLK%
14.1	8.6	1.5	9.9	1.7	0.4

PER	ORTG	DRTG	WS/48	VOL
11.96	105.4	110.6	0.064	0.343

- No injury history, fell out of Detroit's rotation late in the season, resulted in a lot of DNPs
- More of an undersized two guard, not especially efficient as a scorer
- Takes a lot of lower percentage long twos, below mid-range shooter overall
- Inconsistent three-point shooter, percentage has hovered around the league average for his career
- Very solid at defending both guard spots, good rebounder for his size, uses active hands to get steals

Jose Calderon

	Height	Weight	Cap #	Years Left
	6'3"	210	$1.513M	0

Similar at Age 36

		Season	SIMsc
1	Mario Elie	1999-00	894.2
2	Terry Porter	1999-00	890.4
3	Chauncey Billups	2012-13	886.6
4	Jon Barry	2005-06	878.3
5	Anthony Parker	2011-12	876.3
6	Ray Allen*	2011-12	873.6
7	Dell Curry	2000-01	872.4
8	Brad Davis	1991-92	869.8
9	Mitch Richmond	2001-02	865.4
10	Steve Kerr	2001-02	863.3

Baseline Basic Stats

MPG	PTS	AST	REB	BLK	STL
17.8	5.1	2.4	2.0	0.1	0.5

Advanced Metrics

USG%	3PTA/FGA	FTA/FGA	TS%	eFG%	3PT%
13.0	0.461	0.159	0.568	0.540	0.381

AST%	TOV%	OREB%	DREB%	STL%	BLK%
19.6	17.8	1.7	10.8	1.5	0.4

PER	ORTG	DRTG	WS/48	VOL	
10.99	110.8	109.7	0.074	0.515	

- Aging veteran in the twilight of his career, still productive in a limited role with Cleveland last season
- No longer quick enough to be a primary ball handler, Assist Percentage has declined rapidly
- Effective in limited situations as a pick-and-roll ball handler
- Low volume spot-up shooter at this stage of his career
- According to the NBA, the best per-possession spot-up player in the league last season
- Actually posted a career high True Shooting Percentage last season, made 46.4% of his threes
- Historically been a below average defender that struggles on the ball due to a lack of quickness
- Was hidden in favorable matchups last season, played decent position defense

Jon Leuer

	Height	Weight	Cap #	Years Left
	6'10"	228	$10.003M	1

Similar at Age 28

		Season	SIMsc
1	Jonas Jerebko	2015-16	930.4
2	Kent Benson	1982-83	928.3
3	Scott Hastings	1988-89	923.3
4	Jeff Wilkins	1983-84	922.3
5	Greg Foster	1996-97	919.2
6	Edgar Jones	1984-85	916.2
7	Charles D. Smith	1993-94	911.0
8	Marty Conlon	1995-96	911.0
9	Gerard King	2000-01	910.7
10	Jim Petersen	1990-91	908.5

Baseline Basic Stats

MPG	PTS	AST	REB	BLK	STL
19.2	7.3	1.0	4.2	0.5	0.4

Advanced Metrics

USG%	3PTA/FGA	FTA/FGA	TS%	eFG%	3PT%
17.0	0.138	0.323	0.538	0.480	0.243

AST%	TOV%	OREB%	DREB%	STL%	BLK%
7.7	12.7	6.7	18.5	1.0	1.7

PER	ORTG	DRTG	WS/48	VOL
12.55	107.1	108.0	0.087	0.375

- Missed most of last season due to a sprained left ankle
- When healthy, low usage big man that predominantly shoots from mid-range with decent efficiency
- Can make threes, but his percentages have been inconsistent throughout his career
- Effectively scored on post-ups in his last healthy season
- Decent position defender on the interior, solid rebounder
- Limited shot blocking skills, below average rim protector

Henry Ellenson

	Height	Weight	Cap #	Years Left
	6'11"	245	$1.857M	Team Option

Similar at Age __21__

		Season	SIMsc
1	Trey Lyles	2016-17	900.4
2	Trey Thompkins	2011-12	890.7
3	Perry Jones	2012-13	882.0
4	Ryan Anderson	2009-10	877.9
5	Bobby Portis	2016-17	871.7
6	Yi Jianlian	2008-09	866.0
7	Jackie Butler	2006-07	856.1
8	Luke Babbitt	2010-11	854.6
9	Damir Markota	2006-07	854.5
10	Jordan Hamilton	2011-12	849.8

Baseline Basic Stats

MPG	PTS	AST	REB	BLK	STL
19.5	9.0	1.0	4.5	0.4	0.4

Advanced Metrics

USG%	3PTA/FGA	FTA/FGA	TS%	eFG%	3PT%
22.2	0.297	0.222	0.502	0.468	0.353

AST%	TOV%	OREB%	DREB%	STL%	BLK%
9.4	12.2	6.0	20.7	0.9	0.8

PER	ORTG	DRTG	WS/48	VOL
12.16	100.0	108.9	0.042	0.669

- Has not played much in two seasons, has only played a total of 475 minutes

- Spent most of last season at the end of Detroit's bench

- Likely future role is as a stretch big, still struggled to adjust to the NBA three-point line, more of a mid-range shooter at this stage

- Limited defensively, not really a rim protector and is lacking in mobility, very good defensive rebounder

Newcomers

Bruce Brown, Jr.	Height	Weight	Cap #	Years Left
	6'5"	202	$0.838M	2

Baseline Basic Stats

MPG	PTS	AST	REB	BLK	STL
11.5	3.5	1.1	1.4	0.1	0.4

Advanced Metrics

USG%	3PTA/FGA	FTA/FGA	TS%	eFG%	3PT%
16.5	0.211	0.263	0.463	0.425	0.279

AST%	TOV%	OREB%	DREB%	STL%	BLK%
10.6	12.6	4.3	11.5	1.8	1.0

PER	ORTG	DRTG	WS/48	VOL
9.52	96.0	107.2	0.035	N/A

- Drafted by Detroit in the second round with the 42nd overall pick
- Showed promise as a defender at Summer League
- Was better on the ball than he was in college, active help defender that posted good steals, blocks and rebound rates
- Displayed some playmaking skills, but was inefficient as a scorer
- Shot below 30% from the field at Summer League
- Could benefit from some additional seasoning in the G-League to improve his shooting

Khyri Thomas

	Height	Weight	Cap #	Years Left
	6'3"	210	$0.838M	2

Baseline Basic Stats

MPG	PTS	AST	REB	BLK	STL
10.8	3.5	1.0	1.2	0.1	0.4

Advanced Metrics

USG%	3PTA/FGA	FTA/FGA	TS%	eFG%	3PT%
14.9	0.233	0.251	0.435	0.401	0.303

AST%	TOV%	OREB%	DREB%	STL%	BLK%
9.5	11.9	2.9	10.7	1.8	0.7

PER	ORTG	DRTG	WS/48	VOL
7.41	91.3	110.9	0.002	N/A

- Drafted by Philadelphia with the 38th pick, then traded to Detroit
- Flashed potential as a stay-at-home on-ball defender at Summer League, used active hands to get steals
- Showed some effectiveness as a low volume spot-up shooter, was 5-for-11 on threes, but settled for too many low percentage mid-range shots
- Was utilized in a catch-and-shoot role, didn't look to make plays for others, effective at limiting turnovers

INDIANA PACERS

<u>Last Season</u>: 48 – 34, Lost 1st Round to Cleveland (3 – 4)

<u>Offensive Rating</u>: 109.5, 11th in NBA   <u>Defensive Rating</u>: 108.1, 13th in NBA

<u>Primary Executive</u>: Kevin Pritchard, President of Basketball Operations

<u>Head Coach</u>: Nate McMillan

Key Roster Changes

Subtractions	**Additions**
Lance Stephenson, free agency	Aaron Holiday, draft
Glenn Robinson III, free agency	Alize Johnson, draft
Trevor Booker, free agency	Doug McDermott, free agency
Joe Young, free agency	Tyreke Evans, free agency
Al Jefferson, waived	Kyle O'Quinn, free agency
Alex Poythress, waived	

RAFER Projected Win Total: 41.6

Projected Best Five-Man Unit	**Other Rotation Players**
1. Darren Collison	Tyreke Evans
2. Victor Oladipo	Cory Joseph
3. Bojan Bogdanovic	Doug McDermott
4. Thaddeus Young	Domantas Sabonis
5. Myles Turner	Kyle O'Quinn

Remaining Roster

- T.J. Leaf
- Ike Anigbogu
- Aaron Holiday
- Alize Johnson
- Edmond Sumner, 23, 6'6", 176, Xavier (Two-Way)
- C.J. Wilcox, 28, 6'5", 195, Washington (Two-Way)
- Elijah Stewart, 23, 6'5", 194, USC (Exhibit 10)

Season Forecast

The system's projection of the Indiana Pacers came as a shock because they played a very competitive series against Cleveland in last season's playoffs and their roster is relatively young. However, their primary rotation consists of several players coming off atypical career years. For instance, Darren Collison had the best season of his career as a 30-year old and Tyreke Evans' production spiked up significantly after being plagued by injuries in the previous two seasons. Then most notably, Victor Oladipo improved dramatically to being an All-Star level player after a considerable down year in Oklahoma City the year before. Therefore, the system suggests that there is some potential that a few of these players could regress to their means, which could cause Indiana to drop a few wins in the standings, leaving them in a position to have to compete for one of the lower playoff seeds. However, it is very possible that they could outperform these projections because according to the eye test, the improvements from Oladipo appear to be fairly permanent and not a fluke. If this is the case, then Indiana could be a solid playoff team that could be in the mix for a top-four seed in the Eastern Conference.

Indiana was a solid team on both sides of the ball last season, finishing in the upper half of the league in both Offensive and Defensive Rating. Most likely, the system projects that the Pacers will maintain their offensive efficiency because the players in their expected rotation have more established track records on that side of the ball. Stylistically, the Pacers will continue to attack opponents with their pick-and-roll heavy system that features Oladipo as their main ball handler and three solid roll man options in Myles Turner, Domantas Sabonis and new acquisition Kyle O'Quinn. They also picked up a couple of additional outside shooting threats in Evans and Doug McDermott to give them more spacing. As a result, their offense could be a bit better than it was a season ago. The main question for the Pacers is if their defense will continue to be above average. The team is deeper than it was last year, but as it was mentioned earlier, their rotation mainly consists of offensive minded players with only a few players with reliable defensive reputations, Oladipo and Cory Joseph in particular. Therefore, the possibility exists that some of the other players in rotation could revert back to their historical tendencies and cause the team's defense to regress a bit. However, head coach, Nate McMillan has been a decent defensive coach in his years in Indiana and Portland. The only times that his teams finished in the bottom third of the league in Defensive Rating were when he was about to be fired or when his teams were clearly rebuilding. Because of that, the Pacers should probably be around average on defense at worst. In general, Indiana is a talented team that could outperform these analytical projections and be a solid playoff team in the East. If their play falls in line with last season's performance, they could possibly win a round in the playoffs if they get a favorable matchup. However, if the players in their rotation regress to their career averages, it could be a tough season with them finishing with a record closer to 0.500 and fighting for a lower playoff seed.

Veterans

Victor Oladipo

	Height	Weight	Cap #	Years Left
	6'5"	214	$21.000M	2

Similar at Age **25**

		Season	SIMsc
1	Bonzi Wells	2001-02	933.3
2	Gerald Wallace	2007-08	920.1
3	Jason Richardson	2005-06	914.6
4	Ray Allen*	2000-01	910.7
5	Stephen Jackson	2003-04	905.2
6	Gerald Henderson	2012-13	904.5
7	J.R. Smith	2010-11	904.5
8	Vince Carter	2001-02	903.4
9	Kawhi Leonard	2016-17	903.3
10	Randy Foye	2008-09	902.7

Baseline Basic Stats

MPG	PTS	AST	REB	BLK	STL
32.8	16.4	3.2	4.4	0.4	1.2

Advanced Metrics

USG%	3PTA/FGA	FTA/FGA	TS%	eFG%	3PT%
24.4	0.330	0.239	0.554	0.517	0.377

AST%	TOV%	OREB%	DREB%	STL%	BLK%
17.1	12.0	2.6	13.3	2.3	1.2

PER	ORTG	DRTG	WS/48	VOL
17.80	108.1	105.8	0.118	0.360

- Breakout season in his fifth year, posted career highs almost across the board
- Won the 2017-18 Most Improved Player award, made his first All-Star team
- Increased his efficiency in a higher usage role
- Most effective with the ball in his hands as an isolation scorer and pick-and-roll ball handler
- Shot a career high 37.1% on threes, made 69% of his shots inside of three feet, showed solid playmaking skills
- Excellent on-ball defending wing player, very active help defender
- Lead the league in Steal Percentage, posted career highs in Block Percentage and Defensive Rebound Percentage

Myles Turner

	Height	Weight	Cap #	Years Left
	6'11"	243	$3.410M	0

Similar at Age **21**

		Season	SIMsc
1	Andray Blatche	2007-08	909.5
2	Charlie Villanueva	2005-06	908.1
3	Darko Milicic	2006-07	906.6
4	Benoit Benjamin	1985-86	902.8
5	Spencer Hawes	2009-10	901.2
6	Kristaps Porzingis	2016-17	897.8
7	Yi Jianlian	2008-09	897.3
8	LaMarcus Aldridge	2006-07	896.4
9	Derrick Favors	2012-13	892.4
10	Mike Gminski	1980-81	890.1

Baseline Basic Stats

MPG	PTS	AST	REB	BLK	STL
27.3	11.1	1.3	6.5	1.8	0.6

Advanced Metrics

USG%	3PTA/FGA	FTA/FGA	TS%	eFG%	3PT%
18.5	0.135	0.283	0.546	0.509	0.332

AST%	TOV%	OREB%	DREB%	STL%	BLK%
7.4	11.9	6.5	18.6	1.2	4.4

PER	ORTG	DRTG	WS/48	VOL	
15.10	107.8	106.4	0.110	0.355	

- Solid in his third year, regular season performance dipped a bit, played effectively in the playoffs
- Missed some games due to a concussion and an elbow injury
- Fairly effective as the roll man in pick-and-roll situations, struggled a little bit to finish shots inside
- Shooting percentage inside of three feet dropped by about 10% to 61.4% last season
- Improved three-point percentage to almost league average on 157 attempts last season
- Good rim protector, one of the best shot blockers in the league, solid rebounder, sometimes struggles to defend on the ball

Darren Collison

	Height	Weight	Cap #	Years Left
	6'0"	160	$10.000M	0

Similar at Age **30**

		Season	SIMsc
1	Chris Whitney	2001-02	939.5
2	Dana Barros	1997-98	934.2
3	Aaron Brooks	2014-15	925.8
4	Michael Adams	1992-93	920.3
5	Luke Ridnour	2011-12	919.2
6	Chucky Atkins	2004-05	913.8
7	Dee K. Brown	1998-99	905.1
8	Johnny Dawkins	1993-94	905.0
9	Scott Skiles	1994-95	904.3
10	Sherman Douglas	1996-97	903.2

Baseline Basic Stats

MPG	PTS	AST	REB	BLK	STL
24.0	9.8	3.9	1.9	0.1	0.9

Advanced Metrics

USG%	3PTA/FGA	FTA/FGA	TS%	eFG%	3PT%
18.8	0.312	0.233	0.562	0.522	0.402

AST%	TOV%	OREB%	DREB%	STL%	BLK%
25.4	13.0	1.7	7.5	1.9	0.4

PER	ORTG	DRTG	WS/48	VOL
15.65	114.3	110.4	0.115	0.319

- Entering his age-31 season, coming off his best year in the NBA, some decline or regression risk
- Good playmaking point guard that avoids turnovers
- Effective last season as a pick-and-roll ball handler
- Efficient shooter, has shot over 40% on threes in each of the last three seasons
- Led the NBA in Three-Point Percentage at 46.8% last season
- Good at using the threat of his shot to create driving lanes to go by defenders in isolation situations
- Average position defender despite smallish size, posted a career high in Steal Percentage last season

Bojan Bogdanovic

	Height	Weight	Cap #	Years Left
	6'7"	216	$10.500M	0

Similar at Age 28

		Season	SIMsc
1	Eric Piatkowski	1998-99	949.7
2	Morris Peterson	2005-06	939.7
3	Tracy Murray	1999-00	931.5
4	Sam Mack	1998-99	930.8
5	Peja Stojakovic	2005-06	928.4
6	Jason Richardson	2008-09	926.0
7	Glen Rice	1995-96	924.1
8	Roger Mason	2008-09	922.2
9	Quentin Richardson	2008-09	917.9
10	J.R. Smith	2013-14	915.8

Baseline Basic Stats

MPG	PTS	AST	REB	BLK	STL
27.4	11.7	1.7	3.4	0.2	0.7

Advanced Metrics

USG%	3PTA/FGA	FTA/FGA	TS%	eFG%	3PT%
18.8	0.504	0.223	0.573	0.535	0.391

AST%	TOV%	OREB%	DREB%	STL%	BLK%
8.5	10.4	1.8	11.8	1.1	0.4

PER	ORTG	DRTG	WS/48	VOL	
13.00	109.9	109.7	0.093	0.308	

- Entering his age-29 season, coming off the best season of his four-year career
- Developed into a very effective three-and-D wing player
- Mainly used as a spot-up shooter that could also run off screens
- Posted the highest True Shooting Percentage of his career while playing a lower volume role
- Shot a career-best 40.2% on threes last season
- Effective in a limited amount of possessions as a pick-and-roll ball handler
- Solid stay-at-home on-ball defender, improved as an overall defender from his previous seasons

Thaddeus Young

	Height	Weight	Cap #	Years Left
	6'8"	220	$13.764M	0

Similar at Age **29**

		Season	SIMsc
1	George Lynch	1999-00	937.0
2	Shawn Marion	2007-08	927.7
3	Ken Norman	1993-94	924.3
4	Luol Deng	2014-15	917.1
5	Rudy Gay	2015-16	915.7
6	Gerald Wallace	2011-12	909.6
7	Bryon Russell	1999-00	903.7
8	Jerome Kersey	1991-92	902.3
9	Wilson Chandler	2016-17	900.5
10	Grant Long	1995-96	900.3

Baseline Basic Stats

MPG	PTS	AST	REB	BLK	STL
28.9	10.6	1.7	5.8	0.4	1.1

Advanced Metrics

USG%	3PTA/FGA	FTA/FGA	TS%	eFG%	3PT%
17.3	0.198	0.167	0.520	0.501	0.332

AST%	TOV%	OREB%	DREB%	STL%	BLK%
8.7	11.5	7.2	15.5	2.2	1.1

PER	ORTG	DRTG	WS/48	VOL
13.72	105.6	107.0	0.083	0.263

- Heading into his 30s, production over the last two seasons has been down from his career averages

- Some decline risk, maybe feeling the aftereffects of a heavy workload throughout his 20s

- No major injury history, has averaged over 30 minutes per game in each of the last six seasons

- Still a versatile defender that can guard multiple positions

- Steal Percentage is still consistent with his career average

- Diminishing athleticism has hurt him offensively, now a lower volume player

- Attempting fewer shots inside of three feet, below break-even three-point for his career

- Below average in almost every half court situation, still good at running the floor to finish plays in transition

Tyreke Evans

	Height	Weight	Cap #	Years Left
	6'6"	220	$12.400M	0

Similar at Age 28

		Season	SIMsc
1	Ray Allen*	2003-04	906.5
2	Manu Ginobili	2005-06	899.9
3	Josh Howard	2008-09	899.1
4	Michael Redd	2007-08	897.9
5	Jim Jackson	1998-99	897.4
6	Devin Brown	2006-07	895.9
7	Gerald Henderson	2015-16	892.2
8	Jason Richardson	2008-09	890.7
9	Caron Butler	2008-09	889.2
10	Mike Dunleavy, Jr.	2008-09	887.1

Baseline Basic Stats

MPG	PTS	AST	REB	BLK	STL
31.5	15.7	3.3	4.4	0.3	1.1

Advanced Metrics

USG%	3PTA/FGA	FTA/FGA	TS%	eFG%	3PT%
24.3	0.358	0.255	0.538	0.496	0.379

AST%	TOV%	OREB%	DREB%	STL%	BLK%
23.1	11.9	2.9	14.3	1.8	0.9

PER	ORTG	DRTG	WS/48	VOL
16.98	107.3	108.5	0.100	0.422

- Coming off his best season in the NBA at age 28, posted career highs almost across the board
- Missed parts of the 2015-16 and 2016-17 seasons due to a right knee injury that required surgery
- Historically has been a slashing combo guard with good playmaking skills
- Effective as a pick-and-roll ball handler and good at beating his man off the dribble in isolation situations
- Posted a career high in True Shooting Percentage last season
- Took fewer mid-range shots and increased his three-point attempt rate, shot a career high 39.9% on threes last season
- Solid defensively, can guard multiple positions, better at defending wing players, good defensive rebounding guard
- Knee injury has forced him to be more of a stay-at-home defender

Cory Joseph

	Height	Weight	Cap #	Years Left
	6'3"	185	$7.945M	0

Similar at Age 26

		Season	SIMsc
1	Luther Head	2008-09	935.3
2	Craig Hodges	1986-87	932.3
3	Tony Smith	1994-95	931.9
4	Anthony Goldwire	1997-98	928.6
5	Norris Cole	2014-15	927.1
6	Antonio Daniels	2001-02	925.9
7	Kyle Macy	1983-84	921.8
8	Ronald Murray	2005-06	920.4
9	Seth Curry	2016-17	919.7
10	George Hill	2012-13	918.8

Baseline Basic Stats

MPG	PTS	AST	REB	BLK	STL
24.8	9.1	3.4	2.3	0.2	0.9

Advanced Metrics

USG%	3PTA/FGA	FTA/FGA	TS%	eFG%	3PT%
16.8	0.287	0.181	0.520	0.490	0.366

AST%	TOV%	OREB%	DREB%	STL%	BLK%
19.2	12.8	2.0	9.6	1.7	0.6

PER	ORTG	DRTG	WS/48	VOL
12.35	107.4	109.0	0.083	0.438

- Played starter level minutes for the third consecutive season
- Overall production decreased in a lower usage role
- Utilized more like an undersized spot-up shooting two guard
- Shot almost at the league average on threes for the second year in a row
- Decent playmaker, posted lowest Turnover Percentage of his career last season, solid as a pick-and-roll ball handler
- Solid on-ball defender, can defend both guard spots, rebounds well for his size

Domantas Sabonis

	Height	Weight	Cap #	Years Left
	6'11"	240	$2.660M	Team Option

Similar at Age 21

	Player	Season	SIMsc
1	Charlie Villanueva	2005-06	931.4
2	Yi Jianlian	2008-09	930.2
3	Spencer Hawes	2009-10	928.1
4	Rasheed Wallace	1995-96	921.7
5	J.J. Hickson	2009-10	918.3
6	Troy Murphy	2001-02	917.1
7	Cody Zeller	2013-14	916.9
8	Nenad Krstic	2004-05	915.8
9	Noah Vonleh	2016-17	912.7
10	Donte Greene	2009-10	911.6

Baseline Basic Stats

MPG	PTS	AST	REB	BLK	STL
23.9	10.1	1.4	6.0	0.6	0.6

Advanced Metrics

USG%	3PTA/FGA	FTA/FGA	TS%	eFG%	3PT%
19.6	0.102	0.294	0.526	0.489	0.337

AST%	TOV%	OREB%	DREB%	STL%	BLK%
10.7	14.4	8.2	20.0	1.3	1.5

PER	ORTG	DRTG	WS/48	VOL	
13.90	104.7	107.0	0.091	0.307	

- Dramatically improved in his second year after being miscast as a stretch big in Oklahoma City
- Excelled as a rim runner, scored very efficiently on shots inside of three feet
- Playing closer to the basket allowed him to grab offensive rebounds at a significantly higher rate
- Improved his playmaking skills and shot a higher percentage on threes in fewer attempts
- Solid rim protector, uses length to contest shots, very good defensive rebounder
- Below average on-ball defender due to a lack of lateral quickness

Doug McDermott

	Height	Weight	Cap #	Years Left
	6'8"	225	$7.333M	2

Similar at Age 26

		Season	SIMsc
1	Quincy Pondexter	2014-15	928.7
2	Kyle Singler	2014-15	928.7
3	James Jones	2006-07	925.9
4	Bojan Bogdanovic	2015-16	924.3
5	Marvin Williams	2012-13	921.3
6	Luke Babbitt	2015-16	920.5
7	Dennis Scott	1994-95	917.1
8	Jawad Williams	2009-10	916.5
9	Jason Kapono	2007-08	916.3
10	Wilson Chandler	2013-14	915.9

Baseline Basic Stats

MPG	PTS	AST	REB	BLK	STL
22.2	8.3	1.1	2.9	0.2	0.6

Advanced Metrics

USG%	3PTA/FGA	FTA/FGA	TS%	eFG%	3PT%
16.6	0.452	0.159	0.553	0.526	0.395

AST%	TOV%	OREB%	DREB%	STL%	BLK%
7.1	9.0	2.4	11.2	0.9	0.7

PER	ORTG	DRTG	WS/48	VOL	
11.04	108.4	111.9	0.069	0.336	

- Entering his age-27 season, has been on four teams in the last two seasons
- Low usage, rotational shooting specialist, has shot 40.3% on threes for his career
- Primarily used last season as a spot-up shooter, also very good at running the floor in transition to get layups
- Passable defender, decent position defender if given favorable matchups, adequate defensive rebounder

Kyle O'Quinn

	Height	Weight	Cap #	Years Left
	6'10"	240	$4.449M	0

Similar at Age 27

		Season	SIMsc
1	Bernard James	2012-13	896.9
2	Cole Aldrich	2015-16	896.7
3	Alton Lister	1985-86	892.9
4	Melvin Turpin	1987-88	889.8
5	Miles Plumlee	2015-16	885.5
6	Calvin Booth	2003-04	883.8
7	Will Perdue	1992-93	883.0
8	Samuel Dalembert	2008-09	882.9
9	Eric Riley	1997-98	881.7
10	Taj Gibson	2012-13	881.2

Baseline Basic Stats

MPG	PTS	AST	REB	BLK	STL
20.4	7.1	1.1	6.1	1.2	0.5

Advanced Metrics

USG%	3PTA/FGA	FTA/FGA	TS%	eFG%	3PT%
16.8	0.041	0.300	0.568	0.536	0.194

AST%	TOV%	OREB%	DREB%	STL%	BLK%
12.0	16.7	10.3	25.1	1.3	4.5

PER	ORTG	DRTG	WS/48	VOL	
17.22	111.2	105.2	0.129	0.538	

- Very effective per-minute player throughout his career, has never played more than 18 minutes per game
- Efficient at scoring inside of three feet, most effective as a roll man
- Has become a pretty good mid-range shooter, good passing big man that will crash the offensive boards
- Excellent rebounder and shot blocker, defensive impact is uncertain because he's only been on rebuilding teams with bad defenses

T.J. Leaf

	Height	Weight	Cap #	Years Left
	6'10"	222	$2.408M	2 Team Options

Similar at Age 20

		Season	SIMsc
1	Shawne Williams	2006-07	943.9
2	Danilo Gallinari	2008-09	891.9
3	Trey Lyles	2015-16	890.1
4	Chris Wilcox	2002-03	888.3
5	Otto Porter	2013-14	882.3
6	Wilson Chandler	2007-08	878.1
7	Donte Greene	2008-09	877.2
8	Rashard Lewis	1999-00	872.5
9	Jaylen Brown	2016-17	868.0
10	Antonis Fotsis	2001-02	866.2

Baseline Basic Stats

MPG	PTS	AST	REB	BLK	STL
19.8	8.1	1.0	3.6	0.4	0.5

Advanced Metrics

USG%	3PTA/FGA	FTA/FGA	TS%	eFG%	3PT%
17.9	0.361	0.179	0.555	0.533	0.416

AST%	TOV%	OREB%	DREB%	STL%	BLK%
6.2	8.0	5.8	13.8	1.0	1.1

PER	ORTG	DRTG	WS/48	VOL	
13.28	112.6	110.1	0.105	0.431	

- Was on the fringes of Indiana's rotation as a rookie, played 459 minutes
- Showed promise as a spot-up shooter in a low usage role, shot 42.9% on threes in 42 attempts, was open or wide open on almost every attempt
- Most effective as the screener in pick-and-roll situations
- Had difficulties on defense, struggled as an on-ball defender, below average as a rim protector and rebounder

Ike Anigbogu

	Height	Weight	Cap #	Years Left
	6'10"	252	$1.378M	1

Similar at Age 19

		Season	SIMsc
1	Amir Johnson	2006-07	807.1
2	Zaza Pachulia	2003-04	793.9
3	Noah Vonleh	2014-15	791.2
4	Darko Milicic	2004-05	789.5
5	Enes Kanter	2011-12	788.8
6	Jermaine O'Neal	1997-98	788.6
7	Derrick Favors	2010-11	787.8
8	Olumide Oyedeji	2000-01	787.0
9	Kosta Koufos	2008-09	786.1
10	Andre Drummond	2012-13	778.4

Baseline Basic Stats

MPG	PTS	AST	REB	BLK	STL
20.4	7.7	0.8	5.8	1.3	0.6

Advanced Metrics

USG%	3PTA/FGA	FTA/FGA	TS%	eFG%	3PT%
18.8	0.003	0.561	0.587	0.515	0.160

AST%	TOV%	OREB%	DREB%	STL%	BLK%
3.9	14.5	14.9	20.2	1.8	5.9

PER	ORTG	DRTG	WS/48	VOL
21.41	116.7	103.9	0.180	0.745

- Only played 30 minutes in his rookie season, spent some time in the G-League with Fort Wayne
- Very good rebounder and shot blocker in the G-League
- Can eat space inside, limited lateral mobility makes him vulnerable against quicker players
- Efficient inside, mainly did his damage on close shots
- Improved his free throw shooting, shot just over 70% at the free throw line last season in the G-League

Newcomers

Aaron Holiday

	Height	Weight	Cap #	Years Left
	6'1"	185	$1.912M	1 + 2 TO

Baseline Basic Stats

MPG	PTS	AST	REB	BLK	STL
11.3	3.9	1.7	1.0	0.0	0.4

Advanced Metrics

USG%	3PTA/FGA	FTA/FGA	TS%	eFG%	3PT%
19.7	0.282	0.248	0.486	0.446	0.331

AST%	TOV%	OREB%	DREB%	STL%	BLK%
23.5	19.9	2.5	7.6	2.0	0.3

PER	ORTG	DRTG	WS/48	VOL
9.99	95.8	108.6	0.024	N/A

- Drafted by Indiana in the first round with the 23rd overall pick
- Decent showing at Summer League, probably was a bit over-extended in a high usage role
- Got assists at a high rate, but was rather turnover prone and he struggled to shoot efficiently
- Shot below 35% from the field and below 30% on threes
- Active defensively, posted high Steal, Rebound and Block Percentages at Summer League
- A bit unlikely that he'll crack Indiana's rotation right away, could benefit from additional seasoning in the G-League

Alize Johnson

	Height	Weight	Cap #	Years Left
	6'9"	212	$0.838M	0

Baseline Basic Stats

MPG	PTS	AST	REB	BLK	STL
10.5	3.4	0.7	1.6	0.1	0.3

Advanced Metrics

USG%	3PTA/FGA	FTA/FGA	TS%	eFG%	3PT%
15.5	0.270	0.243	0.460	0.412	0.317

AST%	TOV%	OREB%	DREB%	STL%	BLK%
7.8	11.8	7.5	12.8	1.5	0.5

PER	ORTG	DRTG	WS/48	VOL
9.33	98.7	108.7	0.038	N/A

- Drafted by Indiana in the second round with the 50th overall pick
- Very strong showing at Las Vegas Summer League
- Excellent rebounder on both ends, showed some ability to defend multiple positions
- Played more of a stay-at-home style of defense
- Showed decent passing skills, limited turnovers, drew fouls at a high rate, but struggled to shoot efficiently from the field
- Outside chance to get minutes in Indiana as an energy player or defensive specialist, but could benefit from some time in the G-League to improve his shooting

CLEVELAND CAVALIERS

Last Season: 50 – 32, Lost NBA Finals to Golden State (0 – 4)

Offensive Rating: 112.9, 5th in NBA

Defensive Rating: 111.9, 29th in NBA

Primary Executive: Koby Altman, General Manager

Head Coach: Tyronn Lue

Key Roster Changes

Subtractions	Additions
LeBron James, free agency	Collin Sexton, draft
Jeff Green, free agency	Sam Dekker, trade
Jose Calderon, free agency	Channing Frye, free agency
Kendrick Perkins, waived	David Nwaba, free agency

RAFER Projected Win Total: 40.4

Projected Best Five-Man Unit
1. George Hill
2. David Nwaba
3. Kyle Korver
4. Kevin Love
5. Larry Nance, Jr.

Other Rotation Players
J.R. Smith
Tristan Thompson
Jordan Clarkson
Collin Sexton
Cedi Osman
Sam Dekker

Remaining Roster

- Rodney Hood
- Channing Frye
- Ante Zizic
- Isaiah Taylor
- Kobi Simmons - not profiled, signed right before the book was finalized
- John Holland, 30, 6'5", 205, Boston University (Two-Way)
- Billy Preston, 21, 6'10", 240, Redondo Beach, CA (Two-Way)

Season Forecast

The Cleveland Cavaliers are left to figure out a new direction with their franchise after LeBron James elected to sign elsewhere in free agency for the second time this summer, this time going to the Lakers. Unlike the first time when James left in the summer of 2010, the Cavaliers have more talent on the roster. More specifically, they still have an All-Star in Kevin Love to build around for the next few years, as the team was able to sign him to a four-year extension later in the summer. However, the rest of their roster is comprised of players that don't exactly have reliable profiles because every other complementary player either has some kind of injury history, inconsistencies in production, inexperience or advanced age. Therefore, no matter how much head coach, Tyronn Lue tweaks the rotation, the team is not likely to make the playoffs, but they still could be a more competitive unit in the Eastern Conference.

Stylistically, Cleveland is going to have to change its lineups to better complement Love's skill set. In the past few seasons with LeBron James, Love had to play a lot of minutes as a center because the team was extremely efficient offensively with four shooters around James, even though they were put at a significant disadvantage on defense. Now that James is gone, the team would be better served by going to a more traditional lineup with Love at the four alongside another big man, ideally Larry Nance, Jr. This would help to cover up some of Love's deficiencies as a defender and allow him to concentrate more on creating offense for himself and others. They could also make a subtle change to their perimeter rotation by giving more minutes to the newly acquired David Nwaba, as he has shown some promise as a defender in his two years with the Bulls and Lakers and he might be able to improve Cleveland's defense a bit. Any kind of improvement on the defensive end could help Cleveland stay competitive this season. After all, their offensive efficiency is probably going to take a considerable hit, now that James is not in the lineup to generate easy shots. Therefore, moving to a more defensive oriented lineup could somewhat make up for that potential drop-off. From there, Tyronn Lue is going to have to make a difficult decision with J.R. Smith. Smith has been a major part of the team's rotation throughout Cleveland's run with James, but his production has declined significantly in the last two seasons, possibly due to his relatively advancing age. Also, he's a bit of an unpredictable character that has shown some dysfunctional tendencies when placed in a non-winning environment. With the Cavs in something of a rebuilding phase, Smith is probably not a great fit for this roster. The team might be better off by phasing him out and giving some of his minutes to younger players like Nwaba, Cedi Osman or Sam Dekker. At best, if the team's defense improves incrementally and Love produces at a level close to his years with Minnesota, then the Cavs could be a competitive team that finishes just outside of the playoff picture. However, if things go wrong in any way, then this season could be a tough one for Cleveland and they could spend the bulk of the season in the lottery with a win total in the 30s.

Veterans

Kevin Love

	Height	Weight	Cap #	Years Left
	6'10"	260	$24.119M	4

<u>Similar at Age</u> <u>29</u>

	Player	Season	SIMsc
1	Troy Murphy	2009-10	902.3
2	Carlos Boozer	2010-11	896.7
3	Marreese Speights	2016-17	892.7
4	Mehmet Okur	2008-09	891.5
5	Amar'e Stoudemire	2011-12	886.6
6	Ersan Ilyasova	2016-17	886.6
7	Zach Randolph	2010-11	885.5
8	Al Harrington	2009-10	876.3
9	Al Jefferson	2013-14	876.2
10	Terry Mills	1996-97	863.6

Baseline Basic Stats

MPG	PTS	AST	REB	BLK	STL
29.3	14.7	1.8	8.1	0.5	0.7

Advanced Metrics

USG%	3PTA/FGA	FTA/FGA	TS%	eFG%	3PT%
23.2	0.363	0.294	0.571	0.522	0.395

AST%	TOV%	OREB%	DREB%	STL%	BLK%
9.4	10.3	7.3	26.8	1.3	1.3

PER	ORTG	DRTG	WS/48	VOL	
19.10	113.5	105.8	0.155	0.451	

- Still an All-Star level big man despite playing a secondary role for the last four seasons, will now be the primary scoring option
- Missed games in the last two seasons due to a knee injury and a fractured left hand
- Has had multiple concussions over the last three seasons
- Efficient scoring big man, has had to play more of a stretch role, excellent in spot-up situations last season
- Good three-point shooter, posted his highest True Shooting Percentage of his career, good passing big man
- Very good post-up player and effective as the screener in pick-and-roll situations
- Elite defensive rebounder, will probably get more opportunities to crash the offensive glass
- Below average defender, not much of a rim protector, more mobile than he was in Minnesota

George Hill

	Height	Weight	Cap #	Years Left
	6'2"	180	$19.000M	1

Similar at Age 31

		Season	SIMsc
1	Luke Ridnour	2012-13	935.5
2	Devin Harris	2014-15	933.1
3	Sidney Moncrief	1988-89	926.5
4	Mike James	2006-07	923.9
5	Monta Ellis	2016-17	922.2
6	Anthony Johnson	2005-06	920.2
7	Danny Ainge	1990-91	919.8
8	John Starks	1996-97	918.4
9	Howard Eisley	2003-04	914.9
10	Jason Terry	2008-09	914.7

Baseline Basic Stats

MPG	PTS	AST	REB	BLK	STL
24.1	9.6	3.0	2.1	0.2	0.9

Advanced Metrics

USG%	3PTA/FGA	FTA/FGA	TS%	eFG%	3PT%
18.9	0.378	0.253	0.554	0.515	0.387

AST%	TOV%	OREB%	DREB%	STL%	BLK%
19.2	12.9	2.0	8.8	1.8	0.8

PER	ORTG	DRTG	WS/48	VOL	
14.14	110.0	109.1	0.107	0.404	

- In his early 30s, some decline risk, missed most of the 2016-17 season due to a toe injury and strained groin
- Performance over the last five years has been inconsistent, struggled last season in a lower usage role
- Has had his best years in a higher usage role, better playmaker when he gets more touches
- Most effective as a pick-and-roll ball handler, can also use the threat of his shot to beat defenders off the dribble in isolation situations
- Typically an efficient shooter that makes threes at an above average rate and finishes a high percentage of his shots at the rim
- When healthy, good defensive guard that possesses the versatility to defend taller wing players as well as quicker guards

J.R. Smith

	Height	Weight	Cap #	Years Left
	6'6"	220	$14.720M	1

Similar at Age 32

		Season	SIMsc
1	Dan Majerle	1997-98	947.1
2	Alan Anderson	2014-15	944.2
3	Caron Butler	2012-13	919.7
4	Keith Bogans	2012-13	914.9
5	Morris Peterson	2009-10	913.8
6	John Salmons	2011-12	911.4
7	Anthony Parker	2007-08	909.7
8	Jud Buechler	2000-01	908.5
9	Maurice Evans	2010-11	907.5
10	Jason Richardson	2012-13	906.2

Baseline Basic Stats

MPG	PTS	AST	REB	BLK	STL
24.1	7.6	1.7	3.0	0.2	0.7

Advanced Metrics

USG%	3PTA/FGA	FTA/FGA	TS%	eFG%	3PT%
14.1	0.652	0.117	0.530	0.515	0.368

AST%	TOV%	OREB%	DREB%	STL%	BLK%
10.0	10.5	1.7	11.4	1.5	0.7

PER	ORTG	DRTG	WS/48	VOL	
9.70	105.1	110.3	0.051	0.465	

- Entering his age-33 season, production over the last four years in down from his career averages
- Missed a large chunk of the 2016-17 season due to a fractured right thumb
- Still a solid three-point shooter, but has become a one-dimensional, lower volume catch-and-shoot player at this stage
- Rarely goes to the basket, limited playmaking skills, takes a lot of contested three-pointers
- Doesn't offer much value defensively, below average as a position defender, Steal Percentage has been steadily declining

Kyle Korver

	Height	Weight	Cap #	Years Left
	6'7"	210	$7.560M	1

Similar at Age 36

		Season	SIMsc
1	Richard Jefferson	2016-17	894.5
2	Mike Dunleavy, Jr.	2016-17	892.5
3	Michael Finley	2009-10	884.6
4	Ray Allen*	2011-12	883.0
5	James Jones	2016-17	880.4
6	Dan Majerle	2001-02	879.0
7	Eric Piatkowski	2006-07	878.0
8	Brent Barry	2007-08	877.1
9	Anthony Parker	2011-12	876.4
10	Tyrone Corbin	1998-99	872.9

Baseline Basic Stats

MPG	PTS	AST	REB	BLK	STL
21.0	7.0	1.3	2.4	0.3	0.5

Advanced Metrics

USG%	3PTA/FGA	FTA/FGA	TS%	eFG%	3PT%
15.2	0.685	0.127	0.599	0.576	0.397

AST%	TOV%	OREB%	DREB%	STL%	BLK%
8.7	10.9	1.0	11.8	1.1	1.2

PER	ORTG	DRTG	WS/48	VOL	
11.36	110.4	110.4	0.072	0.512	

- Entering his age-37 season, but his overall production is still consistent with his career averages

- Pretty durable over the last six seasons aside from a minor foot injury in the 2016-17 season

- Still one of the best three-point shooters in the league

- Has led the NBA in Three-Point Percentage in three of the last five years

- Great at running off screens and one of the best spot-up shooters in the NBA

- Decent position defender if given favorable matchups, fairly effective on the defensive glass

Larry Nance, Jr.

	Height	Weight	Cap #	Years Left
	6'9"	230	$2.272M	0

Similar at Age 25

		Season	SIMsc
1	Loy Vaught	1993-94	921.2
2	Luc Mbah a Moute	2011-12	920.0
3	Pete Chilcutt	1993-94	918.9
4	JaMychal Green	2015-16	913.2
5	Adam Keefe	1995-96	912.8
6	Andrew DeClercq	1998-99	912.2
7	Charles Shackleford	1991-92	911.5
8	Anderson Varejao	2007-08	911.5
9	Tony Battie	2001-02	907.8
10	Josh Powell	2007-08	903.8

Baseline Basic Stats

MPG	PTS	AST	REB	BLK	STL
23.6	7.9	1.1	6.0	0.6	0.8

Advanced Metrics

USG%	3PTA/FGA	FTA/FGA	TS%	eFG%	3PT%
15.1	0.079	0.306	0.573	0.544	0.264

AST%	TOV%	OREB%	DREB%	STL%	BLK%
8.5	11.7	9.8	20.0	2.2	1.9

PER	ORTG	DRTG	WS/48	VOL	
16.40	117.0	105.7	0.144	0.329	

- Improved significantly in his third year, had a career best season
- Production increased after the trade to Cleveland
- High efficiency, low volume scorer, does most of his damage inside of three feet
- Very effective as the screener in pick-and-roll situations
- Draws fouls at a much higher rate, crashed the offensive glass more often last season
- Very good defensive rebounder, solid shot blocker, uses active hands to frequently get steals
- Below average on-ball defender, somewhat foul prone, undersized to defend interior players

Tristan Thompson

	Height	Weight	Cap #	Years Left
	6'8"	225	$17.470M	1

Similar at Age 26

		Season	SIMsc
1	Lavoy Allen	2015-16	932.0
2	Kenneth Faried	2015-16	924.2
3	Larry Smith	1983-84	921.5
4	Cliff Levingston	1986-87	906.2
5	Chucky Brown	1994-95	906.2
6	Olden Polynice	1990-91	904.8
7	Kurt Rambis	1984-85	904.1
8	Carl Herrera	1992-93	903.7
9	Ed Davis	2015-16	903.2
10	Willie Reed	2016-17	903.2

Baseline Basic Stats

MPG	PTS	AST	REB	BLK	STL
21.5	6.9	0.9	6.1	0.5	0.6

Advanced Metrics

USG%	3PTA/FGA	FTA/FGA	TS%	eFG%	3PT%
13.4	0.016	0.399	0.559	0.539	0.147

AST%	TOV%	OREB%	DREB%	STL%	BLK%
5.5	12.6	12.1	21.0	1.0	1.7

PER	ORTG	DRTG	WS/48	VOL
13.88	117.4	109.2	0.120	0.366

- Coming off his worst season since his rookie year, missed parts of last season due to a strained calf and sprained right ankle
- When healthy, low volume, high efficiency rim runner that is one of the best offensive rebounders in the league
- Good defensive rebounder, can protect the rim but shot blocking rates tend to fluctuate on a year-to-year basis
- Shows enough mobility to defend on the perimeter when healthy, can struggle with interior post defense

Jordan Clarkson

	Height	Weight	Cap #	Years Left
	6'5"	193	$12.500M	1

Similar at Age 25

		Season	SIMsc
1	Derek Anderson	1999-00	940.6
2	Jordan Crawford	2013-14	938.4
3	Marco Belinelli	2011-12	934.8
4	Lucious Harris	1995-96	931.5
5	Michael Dickerson	2000-01	930.3
6	Courtney Lee	2010-11	928.2
7	John Long	1981-82	927.1
8	Darrell Griffith	1983-84	927.0
9	Nick Young	2010-11	927.0
10	Terry Furlow	1979-80	926.5

Baseline Basic Stats

MPG	PTS	AST	REB	BLK	STL
29.4	14.6	2.7	3.1	0.2	0.9

Advanced Metrics

USG%	3PTA/FGA	FTA/FGA	TS%	eFG%	3PT%
23.8	0.321	0.215	0.535	0.497	0.356

AST%	TOV%	OREB%	DREB%	STL%	BLK%
16.6	11.0	2.7	9.3	1.6	0.4

PER	ORTG	DRTG	WS/48	VOL	
15.35	106.4	110.4	0.084	0.356	

- Regular season production improved to a level close to his rookie season in 2014-15, struggled in the playoffs
- Higher volume combo guard with decent playmaking skills that allowed him to be effective as a pick-and-roll ball handler
- Posted his highest True Shooting Percentage last season, shot 40.7% on threes after the trade to Cleveland, excelled as a spot-up shooter last season
- Decent position defender that defends both guard spots, much better at defending taller wings than quicker point guards

Cedi Osman

	Height	Weight	Cap #	Years Left
	6'8"	210	$2.775M	1

Similar at Age **22**

		Season	SIMsc
1	Sasha Pavlovic	2005-06	932.4
2	Jason Kapono	2003-04	920.3
3	Caris LeVert	2016-17	917.9
4	Antoine Wright	2006-07	917.7
5	Maurice Harkless	2015-16	916.3
6	Hollis Thompson	2013-14	914.4
7	Rodney Hood	2014-15	914.0
8	Paul Zipser	2016-17	913.2
9	Bill Walker	2009-10	911.6
10	Kedrick Brown	2003-04	906.9

Baseline Basic Stats

MPG	PTS	AST	REB	BLK	STL
22.8	8.5	1.4	3.1	0.3	0.7

Advanced Metrics

USG%	3PTA/FGA	FTA/FGA	TS%	eFG%	3PT%
17.2	0.437	0.209	0.558	0.540	0.372

AST%	TOV%	OREB%	DREB%	STL%	BLK%
10.4	11.9	3.0	13.5	1.5	0.8

PER	ORTG	DRTG	WS/48	VOL	
11.68	107.4	110.7	0.076	0.389	

- Was on the fringes of Cleveland's rotation last season as a rookie, played 672 minutes
- Flashed potential as a complementary role player on offense
- Shot efficiently in a low volume, spot-up role, posted a 57.7% True Shooting Percentage and a 36.8% Three-Point Percentage
- Struggled to make free throws, was only 26-for-46 last season
- Effective in a small sample of possessions as a pick-and-roll ball handler
- Solid stay-at-home wing defender if given favorable matchups
- Posted a solid Steal Percentage, good defensive rebounder

David Nwaba

	Height	Weight	Cap #	Years Left
	6'4"	209	$1.513M	0

Similar at Age 25

		Season	SIMsc
1	Greg Buckner	2001-02	946.7
2	Kenny Battle	1989-90	918.0
3	Vincent Askew	1991-92	915.5
4	Blue Edwards	1990-91	909.0
5	Todd Lichti	1991-92	907.1
6	T.R. Dunn	1980-81	901.3
7	Dahntay Jones	2005-06	899.7
8	Danny Vranes	1983-84	898.7
9	Joel Kramer	1980-81	897.2
10	Kenny Walker	1989-90	896.2

Baseline Basic Stats

MPG	PTS	AST	REB	BLK	STL
22.0	7.7	1.6	3.6	0.3	0.9

Advanced Metrics

USG%	3PTA/FGA	FTA/FGA	TS%	eFG%	3PT%
15.4	0.106	0.394	0.562	0.519	0.316

AST%	TOV%	OREB%	DREB%	STL%	BLK%
9.6	12.4	5.6	13.4	2.0	1.2

PER	ORTG	DRTG	WS/48	VOL
13.22	112.6	109.3	0.096	0.287

- Regular rotation player for the first time in his second year in the NBA
- True defensive impact is uncertain because he has spent his two-year career on rebuilding teams
- Flashed some potential to defend both guard spots
- Has been an active help defender with good rebound and block rates, Steal Percentage is solid
- Low volume scoring guard that relies on slashing inside to finish close shots or draw fouls at a high rate
- Most effective as a cutter off the ball last season
- Outside shooting still needs improvement, but he was a break-even three-point shooter last season

Sam Dekker

	Height	Weight	2018 Cap #	Years Left
	81	230	$2.760M	0

Similar at Age 23

	Player	Season	SIMsc
1	Larry Nance, Jr.	2015-16	926.1
2	Terence Morris	2001-02	917.2
3	Kyle Anderson	2016-17	917.1
4	Chris Singleton	2012-13	914.4
5	Marcus Morris	2012-13	913.8
6	Omri Casspi	2011-12	911.3
7	Marvin Williams	2009-10	910.0
8	Pete Chilcutt	1991-92	908.3
9	Ersan Ilyasova	2010-11	907.2
10	Perry Jones	2014-15	906.6

Baseline Basic Stats

MPG	PTS	AST	REB	BLK	STL
19.9	6.6	1.1	3.8	0.4	0.7

Advanced Metrics

USG%	3PTA/FGA	FTA/FGA	TS%	eFG%	3PT%
14.9	0.310	0.220	0.526	0.501	0.264

AST%	TOV%	OREB%	DREB%	STL%	BLK%
7.8	10.2	5.7	15.7	1.8	1.2

PER	ORTG	DRTG	WS/48	VOL
13.26	106.3	108.4	0.102	0.401

- Had to a play reduced role with Clippers last season after being a regular rotation player for Houston the season before
- Low usage player that really struggled with his outside shot last season
- Was moderately efficient because he took more shots inside and draw more fouls
- Might be better in motion than as a stationary player, very good cutter over the last two seasons
- Middling overall position defender, can be decent if given favorable matchups, rebounds fairly well for his size

Rodney Hood

	Height	Weight	2018 Cap #	Years Left
	6'8"	215	$3.400M	0

Similar at Age 25

		Season	SIMsc
1	Jason Kapono	2006-07	931.0
2	Kyle Korver	2006-07	928.9
3	Bojan Bogdanovic	2014-15	926.1
4	Jarvis Hayes	2006-07	924.1
5	Glen Rice	1992-93	924.0
6	Peja Stojakovic	2002-03	923.8
7	Dennis Scott	1993-94	923.7
8	Tracy Murray	1996-97	923.6
9	C.J. Miles	2012-13	923.6
10	Sam Mack	1995-96	922.6

Baseline Basic Stats

MPG	PTS	AST	REB	BLK	STL
26.5	12.4	1.6	3.3	0.2	0.7

Advanced Metrics

USG%	3PTA/FGA	FTA/FGA	TS%	eFG%	3PT%
21.9	0.445	0.187	0.548	0.514	0.384

AST%	TOV%	OREB%	DREB%	STL%	BLK%
10.1	9.1	2.0	11.1	1.4	0.6

PER	ORTG	DRTG	WS/48	VOL	
14.04	107.9	109.1	0.096	0.407	

- Rotation player for Utah and Cleveland during the regular season
- Fell out of the playoff rotation for Cleveland after refusing to enter a second round game against Toronto
- Above average three-point shooter for his career, most effective as a spot-up shooter, can also run off screens
- Score-first mentality with the ball in his hands, doesn't really look to pass
- Effective at taking pull-up mid-range jumpers or quick no dribble threes in isolation situations
- Good as a pick-and-roll ball handler by drawing shooting fouls on over-aggressive defenders
- Middling overall as an on-ball defending wing last season, better in Utah than in Cleveland
- More of a stay-at-home defender, doesn't get really get steals or blocks, decent defensive rebounder

Channing Frye

	Height	Weight	Cap #	Years Left
	6'11"	248	$1.513M	0

Similar at Age 34

	Player	Season	SIMsc
1	Brad Miller	2010-11	905.6
2	Bill Laimbeer	1991-92	892.0
3	Matt Bonner	2014-15	889.7
4	Danny Ferry	2000-01	869.3
5	Matt Barnes	2014-15	868.1
6	Christian Laettner	2003-04	861.9
7	Rasheed Wallace	2008-09	858.1
8	Mike Dunleavy, Jr.	2014-15	856.2
9	Dirk Nowitzki	2012-13	853.4
10	Chuck Person	1998-99	851.7

Baseline Basic Stats

MPG	PTS	AST	REB	BLK	STL
17.2	5.9	0.9	3.0	0.3	0.4

Advanced Metrics

USG%	3PTA/FGA	FTA/FGA	TS%	eFG%	3PT%
15.2	0.582	0.144	0.582	0.559	0.371

AST%	TOV%	OREB%	DREB%	STL%	BLK%
7.6	9.3	3.4	18.6	1.1	1.8

PER	ORTG	DRTG	WS/48	VOL
12.94	114.0	109.0	0.112	0.585

- Entering his age-35 season, considerable decline risk, played sparingly last season for Cleveland and the Lakers
- Situational, low volume shooting specialist at this stage
- Three-Point Percentage last season was at a career low in Cleveland last season, but it did improve in limited minutes with the Lakers in the second half
- Mainly a spot-up shooter, was effective in a small sample of post-ups last season with the Lakers
- Below average overall position defender with limited mobility due to his age, not really a rim protector, adequate defensive rebounder

Ante Zizic

	Height	Weight	Cap #	Years Left
	6'11"	250	$1.953M	2 Team Options

Similar at Age 21

		Season	SIMsc
1	Robin Lopez	2009-10	909.6
2	Jelani McCoy	1998-99	889.2
3	JaVale McGee	2008-09	882.5
4	Jermaine O'Neal	1999-00	881.7
5	LaMarcus Aldridge	2006-07	881.2
6	DeAndre Jordan	2009-10	880.5
7	Greg Oden	2008-09	870.4
8	Kosta Koufos	2010-11	868.9
9	Benoit Benjamin	1985-86	867.8
10	Darko Milicic	2006-07	864.3

Baseline Basic Stats

MPG	PTS	AST	REB	BLK	STL
20.8	8.3	0.7	5.8	1.4	0.4

Advanced Metrics

USG%	3PTA/FGA	FTA/FGA	TS%	eFG%	3PT%
18.3	0.001	0.422	0.655	0.631	0.013

AST%	TOV%	OREB%	DREB%	STL%	BLK%
5.3	14.1	11.8	19.4	0.8	4.4

PER	ORTG	DRTG	WS/48	VOL	
20.06	123.3	107.0	0.177	0.524	

- Seldomly played in his rookie season, spent time in the G-League with the Canton Charge, played 214 minutes in the NBA
- Posted efficient rate statistics in the G-League and in his limited minutes in the NBA
- Flashed effectiveness as a rim runner that made 75.8% of his shots from inside of ten feet in the NBA
- Also drew fouls at a high rate and made 72.4% of his free throws
- Showed potential as a rim protector with high blocks and rebound rates in the G-League as well as a high Block Percentage in his limited NBA minutes

Isaiah Taylor

	Height	Weight	Cap #	Years Left
	6'3"	170	$1.513M	0

Similar at Age 23

		Season	SIMsc
1	Kevin Pritchard	1990-91	903.2
2	Scott Haffner	1989-90	898.4
3	Mickey Dillard	1981-82	896.6
4	Reggie Carter	1980-81	893.5
5	Steve Kerr	1988-89	890.2
6	Milt Palacio	2001-02	889.0
7	Kiwane Garris	1997-98	886.7
8	Leon Wood	1985-86	885.8
9	Jeff Taylor	1982-83	885.2
10	Eric Maynor	2010-11	885.0

Baseline Basic Stats

MPG	PTS	AST	REB	BLK	STL
17.7	5.6	2.6	1.7	0.1	0.6

Advanced Metrics

USG%	3PTA/FGA	FTA/FGA	TS%	eFG%	3PT%
15.3	0.272	0.277	0.468	0.426	0.254

AST%	TOV%	OREB%	DREB%	STL%	BLK%
22.8	14.3	2.4	6.9	1.5	0.8

PER	ORTG	DRTG	WS/48	VOL
10.11	100.2	112.9	0.037	0.676

- Became a regular part of Atlanta's rotation in his second year
- Solid playmaking point guard that score at the rim and draw fouls
- Overall scoring is inefficient due to a lack of a reliable outside shot
- Largely ineffective in most offensive situations, most effective in a limited sample of possessions when running off screens
- More of a position defender, can defend both guard spots
- Struggles a bit against quicker point guards, had more success with taller two guards

Collin Sexton

	Height	Weight	Cap #	Years Left
	6'3"	190	$4.069M	1 + 2 TO

Baseline Basic Stats

MPG	PTS	AST	REB	BLK	STL
31.5	14.5	4.8	3.3	0.2	0.9

Advanced Metrics

USG%	3PTA/FGA	FTA/FGA	TS%	eFG%	3PT%
24.3	0.283	0.259	0.504	0.460	0.345

AST%	TOV%	OREB%	DREB%	STL%	BLK%
26.4	15.0	2.8	9.4	1.5	0.5

PER	ORTG	DRTG	WS/48	VOL
14.09	100.4	111.1	0.039	N/A

- Drafted by Cleveland in the first round with the 8th overall pick
- Strong showing at Summer League, figures to be a primary part of Cleveland's rotation next season
- Scored points in volume with middling efficiency, drew fouls at a high rate
- Struggled to shoot a high percentage on outside shots, showed decent playmaking skills
- Played with high energy, more of a position defender, decent on-ball defender
- Solid on the defensive glass at Summer League

BROOKLYN NETS

<u>Last Season</u>: 28 – 54, Missed the Playoffs

<u>Offensive Rating</u>: 106.9, 21st in NBA

<u>Defensive Rating</u>: 110.6, 22nd in NBA

<u>Primary Executive</u>: Sean Marks, General Manager

<u>Head Coach</u>: Kenny Atkinson

Key Roster Changes

Subtractions
Jeremy Lin, trade
Isaiah Whitehead, trade
Timofey Mozgov, trade
Nik Stauskas, free agency
Jahlil Okafor, free agency
Quincy Acy, free agency
Dante Cunningham, free agency

Additions
Dzanan Musa, draft
Rodions Kurucs, draft
Kenneth Faried, trade
Jared Dudley, trade
Ed Davis, free agency
Shabazz Napier, free agency
Treveon Graham, free agency

RAFER Projected Win Total: 36.8

Projected Best Five-Man Unit
1. Spencer Dinwiddie
2. Allen Crabbe
3. DeMarre Carroll
4. Rondae Hollis-Jefferson
5. Jarrett Allen

Other Rotation Players
Joe Harris
Caris LeVert
D'Angelo Russell
Ed Davis
Shabazz Napier

Remaining Roster

- Treveon Graham
- Kenneth Faried
- Jared Dudley
- Dzanan Musa
- Rodions Kurucs
- Alan Williams, 26, 6'8", 260, UC-Santa Barbara (Two-Way)
- Theo Pinson, 23, 6'6", 220, North Carolina (Exhibit 10)
- Jordan McLaughlin, 22, 6'1", 185, USC (Exhibit 10)
- Mitch Creek, 26, 6'5", 216, Australia (Exhibit 10)

Season Forecast

The Brooklyn Nets didn't make any splashy moves this summer, as the team is still in a rebuilding mode. However, the Nets were able to quietly add a couple of extra contributors to make them a bit more competitive in Ed Davis and Shabazz Napier. Additionally, the system projects to be an interesting team this season because there's considerable potential for them to improve significantly as a result of some internal growth from key players in their rotation. Six of their projected rotation players above are going to be between the ages of 23 to 27, which is noteworthy because that specific age range is usually when NBA players start to approach their peak and make large jumps in their development. With this in mind, the Nets could get some major improvement from a few of these six, which include three of the team's best players such as Spencer Dinwiddie, Caris LeVert and Rondae Hollis-Jefferson. If those players show considerable improvement this season, Brooklyn could see its win total increase to somewhere in the mid-30s, making them still a lottery team, but a little more competitive than last season.

From a style of play standpoint, the Nets are likely to see the most improvement on the offensive side of the ball. In the past two seasons under head coach, Kenny Atkinson, Brooklyn has been shuffling players in and out hoping to find some pieces to fit a pace-and-space system. Last season, they appeared to have found a few interesting pieces to work with, as players Dinwiddie and Joe Harris seemed to thrive in their system. Also, their offense improved incrementally in Atkinson's second year, going from 28th in Offensive Rating in 2016-17 to 21st in the league in this metric last season. With much of the team's rotation being in a developmental stage where significant improvement is possible, the team could see its offense reach another level where it could be around the league average if things break according to the projection model. If there's any stagnation in the development of their key younger players, the Nets would likely be one of the worst teams in the league once again because their defense over the last two seasons has basically stayed the same. They did make a few changes to the back-end of their roster, but most of their additions are around average defenders. Therefore, the team's defense is likely to remain a bottom third defense in the league. Overall, the Nets don't have any big names on the roster, but they do have a lot of younger, still developing players that could show enough growth to allow the team to sneak up on opponents and possibly scratch out a few more wins. They still aren't likely to make the playoffs, even in the Eastern Conference, but they could give their fan base a small glimmer of hope for the first time in many years this season.

Veterans

Spencer Dinwiddie

	Height	Weight	Cap #	Years Left
	6'6"	200	$1.656M	0

Similar at Age **24**

		Season	SIMsc
1	Alexey Shved	2012-13	929.0
2	Greivis Vasquez	2010-11	920.6
3	Chauncey Billups	2000-01	915.4
4	George McCloud	1991-92	912.2
5	Jerryd Bayless	2012-13	910.9
6	Austin Rivers	2016-17	908.4
7	Tim Hardaway, Jr.	2016-17	907.3
8	Evan Fournier	2016-17	906.4
9	Khalid Reeves	1996-97	903.0
10	Martell Webster	2010-11	901.2

Baseline Basic Stats

MPG	PTS	AST	REB	BLK	STL
28.1	11.9	3.6	3.0	0.2	0.9

Advanced Metrics

USG%	3PTA/FGA	FTA/FGA	TS%	eFG%	3PT%
19.9	0.412	0.336	0.534	0.478	0.337

AST%	TOV%	OREB%	DREB%	STL%	BLK%
26.0	12.8	2.2	10.5	1.5	0.7

PER	ORTG	DRTG	WS/48	VOL	
14.71	110.4	110.7	0.102	0.274	

- Had a career best season in his fourth year in the NBA, entering his prime years
- Good playmaker that limits turnovers
- Effective with the ball in his hands as a pick-and-roll ball handler, good in isolation situations
- Outside shot still needs improvement, historically a below break-even three-point shooter
- Can attack aggressive closeouts by getting to the rim to draw shooting fouls
- Around an average on-ball defender, can defend both guard spots, solid defensive rebounder for his size

Allen Crabbe

	Height	Weight	Cap #	Years Left
	6'6"	210	$18.500M	Player Option

Similar at Age 25

		Season	SIMsc
1	Brandon Rush	2010-11	940.7
2	Danny Green	2012-13	938.5
3	Anthony Morrow	2010-11	934.5
4	Kyle Korver	2006-07	930.0
5	Bojan Bogdanovic	2014-15	928.2
6	C.J. Miles	2012-13	926.3
7	Terrence Ross	2016-17	924.5
8	Arron Afflalo	2010-11	920.9
9	Gordan Giricek	2002-03	920.5
10	Chris Mills	1994-95	919.0

Baseline Basic Stats

MPG	PTS	AST	REB	BLK	STL
25.5	10.1	1.4	3.0	0.4	0.7

Advanced Metrics

USG%	3PTA/FGA	FTA/FGA	TS%	eFG%	3PT%
17.6	0.551	0.181	0.567	0.537	0.394

AST%	TOV%	OREB%	DREB%	STL%	BLK%
8.3	9.0	1.6	11.9	1.3	1.1

PER	ORTG	DRTG	WS/48	VOL	
12.43	110.4	110.5	0.082	0.382	

- Played starter level minutes for the third consecutive year, had his most productive season in the NBA
- Three-and-D wing player entering his prime years
- Primarily a low volume, catch-and-shoot player, good three-point shooter with a career Three-Point Percentage of 39.7%
- Utilized as a spot-up shooter that can also come off screens
- Mainly a stay-at-home position defender, plays good on-ball defense against opposing wings, good defensive rebounder

DeMarre Carroll

	Height	Weight	Cap #	Years Left
	6'8"	212	$15.400M	0

Similar at Age **31**

		Season	SIMsc
1	Rashard Lewis	2010-11	930.9
2	Chuck Person	1995-96	927.0
3	James Posey	2007-08	925.4
4	Luol Deng	2016-17	919.4
5	George McCloud	1998-99	917.3
6	Alan Anderson	2013-14	916.7
7	Chris Morris	1996-97	916.5
8	Bryon Russell	2001-02	915.9
9	Peja Stojakovic	2008-09	915.4
10	Eric Piatkowski	2001-02	915.1

Baseline Basic Stats

MPG	PTS	AST	REB	BLK	STL
23.6	8.7	1.4	3.8	0.3	0.6

Advanced Metrics

USG%	3PTA/FGA	FTA/FGA	TS%	eFG%	3PT%
17.4	0.482	0.242	0.537	0.501	0.371

AST%	TOV%	OREB%	DREB%	STL%	BLK%
9.0	10.3	4.2	15.4	1.5	1.0

PER	ORTG	DRTG	WS/48	VOL
12.80	108.0	107.6	0.090	0.336

- Had a bounce-back year with the Nets after two lackluster seasons in Toronto
- Durable for the past two seasons, missed most of the 2015-16 with a right knee injury that required surgery
- When healthy, low usage spot-up shooter that makes threes at a league average rate, will also draw fouls inside
- Good at cutting to the rim, effective in a small sample of pick-and-roll possessions as both the screener and ball handler last season
- Solid on-ball defender that can guard multiple positions, good defensive rebounder

Rondae Hollis-Jefferson

	Height	Weight	Cap #	Years Left
	6'7"	220	$2.470M	0

Similar at Age 23

		Season	SIMsc
1	Luol Deng	2008-09	932.7
2	Michael Brooks	1981-82	924.3
3	George L. Johnson	1979-80	923.3
4	Caron Butler	2003-04	922.4
5	Lamond Murray	1996-97	917.3
6	Morris Peterson	2000-01	917.0
7	Mike O'Koren	1981-82	913.9
8	Tyreke Evans	2012-13	913.1
9	Willie Burton	1991-92	912.1
10	Gerald Henderson	2010-11	911.3

Baseline Basic Stats

MPG	PTS	AST	REB	BLK	STL
31.3	14.1	2.4	5.9	0.5	1.2

Advanced Metrics

USG%	3PTA/FGA	FTA/FGA	TS%	eFG%	3PT%
20.9	0.121	0.379	0.551	0.495	0.290

AST%	TOV%	OREB%	DREB%	STL%	BLK%
13.5	12.5	5.8	18.0	1.9	1.5

PER	ORTG	DRTG	WS/48	VOL	
16.88	109.3	107.1	0.119	0.384	

- Entering his age-24 season, improved in his third year to have his highest level of production as a pro
- Took on a higher volume role, got to the free throw line at a high rate, showed a greatly improved mid-range jumper
- Continued to improve his playmaking skills while posting a career best in Turnover Percentage
- Most effective as a roll man, could post-up smaller perimeter players, good in isolations if given a mismatch
- Solid overall defender, can guard multiple positions, better at handling interior players at this stage
- Became more of a position defender last season, can occasionally block shots, good defensive rebounder

Jarrett Allen

	Height	Weight	Cap #	Years Left
	6'10"	234	$2.034M	2 TO

Similar at Age 19

		Season	SIMsc
1	Derrick Favors	2010-11	914.5
2	Jermaine O'Neal	1997-98	900.8
3	Myles Turner	2015-16	900.2
4	Chris Bosh	2003-04	896.9
5	Josh Smith	2004-05	892.2
6	Tyson Chandler	2001-02	885.5
7	Anthony Davis	2012-13	884.5
8	Bismack Biyombo	2011-12	883.1
9	Dwight Howard	2004-05	880.2
10	Kevin Garnett	1995-96	876.2

Baseline Basic Stats

MPG	PTS	AST	REB	BLK	STL
26.1	10.5	1.0	7.2	1.4	0.6

Advanced Metrics

USG%	3PTA/FGA	FTA/FGA	TS%	eFG%	3PT%
18.6	0.032	0.394	0.614	0.569	0.355

AST%	TOV%	OREB%	DREB%	STL%	BLK%
7.2	13.6	10.2	21.7	1.2	4.0

PER	ORTG	DRTG	WS/48	VOL	
19.57	118.1	106.5	0.161	0.470	

- Strong rookie season as a regular part of Brooklyn's rotation
- Mainly a low volume, rim runner that scored efficiently inside, shot just under 70% on shots inside of three feet
- Primarily used as a roll man and cutter
- Very good offensive rebounder, drew lots of fouls, good free throw shooter
- Flashed some stretch potential by shooting a break-even percentage on threes in very limited number of attempts
- Has promise as a rim protector, good rebounder and shot blocker
- Body is still filling out, has some struggles as a position defender

D'Angelo Russell

	Height	Weight	Cap #	Years Left
	6'5"	195	$7.020M	0

Similar at Age 21

		Season	SIMsc
1	Tony Wroten	2014-15	898.7
2	Marcus D. Williams	2006-07	893.0
3	Dion Waiters	2012-13	892.2
4	Archie Goodwin	2015-16	889.4
5	Evan Fournier	2013-14	884.5
6	Ben Gordon	2004-05	884.3
7	Brandon Knight	2012-13	883.1
8	Terrence Ross	2012-13	881.9
9	Manny Harris	2010-11	881.8
10	Alec Burks	2012-13	880.1

Baseline Basic Stats

MPG	PTS	AST	REB	BLK	STL
28.5	14.4	3.7	3.1	0.2	1.0

Advanced Metrics

USG%	3PTA/FGA	FTA/FGA	TS%	eFG%	3PT%
25.7	0.301	0.226	0.514	0.478	0.335

AST%	TOV%	OREB%	DREB%	STL%	BLK%
26.9	14.9	2.1	10.9	1.8	0.6

PER	ORTG	DRTG	WS/48	VOL	
14.26	101.5	111.1	0.040	0.380	

- Missed two months last season due to a bruised left knee that required surgery
- Very good playmaking guard, Assist Percentage has increased in each of his three seasons, effective as a pick-and-roll ball handler
- Middling shooting efficiency, above average in isolation situations, but infrequently gets to the rim, takes a high volume of inefficient mid-range shots
- Above break-even three-point shooter for his career, much better in the corners
- Below average overall defender, lateral mobility slowed by the knee injury, good defensive rebounding guard

Joe Harris

	Height	Weight	Cap #	Years Left
	6'6"	225	$7.692M	1

Similar at Age 26

		Season	SIMsc
1	Quincy Pondexter	2014-15	938.0
2	Quentin Richardson	2006-07	925.6
3	Mickael Pietrus	2008-09	921.7
4	Sam Mack	1996-97	919.0
5	Danny Green	2013-14	918.8
6	Morris Peterson	2003-04	909.2
7	Dennis Scott	1994-95	908.7
8	Keith Bogans	2006-07	907.8
9	Kyle Singler	2014-15	907.2
10	Martell Webster	2012-13	907.1

Baseline Basic Stats

MPG	PTS	AST	REB	BLK	STL
24.2	9.1	1.3	3.3	0.3	0.6

Advanced Metrics

USG%	3PTA/FGA	FTA/FGA	TS%	eFG%	3PT%
16.9	0.599	0.164	0.572	0.548	0.391

AST%	TOV%	OREB%	DREB%	STL%	BLK%
9.6	11.6	2.4	12.7	1.1	0.7

PER	ORTG	DRTG	WS/48	VOL
11.86	108.7	110.5	0.081	0.405

- Had a career best season in his fourth year in the NBA
- Low volume three-point specialist, has shot 40.6% on threes over the last two seasons in Brooklyn
- Great at making spot-up jumpers and running off screens
- Decent position defender if given favorable matchups, solid defensive rebounder

Caris LeVert

	Height	Weight	Cap #	Years Left
	6'7"	203	$1.703M	1

Similar at Age 23

		Season	SIMsc
1	Mike Miller	2003-04	944.7
2	Steve Smith	1992-93	934.9
3	Mike O'Koren	1981-82	926.3
4	Chris Douglas-Roberts	2009-10	919.2
5	Sasha Pavlovic	2006-07	918.7
6	Josh Richardson	2016-17	915.1
7	Landry Fields	2011-12	913.4
8	Wesley Johnson	2010-11	912.6
9	Morris Peterson	2000-01	912.0
10	Lewis Lloyd	1982-83	911.1

Baseline Basic Stats

MPG	PTS	AST	REB	BLK	STL
26.6	11.4	2.6	3.3	0.3	0.9

Advanced Metrics

USG%	3PTA/FGA	FTA/FGA	TS%	eFG%	3PT%
20.9	0.398	0.247	0.541	0.505	0.352

AST%	TOV%	OREB%	DREB%	STL%	BLK%
19.1	13.5	2.6	11.7	1.9	0.8

PER	ORTG	DRTG	WS/48	VOL	
14.18	106.0	109.8	0.081	0.390	

- Increased his overall production in a larger role in his second season in the NBA

- Greatly improved as a playmaker, almost doubled his Assist Percentage from his rookie season

- Gets to the free throw line at a solid rate, improved his Three-Point Percentage to above break-even, took too many inefficient mid-range shots

- Most effective at finishing plays in transition, can slash to the rim on isolations, slightly above average spot-up shooter

- Solid on-ball wing defender, gets steals at a fairly high rate, good rebounding wing player

Ed Davis

	Height	Weight	Cap #	Years Left
	6'10"	225	$4.449M	0

Similar at Age **28**

		Season	SIMsc
1	Anderson Varejao	2010-11	934.8
2	Ian Mahinmi	2014-15	931.2
3	Anthony Miller	1999-00	927.4
4	Nazr Mohammed	2005-06	925.2
5	Scott Williams	1996-97	922.6
6	Corie Blount	1996-97	918.7
7	Major Jones	1981-82	916.2
8	Mark Acres	1990-91	912.9
9	Dave Greenwood	1985-86	910.0
10	Chris Gatling	1995-96	908.1

Baseline Basic Stats

MPG	PTS	AST	REB	BLK	STL
20.1	6.3	0.8	5.7	0.7	0.5

Advanced Metrics

USG%	3PTA/FGA	FTA/FGA	TS%	eFG%	3PT%
13.0	0.004	0.446	0.569	0.536	0.110

AST%	TOV%	OREB%	DREB%	STL%	BLK%
5.6	15.9	12.1	23.5	1.3	2.5

PER	ORTG	DRTG	WS/48	VOL	
13.95	114.7	105.5	0.125	0.364	

- Veteran rotational big man entering his age-29 season, production slightly below his career averages, some decline risk
- Durable for the most part, missed chunks of the 2016-17 season due to injuries to his ankle, wrist and shoulder
- Historically, a low volume, high efficiency rim runner that draws fouls and grabs offensive rebounds at a high rate
- Excelled at the running the floor in transition, above average as a screener in pick-and-roll situations
- Decent interior defender, can provide some rim protection, but shot blocking rates are declining to below his career averages
- Very good defensive rebounder, decent as a position defender

Shabazz Napier

	Height	Weight	Cap #	Years Left
	6'1"	180	$1.621M	Team Option

Similar at Age 26

		Season	SIMsc
1	Eddie House	2004-05	941.1
2	Toney Douglas	2012-13	935.7
3	C.J. Watson	2010-11	932.9
4	Lou Williams	2012-13	930.7
5	Brandon Jennings	2015-16	926.4
6	James Robinson	1996-97	916.9
7	Shammond Williams	2001-02	915.7
8	A.J. Price	2012-13	915.1
9	Seth Curry	2016-17	912.9
10	Bobby Jackson	1999-00	912.9

Baseline Basic Stats

MPG	PTS	AST	REB	BLK	STL
22.2	9.1	3.0	2.2	0.1	0.9

Advanced Metrics

USG%	3PTA/FGA	FTA/FGA	TS%	eFG%	3PT%
20.4	0.424	0.249	0.530	0.487	0.374

AST%	TOV%	OREB%	DREB%	STL%	BLK%
19.7	13.4	1.8	9.7	2.3	0.5

PER	ORTG	DRTG	WS/48	VOL
14.18	105.8	107.4	0.079	0.367

- Coming off a career best season in his fourth year in the NBA
- Utilized more as an off-ball guard in Portland last season, still an effective playmaker that limited turnovers
- Excellent at spotting up and coming off screens, ranked in the 94th percentile at shooting off screens according to the NBA
- Posted his highest True Shooting Percentage, good three-point shooter that drew fouls and shot 84.1% at the free throw line
- Slightly below average position defender, but defends aggressively to get steals at a high rate, rebounds well for a smaller guard

Treveon Graham

	Height	Weight	Cap #	Years Left
	6'6"	220	$1.513M	1

Similar at Age **24**

		Season	SIMsc
1	Quincy Pondexter	2012-13	938.5
2	Yakhouba Diawara	2006-07	910.9
3	Cartier Martin	2008-09	909.6
4	Martell Webster	2010-11	908.8
5	Dahntay Jones	2004-05	907.0
6	Solomon Hill	2015-16	905.7
7	Bobby R. Jones	2007-08	902.9
8	Jared Dudley	2009-10	899.4
9	Arron Afflalo	2009-10	898.6
10	Reggie Bullock	2015-16	897.8

Baseline Basic Stats

MPG	PTS	AST	REB	BLK	STL
18.8	6.0	0.9	2.3	0.2	0.5

Advanced Metrics

USG%	3PTA/FGA	FTA/FGA	TS%	eFG%	3PT%
13.2	0.441	0.286	0.559	0.525	0.413

AST%	TOV%	OREB%	DREB%	STL%	BLK%
7.5	9.6	3.6	9.8	1.4	0.5

PER	ORTG	DRTG	WS/48	VOL	
10.17	113.5	110.8	0.084	0.283	

- Cracked Charlotte's regular rotation in his second year, played 1050 minutes overall

- Fairly effective as a low usage spot-up shooter, made 41.2% of his threes in 97 attempts

- Was most successful at running the floor in transition and shooting spot-up jumpers

- Tasked to guard multiple positions, but still below average as an on-ball defender, solid Steal Percentage

Kenneth Faried

	Height	Weight	Cap #	Years Left
	6'8"	228	$13.764M	0

Similar at Age 28

		Season	SIMsc
1	Major Jones	1981-82	929.4
2	Anderson Varejao	2010-11	921.7
3	Lawrence Funderburke	1998-99	920.9
4	Kris Humphries	2013-14	917.4
5	Kurt Thomas	2000-01	914.8
6	Kermit Washington	1979-80	914.1
7	Drew Gooden	2009-10	913.6
8	Kenny Gattison	1992-93	913.1
9	Stromile Swift	2007-08	910.5
10	Nazr Mohammed	2005-06	908.6

Baseline Basic Stats

MPG	PTS	AST	REB	BLK	STL
21.0	7.9	0.9	5.9	0.6	0.5

Advanced Metrics

USG%	3PTA/FGA	FTA/FGA	TS%	eFG%	3PT%
17.5	0.018	0.370	0.547	0.509	0.117

AST%	TOV%	OREB%	DREB%	STL%	BLK%
6.5	12.0	13.4	21.6	1.3	2.1

PER	ORTG	DRTG	WS/48	VOL	
16.37	113.1	107.3	0.124	0.430	

- Fell out of the rotation in Denver last season, suffered a lower back injury at the end of the 2016-17 season
- When healthy, low volume, high efficiency rim runner that draws fouls, does most of his damage inside of three feet
- Best used as a roll man, good at running the floor in transition
- Excellent rebounder on both ends, solid shot blocker
- Struggles to play position defense, a bit undersized against interior players, can be over-aggressive on the perimeter, somewhat foul prone

Jared Dudley

	Height	Weight	Cap #	Years Left
	6'7"	225	$9.530M	0

Similar at Age **32**

		Season	SIMsc
1	Jud Buechler	2000-01	919.3
2	Bryon Russell	2002-03	907.6
3	Richard Jefferson	2012-13	905.3
4	Devean George	2009-10	905.3
5	Dan Majerle	1997-98	901.7
6	Morris Peterson	2009-10	901.6
7	Alan Anderson	2014-15	898.3
8	Shane Battier	2010-11	893.6
9	James Posey	2008-09	893.3
10	Walt Williams	2002-03	893.0

Baseline Basic Stats

MPG	PTS	AST	REB	BLK	STL
19.9	5.9	1.3	2.7	0.2	0.6

Advanced Metrics

USG%	3PTA/FGA	FTA/FGA	TS%	eFG%	3PT%
12.2	0.662	0.214	0.558	0.532	0.366

AST%	TOV%	OREB%	DREB%	STL%	BLK%
12.5	14.7	1.9	13.1	1.5	1.0

PER	ORTG	DRTG	WS/48	VOL	
9.67	109.3	111.0	0.066	0.472	

- Entering his age-33 season, production has been declining for the last four seasons, fell out of the rotation in Phoenix last season
- Very low volume spot-up shooter that still makes threes at a high percentage, has decent playmaking skills
- Not effective in any other offensive situation except spot-ups
- Offers little defensive value due to diminishing athleticism, below average position defender that needs to be hidden, solid on the defensive boards

Dzanan Musa

		Height	Weight	Cap #	Years Left
		6'10"	195	$1.632M	1 + 2 TO

Baseline Basic Stats

MPG	PTS	AST	REB	BLK	STL
21.7	8.1	1.5	3.2	0.3	0.7

Advanced Metrics

USG%	3PTA/FGA	FTA/FGA	TS%	eFG%	3PT%
18.6	0.429	0.316	0.530	0.488	0.290

AST%	TOV%	OREB%	DREB%	STL%	BLK%
13.3	12.0	2.8	12.7	1.7	0.7

PER	ORTG	DRTG	WS/48	VOL	
12.56	101.5	103.0	0.078	0.562	

- Drafted by Brooklyn in the first round with the 29th overall pick
- Stats translated from the Adriatic League, played with Cedevita last season
- Productive in a high usage offensive role, played well as a slashing wing that scored inside and drew fouls
- Showed solid playmaking skills, needs to improve his outside shot, below break-even three-point shooter
- Below average on-ball defender, more of a help defender at this stage
- Rebounds well despite a thin frame, gets steals at a high rate
- Could benefit from some additional seasoning in the G-League

Rodions Kurucs

	Height	Weight	Cap #	Years Left
	6'9"	220	$1.600M	3

Baseline Basic Stats

MPG	PTS	AST	REB	BLK	STL
19.6	7.1	1.2	3.1	0.3	0.6

Advanced Metrics

USG%	3PTA/FGA	FTA/FGA	TS%	eFG%	3PT%
17.1	0.379	0.231	0.505	0.479	0.336

AST%	TOV%	OREB%	DREB%	STL%	BLK%
11.6	12.4	3.9	11.4	2.3	1.6

PER	ORTG	DRTG	WS/48	VOL	
12.79	96.1	94.2	0.081	0.490	

- Drafted by Brooklyn in the second round with the 40th overall pick
- Played with FC Barcelona II in LEB Gold, translated LEB Gold stats
- Higher usage player, scored efficiently inside, drew fouls, shot a break-even three-point percentage in the LEB Gold
- Improved his passing skills, but still was turnover prone
- Active help defender, posted high Steal and Block Percentages, struggles as an on-ball defender
- Not quite ready to land a spot in Brooklyn's rotation, additional seasoning in the G-League could be beneficial

NEW YORK KNICKS

Last Season: 29 – 53, Missed the Playoffs

Offensive Rating: 107.1, 20th in NBA

Defensive Rating: 110.7, 23rd in NBA

Primary Executive: Steve Mills, Team President

Head Coach: David Fizdale

Key Roster Changes

Subtractions
Kyle O'Quinn, free agency
Michael Beasley, free agency
Jarrett Jack, free agency
Troy Williams, waived

Additions
Kevin Knox, draft
Mitchell Robinson, draft
Mario Hezonja, free agency
Noah Vonleh, free agency

RAFER Projected Win Total: 33.8

Projected Best Five-Man Unit
1. Trey Burke
2. Courtney Lee
3. Tim Hardaway, Jr.
4. Kristaps Porzingis
5. Enes Kanter

Other Rotation Players
Frank Ntilikina
Emmanuel Mudiay
Kevin Knox
Mario Hezonja
Mitchell Robinson
Noah Vonleh

Remaining Roster

- Ron Baker
- Damyean Dotson
- Lance Thomas
- Joakim Noah – likely will be waived after publication
- Luke Kornet
- Isaiah Hicks, 24, 6'9", 233, North Carolina (Two-Way)
- Allonzo Trier, 23, 6'5", 205, Arizona (Two-Way)
- Kadeem Allen, 26, 6'3", 192, Arizona (Exhibit 10)

Season Forecast

The system's projection of the New York Knicks represents a best-case scenario because it includes about a half season of Kristaps Porzingis, which would likely be the most that he could play if he makes a fast recovery from tearing his ACL in February of last season. However, it's more likely that he'll miss most of the season if not all of it because teams are more cautious these days about bringing players back from injury, especially All-Stars like Porzingis. The Knicks probably weren't going to compete for the playoffs even with a healthy Porzingis, but if he is not in the lineup for most of the season, they will most likely finish towards the bottom of the standings in the Eastern Conference.

Because the Knicks are still going to be in a rebuilding phase, they probably should place a greater emphasis on developing their young players. This could mean that veterans like Courtney Lee, Tim Hardaway, Jr. and Enes Kanter could have their minutes cut a bit in favor of younger players or the team could play them for the first half of the season with the hope of building their trade value to possibly sell them off at the trade deadline. The latter seems like the most likely scenario and it would allow the Knicks to ease their young players into the lineup. From there, the Knicks are probably going to finish in the bottom third of the league on both sides of the ball, but they might show some flashes of promise on defense. Head coach, David Fizdale has only coached one full season in the NBA, but he has spent most of his career as an assistant coach in a defensive oriented environment in Miami. Therefore, it's probable that he could look to place a greater emphasis on defense in New York, which could be a good fit for the team's young players. After all, their primary young players like Kevin Knox, Mitchell Robinson and Frank Ntilikina have shown potential as long, versatile, multi-positional defenders. On the offensive end, the missing presence of Porzingis could hurt them a great deal because they wouldn't have a reliable primary scoring option to take pressure off the others and allow the team to generate more efficient shots. Therefore, the Knicks will likely struggle to consistently create offense because the rest of the roster is better suited to playing in complementary roles. Overall, the primary goal for the Knicks is to help their base of young talent grow to better complement Kristaps Porzingis if and when he fully recovers from his ACL injury. Their season would be considered a success if players like Ntilikina, Knox, Robinson and possibly Emmanuel Mudiay or Mario Hezonja improve to the point where they are clearly on the path to being reliable pieces of New York's future rotation. Otherwise, if the development of their base of young talent is stunted in any way, they may have to decide to change course and make a drastic change.

Veterans

Kristaps Porzingis

	Height	Weight	Cap #	Years Left
	7'3"	240	$5.697M	0

Similar at Age **22**

		Season	SIMsc
1	Zydrunas Ilgauskas	1997-98	875.8
2	Frank Kaminsky	2015-16	855.4
3	Rik Smits	1988-89	851.9
4	Yi Jianlian	2009-10	851.3
5	LaMarcus Aldridge	2007-08	850.0
6	Dirk Nowitzki	2000-01	842.3
7	Marcus Camby	1996-97	841.5
8	Andrea Bargnani	2007-08	838.6
9	Channing Frye	2005-06	837.8
10	Duane Causwell	1990-91	836.0

Baseline Basic Stats

MPG	PTS	AST	REB	BLK	STL
29.1	14.9	1.4	6.5	1.6	0.7

Advanced Metrics

USG%	3PTA/FGA	FTA/FGA	TS%	eFG%	3PT%
25.7	0.214	0.277	0.547	0.505	0.389

AST%	TOV%	OREB%	DREB%	STL%	BLK%
7.5	9.6	6.0	17.6	1.2	4.8

PER	ORTG	DRTG	WS/48	VOL	
18.93	108.2	107.6	0.116	0.210	

- Was in the middle of his best season in the NBA in his third year, made his first All-Star team
- Missed the second half of last season due to a torn ACL in his left knee, will miss most of this season as well
- Versatile offensive big man, very good post-up player and cutter
- Good three-point shooter that can come off screens and knock down spot-up jumpers
- Shoots over 40% on threes from the corners
- Excellent rim protector, led the NBA in Block Percentage, solid defensive rebounder and position defender
- When healthy, has solid lateral mobility to defend on the perimeter

Tim Hardaway, Jr.

	Height	Weight	Cap #	Years Left
	6'6"	205	$17.325M	1 + PO

Similar at Age **25**

		Season	SIMsc
1	Gordan Giricek	2002-03	944.6
2	Marcus Thornton	2012-13	941.1
3	Nick Young	2010-11	939.8
4	C.J. Miles	2012-13	933.0
5	Allan Houston	1996-97	932.9
6	Courtney Lee	2010-11	928.3
7	Kyle Korver	2006-07	928.0
8	Wesley Person	1996-97	928.0
9	Brandon Rush	2010-11	927.8
10	Reggie Williams	2011-12	924.5

Baseline Basic Stats

MPG	PTS	AST	REB	BLK	STL
26.8	12.7	1.7	3.0	0.3	0.8

Advanced Metrics

USG%	3PTA/FGA	FTA/FGA	TS%	eFG%	3PT%
22.0	0.448	0.213	0.550	0.514	0.360

AST%	TOV%	OREB%	DREB%	STL%	BLK%
12.2	9.4	1.9	10.7	1.6	0.7

PER	ORTG	DRTG	WS/48	VOL
14.50	108.0	109.3	0.092	0.331

- Heading into his prime years, production slowed due to injuries his left leg and left ankle
- Has taken on a higher volume offensive role with the Knicks, has shown improved playmaking skills, above average in isolation situations
- Moderately efficient shooter, good mid-range shooter, but inconsistent three-point shooter
- Better at coming off screens than making stand-still jumpers
- Decent on-ball defending wing player, more of a stay-at-home defender
- Posted the highest Steal Percentage of his career last season

Courtney Lee

	Height	Weight	Cap #	Years Left
	6'5"	200	$12.254M	1

Similar at Age 32

		Season	SIMsc
1	Raja Bell	2008-09	960.0
2	Anthony Peeler	2001-02	939.1
3	Anthony Parker	2007-08	934.4
4	Steve Smith	2001-02	932.0
5	Ray Allen*	2007-08	928.7
6	Dell Curry	1996-97	924.7
7	Roger Mason	2012-13	922.7
8	Mario Elie	1995-96	920.7
9	Cuttino Mobley	2007-08	914.1
10	Wesley Person	2003-04	910.0

Baseline Basic Stats

MPG	PTS	AST	REB	BLK	STL
27.3	10.1	2.1	2.7	0.2	0.8

Advanced Metrics

USG%	3PTA/FGA	FTA/FGA	TS%	eFG%	3PT%
15.8	0.413	0.168	0.554	0.522	0.385

AST%	TOV%	OREB%	DREB%	STL%	BLK%
11.7	10.6	1.8	9.4	1.5	0.6

PER	ORTG	DRTG	WS/48	VOL	
11.96	110.3	110.3	0.086	0.370	

- Entering his age-33 season, production still consistent with career averages, mild decline risk
- Primarily a low usage spot-up shooter, shot over 40% on threes in each of the last two seasons
- Can beat over-aggressive defenders off the ball on cuts to the rim
- Has shown improved passing skills in his tenure in New York, had success last season as a pick-and-roll ball handler
- Solid stay-at-home on-ball wing defender, Steal Percentage is still around his career average

Enes Kanter

	Height	Weight	Cap #	Years Left
	6'11"	262	$18.623M	0

Similar at Age __25__

		Season	SIMsc
1	Greg Monroe	2015-16	907.7
2	Joe Kleine	1986-87	904.0
3	Tyler Zeller	2014-15	900.6
4	Brian Grant	1997-98	893.8
5	Al Jefferson	2009-10	891.5
6	Mehmet Okur	2004-05	890.9
7	Carlos Boozer	2006-07	884.0
8	Marreese Speights	2012-13	883.3
9	Jamaal Magloire	2003-04	882.6
10	Jason Thompson	2011-12	882.4

Baseline Basic Stats

MPG	PTS	AST	REB	BLK	STL
26.0	12.7	1.4	8.0	0.8	0.5

Advanced Metrics

USG%	3PTA/FGA	FTA/FGA	TS%	eFG%	3PT%
22.7	0.033	0.316	0.590	0.545	0.208

AST%	TOV%	OREB%	DREB%	STL%	BLK%
9.1	12.3	13.2	25.2	1.0	2.1

PER	ORTG	DRTG	WS/48	VOL	
21.58	116.8	106.8	0.170	0.401	

- Tied for his career best in PER in his first season as a full-time starter with the Knicks

- Highly efficient in a moderate volume role, led the NBA in Offensive Rebound Percentage

- Most effective as a post-up player, greatly improved as a mid-range shooter and passer

- Excellent defensive rebounder, 7th in the NBA last season in Defensive Rebound Percentage

- Struggles as an interior defender, limited rim protection skills, below average in position defense

Frank Ntilikina

	Height	Weight	Cap #	Years Left
	6'5"	190	$4.156M	2 Team Options

Similar at Age 19

		Season	SIMsc
1	Jrue Holiday	2009-10	916.3
2	D'Angelo Russell	2015-16	906.4
3	Zach LaVine	2014-15	903.9
4	Dante Exum	2014-15	901.7
5	Emmanuel Mudiay	2015-16	892.3
6	Tony Parker	2001-02	889.5
7	Shaun Livingston	2004-05	880.0
8	Archie Goodwin	2013-14	878.1
9	Marquis Teague	2012-13	873.6
10	Tyus Jones	2015-16	873.0

Baseline Basic Stats

MPG	PTS	AST	REB	BLK	STL
23.2	9.6	2.7	2.5	0.2	0.8

Advanced Metrics

USG%	3PTA/FGA	FTA/FGA	TS%	eFG%	3PT%
19.6	0.290	0.198	0.512	0.482	0.385

AST%	TOV%	OREB%	DREB%	STL%	BLK%
21.7	16.2	2.2	10.1	2.0	0.7

PER	ORTG	DRTG	WS/48	VOL	
11.90	101.1	111.2	0.036	0.403	

- Was a regular part of New York's rotation as a rookie
- Flashed promise as a solid on-ball defender that could defend multiple positions, posted a good Steal Percentage
- Decent playmaking skills, highly turnover prone
- Shot very inefficiently, struggled to get to the rim or draw fouls, shot less than 35% on all shots beyond ten feet
- Above average in spot-up situations according to the NBA, made 37.5% of his corner threes last season

Emmanuel Mudiay

	Height	Weight	Cap #	Years Left
	6'5"	200	$4.294M	0

Similar at Age 21

		Season	SIMsc
1	Archie Goodwin	2015-16	942.9
2	Dion Waiters	2012-13	926.1
3	Austin Rivers	2013-14	924.5
4	Alec Burks	2012-13	917.9
5	Manny Harris	2010-11	917.2
6	Marcus D. Williams	2006-07	914.9
7	Rodney Stuckey	2007-08	910.3
8	Tyreke Evans	2010-11	909.4
9	Jerryd Bayless	2009-10	908.0
10	Ray Allen*	1996-97	906.8

Baseline Basic Stats

MPG	PTS	AST	REB	BLK	STL
25.4	12.0	3.0	2.9	0.2	0.8

Advanced Metrics

USG%	3PTA/FGA	FTA/FGA	TS%	eFG%	3PT%
22.8	0.217	0.263	0.498	0.454	0.314

AST%	TOV%	OREB%	DREB%	STL%	BLK%
22.3	14.9	2.6	10.0	1.6	0.6

PER	ORTG	DRTG	WS/48	VOL	
12.53	100.8	112.9	0.028	0.373	

- Production has incrementally improved in each of his three seasons

- High usage combo guard with solid playmaking skills and will draw fouls

- A little turnover prone, very inefficient shooter, has shot below 36% on all shots beyond three feet

- Below average in virtually every offensive situation

- Struggles as an on-ball defender, solid rebounding guard, gets steals at a decent rate

Mario Hezonja

	Height	Weight	Cap #	Years Left
	6'8"	215	$6.500M	0

Similar at Age **22**

		Season	SIMsc
1	Rodney Hood	2014-15	942.8
2	Chase Budinger	2010-11	931.9
3	Mike Dunleavy, Jr.	2002-03	930.5
4	Khris Middleton	2013-14	929.1
5	Paul Zipser	2016-17	927.9
6	Taurean Prince	2016-17	926.2
7	C.J. Miles	2009-10	924.2
8	Mike Miller	2002-03	923.2
9	Vladimir Radmanovic	2002-03	922.3
10	Norman Powell	2015-16	916.4

Baseline Basic Stats

MPG	PTS	AST	REB	BLK	STL
25.3	10.4	1.7	4.0	0.4	0.9

Advanced Metrics

USG%	3PTA/FGA	FTA/FGA	TS%	eFG%	3PT%
19.8	0.401	0.181	0.528	0.497	0.348

AST%	TOV%	OREB%	DREB%	STL%	BLK%
11.2	12.0	3.0	15.0	1.9	1.2

PER	ORTG	DRTG	WS/48	VOL	
12.88	101.7	107.9	0.067	0.363	

- Vastly improved in his third season, had his best year in the NBA last season with Orlando
- Effective as a low volume catch-and-shoot player, greatly reduced his Turnover Percentage last season
- Dramatically improved his ability to finish close shots and make long twos, shot a break-even percentage on threes
- Most effective as a spot-up shooter and cutter, had success in the pick-and-roll as both the ball handler and screener
- Posted a career high in Defensive Rebound Percentage, could passably defend multiple positions if given favorable matchups

Trey Burke

	Height	Weight	Cap #	Years Left
	6'0"	190	$1.795M	0

Similar at Age 25

		Season	SIMsc
1	Tony Delk	1998-99	932.1
2	J.J. Barea	2009-10	911.6
3	Jordan Farmar	2011-12	910.0
4	Jameer Nelson	2007-08	905.3
5	Mo Williams	2007-08	902.7
6	Trevor Ruffin	1995-96	900.4
7	Ty Lawson	2012-13	892.6
8	Patty Mills	2013-14	891.9
9	Jannero Pargo	2004-05	891.7
10	Tierre Brown	2004-05	891.4

Baseline Basic Stats

MPG	PTS	AST	REB	BLK	STL
22.5	9.8	3.5	2.1	0.1	0.6

Advanced Metrics

USG%	3PTA/FGA	FTA/FGA	TS%	eFG%	3PT%
22.1	0.331	0.166	0.554	0.527	0.380

AST%	TOV%	OREB%	DREB%	STL%	BLK%
27.1	12.2	1.7	8.0	1.3	0.3

PER	ORTG	DRTG	WS/48	VOL	
16.23	111.5	109.4	0.113	0.420	

- Thrived in a late season stint with the Knicks after a strong showing with their G-League team in Westchester
- Demonstrated greatly improved playmaking and ball control skills
- Very effective as the ball handler in pick-and-roll situations
- Continued to shoot well from mid-range and at the three-point line
- Dramatically improved his ability to finish shots at the rim
- Good spot-up shooter, excellent at coming off screens last season
- Ranked by the NBA in the 99th percentile at scoring off screens on a per-possession basis
- Smallish frame limits him defensively, below average position defender, decent rebounder for a player of his size

Noah Vonleh

	Height	Weight	Cap #	Years Left
	6'10"	240	$1.513M	0

Similar at Age 22

		Season	SIMsc
1	Jarell Martin	2016-17	920.9
2	Loy Vaught	1990-91	913.6
3	Charlie Villanueva	2006-07	909.2
4	Josh McRoberts	2009-10	908.9
5	Thomas Robinson	2013-14	908.8
6	Rick Mahorn	1980-81	906.6
7	Cal Bowdler	1999-00	902.4
8	Perry Jones	2013-14	902.2
9	Jonas Jerebko	2009-10	901.8
10	Raef LaFrentz	1998-99	901.2

Baseline Basic Stats

MPG	PTS	AST	REB	BLK	STL
22.0	7.7	1.2	5.4	0.7	0.5

Advanced Metrics

USG%	3PTA/FGA	FTA/FGA	TS%	eFG%	3PT%
15.7	0.185	0.268	0.532	0.507	0.342

AST%	TOV%	OREB%	DREB%	STL%	BLK%
7.6	12.9	7.8	22.6	1.2	2.1

PER	ORTG	DRTG	WS/48	VOL	
13.18	107.1	105.7	0.097	0.365	

- Fell out of the rotation in Portland, playing time increased after the trade to Chicago
- Low volume big man that can draw fouls and crash the offensive glass
- Middling efficiency as a scorer, heavily reliant on his mid-range jumper
- Below break-even three-point shooter, doesn't get many shots around the rim
- Very good defensive rebounder, solid on-ball defender, limited as a rim protector because he doesn't really block shots

Ron Baker

	Height	Weight	Cap #	Years Left
	6'4"	220	$4.544M	0

Similar at Age 24

		Season	SIMsc
1	Gerald Madkins	1993-94	906.0
2	Lamar Patterson	2015-16	905.1
3	Fred Jones	2003-04	903.5
4	Carlos Clark	1984-85	891.1
5	Aaron McKie	1996-97	889.8
6	Fred Hoiberg	1996-97	885.9
7	Kostas Papanikolaou	2014-15	879.5
8	Iman Shumpert	2014-15	879.2
9	Coby Karl	2007-08	877.8
10	Jerian Grant	2016-17	876.4

Baseline Basic Stats

MPG	PTS	AST	REB	BLK	STL
22.4	7.4	2.6	2.6	0.2	0.9

Advanced Metrics

USG%	3PTA/FGA	FTA/FGA	TS%	eFG%	3PT%
15.0	0.444	0.306	0.514	0.463	0.336

AST%	TOV%	OREB%	DREB%	STL%	BLK%
18.1	16.6	2.1	9.7	2.2	0.9

PER	ORTG	DRTG	WS/48	VOL
11.02	104.5	110.3	0.059	0.700

- Missed most of last season due to a dislocated right shoulder
- Extremely low volume combo guard that will draw fouls and shows decent playmaking skills
- Highly turnover prone, struggles to make shots from the field, below break-even three-point shooter
- Good at cutting to the rim when healthy, better in spot-up situations last season
- High energy defender that defends both guard spots, better at handling wing players
- Very active to get steals and contest shots

Damyean Dotson

	Height	Weight	Cap #	Years Left
	6'6"	205	$1.378M	1

Similar at Age 23

	Player	Season	SIMsc
1	Reggie Williams	2009-10	939.9
2	Tim Hardaway, Jr.	2015-16	936.9
3	Bryce Dejean-Jones	2015-16	926.2
4	Darrun Hilliard	2016-17	922.4
5	Bill Walker	2010-11	919.0
6	Brandon Rush	2008-09	917.1
7	Chase Budinger	2011-12	914.7
8	Kareem Rush	2003-04	914.3
9	Orlando Johnson	2012-13	914.3
10	Chris Johnson	2013-14	914.1

Baseline Basic Stats

MPG	PTS	AST	REB	BLK	STL
21.4	7.9	1.3	2.6	0.2	0.6

Advanced Metrics

USG%	3PTA/FGA	FTA/FGA	TS%	eFG%	3PT%
17.4	0.458	0.162	0.544	0.522	0.355

AST%	TOV%	OREB%	DREB%	STL%	BLK%
10.0	9.9	2.1	14.5	1.4	0.6

PER	ORTG	DRTG	WS/48	VOL	
11.97	106.8	110.9	0.065	0.385	

- Was on the fringes of New York's rotation, spent time with Westchester in the G-League
- Lower volume spot-up shooter in the NBA, shot a below break-even percentage on threes in limited attempts
- Took on higher usage in the G-League and shot much higher percentages, flashed some playmaking skills
- Stay-at-home defender, solid position defending wing player if given favorable matchups

Lance Thomas

	Height	Weight	Cap #	Years Left
	6'8"	225	$7.120M	1

Similar at Age **29**

		Season	SIMsc
1	Devean George	2006-07	927.1
2	James Jones	2009-10	926.4
3	Mickael Gelabale	2012-13	918.0
4	Tracy Murray	2000-01	917.9
5	Eric Piatkowski	1999-00	916.4
6	Travis Outlaw	2013-14	914.0
7	David Benoit	1997-98	913.8
8	Jonas Jerebko	2016-17	911.9
9	Luc Mbah a Moute	2015-16	911.7
10	Pat Garrity	2005-06	911.3

Baseline Basic Stats

MPG	PTS	AST	REB	BLK	STL
18.8	5.9	0.8	2.6	0.2	0.5

Advanced Metrics

USG%	3PTA/FGA	FTA/FGA	TS%	eFG%	3PT%
12.8	0.458	0.204	0.539	0.505	0.408

AST%	TOV%	OREB%	DREB%	STL%	BLK%
5.4	10.1	3.5	11.9	1.2	0.9

PER	ORTG	DRTG	WS/48	VOL
9.16	108.8	110.8	0.065	0.366

- Has been a regular rotation player for the Knicks in the last three seasons, production has steadily declined
- Extremely low volume offensive player that has made more than 40% of his threes in each of the last three seasons
- Almost strictly a spot-up shooter, not effective in any other offensive situation
- Solid stay-at-home on-ball defender that can defend multiple positions

Joakim Noah

	Height	Weight	Cap #	Years Left
	6'11"	232	$18.530M	1

Similar at Age 32

		Season	SIMsc
1	Zaza Pachulia	2016-17	903.6
2	Louis Amundson	2014-15	883.7
3	Dan Gadzuric	2010-11	880.6
4	Greg Anderson	1996-97	880.6
5	Chris Dudley	1997-98	878.9
6	Charles Shackleford	1998-99	878.5
7	Ben Coleman	1993-94	873.4
8	Duane Causwell	2000-01	871.8
9	Jeff Foster	2008-09	870.0
10	Coby Dietrick	1980-81	868.4

Baseline Basic Stats

MPG	PTS	AST	REB	BLK	STL
15.2	4.1	0.8	4.5	0.6	0.4

Advanced Metrics

USG%	3PTA/FGA	FTA/FGA	TS%	eFG%	3PT%
14.5	0.004	0.354	0.507	0.496	0.032

AST%	TOV%	OREB%	DREB%	STL%	BLK%
11.4	19.7	14.7	22.6	1.7	3.4

PER	ORTG	DRTG	WS/48	VOL
14.20	105.4	105.8	0.091	0.454

- Severely hampered by injuries to his shoulder and knee in the previous two seasons
- Only played 40 total minutes last season
- Exiled from the Knicks last season after an altercation with former head coach, Jeff Hornacek
- Rebounds and blocks shots at a high rate, defensive impact is negatively impacted by his limited mobility due to injury and age
- Still a good passing big man, but physical limitations make him unable to efficiently finish shots inside, resulting in very low True Shooting Percentages
- Likely to be waived after publication of this book

Luke Kornet

	Height	Weight	Cap #	Years Left
	7'1"	250	$1.619M	0

Similar at Age **22**

		Season	SIMsc
1	Frank Kaminsky	2015-16	867.8
2	Oleksiy Pecherov	2007-08	857.0
3	Raef LaFrentz	1998-99	856.8
4	Ryan Anderson	2010-11	851.8
5	Meyers Leonard	2014-15	850.8
6	Robin Lopez	2010-11	844.1
7	Spencer Hawes	2010-11	842.6
8	Richaun Holmes	2015-16	842.0
9	Perry Jones	2013-14	840.6
10	Alexis Ajinca	2010-11	838.1

Baseline Basic Stats

MPG	PTS	AST	REB	BLK	STL
20.3	8.1	1.2	4.6	0.8	0.4

Advanced Metrics

USG%	3PTA/FGA	FTA/FGA	TS%	eFG%	3PT%
19.1	0.433	0.164	0.524	0.500	0.369

AST%	TOV%	OREB%	DREB%	STL%	BLK%
10.7	10.2	5.3	17.7	1.0	3.5

PER	ORTG	DRTG	WS/48	VOL	
14.18	106.0	107.7	0.092	0.588	

- Played on a two-way contract last season for the Knicks, spent most of the season with Westchester in the G-League
- Showed promise as a low volume, stretch big, made 44% of his threes in the G-League
- Shot an above break-even percentage on threes in limited attempts in the NBA
- Effective in a small sample of minutes at cutting to the basket
- Below average as a position defender, adequate rebounder, blocked shots at a high rate in both the NBA and the G-League

Newcomers

Kevin Knox

	Height	Weight	Cap #	Years Left
	6'9"	215	$3.740M	1 + 2 TO

Baseline Basic Stats

MPG	PTS	AST	REB	BLK	STL
25.4	9.7	1.7	3.7	0.4	0.8

Advanced Metrics

USG%	3PTA/FGA	FTA/FGA	TS%	eFG%	3PT%
19.3	0.256	0.277	0.517	0.478	0.341

AST%	TOV%	OREB%	DREB%	STL%	BLK%
10.8	12.2	4.7	11.9	1.6	1.1

PER	ORTG	DRTG	WS/48	VOL
12.76	103.6	108.9	0.067	N/A

- Drafted by New York in the first round with the 10th pick
- Solid showing at the Las Vegas Summer League
- Played a very high usage role, scored in volume, made threes at an average rate, flashed some playmaking skills
- Somewhat turnover prone and was inefficient as an overall shooter, took a lot of inefficient long twos
- Played with high energy, but did not stand out as an on-ball defender
- Decent as a defensive rebounder

Mitchell Robinson

	Height	Weight	Cap #	Years Left
	7'0"	225	$1.524M	2 + TO

Baseline Basic Stats

MPG	PTS	AST	REB	BLK	STL
18.6	6.0	0.5	4.9	1.6	0.4

Advanced Metrics

USG%	3PTA/FGA	FTA/FGA	TS%	eFG%	3PT%
13.9	0.006	0.283	0.580	0.573	0.114

AST%	TOV%	OREB%	DREB%	STL%	BLK%
2.8	7.7	17.4	19.1	1.5	8.7

PER	ORTG	DRTG	WS/48	VOL	
20.05	124.7	103.5	0.152	0.592	

- Drafted by New York in the second round with 36th overall pick
- Limited statistical information, very small sample size, projection uses translated Summer League stats
- Very strong performance at Summer League
- Flashed potential as a rim protecting big man, blocked shots and rebounded at a very high rate
- Generally maintained solid positioning, fouled at an extremely high rate
- Mainly effective offensively as a low volume rim runner that scored at the rim
- Extremely active and aggressive offensive rebounder
- Other skills need work, shot below 50% on free throws, did not record an assist in the entire tournament

ORLANDO MAGIC

Last Season: 25 – 57, Missed the Playoffs

Offensive Rating: 105.2, 25th in NBA   Defensive Rating: 110.1, 18th in NBA

Primary Executive: Jeff Weltman, President of Basketball Operations

Head Coach: Steve Clifford

Key Roster Changes

Subtractions	Additions
Bismack Biyombo, trade	Mohamed Bamba, draft
Rodney Purvis, trade	Melvin Frazier, draft
Arron Afflalo, free agency	Jerian Grant, trade
Mario Hezonja, free agency	Timofey Mozgov, trade
Marreese Speights, free agency	Jarell Martin, trade
Shelvin Mack, waived	Isaiah Briscoe, free agency

RAFER Projected Win Totals: 31.1

Projected Best Five-Man Unit	Other Rotation Players
1. Jerian Grant	D.J. Augustin
2. Evan Fournier	Terrence Ross
3. Jonathon Simmons	Jonathan Isaac
4. Aaron Gordon	Mohamed Bamba
5. Nikola Vucevic	

Remaining Roster

- Wesley Iwundu
- Melvin Frazier
- Isaiah Briscoe
- Jarell Martin
- Khem Birch
- Timofey Mozgov
- Amile Jefferson, 26, 6'9", 224, Duke (Two-Way)
- Troy Caupain, 23, 6'4", 210, Cincinnati (Two-Way)
- B.J. Johnson, 23, 6'7", 200, LaSalle (Exhibit 10)
- Gabe York, 25, 6'3", 190, Arizona (Exhibit 10)

Season Forecast

The Orlando Magic took small steps to carve out an identity for themselves this summer. They did this by switching out some players from the previous regime like Bismack Biyombo and Mario Hezonja for ones with more length and athleticism like incoming lottery pick, Mohamed Bamba and point guard, Jerian Grant. The intent behind these acquisitions was the Magic could build a solid defensive unit that utilizes a roster of long, versatile athletes that could aggressively defend multiple positions to make themselves more competitive. This line of thinking is also why they hired Steve Clifford as their head coach because of his reputation as a high-level defensive mind as a result of his work as an assistant with both of the Van Gundy brothers. However, Orlando is unlikely to fully execute this vision right now because their roster is still young and unproven. Therefore, they may flash some potential at times, but most likely, the Magic will finish near the bottom of the Eastern Conference.

At the defensive end, Orlando could get a boost because they will inject some younger and more athletic players in their rotation. In particular, Bamba is probably going to figure heavily into the lineup, as they will try to groom him to be the future anchor of their defense. He could make positive contributions right away because of his extraordinary 7'10" wingspan and excellent shot blocking skills. He will take his fair share of lumps because he's still unpolished as a position defender, but steady playing time should allow him to make a quicker adjustment to the NBA. In addition to Bamba, the trade for Grant gives them a taller point guard that allows the team to have length at every position. It also allows them to switch screens more aggressively because they can produce a five-man unit where each player can defend multiple positions. Finally, a healthy Jonathan Isaac should also be a boost to their defense because he would give them a versatile, 6'10" forward that could defend both perimeter and interior players. His on-ball defense looked to be significantly improved at this year's Summer League. Offensively, the Magic are still going to struggle to score points because they simply don't have a reliable shot creator and Clifford isn't especially known for implementing creative offensive schemes to maximize talent. Therefore, they will have difficulties in generating efficient offense because they don't have any plus-level playmakers and they haven't been a great shooting team either. As a result, Orlando will probably have a bottom third level offensive team. In general, Orlando has taken a positive step by moving towards building a team with a clear identity, but they are still at least a season or two away from realizing their vision. In all likelihood, they will spend another season as a lottery team, but they finally may have a few solid building blocks to move forward and eventually become competitive in the Eastern Conference.

Veterans

Aaron Gordon

	Height	Weight	Cap #	Years Left
	6'9"	225	$21.591M	3

Similar at Age **22**

		Season	SIMsc
1	Tobias Harris	2014-15	945.4
2	Dario Saric	2016-17	935.7
3	Ersan Ilyasova	2009-10	928.9
4	Peja Stojakovic	1999-00	927.4
5	Marvin Williams	2008-09	927.0
6	Omri Casspi	2010-11	926.6
7	Vladimir Radmanovic	2002-03	925.8
8	Hedo Turkoglu	2001-02	924.1
9	Tim Thomas	1999-00	921.5
10	Mike Miller	2002-03	919.5

Baseline Basic Stats

MPG	PTS	AST	REB	BLK	STL
30.3	14.0	1.8	5.4	0.6	0.9

Advanced Metrics

USG%	3PTA/FGA	FTA/FGA	TS%	eFG%	3PT%
21.9	0.309	0.255	0.543	0.507	0.344

AST%	TOV%	OREB%	DREB%	STL%	BLK%
10.4	9.9	4.9	16.8	1.5	1.6

PER	ORTG	DRTG	WS/48	VOL	
16.08	107.6	107.8	0.103	0.321	

- Had a bounce back season in his fourth year after playing out of position at the three the season before
- Missed games due to a series of injuries which included a strained calf, strained hip flexor and a concussion
- Explosive dunker, maintained efficiency in a higher volume role, above average post-up player
- Very good on rim running plays, excelled as a roll man and cutter
- Improved his three-point shot to a break-even level, steadily increased his Assist Percentage
- Solid position defender that can guard both forward positions, good rebounder, occasionally blocks shots

Evan Fournier

	Height	Weight	Cap #	Years Left
	6'6"	190	$17.000M	1 + PO

Similar at Age 25

		Season	SIMsc
1	Nick Young	2010-11	940.3
2	Allan Houston	1996-97	933.7
3	Marco Belinelli	2011-12	931.3
4	Al Wood	1983-84	929.3
5	Gordan Giricek	2002-03	928.2
6	Michael Dickerson	2000-01	927.0
7	Leandro Barbosa	2007-08	924.2
8	Jordan Crawford	2013-14	923.5
9	Jamal Crawford	2005-06	922.2
10	Steve Smith	1994-95	921.6

Baseline Basic Stats

MPG	PTS	AST	REB	BLK	STL
30.1	14.5	2.6	3.0	0.2	0.9

Advanced Metrics

USG%	3PTA/FGA	FTA/FGA	TS%	eFG%	3PT%
22.5	0.374	0.257	0.558	0.513	0.367

AST%	TOV%	OREB%	DREB%	STL%	BLK%
14.9	10.9	2.1	8.9	1.5	0.5

PER	ORTG	DRTG	WS/48	VOL	
14.84	108.8	110.8	0.095	0.336	

- Had his best season in the NBA in his sixth year, missed games due to a sprained right ankle and a sprained MCL in his left knee
- Scores efficiently in a higher usage role, very good three-point shooter throughout his career
- Decent playmaker that limits turnovers, excellent at cutting to the rim off the ball
- Effective with the ball in his hands on isolation plays and as a pick-and-roll ball handler
- Passable defender, needs to be hidden, plays adequate position defense if given favorable matchups

Nikola Vucevic

	Height	Weight	Cap #	Years Left
	6'10"	240	$12.750M	0

Similar at Age 27

		Season	SIMsc
1	Jordan Hill	2014-15	909.6
2	Al Horford	2013-14	903.5
3	LaMarcus Aldridge	2012-13	901.4
4	David West	2007-08	899.9
5	Derrick Coleman	1994-95	898.6
6	Andray Blatche	2013-14	897.7
7	Herb Williams	1985-86	893.1
8	Blake Griffin	2016-17	892.7
9	Chris Webber	2000-01	891.2
10	Rasheed Wallace	2001-02	890.7

Baseline Basic Stats

MPG	PTS	AST	REB	BLK	STL
33.8	18.4	2.8	8.7	1.1	0.9

Advanced Metrics

USG%	3PTA/FGA	FTA/FGA	TS%	eFG%	3PT%
25.4	0.141	0.184	0.527	0.500	0.313

AST%	TOV%	OREB%	DREB%	STL%	BLK%
16.9	10.2	7.0	25.1	1.5	2.5

PER	ORTG	DRTG	WS/48	VOL	
19.50	106.3	104.6	0.110	0.356	

- Highly productive, starting level big man in his prime, missed two months due to a broken hand
- Skilled offensively, good mid-range shooter that can occasionally hit a three, very good passing big man
- Going to the offensive glass less frequently, still scores on a high percentage of his put-backs
- Good defensive rebounder and shot blocker, struggles as an on-ball position defender due to a lack of mobility and athleticism

Jonathon Simmons

	Height	Weight	Cap #	Years Left
	6'6"	195	$6.000M	1

Similar at Age 28

		Season	SIMsc
1	Marquis Daniels	2008-09	935.4
2	Anthony Bowie	1991-92	934.7
3	Raja Bell	2004-05	934.5
4	Ricky Davis	2007-08	930.6
5	Derek Smith	1989-90	927.6
6	Vincent Askew	1994-95	925.4
7	Willie Green	2009-10	923.5
8	Johnny Newman	1991-92	922.3
9	Anfernee Hardaway	1999-00	921.1
10	Albert King	1987-88	920.0

Baseline Basic Stats

MPG	PTS	AST	REB	BLK	STL
25.2	10.5	2.2	2.9	0.2	0.8

Advanced Metrics

USG%	3PTA/FGA	FTA/FGA	TS%	eFG%	3PT%
19.3	0.308	0.279	0.542	0.500	0.334

AST%	TOV%	OREB%	DREB%	STL%	BLK%
12.7	13.3	2.7	9.9	1.5	0.8

PER	ORTG	DRTG	WS/48	VOL	
11.99	104.5	109.1	0.065	0.316	

- Became a regular starter for the first time in his three-year career, had his best season as a pro
- Still recovering from right wrist surgery, timetable to return is currently uncertain
- Played a higher usage role in Orlando, slashing wing that drew fouls, made threes at a break-even rate and showed decent playmaking skills
- Most effective in spot-up situations or as a cutter off the ball
- Solid high energy wing defender that can guard multiple positions, more of a stay-at-home position defender

Jerian Grant

	Height	Weight	Cap #	Years Left
	6'4"	195	$2.639M	0

	Similar at Age	25	
	Player	Season	SIMsc
1	Antonio Daniels	2000-01	948.8
2	Rex Walters	1995-96	939.2
3	Jordan Crawford	2013-14	932.2
4	Jerryd Bayless	2013-14	930.9
5	Doug Overton	1994-95	929.1
6	Khalid Reeves	1997-98	923.6
7	Matthew Dellavedova	2015-16	922.4
8	Chauncey Billups	2001-02	919.9
9	Fred Jones	2004-05	919.1
10	Rick Brunson	1997-98	918.5

Baseline Basic Stats

MPG	PTS	AST	REB	BLK	STL
22.1	8.3	2.9	2.1	0.2	0.7

Advanced Metrics

USG%	3PTA/FGA	FTA/FGA	TS%	eFG%	3PT%
18.1	0.373	0.309	0.534	0.483	0.340

AST%	TOV%	OREB%	DREB%	STL%	BLK%
23.3	13.4	1.8	9.5	1.8	0.5

PER	ORTG	DRTG	WS/48	VOL	
13.74	109.5	109.1	0.104	0.460	

- Has steadily improved in each of his three seasons, had a career best season last year as a regular rotation player for Chicago
- Low usage point guard, dramatically increased his Assist Percentage
- Very good at turning the corner and drawing fouls as a pick-and-roll ball handler
- Shot 64% on shots inside of three feet, good mid-range shooter, only about break-even as a three-point shooter
- Can defend both guard spots, better at handling taller wings
- Can struggle to contain quicker point guards, gets steals at a fairly high rate

D.J. Augustin

	Height	Weight	Cap #	Years Left
	6'0"	180	$7.250M	1

Similar at Age 30

		Season	SIMsc
1	Jason Williams	2005-06	938.8
2	Scott Skiles	1994-95	933.1
3	C.J. Watson	2014-15	931.2
4	Chris Whitney	2001-02	931.2
5	Kenny Smith	1995-96	924.5
6	J.J. Barea	2014-15	915.7
7	Travis Best	2002-03	914.6
8	John Crotty	1999-00	913.7
9	George Hill	2016-17	913.7
10	Howard Eisley	2002-03	905.9

Baseline Basic Stats

MPG	PTS	AST	REB	BLK	STL
23.2	9.1	3.6	2.0	0.1	0.7

Advanced Metrics

USG%	3PTA/FGA	FTA/FGA	TS%	eFG%	3PT%
18.5	0.476	0.280	0.560	0.513	0.381

AST%	TOV%	OREB%	DREB%	STL%	BLK%
23.4	15.1	1.6	8.3	1.5	0.2

PER	ORTG	DRTG	WS/48	VOL
13.63	110.0	111.7	0.081	0.399

- Some age-related decline risk, maintained his level of production in his age-30 season last year
- Effective offensively, solid playmaker in a low volume role
- Posted the highest True Shooting Percentage of his career
- Made 41.9% of his threes, shot over 50% on long twos and drew fouls at a high rate
- Excellent spot-up shooter that could also come off screens and cut to the rim
- Good at using the threat of his shot to get by defenders in isolation situations and as a pick-and-roll ball handler
- Historically limited defensively due to his small stature
- Played competent position defense against second unit point guards last season

Terrence Ross

	Height	Weight	Cap #	Years Left
	6'6"	195	$10.500M	0

Similar at Age 26

		Season	SIMsc
1	Justin Holiday	2015-16	943.9
2	C.J. Miles	2013-14	929.9
3	Rudy Fernandez	2011-12	929.3
4	Brent Barry	1997-98	929.1
5	Courtney Lee	2011-12	926.1
6	Sasha Vujacic	2010-11	923.5
7	Mickael Pietrus	2008-09	922.1
8	Dorell Wright	2011-12	920.3
9	Wesley Person	1997-98	920.1
10	Danny Green	2013-14	914.7

Baseline Basic Stats

MPG	PTS	AST	REB	BLK	STL
23.7	9.3	1.5	2.8	0.4	0.8

Advanced Metrics

USG%	3PTA/FGA	FTA/FGA	TS%	eFG%	3PT%
18.2	0.495	0.173	0.535	0.506	0.363

AST%	TOV%	OREB%	DREB%	STL%	BLK%
9.4	10.3	1.8	11.0	1.9	1.4

PER	ORTG	DRTG	WS/48	VOL
12.15	103.8	108.9	0.072	0.403

- Production limited, missed most of last season due to a sprained MCL in his right knee and a fractured right leg
- When healthy, low usage spot-up shooter that makes threes at a league average rate, uses athleticism to explosively dunk in transition
- Was only effective as a pick-and-roll ball handler last season, struggled in almost every other offensive situation
- Decent on-ball defending wing, good rebounder despite thin frame, posts an above average Steal Percentage

Jonathan Isaac

	Height	Weight	Cap #	Years Left
	6'10"	210	$4.969M	2 Team Options

Similar at Age 20

		Season	SIMsc
1	Paul George	2010-11	884.5
2	Chris McCullough	2015-16	882.6
3	Al-Farouq Aminu	2010-11	873.0
4	Antonis Fotsis	2001-02	868.4
5	Travis Outlaw	2004-05	867.2
6	Eddie Griffin	2002-03	864.9
7	DerMarr Johnson	2000-01	864.8
8	Maurice Harkless	2013-14	861.5
9	Jerami Grant	2014-15	854.7
10	Rashard Lewis	1999-00	851.0

Baseline Basic Stats

MPG	PTS	AST	REB	BLK	STL
22.3	8.1	1.3	4.1	0.6	0.8

Advanced Metrics

USG%	3PTA/FGA	FTA/FGA	TS%	eFG%	3PT%
17.5	0.344	0.202	0.507	0.475	0.371

AST%	TOV%	OREB%	DREB%	STL%	BLK%
8.0	12.7	4.1	16.0	2.2	2.8

PER	ORTG	DRTG	WS/48	VOL	
12.47	98.3	106.3	0.069	0.577	

- Missed most of his rookie season due to injuries to his right ankle
- More advanced as a help defender than a position defender, posted a high Steal and Block Percentage, solid defensive rebounder
- Can defend perimeter and interior players, thin frame makes him better suited to defending on the perimeter
- Struggled to shoot efficiently in a low usage role, displayed limited playmaking skills
- Took too many inefficient mid-range shots, infrequently took shots close to the basket, did shoot an above break-even percentage on threes in limited attempts
- Mainly effective at cutting to the rim in a half-court set and running the floor to finish plays in transition

Wesley Iwundu

	Height	Weight	Cap #	Years Left
	6'7"	193	$1.378M	Team Option

Similar at Age 23

		Season	SIMsc
1	Quinton Ross	2004-05	927.5
2	Antoine Wright	2007-08	919.6
3	Jeryl Sasser	2002-03	916.6
4	Mickael Gelabale	2006-07	912.9
5	John Salmons	2002-03	911.3
6	Chris Douglas-Roberts	2009-10	908.3
7	Tony Snell	2014-15	907.4
8	Pace Mannion	1983-84	906.7
9	Rodney Carney	2007-08	906.3
10	Axel Toupane	2015-16	905.5

Baseline Basic Stats

MPG	PTS	AST	REB	BLK	STL
19.0	6.2	1.2	2.5	0.3	0.6

Advanced Metrics

USG%	3PTA/FGA	FTA/FGA	TS%	eFG%	3PT%
14.3	0.253	0.231	0.511	0.475	0.274

AST%	TOV%	OREB%	DREB%	STL%	BLK%
9.2	11.0	3.8	11.3	1.7	0.9

PER	ORTG	DRTG	WS/48	VOL	
10.25	104.5	110.6	0.060	0.398	

- Cracked Orlando's rotation in his rookie season, played 1020 minutes
- Flashed defensive versatility by guarding both forward spots
- Better suited to defending wings on the perimeter at this stage, solid rebounder
- Had difficulties shooting efficiently in a very low volume role, could not make shots outside of three feet
- Very good cutter that took 39% of his shots from inside of three feet and made almost 64% of those shots

Jarell Martin

	Height	Weight	Cap #	Years Left
	6'10"	239	$2.416M	0

Similar at Age 23

		Season	SIMsc
1	Alaa Abdelnaby	1991-92	937.1
2	Yi Jianlian	2010-11	933.5
3	Terry Mills	1990-91	931.2
4	Cherokee Parks	1995-96	929.3
5	Adreian Payne	2014-15	928.9
6	Jordan Hill	2010-11	928.8
7	Josh McRoberts	2010-11	928.0
8	Acie Earl	1993-94	926.9
9	Mehmet Okur	2002-03	925.6
10	Jim Petersen	1985-86	924.1

Baseline Basic Stats

MPG	PTS	AST	REB	BLK	STL
19.6	7.6	1.0	4.8	0.6	0.5

Advanced Metrics

USG%	3PTA/FGA	FTA/FGA	TS%	eFG%	3PT%
18.2	0.146	0.290	0.536	0.493	0.348

AST%	TOV%	OREB%	DREB%	STL%	BLK%
7.2	13.3	8.2	18.9	1.3	2.2

PER	ORTG	DRTG	WS/48	VOL	
13.51	106.0	107.4	0.092	0.366	

- Played regular rotation minutes for Memphis for the first time in his three-year career last season
- Utilized in a low usage role, pre-dominantly a middling mid-range shooter
- Could draw fouls and shoot threes at an above break-even rate
- Rated as below average in almost every offensive situation last season
- Below average position defender, active help defender that could block shots and grab defensive rebounds at a solid rate

Khem Birch

	Height	Weight	Cap #	Years Left
	6'9"	220	$1.378M	0

Similar at Age 25

		Season	SIMsc
1	Aaron Williams	1996-97	931.3
2	Lavoy Allen	2014-15	922.1
3	Dominic McGuire	2010-11	917.9
4	Adam Keefe	1995-96	917.8
5	Ray Tolbert	1983-84	915.1
6	Vernon Macklin	2011-12	914.7
7	Antonio Davis	1993-94	912.6
8	Carl Herrera	1991-92	911.1
9	Marty Conlon	1992-93	904.9
10	Anthony Avent	1994-95	904.8

Baseline Basic Stats

MPG	PTS	AST	REB	BLK	STL
18.6	5.9	0.8	4.7	0.5	0.4

Advanced Metrics

USG%	3PTA/FGA	FTA/FGA	TS%	eFG%	3PT%
14.1	0.001	0.432	0.562	0.516	0.066

AST%	TOV%	OREB%	DREB%	STL%	BLK%
7.3	13.6	11.5	19.6	1.2	2.1

PER	ORTG	DRTG	WS/48	VOL	
14.46	116.0	107.3	0.116	0.326	

- Found his way onto the fringes of Orlando's rotation after starting the season with Lakeland in the G-League
- Low usage rim running big man that scores efficiently as a roll man
- Draws fouls, made almost 69% of his free throws, decent passing big man
- Good rebounder on both ends, above average shot blocker, struggles in position defense due to being slightly undersized

Timofey Mozgov

	Height	Weight	Cap #	Years Left
	7'1"	250	$16.000M	1

Similar at Age 31

		Season	SIMsc
1	Rasho Nesterovic	2007-08	910.5
2	Kelvin Cato	2005-06	892.8
3	Paul Mokeski	1987-88	892.7
4	Greg Dreiling	1994-95	892.3
5	Zeljko Rebraca	2003-04	892.0
6	Benoit Benjamin	1995-96	890.4
7	Luc Longley	1999-00	888.4
8	Sam Bowie	1992-93	887.8
9	Samuel Dalembert	2012-13	886.5
10	Francisco Elson	2007-08	885.7

Baseline Basic Stats

MPG	PTS	AST	REB	BLK	STL
15.5	5.0	0.6	3.9	0.6	0.3

Advanced Metrics

USG%	3PTA/FGA	FTA/FGA	TS%	eFG%	3PT%
15.9	0.073	0.291	0.562	0.521	0.080

AST%	TOV%	OREB%	DREB%	STL%	BLK%
5.8	18.6	9.6	18.8	1.0	2.9

PER	ORTG	DRTG	WS/48	VOL	
12.03	104.9	109.5	0.060	0.491	

- Played seldomly for Brooklyn last season, production has been in decline

- Typically a low volume, big body rim runner that scores from close range, limited post-up game

- Mainly scores on cuts to the rim or on put-backs, decent offensive rebounder

- Offensive Rebound Percentage has been down from his career average for the last three seasons

- Solid rebounder and shot blocker, severe lack of mobility makes him a liability on defense

Newcomers

Mohamed Bamba

	Height	Weight	Cap #	Years Left
	7'0"	225	$4.865M	1 + 2 TO

Baseline Basic Stats

MPG	PTS	AST	REB	BLK	STL
24.9	9.7	0.8	6.2	1.3	0.6

Advanced Metrics

USG%	3PTA/FGA	FTA/FGA	TS%	eFG%	3PT%
19.2	0.050	0.332	0.525	0.490	0.330

AST%	TOV%	OREB%	DREB%	STL%	BLK%
5.4	12.7	10.4	18.6	1.3	3.8

PER	ORTG	DRTG	WS/48	VOL
15.15	105.3	106.7	0.086	N/A

- Drafted by Orlando in the first round with the 6th overall pick
- Strong performance at Las Vegas Summer League
- Flashed potential as a rim protector by blocking shots at a high rate, decent defensive rebounder, showed improvement as a position defender
- Primarily a low volume rim runner, mainly scored on dunks, crashed the offensive glass
- Went 2-for-4 on threes, did not get to the free throw line at all in his minutes at Summer League

Melvin Frazier

	Height	Weight	Cap #	Years Left
	6'6"	200	$1.050M	1 + TO

Baseline Basic Stats

MPG	PTS	AST	REB	BLK	STL
10.4	3.4	0.8	1.3	0.2	0.4

Advanced Metrics

USG%	3PTA/FGA	FTA/FGA	TS%	eFG%	3PT%
17.1	0.240	0.298	0.501	0.456	0.291

AST%	TOV%	OREB%	DREB%	STL%	BLK%
9.2	12.1	3.1	12.7	2.0	1.2

PER	ORTG	DRTG	WS/48	VOL
10.90	99.9	107.2	0.056	N/A

- Drafted by Orlando in the second round with the 35th overall pick
- Struggled overall at Summer League, needs additional seasoning in the G-League
- Played with high energy on defense, showed promise as an on-ball defender, active to get steals, rotate to block shots and grab defensive rebounds
- Had trouble adjusting to a low usage role, shot below 30% from the field, did not make a three, committed turnovers at a high rate

Isaiah Briscoe

		Height	Weight	Cap #	Years Left
		6'3"	224	$0.838M	3

Baseline Basic Stats

MPG	PTS	AST	REB	BLK	STL
20.0	6.6	1.9	3.3	0.2	0.7

Advanced Metrics

USG%	3PTA/FGA	FTA/FGA	TS%	eFG%	3PT%
15.0	0.216	0.255	0.465	0.439	0.334

AST%	TOV%	OREB%	DREB%	STL%	BLK%
15.4	12.3	3.3	13.2	1.9	0.4

PER	ORTG	DRTG	WS/48	VOL	
12.26	91.9	81.3	0.110	0.675	

- Played with BC Kalev in Estonia last season, stats translated from the Estonian KML
- Solid playmaking skills, was turnover prone at Summer League
- Mainly relied on slashing to the rim to finish inside or draw fouls
- Made 39% of his threes in Estonia, but struggled with his outside shot at Summer League
- Energetic defensive point guard, uses active hands to get steals, rebounds very well for his size, decent on-ball defender

ATLANTA HAWKS

Last Season: 24 – 58, Missed the Playoffs

Offensive Rating: 105.0, 26th in NBA   Defensive Rating: 110.6, 21st in NBA

Primary Executive: Travis Schlenk, General Manager and Head of Basketball Operations

Head Coach: Lloyd Pierce

Key Roster Changes

Subtractions
Dennis Schroder, trade
Mike Muscala, trade
Damion Lee, free agency
Malcolm Delaney, free agency
Jaylen Morris, waived
Antonius Cleveland, waived
Isaiah Taylor, waived

Additions
Trae Young, draft
Kevin Huerter, draft
Omari Spellman, draft
Jeremy Lin, trade
Justin Anderson, trade
Alex Len, free agency
Vince Carter, free agency
Daniel Hamilton, free agency

RAFER Projected Win Total: 24.8

Projected Best Five-Man Unit
1. Jeremy Lin
2. Kent Bazemore
3. Taurean Prince
4. John Collins
5. Alex Len

Other Rotation Players
Trae Young
Dewayne Dedmon
Justin Anderson
Kevin Huerter
Omari Spellman
Vince Carter
Tyler Dorsey

Remaining Roster

- DeAndre' Bembry
- Miles Plumlee
- Daniel Hamilton
- Alex Poythress, 25, 6'7", 238, Kentucky (Two-Way)
- Jaylen Adams, 22, 6'2", 190, St. Bonaventure (Two-Way)
- Thomas Robinson, 27, 6'10", 237, Kansas (Exhibit 10)

Season Forecast

The Atlanta Hawks have officially turned the page on the Mike Budenholzer era, as they allowed him to leave for Milwaukee this summer. Right now, they are beginning to launch a new rebuilding project under new head coach, Lloyd Pierce, a former assistant with the Philadelphia 76ers. Pierce was part of Philadelphia's rebuilding project from the beginning, so it's very likely that the process will follow a similar pattern in Atlanta. Specifically, they are likely to provide ample playing time and developmental opportunities to their young players while shuffling around other pieces on the roster to either add assets or shed payroll. In all likelihood, the Hawks will remain at the bottom of the NBA's standings to position themselves for a high draft pick in the 2019 NBA Draft.

From a personnel standpoint, the Hawks made a very bold decision to essentially pass on a more polished prospect in Luka Doncic in favor of trading down for Trae Young. After all, Doncic was rated by some as the top overall prospect in the last draft and could have been a fit for them as a primary ball handler. However, they decided to make the move to acquire Young and an additional draft pick with the intention of finding pieces to build a team in the image of the Golden State Warriors, as that was where GM Travis Schlenk and Pierce had previously worked together in 2010 to 2011. Even with this in mind, the Hawks are very far from realizing anything close to this vision because Young and their other young players are still unpolished and in need of some serious development. Offensively, they showed promise at Summer League of being a unit that could be effective at using ball movement to generate open shots. If Young lets the game come to him and plays with more of a pass-first mentality, his development could be accelerated because he displayed great vision and passing skills in Vegas this past July. From there, John Collins could provide them with some effective inside scoring using his abilities as a roll man in pick-and-roll situations and Omari Spellman could space the floor as a stretch big. Finally, though he was unable to play in Vegas due to injury, Kevin Huerter could give them another decent perimeter shooter. Defensively, they are likely to struggle mightily because their rotation will likely feature a lot of younger players and young teams tend to struggle to pick up defensive rotation schemes. Also, the veterans that they brought in don't really have much of a defensive reputation at their current career stage, so it's not likely that their defense will improve much, if at all. Overall, winning is not going to be much of a priority with the Hawks this season and they will probably be one of the worst teams in the league. Their season would be considered a success if their younger core players can establish some strengths to serve as building blocks for future improvement down the line.

Veterans

Kent Bazemore

	Height	Weight	Cap #	Years Left
	6'5"	201	$18.090M	Player Option

Similar at Age 28

		Season	SIMsc
1	Bobby Phills	1997-98	919.5
2	Rodney Stuckey	2014-15	914.3
3	Bob Sura	2001-02	910.8
4	Derek Anderson	2002-03	907.5
5	Nick Anderson	1995-96	905.5
6	Devin Brown	2006-07	905.2
7	Aaron McKie	2000-01	905.1
8	Voshon Lenard	2001-02	903.8
9	Ben Gordon	2011-12	903.1
10	Kerry Kittles	2002-03	899.5

Baseline Basic Stats

MPG	PTS	AST	REB	BLK	STL
29.7	12.1	3.1	3.6	0.4	1.2

Advanced Metrics

USG%	3PTA/FGA	FTA/FGA	TS%	eFG%	3PT%
20.3	0.388	0.267	0.523	0.480	0.358

AST%	TOV%	OREB%	DREB%	STL%	BLK%
17.3	14.6	2.4	12.1	2.3	1.6

PER	ORTG	DRTG	WS/48	VOL	
13.41	101.5	106.3	0.072	0.275	

- Had a career best season at age-28, missed the last month of the season due to a bone bruise in his right knee
- Took on a higher usage role, increased his Assist Percentage, also was a bit more turnover prone
- Scored efficiently by shooting a career high 39.4% on threes, got to the free throw line at a higher rate
- Most effective off the ball as a spot-up shooter that could run off screens and cut to the rim
- Solid on-ball wing defender, active to contest shots, gets steals at a high rate, good defensive rebounding wing player

Taurean Prince

	Height	Weight	Cap #	Years Left
	6'8"	220	$2.527M	Team Option

Similar at Age 23

		Season	SIMsc
1	Sasha Pavlovic	2006-07	951.1
2	Mike Miller	2003-04	940.4
3	Cleanthony Early	2014-15	934.3
4	James Posey	1999-00	928.9
5	Jumaine Jones	2002-03	924.7
6	Wilson Chandler	2010-11	924.5
7	Mike Dunleavy Jr.	2003-04	924.1
8	Omri Casspi	2011-12	923.4
9	Rodney Hood	2015-16	922.9
10	Danilo Gallinari	2011-12	919.1

Baseline Basic Stats

MPG	PTS	AST	REB	BLK	STL
29.2	12.4	2.2	4.5	0.5	0.9

Advanced Metrics

USG%	3PTA/FGA	FTA/FGA	TS%	eFG%	3PT%
20.5	0.455	0.221	0.544	0.506	0.369

AST%	TOV%	OREB%	DREB%	STL%	BLK%
12.4	13.3	3.0	14.7	1.7	1.5

PER	ORTG	DRTG	WS/48	VOL	
13.48	103.9	108.7	0.068	0.326	

- Improved in his second season, started all 82 games for Atlanta last season
- Increased his scoring efficiency in a higher volume role, made 38.5% of his threes, showed improved passing skills
- Better in motion than as a stationary player, excelled at coming off screens or cutting to the rim
- Tasked to defend both forward spots, slightly below average as a stay-at-home position defender
- Better at handling wing players, solid rebounder

John Collins

	Height	Weight	Cap #	Years Left
	6'10"	235	$2.299M	2 Team Options

Similar at Age 20

		Season	SIMsc
1	Derrick Favors	2011-12	924.5
2	Andris Biedrins	2006-07	914.1
3	Jonas Valanciunas	2012-13	911.9
4	Andray Blatche	2006-07	907.1
5	Tyson Chandler	2002-03	903.3
6	J.J. Hickson	2008-09	903.0
7	Jackie Butler	2005-06	900.9
8	Aaron Gordon	2015-16	899.5
9	Nikola Jokic	2015-16	899.5
10	Serge Ibaka	2009-10	895.7

Baseline Basic Stats

MPG	PTS	AST	REB	BLK	STL
25.2	10.4	1.2	7.4	1.2	0.7

Advanced Metrics

USG%	3PTA/FGA	FTA/FGA	TS%	eFG%	3PT%
19.4	0.049	0.326	0.601	0.572	0.338

AST%	TOV%	OREB%	DREB%	STL%	BLK%
8.9	12.9	10.4	22.4	1.3	3.2

PER	ORTG	DRTG	WS/48	VOL	
19.15	116.7	105.3	0.161	0.326	

- Excellent in his rookie season, was named to the All-Rookie second team
- Played very well on offense, excelled at scoring inside of three feet, frequently crashed the offensive glass
- Most effective at cutting to the basket or rolling to the rim
- Flashed some stretch potential by making threes at an above break-even rate
- Very good defensive rebounder and shot blocker, played decent position defense

Dewayne Dedmon

	Height	Weight	Cap #	Years Left
	7'0"	255	$6.300M	0

Similar at Age 28

		Season	SIMsc
1	Timofey Mozgov	2014-15	898.5
2	Paul Mokeski	1984-85	896.5
3	Samuel Dalembert	2009-10	893.7
4	Raef LaFrentz	2004-05	891.1
5	Joe Kleine	1989-90	887.8
6	Nick Collison	2008-09	887.6
7	Marcin Gortat	2012-13	887.4
8	Kelvin Cato	2002-03	886.6
9	Spencer Hawes	2016-17	883.6
10	Blair Rasmussen	1990-91	882.0

Baseline Basic Stats

MPG	PTS	AST	REB	BLK	STL
21.1	7.1	0.8	5.7	0.9	0.5

Advanced Metrics

USG%	3PTA/FGA	FTA/FGA	TS%	eFG%	3PT%
15.5	0.143	0.242	0.580	0.553	0.360

AST%	TOV%	OREB%	DREB%	STL%	BLK%
6.9	14.4	8.5	24.9	1.2	3.2

PER	ORTG	DRTG	WS/48	VOL	
14.54	111.3	104.8	0.116	0.358	

- Solid in his fifth season in the NBA, production still at a level above his career averages
- Effective in a completely different role in Atlanta as a stretch big after being a rim runner with other teams
- Took threes in much greater frequency and converted them at almost a league average percentage
- Excellent rebounder, shot blocking rates have declined in each of the last three seasons, below average position defender

Alex Len

	Height	Weight	Cap #	Years Left
	7'1"	255	$4.146M	2

Similar at Age 24

		Season	SIMsc
1	Tyler Zeller	2013-14	932.5
2	Sam Bowie	1985-86	919.5
3	Jamaal Magloire	2002-03	917.3
4	Felton Spencer	1991-92	916.2
5	Chris Mihm	2003-04	915.1
6	Marc Gasol	2008-09	914.0
7	Brendan Haywood	2003-04	913.1
8	Blair Rasmussen	1986-87	907.1
9	Andrew Bogut	2008-09	903.9
10	Nene Hilario	2006-07	903.6

Baseline Basic Stats

MPG	PTS	AST	REB	BLK	STL
25.2	9.8	1.1	7.0	1.3	0.5

Advanced Metrics

USG%	3PTA/FGA	FTA/FGA	TS%	eFG%	3PT%
17.7	0.009	0.461	0.575	0.528	0.268

AST%	TOV%	OREB%	DREB%	STL%	BLK%
7.7	13.9	11.0	23.7	1.0	3.8

PER	ORTG	DRTG	WS/48	VOL	
17.55	114.4	106.9	0.133	0.339	

- Had a career best season in his fifth year in the NBA at age 24
- Played a lower usage role, posted the best True Shooting Percentage of his career last season
- Excelled as a rim runner, displayed above average post-up skills, frequently crashed the offensive glass
- Cut his turnover rate significantly and showed improved passing skills
- Very good rebounder and shot blocker, consistently below average as a position defender

Jeremy Lin

	Height	Weight	Cap #	Years Left
	6'3"	200	$13.768M	0

Similar at Age 29

		Season	SIMsc
1	Andrew Toney	1986-87	898.8
2	Ben Gordon	2012-13	894.8
3	Sam Cassell	1998-99	893.1
4	John Crotty	1998-99	876.8
5	Ricky Sobers	1981-82	876.5
6	Doug Overton	1998-99	875.9
7	Steve Francis	2006-07	871.8
8	Jarrett Jack	2012-13	867.6
9	Ramon Sessions	2015-16	867.4
10	Robert Pack	1998-99	865.5

Baseline Basic Stats

MPG	PTS	AST	REB	BLK	STL
24.9	11.5	4.1	2.3	0.2	0.8

Advanced Metrics

USG%	3PTA/FGA	FTA/FGA	TS%	eFG%	3PT%
24.6	0.244	0.349	0.541	0.469	0.388

AST%	TOV%	OREB%	DREB%	STL%	BLK%
26.4	15.7	1.3	6.9	1.3	0.6

PER	ORTG	DRTG	WS/48	VOL	
14.45	105.1	112.2	0.074	0.594	

- Missed most of the last two seasons due to injuries to his back, hamstring and a ruptured patella tendon in right knee
- Historically, a slashing point guard that draws fouls at a high rate and has good playmaking skills
- Solid pick-and-roll ball handler when healthy
- Can keep defenses honest by knocking down threes at a rate that hovers around league average
- Decent position defender before the injuries, uncertain if his lateral quickness is affected
- In the season prior to last year, he showed that he could occasionally guard shorter wing players, gets steals at an above average rate

Justin Anderson

	Height	Weight	Cap #	Years Left
	6'6"	228	$2.516M	0

Similar at Age **24**

		Season	SIMsc
1	Lazar Hayward	2010-11	948.5
2	Chase Budinger	2012-13	932.9
3	Quincy Pondexter	2012-13	924.4
4	Carlos Delfino	2006-07	923.4
5	Kelenna Azubuike	2007-08	921.2
6	Cartier Martin	2008-09	914.7
7	Eric Piatkowski	1994-95	912.8
8	Brian Cook	2004-05	912.0
9	James Jones	2004-05	911.2
10	Jarvis Hayes	2005-06	909.6

Baseline Basic Stats

MPG	PTS	AST	REB	BLK	STL
20.2	7.6	1.1	3.1	0.3	0.6

Advanced Metrics

USG%	3PTA/FGA	FTA/FGA	TS%	eFG%	3PT%
18.5	0.462	0.230	0.537	0.500	0.337

AST%	TOV%	OREB%	DREB%	STL%	BLK%
8.5	9.7	4.6	14.6	1.5	1.1

PER	ORTG	DRTG	WS/48	VOL	
12.91	107.4	108.3	0.098	0.423	

- On the fringes of Philadelphia's rotation last season, missed parts of the season due to shin splints and a sprained right ankle
- Efficient in a low volume role, 76.6% of his shots were either at the rim or behind the three-point line
- Made 67.2% of his shots inside of three feet, just below break-even on threes
- Only effective last season as a cutter, ranked by the NBA in the 93rd percentile on a per-possession basis
- Decent on-ball wing defender, mainly a stay-at-home guy, good rebounder for his size

Vince Carter

	Height	Weight	Cap #	Years Left
	6'6"	215	$2.394M	0

Similar at Age **41**

No Comps Available

Baseline Basic Stats

MPG	PTS	AST	REB	BLK	STL
19.0	6.8	1.5	2.5	0.3	0.6

Advanced Metrics

USG%	3PTA/FGA	FTA/FGA	TS%	eFG%	3PT%
12.4	1.000	0.201	0.524	0.494	0.000

AST%	TOV%	OREB%	DREB%	STL%	BLK%
8.5	12.5	2.7	16.7	1.3	2.2

PER	ORTG	DRTG	WS/48	VOL	
10.43	104.2	114.8	0.045	0.666	

- The only wing player to play in the NBA in his age-41 season in the modern three-point era
- Projection extremely volatile because only big guys have played at this age, no reliable comps
- Projected stats are not especially reliable as a result, some fluky rate stats due to the rarity of his profile
- Low usage spot-up shooter at this advanced stage of his career
- Has been an above break-even three-point shooter over the last four seasons
- Still can run the floor to finish plays in transition
- Effective in pick-and-roll situations as both the ball handler and screener last season in a small sample of possessions
- Showed an ability to defend fours as well as wing players
- Slightly below average on-ball defender due to his diminishing lateral quickness
- Posted high Steal, Block and Defensive Rebound Percentages last season

Tyler Dorsey

	Height	Weight	Cap #	Years Left
	6'5"	183	$1.378M	0

Similar at Age 21

		Season	SIMsc
1	Zach LaVine	2016-17	929.8
2	Jeremy Lamb	2013-14	924.2
3	Marco Belinelli	2007-08	923.6
4	Evan Fournier	2013-14	921.3
5	Manny Harris	2010-11	919.3
6	Dante Exum	2016-17	910.1
7	Terrence Ross	2012-13	908.2
8	Daequan Cook	2008-09	897.4
9	Patrick McCaw	2016-17	893.1
10	Kentavious Caldwell-Pope	2014-15	890.9

Baseline Basic Stats

MPG	PTS	AST	REB	BLK	STL
21.5	9.2	1.4	2.4	0.1	0.7

Advanced Metrics

USG%	3PTA/FGA	FTA/FGA	TS%	eFG%	3PT%
18.7	0.387	0.216	0.535	0.502	0.367

AST%	TOV%	OREB%	DREB%	STL%	BLK%
11.5	9.5	1.9	10.8	1.4	0.4

PER	ORTG	DRTG	WS/48	VOL	
11.49	106.3	111.8	0.066	0.303	

- On the fringes of Atlanta's rotation last season, played 974 minutes

- Moderate usage player, showed decent playmaking skills, struggled with shooting efficiency

- Took a lot of lower percentage mid-range shots, but shot just over the league average on threes

- Had some success in spot-up situations and when coming off screens

- Could also use the threat of his shot to occasionally get to the rim in isolation situations

- Was hidden in favorable matchups, played passable position defense, solid defensive rebounder

DeAndre' Bembry

	Height	Weight	Cap #	Years Left
	6'6"	210	$1.635M	Team Option

Similar at Age 23

		Season	SIMsc
1	John Salmons	2002-03	924.8
2	Thabo Sefolosha	2007-08	918.2
3	Mardy Collins	2007-08	916.6
4	Bryce Dejean-Jones	2015-16	915.1
5	James Anderson	2012-13	913.3
6	Mike Sanders	1983-84	905.7
7	Kevin Loder	1982-83	902.2
8	Darrun Hilliard	2016-17	901.3
9	Landry Fields	2011-12	901.2
10	Reece Gaines	2003-04	900.2

Baseline Basic Stats

MPG	PTS	AST	REB	BLK	STL
21.7	7.1	1.9	3.2	0.3	0.9

Advanced Metrics

USG%	3PTA/FGA	FTA/FGA	TS%	eFG%	3PT%
16.5	0.239	0.222	0.512	0.489	0.289

AST%	TOV%	OREB%	DREB%	STL%	BLK%
13.2	16.2	3.4	13.5	2.0	1.3

PER	ORTG	DRTG	WS/48	VOL	
10.62	98.0	108.3	0.040	0.474	

- Played sparingly for the Hawks last season, has only played 826 total minutes in two seasons
- Lower usage player with some playmaking skills, but highly turnover prone
- Does not score efficiently, a below 60% free throw shooter, inconsistent at finishing close shots
- Shot an above average percentage on threes in a limited number of attempts
- Solid defensive potential, above average on-ball wing defender
- Active in help defense, gets steals and blocks at a high rate, very good defensive rebounder

Miles Plumlee

	Height	Weight	Cap #	Years Left
	6'10"	245	$12.500M	1

Similar at Age **29**

		Season	SIMsc
1	Emeka Okafor	2011-12	936.2
2	Brian Skinner	2005-06	935.0
3	Clemon Johnson	1985-86	924.4
4	Art Long	2001-02	920.1
5	Corie Blount	1997-98	918.6
6	Mark Bryant	1994-95	916.9
7	Melvin Turpin	1989-90	916.7
8	Alan Henderson	2001-02	915.4
9	Andrew DeClercq	2002-03	913.4
10	Chris Wilcox	2011-12	907.8

Baseline Basic Stats

MPG	PTS	AST	REB	BLK	STL
17.7	4.9	0.7	4.6	0.6	0.4

Advanced Metrics

USG%	3PTA/FGA	FTA/FGA	TS%	eFG%	3PT%
13.1	0.002	0.345	0.542	0.519	0.018

AST%	TOV%	OREB%	DREB%	STL%	BLK%
6.1	18.7	9.8	18.3	1.2	2.6

PER	ORTG	DRTG	WS/48	VOL
10.97	104.8	108.2	0.072	0.281

- A fringe rotation player for Atlanta, played 918 minutes last season
- Very low usage rim runner that scores on dunks and other close shots, will draw fouls, but struggles to make free throws
- Decent rebounder on both ends, can block shots, but block rates have declined significantly in the last two seasons
- Middling as an overall position defender due to limitations in mobility

Daniel Hamilton

	Height	Weight	Cap #	Years Left
	6'7"	195	$1.349M	0

Similar at Age 22

		Season	SIMsc
1	Tim Quarterman	2016-17	855.5
2	Myron Brown	1991-92	832.2
3	Kendall Marshall	2013-14	828.5
4	Marco Belinelli	2008-09	824.2
5	Jeremy Richardson	2006-07	823.0
6	D.J. Kennedy	2011-12	822.7
7	Caris LeVert	2016-17	821.5
8	E'Twaun Moore	2011-12	808.6
9	Vander Blue	2014-15	808.5
10	Devyn Marble	2014-15	806.3

Baseline Basic Stats

MPG	PTS	AST	REB	BLK	STL
17.7	7.1	2.0	2.2	0.2	0.6

Advanced Metrics

USG%	3PTA/FGA	FTA/FGA	TS%	eFG%	3PT%
20.1	0.378	0.138	0.527	0.503	0.377

AST%	TOV%	OREB%	DREB%	STL%	BLK%
32.6	14.1	1.9	15.1	1.9	0.6

PER	ORTG	DRTG	WS/48	VOL
16.36	112.0	108.1	0.134	0.465

- Played on a two-way contract last season for Oklahoma City, spent most of the season with their G-League affiliate
- Took on a high usage role in the G-League, posted a very high Assist Percentage, but was extremely turnover prone
- Scored in volume, got to the foul line at a high rate and made a lot of free throws
- Three-point percentage dropped significantly to well below break-even
- Decent defensively in the G-League, uncertain if it will translate in the NBA, excellent rebounder for his size

Newcomers

Trae Young

	Height	Weight	Cap #	Years Left
	6'2"	180	$5.356M	1 + 2 TO

Baseline Basic Stats

MPG	PTS	AST	REB	BLK	STL
32.1	13.8	5.5	3.1	0.1	1.1

Advanced Metrics

USG%	3PTA/FGA	FTA/FGA	TS%	eFG%	3PT%
22.9	0.294	0.238	0.503	0.462	0.336

AST%	TOV%	OREB%	DREB%	STL%	BLK%
29.0	16.1	2.2	9.1	1.8	0.4

PER	ORTG	DRTG	WS/48	VOL
14.25	100.7	111.2	0.040	N/A

- Drafted by Dallas with the 5th overall pick, then traded to Atlanta
- Mixed overall showing in two Summer Leagues, fared much better in Las Vegas than he did in Utah
- Excelled as a passer, but was still somewhat turnover prone
- Shot very well when he wasn't forcing his offense, made 38.7% of his threes in Las Vegas
- Played with high effort of the defensive end, but appeared to be below average as a position defender
- Effective at playing passing lanes and using active hands to get steals

Kevin Huerter

	Height	Weight	Cap #	Years Left
	6'7"	190	$2.251M	1 + 2 TO

Baseline Basic Stats

MPG	PTS	AST	REB	BLK	STL
21.8	8.0	1.9	2.5	0.2	0.6

Advanced Metrics

USG%	3PTA/FGA	FTA/FGA	TS%	eFG%	3PT%
19.3	0.304	0.239	0.486	0.445	0.339

AST%	TOV%	OREB%	DREB%	STL%	BLK%
14.1	13.0	2.9	10.0	1.5	0.8

PER	ORTG	DRTG	WS/48	VOL
11.82	102.4	110.6	0.049	N/A

- Drafted by Atlanta in the first round with the 19th overall pick
- Missed Summer League due to surgery to repair torn ligaments in his right hand
- Projects to eventually become an outside shooting threat with a solid ability to move off the ball
- Has decent passing skills, but is a little turnover prone
- Defensive ability is uncertain, has more athleticism than initially expected, may still have to be hidden in favorable matchups

Omari Spellman

	Height	Weight	Cap #	Years Left
	6'9"	245	$1.620M	1 + 2 TO

Baseline Basic Stats

MPG	PTS	AST	REB	BLK	STL
15.7	6.1	0.6	3.7	0.5	0.3

Advanced Metrics

USG%	3PTA/FGA	FTA/FGA	TS%	eFG%	3PT%
19.2	0.122	0.247	0.515	0.481	0.337

AST%	TOV%	OREB%	DREB%	STL%	BLK%
6.0	11.9	9.6	18.0	1.2	2.5

PER	ORTG	DRTG	WS/48	VOL
13.62	104.5	107.5	0.069	N/A

- Drafted by Atlanta in the first round with the 30th overall pick
- Solid performance at Summer League
- Flashed better than expected defensive potential, decent position defender with above average mobility
- Solid defensive rebounder that could block shots, used active hands to get steals
- Showed more advanced passing skills, struggled with his shooting efficiency, had trouble adjusting to the longer NBA three-point line

CHICAGO BULLS

Last Season: 27 – 55, Missed the Playoffs

Offensive Rating: 103.8, 28th in NBA

Defensive Rating: 110.9, 24th in NBA

Primary Executive: Gar Forman, General Manager

Head Coach: Fred Hoiberg

Key Roster Changes

Subtractions
Jerian Grant, trade
Noah Vonleh, free agency
David Nwaba, free agency
Sean Kilpatrick, waived
Paul Zipser, waived

Additions
Wendell Carter, Jr., draft
Chandler Hutchison, draft
Antonius Cleveland, waivers
Jabari Parker, free agency

RAFER Projected Win Total: 22.1

Projected Best Five-Man Unit
1. Kris Dunn
2. Justin Holiday
3. Jabari Parker
4. Lauri Markkanen
5. Wendell Carter, Jr.

Other Rotation Players
Zach LaVine
Robin Lopez
Denzel Valentine
Bobby Portis
Chandler Hutchison

Remaining Roster

- Antonio Blakeney
- Cameron Payne
- Cristiano Felicio
- Omer Asik
- Antonius Cleveland (non-guaranteed)
- Ryan Arcidiacono (partially guaranteed)
- Derrick Walton, Jr. (non-guaranteed)
- JaKarr Sampson (partially guaranteed) - not profiled, signed right before the book was finalized
- Rawle Alkins, 21, 6'5", 220, Arizona (Two-Way)

Season Forecast

Though the Chicago Bulls are still in the middle of a rebuild, the team decided to commit to its young core by matching Sacramento's offer sheet to Zach LaVine to lock him up for the next four years. Then, the Bulls signed Chicago native, Jabari Parker to potentially give their rotation a boost. However, his fit is unclear because the team intends to use him as a three when he's spent the bulk of his career as a four. If he adjusts to the position switch, Chicago could improve incrementally, but they'll likely still be out of the playoff mix. In all probability, the Bulls will spend another season at the bottom of the standings in the Eastern Conference with the hope that they can get flashes of potential from Lauri Markkanen and Wendell Carter, Jr. while positioning themselves for a high pick in the next draft.

On paper, Chicago's offense seems like it could improve with the addition of Parker and a full season of LaVine to go along with their two young big men. However, Parker and LaVine are very high usage players that tend to dominate the ball, so the team's offensive flow and ball movement may be disrupted a bit because both players have displayed ball stopper tendencies in the past. Also, distributing touches and shots could be a problem because Kris Dunn can be slow to make his decisions, which means that the ball isn't always going to be moved into positions where the team can effectively attack opposing defenses. This could negatively affect the team's big men because it could be harder for them to get quality touches either inside or in spot-up situations. On the positive side, Parker will give them another consistent outside shooter, so it could open up the floor a bit for his teammates. Most likely, the good and bad will cancel each other out and Chicago will probably score more points in volume, but still be rather inefficient. The defensive end is going to be a major concern because they'll be relying on a lot of young, untested players and neither Parker nor LaVine have established themselves as impact defenders. As a result, Carter will have to take on a lot of defensive responsibilities in his rookie season to serve as an anchor of their defense. He flashed solid potential with a strong performance at Summer League, but he still might not be fully ready for this role right now, as there are still some areas like positioning that he'll need to clean up. With the team's current set of personnel, the Bulls are likely to once again be a bottom third defensive team. Overall, Chicago is most likely set for another season as a lottery team, but they will have to figure out an identity to help them move forward. Right now, the styles of their ball dominant wing players clash a bit with their two young big men. If they can reconcile their stylistic differences and find a way to coexist, the Bulls could be a team to watch in the future. Otherwise, they may have to shuffle some pieces around to find an optimal core to make them a more competitive unit.

Veterans

Lauri Markkanen

	Height	Weight	Cap #	Years Left
	7'0"	230	$4.536M	2 Team Options

Similar at Age 20

		Season	SIMsc
1	Trey Lyles	2015-16	888.4
2	Bobby Portis	2015-16	875.8
3	Dirk Nowitzki	1998-99	870.4
4	Donte Greene	2008-09	868.8
5	Spencer Hawes	2008-09	868.4
6	Yi Jianlian	2007-08	867.3
7	Michael Beasley	2008-09	864.5
8	Ryan Anderson	2008-09	863.6
9	Domantas Sabonis	2016-17	862.7
10	Tim Thomas	1997-98	862.1

Baseline Basic Stats

MPG	PTS	AST	REB	BLK	STL
28.5	14.1	1.6	5.8	0.7	0.7

Advanced Metrics

USG%	3PTA/FGA	FTA/FGA	TS%	eFG%	3PT%
23.3	0.416	0.231	0.563	0.523	0.386

AST%	TOV%	OREB%	DREB%	STL%	BLK%
8.4	8.6	4.1	20.2	1.1	1.6

PER	ORTG	DRTG	WS/48	VOL
17.26	110.4	109.2	0.112	0.363

- Arguably Chicago's best player as a rookie, made the All-Rookie first team last season
- Moderate volume player, primarily used as a stretch big, shot just above league average on threes
- Mainly effective as a spot-up shooter and screener in pick-and-roll
- Good at coming off screens and cutting to the rim, below average on post-ups
- Below average position defender, limited rim protection skills, solid defensive rebounder

Kris Dunn

	Height	Weight	Cap #	Years Left
	6'4"	210	$4.221M	Team Option

Similar at Age 23

		Season	SIMsc
1	Thabo Sefolosha	2007-08	902.3
2	Jason Kidd*	1996-97	899.9
3	Orien Greene	2005-06	897.1
4	Tony Allen	2004-05	895.9
5	Jon Barry	1992-93	894.3
6	Baron Davis	2002-03	892.9
7	Doug Christie	1993-94	892.8
8	Cory Carr	1998-99	892.2
9	Randy Foye	2006-07	889.4
10	Shannon Brown	2008-09	888.5

Baseline Basic Stats

MPG	PTS	AST	REB	BLK	STL
24.8	9.7	3.5	3.3	0.3	1.2

Advanced Metrics

USG%	3PTA/FGA	FTA/FGA	TS%	eFG%	3PT%
20.5	0.294	0.239	0.510	0.478	0.337

AST%	TOV%	OREB%	DREB%	STL%	BLK%
25.7	16.1	2.4	13.6	2.8	1.3

PER	ORTG	DRTG	WS/48	VOL	
14.75	102.2	105.3	0.085	0.536	

- Showed considerable improvement after receiving ample playing time with Chicago
- Missed 30 games due to several injuries including a concussion, patellar tendinitis in his knee, a dislocated finger and a sprained toe
- Significantly increased his Assist Percentage, but was still rather turnover prone
- Shot distribution was almost even across the board, improved as a mid-range shooter and shot almost a break-even percentage on threes
- Could increase his scoring efficiency by getting to the rim more frequently
- High energy defender that rebounds well for his size and gets steals at a high rate
- Below average as a position defender, tends to gamble a bit too much

Zach LaVine

	Height	Weight	Cap #	Years Left
	6'5"	180	$19.500M	3

Similar at Age 22

		Season	SIMsc
1	Jeremy Lamb	2014-15	931.0
2	Jordan Clarkson	2014-15	918.1
3	Nick Young	2007-08	908.9
4	Rex Chapman	1989-90	907.8
5	Jordan Crawford	2010-11	902.6
6	Marco Belinelli	2008-09	900.5
7	Brandon Knight	2013-14	899.7
8	Richard Hamilton	2000-01	897.9
9	Evan Fournier	2014-15	897.7
10	Bradley Beal	2015-16	895.8

Baseline Basic Stats

MPG	PTS	AST	REB	BLK	STL
24.7	12.4	2.1	2.7	0.2	0.8

Advanced Metrics

USG%	3PTA/FGA	FTA/FGA	TS%	eFG%	3PT%
24.6	0.352	0.246	0.542	0.499	0.369

AST%	TOV%	OREB%	DREB%	STL%	BLK%
15.5	9.9	1.8	11.0	1.6	0.6

PER	ORTG	DRTG	WS/48	VOL
15.11	106.6	112.1	0.056	0.358

- Missed most of the first half season because he was still recovering from a torn ACL in his left knee in February 2017
- Missed the last month of this season due to patellar tendinitis in the same knee
- Took on a higher volume role, efficiency dropped, shooting percentages took a hit
- Typically a scoring guard with solid playmaking skills, break-even three-point shooter
- Attacking the basket more in Chicago, drew fouls at a high rate last season
- Most effective with the ball in his hands as a pick-and-roll ball handler and isolation player
- True defensive ability is uncertain, was hidden in favorable matchups in the past
- Increased his Defensive Rebound and Steal Percentage last season

Jabari Parker

	Height	Weight	Cap #	Years Left
	6'8"	235	$20.000M	1

Similar at Age **22**

		Season	SIMsc
1	Tobias Harris	2014-15	924.2
2	Rodney White	2002-03	922.7
3	Luol Deng	2007-08	913.3
4	Lamond Murray	1995-96	910.4
5	Dennis Scott	1990-91	909.4
6	Michael Redd	2001-02	909.1
7	Jeff Green	2008-09	906.2
8	T.J. Warren	2015-16	906.0
9	Michael Beasley	2010-11	904.9
10	Kirk Snyder	2005-06	903.3

Baseline Basic Stats

MPG	PTS	AST	REB	BLK	STL
26.4	12.2	1.6	4.8	0.4	0.8

Advanced Metrics

USG%	3PTA/FGA	FTA/FGA	TS%	eFG%	3PT%
22.4	0.231	0.224	0.548	0.517	0.374

AST%	TOV%	OREB%	DREB%	STL%	BLK%
11.5	9.9	5.4	15.7	1.7	1.2

PER	ORTG	DRTG	WS/48	VOL	
16.73	108.7	109.1	0.097	0.359	

- Has torn the ACL in his left knee twice in four years, missed the first half of this season while recovering from his second ACL tear
- Efficient in a high volume role, has developed into a good mid-range and three-point shooter
- Good pick-and-roll player that is effective as either the screener or ball handler
- Above average in spot-up situations, good at posting up smaller perimeter players
- Passing skills have improved over the last two seasons
- Defended both forward spots in Milwaukee, better at handling fours
- Below average position defender overall, solid defensive rebounder

Robin Lopez

	Height	Weight	Cap #	Years Left
	7'0"	255	$14.358M	0

Similar at Age **29**

		Season	SIMsc
1	Benoit Benjamin	1993-94	912.6
2	Andrew Lang	1995-96	904.4
3	Dave Corzine	1985-86	901.4
4	Blair Rasmussen	1991-92	900.6
5	Mark Blount	2004-05	900.0
6	Rasho Nesterovic	2005-06	897.1
7	Timofey Mozgov	2015-16	895.9
8	Sam Bowie	1990-91	892.7
9	Marcin Gortat	2013-14	891.8
10	Michael Olowokandi	2004-05	889.1

Baseline Basic Stats

MPG	PTS	AST	REB	BLK	STL
24.2	8.9	1.3	5.5	1.0	0.4

Advanced Metrics

USG%	3PTA/FGA	FTA/FGA	TS%	eFG%	3PT%
18.7	0.011	0.170	0.527	0.502	0.171

AST%	TOV%	OREB%	DREB%	STL%	BLK%
9.5	14.1	9.1	14.2	0.7	3.1

PER	ORTG	DRTG	WS/48	VOL
13.57	103.3	110.1	0.067	0.299

- Entering his age-30 season, production over the last two seasons is below his career averages
- Effective on offense in a moderate usage role, drawing fouls at a much lower rate, but made almost 73% of his shots inside of three feet
- Above average or better in post-up situations and scoring on put-backs
- Posted the highest Assist Percentage of his career
- Lack of mobility has made him a liability on defense, below average position defender
- Rebound percentages on both ends have dropped to career lows as well as his Block Percentage

Bobby Portis

	Height	Weight	Cap #	Years Left
	6'11"	230	$2.494M	0

Similar at Age 22

		Season	SIMsc
1	Charlie Villanueva	2006-07	932.5
2	Ersan Ilyasova	2009-10	914.1
3	Kelly Olynyk	2013-14	914.0
4	Tim Thomas	1999-00	908.1
5	Dario Saric	2016-17	907.5
6	Willy Hernangomez	2016-17	898.4
7	Donte Greene	2010-11	897.1
8	Drew Gooden	2003-04	896.9
9	Vladimir Radmanovic	2002-03	895.1
10	Tobias Harris	2014-15	894.0

Baseline Basic Stats

MPG	PTS	AST	REB	BLK	STL
23.3	10.9	1.3	5.3	0.5	0.6

Advanced Metrics

USG%	3PTA/FGA	FTA/FGA	TS%	eFG%	3PT%
22.9	0.258	0.213	0.542	0.510	0.356

AST%	TOV%	OREB%	DREB%	STL%	BLK%
10.6	10.4	7.8	20.4	1.4	1.5

PER	ORTG	DRTG	WS/48	VOL	
17.19	107.9	107.8	0.111	0.171	

- Had a career best season in his third year
- Took on a higher usage role with Chicago's second unit
- Good on the offensive glass, greatly improved playmaking skills
- Improved his outside shooting, very good from mid-range, became almost a league average three-point shooter
- Most effective as a post-up player and above average as a spot-up shooter
- Struggles at playing position defense on the interior, limited rim protection skills, very good rebounder

Justin Holiday

	Height	Weight	Cap #	Years Left
	6'6"	185	$4.385M	0

Similar at Age 28

		Season	SIMsc
1	Brent Barry	1999-00	927.2
2	Courtney Lee	2013-14	923.8
3	Wesley Person	1999-00	922.9
4	Marco Belinelli	2014-15	920.4
5	Rex Chapman	1995-96	919.4
6	Kerry Kittles	2002-03	912.3
7	Anthony Bowie	1991-92	912.1
8	Danny Green	2015-16	909.7
9	George McCloud	1995-96	904.9
10	Wayne Ellington	2015-16	904.5

Baseline Basic Stats

MPG	PTS	AST	REB	BLK	STL
25.4	9.7	2.0	2.9	0.3	0.9

Advanced Metrics

USG%	3PTA/FGA	FTA/FGA	TS%	eFG%	3PT%
17.0	0.551	0.180	0.534	0.502	0.363

AST%	TOV%	OREB%	DREB%	STL%	BLK%
10.9	10.7	1.7	11.9	1.8	1.1

PER	ORTG	DRTG	WS/48	VOL
11.75	104.5	108.7	0.067	0.268

- First season in the league as a regular starter for Chicago
- Productivity decreased due to being overextended in his role
- Decent stay-at-home on-ball wing defender, solid on the defensive boards
- Low volume spot-up shooter that limits turnovers, has some playmaking skills
- Almost a league average three-point shooter for the last two seasons

Denzel Valentine

	Height	Weight	Cap #	Years Left
	6'6"	212	$2.281M	Team Option

Similar at Age 24

		Season	SIMsc
1	James Anderson	2013-14	933.5
2	Kyle Korver	2005-06	919.2
3	Bill Walker	2011-12	918.0
4	Iman Shumpert	2014-15	916.0
5	Reggie Williams	2010-11	915.6
6	John Salmons	2003-04	912.9
7	Danny Green	2011-12	910.4
8	Anthony Morrow	2009-10	910.0
9	Terrence Ross	2015-16	908.8
10	Carlos Delfino	2006-07	908.7

Baseline Basic Stats

MPG	PTS	AST	REB	BLK	STL
24.8	9.6	1.7	3.4	0.4	0.8

Advanced Metrics

USG%	3PTA/FGA	FTA/FGA	TS%	eFG%	3PT%
17.8	0.551	0.131	0.535	0.513	0.381

AST%	TOV%	OREB%	DREB%	STL%	BLK%
13.9	12.1	2.2	15.5	1.6	0.9

PER	ORTG	DRTG	WS/48	VOL	
12.04	104.1	108.9	0.073	0.454	

- Increased his production in his second year, played starter level minutes for Chicago last season
- Dramatically improved as a shooter and playmaker in a low usage role
- Had success as a pick-and-roll ball handler last season
- Posted an Assist-to-Turnover ratio of almost 2.5, improved his Three-Point Percentage to 38.6% last season
- Decent on-ball defending wing, more of a stay-at-home position defender, solid rebounder

Antonio Blakeney

	Height	Weight	Cap #	Years Left
	6'4"	197	$1.349M	1

Similar at Age 21

		Season	SIMsc
1	Marco Belinelli	2007-08	914.7
2	Bracey Wright	2005-06	909.9
3	Malachi Richardson	2016-17	909.5
4	Shannon Brown	2006-07	908.7
5	Keyon Dooling	2001-02	896.9
6	Archie Goodwin	2015-16	894.5
7	Chris Carr	1995-96	891.5
8	Rashad McCants	2005-06	890.5
9	Doron Lamb	2012-13	890.3
10	Dion Waiters	2012-13	888.4

Baseline Basic Stats

MPG	PTS	AST	REB	BLK	STL
17.0	6.7	1.1	1.6	0.1	0.5

Advanced Metrics

USG%	3PTA/FGA	FTA/FGA	TS%	eFG%	3PT%
19.1	0.323	0.284	0.513	0.465	0.333

AST%	TOV%	OREB%	DREB%	STL%	BLK%
11.0	10.0	1.5	8.5	1.6	0.3

PER	ORTG	DRTG	WS/48	VOL	
10.35	102.3	111.2	0.031	0.200	

- Played on a two-way contract last season, spent most of the year with the Windy City Bulls in the G-League
- In the G-League, high volume scoring guard with decent playmaking skills
- Used penetration skills to finish inside or draw fouls, frequently shot threes at an above break-even rate
- Struggled to shoot efficiently in the NBA, percentages significantly lower across the board
- Below average position defender, struggled to handle taller wings, decent rebounding guard

Cameron Payne

	Height	Weight	Cap #	Years Left
	6'3"	185	$3.263M	0

Similar at Age 23

		Season	SIMsc
1	Chris Quinn	2006-07	941.1
2	Damon Jones	1999-00	932.7
3	J.R. Bremer	2003-04	928.6
4	Nolan Smith	2011-12	922.4
5	Quincy Douby	2007-08	919.2
6	Steve Nash	1997-98	916.5
7	A.J. Price	2009-10	915.6
8	Gerald Fitch	2005-06	914.8
9	Erick Green	2014-15	913.5
10	E'Twaun Moore	2012-13	912.7

Baseline Basic Stats

MPG	PTS	AST	REB	BLK	STL
18.8	7.4	2.4	1.9	0.1	0.7

Advanced Metrics

USG%	3PTA/FGA	FTA/FGA	TS%	eFG%	3PT%
19.6	0.433	0.125	0.504	0.482	0.367

AST%	TOV%	OREB%	DREB%	STL%	BLK%
22.8	12.4	2.2	9.4	1.9	0.8

PER	ORTG	DRTG	WS/48	VOL	
12.83	103.9	109.7	0.064	0.410	

- Missed most of the last two seasons due to multiple surgeries to repair a fractured right foot
- Showed improved playmaking and shooting skills in a small sample of games last season
- Shot more efficiently than he did in prior seasons, shot 38.5% on threes, still took a lot of low percentage mid-range shots
- Below average in most offensive situations, but good as a spot-up shooter last season
- Plays good position defense and will pressure his man to get steals
- May be physically limited due to his foot injury

Cristiano Felicio

	Height	Weight	Cap #	Years Left
	6'10"	275	$8.471M	2

Similar at Age 25

		Season	SIMsc
1	Vitaly Potapenko	2000-01	911.5
2	Eric Leckner	1991-92	905.2
3	Nick Collison	2005-06	898.1
4	Victor Alexander	1994-95	896.5
5	Todd MacCulloch	2000-01	891.6
6	Mike Brown	1988-89	891.5
7	Chuck Aleksinas	1984-85	890.2
8	Carl Landry	2008-09	889.2
9	Michael Bradley	2004-05	887.5
10	Mark Bryant	1990-91	886.6

Baseline Basic Stats

MPG	PTS	AST	REB	BLK	STL
20.0	6.5	0.7	4.9	0.5	0.4

Advanced Metrics

USG%	3PTA/FGA	FTA/FGA	TS%	eFG%	3PT%
14.3	0.006	0.377	0.571	0.537	0.080

AST%	TOV%	OREB%	DREB%	STL%	BLK%
7.0	15.1	9.8	17.5	1.1	1.8

PER	ORTG	DRTG	WS/48	VOL	
13.26	112.6	108.7	0.106	0.578	

- Per-minute effectiveness has declined in each of his three seasons, fringe rotation player for Chicago last season
- Extremely low volume rim runner that scores at close range, good as a roll man and cutter
- Draws fouls but his free throw attempt rate has been declining each year
- Below average overall interior defender with limited rim protection skills, also lacks mobility
- Rebound and block rates have decreased each season

Omer Asik

	Height	Weight	Cap #	Years Left
	7'0"	255	$11.287	Player Option

Similar at Age 31

		Season	SIMsc
1	Jarron Collins	2009-10	919.2
2	Joel Przybilla	2010-11	913.4
3	Greg Kite	1992-93	884.1
4	Kelvin Cato	2005-06	879.8
5	Etan Thomas	2009-10	874.2
6	Clemon Johnson	1987-88	873.0
7	Greg Dreiling	1994-95	870.5
8	Dennis Awtrey	1979-80	869.2
9	Joe Kleine	1992-93	868.5
10	Cherokee Parks	2003-04	867.6

Baseline Basic Stats

MPG	PTS	AST	REB	BLK	STL
11.9	1.9	0.3	3.1	0.4	0.2

Advanced Metrics

USG%	3PTA/FGA	FTA/FGA	TS%	eFG%	3PT%
9.2	0.002	0.536	0.438	0.415	-0.024

AST%	TOV%	OREB%	DREB%	STL%	BLK%
2.7	20.9	9.0	21.1	0.7	2.3

PER	ORTG	DRTG	WS/48	VOL	
6.04	91.4	107.4	0.034	0.179	

- Performance has rapidly declined over the course of the last four seasons, likely out of the NBA after this season
- Primarily a low volume rim runner when he was younger
- Deteriorating athleticism makes him unable to finish shots inside
- Severe lack of mobility makes him a liability on defense, no longer the shot blocker he once was
- Still a solid defensive rebounder in his current diminished state

Ryan Arcidiacono

	Height	Weight	Cap #	Years Left
	6'3"	188	$1.349M	0

Similar at Age 23

		Season	SIMsc
1	Kendall Marshall	2014-15	879.3
2	Steve Kerr	1988-89	878.2
3	Randolph Childress	1995-96	872.8
4	Daniel Ewing	2006-07	870.9
5	Corey Gaines	1988-89	869.9
6	Charles R. Jones	1998-99	868.3
7	Damon Jones	1999-00	867.8
8	Shabazz Napier	2014-15	867.0
9	Travis Diener	2005-06	864.4
10	Steve Blake	2003-04	864.0

Baseline Basic Stats

MPG	PTS	AST	REB	BLK	STL
16.5	5.1	2.3	1.4	0.1	0.5

Advanced Metrics

USG%	3PTA/FGA	FTA/FGA	TS%	eFG%	3PT%
12.1	0.650	0.153	0.540	0.515	0.343

AST%	TOV%	OREB%	DREB%	STL%	BLK%
20.3	18.8	0.7	8.0	1.7	0.1

PER	ORTG	DRTG	WS/48	VOL	
9.78	106.8	111.1	0.060	0.415	

- Played last season on a two-way contract, spent most of the year with the Windy City Bulls in the G-League
- Very low volume, pass-first point guard, good playmaker, somewhat turnover prone
- Efficient shooter at both the NBA and G-League levels, shot almost 44% on threes in two G-League seasons, made 80% of twos in the NBA last season
- Very effective in a small sample of possessions as a pick-and-roll ball handler, ranked by the NBA in the 98th percentile on a per-possession basis
- Aggressive defender, plays hard, can stay with opposing point guards, uses active hands to get steals at a fairly high rate

Antonius Cleveland

	Height	Weight	Cap #	Years Left
	6'6"	195	$1.378M	0

<u>Similar at Age</u> 23

		Season	SIMsc
1	Julyan Stone	2011-12	889.7
2	Jamie Watson	1995-96	885.7
3	Keith Askins	1990-91	873.2
4	Carey Scurry	1985-86	863.8
5	Sam Worthen	1980-81	860.5
6	Charles C. Smith	1998-99	859.8
7	Kyle Weaver	2009-10	858.1
8	Doug West	1990-91	856.1
9	David Thirdkill	1983-84	855.8
10	Pace Mannion	1983-84	855.7

Baseline Basic Stats

MPG	PTS	AST	REB	BLK	STL
16.0	5.1	1.4	2.3	0.3	0.7

Advanced Metrics

USG%	3PTA/FGA	FTA/FGA	TS%	eFG%	3PT%
13.6	0.225	0.324	0.534	0.492	0.588

AST%	TOV%	OREB%	DREB%	STL%	BLK%
9.3	18.0	3.3	9.8	2.3	2.2

PER	ORTG	DRTG	WS/48	VOL	
9.38	96.4	107.2	0.059	0.372	

- Initially played on a two-way contract with Dallas, but was claimed off waivers by Atlanta
- Contract for 2018-19 is not guaranteed
- Struggled to adjust to low volume offensive role, highly turnover prone, had trouble making shots from two-point range
- Had difficulties as an on-ball defender, showed promise as a help defender, posted a high Steal and Block Percentage

Derrick Walton, Jr.

	Height	Weight	Cap #	Years Left
	6'1"	189	$1.349M	1

Similar at Age **22**

		Season	SIMsc
1	R.J. Hunter	2015-16	861.8
2	Ronnie Price	2005-06	861.5
3	Isaiah Canaan	2013-14	857.2
4	J.R. Bremer	2002-03	851.8
5	Terry Rozier	2016-17	851.7
6	Damon Jones	1998-99	850.3
7	Joe Crispin	2001-02	841.6
8	A.J. Guyton	2000-01	838.9
9	Daniel Gibson	2008-09	837.1
10	E'Twaun Moore	2011-12	833.1

Baseline Basic Stats

MPG	PTS	AST	REB	BLK	STL
16.1	6.1	1.8	1.7	0.1	0.6

Advanced Metrics

USG%	3PTA/FGA	FTA/FGA	TS%	eFG%	3PT%
14.8	0.544	0.233	0.540	0.491	0.405

AST%	TOV%	OREB%	DREB%	STL%	BLK%
17.5	10.1	1.7	10.0	2.2	1.1

PER	ORTG	DRTG	WS/48	VOL
12.83	115.9	107.4	0.111	0.330

- Played on a two-way contract last season with Miami, spent most of the year with Sioux Falls in the G-League
- Contract for 2018-19 is not guaranteed
- Good playmaking skills, scored efficiently in the G-League by making 37.7% of his threes and 90.2% of his free throws, somewhat turnover prone
- Middling position defender, will pressure his man and use active hands to get steals at a solid rate

Newcomers

Wendell Carter, Jr.

	Height	Weight	Cap #	Years Left
	6'10"	259	$4.441M	1 + 2 TO

Baseline Basic Stats

MPG	PTS	AST	REB	BLK	STL
23.7	9.1	1.1	6.2	0.9	0.5

Advanced Metrics

USG%	3PTA/FGA	FTA/FGA	TS%	eFG%	3PT%
18.9	0.052	0.341	0.527	0.490	0.288

AST%	TOV%	OREB%	DREB%	STL%	BLK%
7.3	14.1	10.6	19.6	1.1	2.9

PER	ORTG	DRTG	WS/48	VOL
14.74	105.1	106.3	0.091	N/A

- Drafted by Chicago in the first round with the 7th overall pick
- Excellent performance at the Las Vegas Summer League
- Efficient scorer that got to the free throw line at a high rate
- Flashed some stretch potential by going 3-for-7 from the three-point line, also displayed good passing skills
- Played effective interior defense, good shot blocker, solid rebounder
- Used length and active hands to occasionally get steals

Chandler Hutchison

	Height	Weight	Cap #	Years Left
	6'7"	197	$1.992M	1 + 2 TO

Baseline Basic Stats

MPG	PTS	AST	REB	BLK	STL
19.3	7.7	1.7	2.7	0.2	0.8

Advanced Metrics

USG%	3PTA/FGA	FTA/FGA	TS%	eFG%	3PT%
20.6	0.144	0.315	0.502	0.456	0.328

AST%	TOV%	OREB%	DREB%	STL%	BLK%
14.5	14.3	5.4	10.8	2.1	0.9

PER	ORTG	DRTG	WS/48	VOL
12.75	100.8	108.5	0.019	N/A

- Drafted by Chicago in the first round with the 22nd overall pick
- Solid showing at Summer League this July
- Shot efficiently in a low volume role, made 8 out of 16 threes
- Drew fouls at a high rate, displayed solid playmaking skills for a wing player
- Struggled with turnovers, shot poorly from two-point range
- Decent on-ball defending wing player, more of a stay-at-home position defender, rebounded well on the defensive glass

PREVIEWING THE WESTERN CONFERENCE

RAFER Rankings

1. Golden State Warriors
2. Houston Rockets
3. Oklahoma City Thunder
4. Minnesota Timberwolves
5. Utah Jazz
6. San Antonio Spurs
7. New Orleans Pelicans
8. Los Angeles Lakers
9. Denver Nuggets
10. Los Angeles Clippers
11. Portland Trail Blazers
12. Dallas Mavericks
13. Memphis Grizzlies
14. Phoenix Suns
15. Sacramento Kings

Rosters are accurate as of September 10, 2018

GOLDEN STATE WARRIORS

<u>Last Season</u>: 58 – 24, 2017-18 NBA Champions

<u>Offensive Rating</u>: 113.6, 3rd in NBA

<u>Defensive Rating</u>: 107.6, 11th in NBA

<u>Primary Executive</u>: Bob Myers, President of Basketball Operations

<u>Head Coach</u>: Steve Kerr

Key Roster Changes

<u>Subtractions</u>	<u>Additions</u>
David West, free agency	Jacob Evans, draft
Zaza Pachulia, free agency	DeMarcus Cousins, free agency
JaVale McGee, free agency	Jonas Jerebko, free agency
Nick Young, free agency	

Note: Patrick McCaw was tendered a qualifying offer, still an unsigned restricted free agent

RAFER Projected Win Total: 61.1

<u>Projected Best Five-Man Unit</u>
1. Stephen Curry
2. Klay Thompson
3. Andre Iguodala
4. Kevin Durant
5. Draymond Green

<u>Other Rotation Players</u>
DeMarcus Cousins
Shaun Livingston
Kevon Looney
Jordan Bell
Jonas Jerebko

Remaining Roster

- Quinn Cook
- Damian Jones
- Jacob Evans
- Damion Lee, 26, 6'6", 210, Louisville (Two-Way)
- Danuel House, 25, 6'7", 207, Texas A&M (Exhibit 10)
- Marcus Derrickson, 22, 6'7", 250, Georgetown (Exhibit 10)
- Alfonzo McKinnie, 26, 6'8", 215, Wisconsin-Green Bay (Exhibit 10)

Season Forecast

The Golden State Warriors have been on an impressive run, winning three championships in the last four seasons. Things don't appear to be slowing down because the Warriors pounced on an opportunity to add four-time All-Star DeMarcus Cousins to an already loaded roster after he inexplicably received no offers on the first day of free agency. Cousins is recovering from an Achilles tear that he suffered in January of last season, so he'll likely join the team mid-season and Golden State has the luxury of bringing him along slowly because they have so much talent on their roster. Because of their combination of talent and continuity in the rest of the rotation, the Warriors will once again be the heavy favorite to win the title this coming season. If they can survive the regular season and stay healthy, they will likely come out of the Western Conference and add another title to their run of success. Otherwise, if any of their key players sustains a critical injury, it may open the door for another team to win the title because their core is a little older and their rotation isn't as deep as it once was.

Besides the obvious infusion of an All-Star level talent, the addition of Cousins will help Golden State keep Andre Iguodala fresh in the post-season. Iguodala is entering his age-35 season and he isn't the dynamic two-way player that he was in his younger days, but his role is still critical to the Warriors' success. Primarily, his presence in the team's closing unit gives them an additional quality wing defender to reduce the overall workloads of Klay Thompson and Kevin Durant. His role also gives the team maximum versatility on defense to switch screens and defend a variety of different lineups. If he isn't worn down at the end of the season, the Warriors can aggressively hold teams down on the defensive end to magnify the impact of their prolific offense. It's hard to say anything about the team's offense that hasn't been said already. In essence, Golden State will once again generate highly efficient offense with great player and ball movement with talent that includes up to five All-Stars, three of the league's best shooters and two league MVPs. The team's only weakness was that they seemed bored and disinterested in last year's regular season. Cousins' presence may work to sharpen the team's focus because everyone will have to make a slight adjustment to allow him to become a cohesive part of their rotation. Generally speaking, the Warriors are in a class by themselves and they are highly likely to win their fourth title in five years. There is some potential that this could be the last title from this group as its currently constituted because they will be pressed against the luxury tax with several key players up for new contracts either this summer or the next. With this in mind, Golden State could come into this season with a greater sense of urgency, leading to a stronger performance in the regular season and a deep championship run.

Veterans

Stephen Curry

	Height	Weight	Cap #	Years Left
	6'3"	185	$37.457M	3

Similar at Age **29**

		Season	SIMsc
1	Mike Conley	2016-17	893.1
2	Devin Harris	2012-13	882.2
3	Jeff Hornacek	1992-93	880.9
4	Jay Humphries	1991-92	880.7
5	Kenny Smith	1994-95	875.5
6	Deron Williams	2013-14	875.1
7	Gilbert Arenas	2010-11	873.4
8	Derek Harper	1990-91	872.7
9	John Starks	1994-95	871.3
10	Dell Curry	1993-94	870.4

Baseline Basic Stats

MPG	PTS	AST	REB	BLK	STL
30.6	16.8	5.0	3.3	0.2	1.3

Advanced Metrics

USG%	3PTA/FGA	FTA/FGA	TS%	eFG%	3PT%
27.1	0.484	0.287	0.603	0.551	0.387

AST%	TOV%	OREB%	DREB%	STL%	BLK%
27.5	13.2	2.5	11.6	2.3	0.4

PER	ORTG	DRTG	WS/48	VOL	
22.01	115.9	106.9	0.261	0.520	

- MVP level point guard entering his age-30 season, missed games due to multiple ankle sprains and a sprained MCL in his left knee
- Projection a bit undershot because there aren't many guards at Curry's size that have matched his level of production
- The NBA's most efficient shooter, led the league in True Shooting Percentage in two of the last three seasons, maintains efficiency at a very high volume
- Excels in every relevant offensive situation, 2nd in the NBA in points scored per game when coming off a screen
- Dynamic playmaker that has reduced his turnover rate
- Can be targeted on the defensive end, slightly below average as an on-ball defender
- Plays passing lanes, will get steals at a solid rate
- Posted the best Defensive Rebound Percentage of his career last season

Kevin Durant

	Height	Weight	Cap #	Years Left
	6'9"	215	$30.000M	Player Option

Similar at Age 29

		Season	SIMsc
1	Rasheed Wallace	2003-04	869.6
2	Larry Bird*	1985-86	869.1
3	Hedo Turkoglu	2008-09	865.8
4	Josh Smith	2014-15	864.4
5	Vince Carter	2005-06	864.2
6	Al Harrington	2009-10	861.4
7	Joe Johnson	2010-11	859.2
8	Carmelo Anthony	2013-14	858.4
9	Chris Bosh	2013-14	858.2
10	Jalen Rose	2001-02	857.2

Baseline Basic Stats

MPG	PTS	AST	REB	BLK	STL
35.0	21.1	4.1	6.6	0.8	1.2

Advanced Metrics

USG%	3PTA/FGA	FTA/FGA	TS%	eFG%	3PT%
27.4	0.308	0.316	0.599	0.547	0.382

AST%	TOV%	OREB%	DREB%	STL%	BLK%
21.5	11.8	2.7	18.8	1.4	2.6

PER	ORTG	DRTG	WS/48	VOL	
22.60	115.3	105.6	0.239	0.639	

- Dynamic MVP level talent, production still in line with his career averages, missed a few games last season due to a fractured rib
- Projection volatile and undershot, not many comps with Durant's body type and production level
- Elite scoring efficiency at a high usage rate, excellent shooter all over the floor, improved his playmaking skills in Golden State
- Very effective in virtually offensive situation
- Very good, versatile defender that guards multiple positions, excellent weak side shot blocker, solid rebounder

Klay Thompson

	Height	Weight	Cap #	Years Left
	6'7"	205	$18.989M	0

Similar at Age 27

		Season	SIMsc
1	Sean Elliott	1995-96	919.4
2	Rasual Butler	2006-07	918.0
3	Glen Rice	1994-95	915.2
4	Bojan Bogdanovic	2016-17	913.0
5	Wesley Johnson	2014-15	912.3
6	Steve Smith	1996-97	910.9
7	C.J. Miles	2014-15	910.8
8	Dale Ellis	1987-88	909.5
9	Wesley Person	1998-99	907.0
10	Josh Howard	2007-08	904.4

Baseline Basic Stats

MPG	PTS	AST	REB	BLK	STL
30.5	15.8	2.1	3.5	0.4	0.8

Advanced Metrics

USG%	3PTA/FGA	FTA/FGA	TS%	eFG%	3PT%
23.6	0.465	0.173	0.577	0.548	0.418

AST%	TOV%	OREB%	DREB%	STL%	BLK%
11.3	9.4	2.2	10.3	1.2	1.0

PER	ORTG	DRTG	WS/48	VOL
16.16	110.2	109.3	0.111	0.484

- Arguably the NBA's best two guard in the prime of his career
- Very efficient shooter in a higher volume role, excellent spot-up shooter
- Has made over 40% of his threes in each of his seven seasons in the NBA
- Led the NBA in most points scored per-game when coming off a screen
- Very good in dribble hand-off situations, above average isolation player
- Excellent on-ball wing defender, more of a stay-at-home guy, solid on the defensive glass

Draymond Green

	Height	Weight	Cap #	Years Left
	6'7"	230	$17.470M	1

Similar at Age **27**

		Season	SIMsc
1	Rick Fox	1996-97	889.2
2	Matt Barnes	2007-08	885.2
3	Carlos Delfino	2009-10	881.3
4	Jared Dudley	2012-13	878.2
5	Bryon Russell	1997-98	876.4
6	Morris Peterson	2004-05	868.5
7	Rodney Rogers	1998-99	863.8
8	Shandon Anderson	2000-01	862.4
9	John Salmons	2006-07	861.7
10	Andre Iguodala	2010-11	860.5

Baseline Basic Stats

MPG	PTS	AST	REB	BLK	STL
29.7	11.0	3.0	5.3	0.6	1.2

Advanced Metrics

USG%	3PTA/FGA	FTA/FGA	TS%	eFG%	3PT%
17.3	0.423	0.287	0.550	0.513	0.338

AST%	TOV%	OREB%	DREB%	STL%	BLK%
22.2	18.2	4.3	18.4	2.1	2.2

PER	ORTG	DRTG	WS/48	VOL	
15.44	110.1	103.8	0.124	0.318	

- Three-time All-Star in his prime, coming off his fourth straight appearance on the NBA's All-Defensive team
- Versatile defender that can defend on the perimeter and inside
- Active help defender that posts high Steal and Block Percentages, good defensive rebounder
- Low usage player with excellent playmaking skills, but a little turnover prone
- Efficient at converting shots inside, but his three-point shooting is below break-even
- Most effectively used as a cutter, below average in other offensive situations

DeMarcus Cousins

	Height	Weight	Cap #	Years Left
	6'11"	270	$5.337M	0

Similar at Age 27

		Season	SIMsc
1	Blake Griffin	2016-17	847.9
2	Tim Duncan	2003-04	836.8
3	Chris Kaman	2009-10	832.2
4	Brook Lopez	2015-16	830.3
5	Kevin Love	2015-16	827.2
6	Chris Webber	2000-01	826.8
7	Al Jefferson	2011-12	821.6
8	Tom Gugliotta	1996-97	820.1
9	Andray Blatche	2013-14	819.0
10	Jermaine O'Neal	2005-06	816.1

Baseline Basic Stats

MPG	PTS	AST	REB	BLK	STL
32.4	17.1	2.7	8.8	1.3	1.0

Advanced Metrics

USG%	3PTA/FGA	FTA/FGA	TS%	eFG%	3PT%
28.6	0.212	0.397	0.561	0.510	0.360

AST%	TOV%	OREB%	DREB%	STL%	BLK%
19.2	14.4	7.3	26.6	1.8	3.0

PER	ORTG	DRTG	WS/48	VOL
21.81	107.6	102.9	0.146	0.429

- Missed the second half of last season due to a torn left Achilles tendon
- Will miss the early portion of this season recovering from this injury
- Elite All-Star level big man when healthy
- Very skilled and versatile offensively, highly efficient scorer, good roll man and post-up player
- About a league average three-point shooter, excellent playmaking skills, draws fouls at a high rate
- Scored the 2nd most Points per Game in spot-up situations by knocking down shots and attacking closeouts to get to the rim to draw shooting fouls
- Lateral mobility is limited, struggles as a position defender
- Can provide some rim protection, good shot blocker, excellent defensive rebounder

Andre Iguodala

	Height	Weight	Cap #	Years Left
	6'6"	207	$16.000M	1

Similar at Age 34

		Season	SIMsc
1	John Salmons	2013-14	912.9
2	Anthony Parker	2009-10	911.3
3	George McCloud	2001-02	910.2
4	Mario Elie	1997-98	907.1
5	Brent Barry	2005-06	901.9
6	Anthony Peeler	2003-04	901.9
7	Brian Shaw	2000-01	899.7
8	Tyrone Corbin	1996-97	899.2
9	Raja Bell	2010-11	898.0
10	Chris Mullin*	1997-98	897.6

Baseline Basic Stats

MPG	PTS	AST	REB	BLK	STL
25.1	7.5	2.6	3.2	0.3	1.0

Advanced Metrics

USG%	3PTA/FGA	FTA/FGA	TS%	eFG%	3PT%
12.6	0.370	0.258	0.556	0.529	0.326

AST%	TOV%	OREB%	DREB%	STL%	BLK%
15.4	13.2	3.6	12.4	1.8	1.6

PER	ORTG	DRTG	WS/48	VOL	
12.76	115.8	106.3	0.121	0.401	

- In his mid-30s and in the decline stage of his career
- Extremely low usage player, still a good playmaking wing that scores efficiently around the basket
- Excellent as a pick-and-roll ball handler
- Struggled with his outside shot last season, Three-Point Percentage was under 30% for the first time in his career
- Better in motion than as a stationary spot-up shooter, fared much better at coming off screens and cutting to the basket
- Still an excellent on-ball wing defender, posted the highest Block Percentage of his career in his age-34 season

Shaun Livingston

	Height	Weight	Cap #	Years Left
	6'7"	182	$8.308M	1

Similar at Age 32

		Season	SIMsc
1	Anthony Bowie	1995-96	935.7
2	David Wingate	1995-96	911.7
3	Bill Hanzlik	1989-90	911.2
4	Paul Pressey	1990-91	908.8
5	Jim Paxson	1989-90	906.5
6	Mike Sanders	1992-93	900.4
7	Gerald Wilkins	1995-96	900.1
8	Anfernee Hardaway	2003-04	899.1
9	Ron Harper	1995-96	898.6
10	George Gervin*	1984-85	898.3

Baseline Basic Stats

MPG	PTS	AST	REB	BLK	STL
17.9	5.7	2.1	1.9	0.3	0.6

Advanced Metrics

USG%	3PTA/FGA	FTA/FGA	TS%	eFG%	3PT%
15.4	0.073	0.222	0.543	0.507	0.197

AST%	TOV%	OREB%	DREB%	STL%	BLK%
16.7	14.9	3.2	9.3	1.7	1.2

PER	ORTG	DRTG	WS/48	VOL
11.61	109.1	108.5	0.092	0.461

- Solid rotational wing player, entering a decline phase as he hits his mid-30s
- Very good playmaker, excellent post-up player
- Scores efficiently by making shots inside of 16 feet, rarely takes an outside jumper
- Effective in isolation situations if he has a mismatch
- Versatile defender that excels at defending both guard spots, more of a position defender at this stage

Kevon Looney

	Height	Weight	Cap #	Years Left
	6'9"	220	$1.513M	0

Similar at Age 21

		Season	SIMsc
1	Ed Davis	2010-11	926.6
2	Donnell Harvey	2001-02	915.4
3	Brandan Wright	2008-09	908.8
4	Darrell Arthur	2009-10	907.8
5	Amir Johnson	2008-09	904.7
6	Stromile Swift	2000-01	898.0
7	Cedric Simmons	2006-07	897.9
8	Patrick Patterson	2010-11	895.8
9	Kenny Williams	1990-91	893.8
10	Kris Humphries	2006-07	891.3

Baseline Basic Stats

MPG	PTS	AST	REB	BLK	STL
21.0	7.2	1.1	5.1	0.8	0.7

Advanced Metrics

USG%	3PTA/FGA	FTA/FGA	TS%	eFG%	3PT%
14.6	0.045	0.344	0.575	0.541	0.228

AST%	TOV%	OREB%	DREB%	STL%	BLK%
8.3	13.0	10.3	17.3	1.7	2.7

PER	ORTG	DRTG	WS/48	VOL	
14.69	117.5	105.2	0.137	0.321	

- Was on the fringes of Golden State's rotation in the regular season, played regular rotational minutes in the playoffs
- On offense, very low volume rim runner, did most of his damage inside of three feet, good at crashing the offensive glass
- Most effective at running the floor for dunks in transition
- Provided solid rim protection, blocked shots at a high rate, decent defensive rebounder
- Slightly below average as a position defender, flashed the potential to guard players inside and on the perimeter

Jordan Bell

	Height	Weight	Cap #	Years Left
	6'9"	224	$1.378M	0

Similar at Age 23

		Season	SIMsc
1	Granville Waiters	1983-84	890.9
2	James Hardy	1979-80	883.8
3	Larry Nance, Jr.	2015-16	881.2
4	Kyle O'Quinn	2013-14	880.5
5	James Johnson	2010-11	880.3
6	Jeremy Evans	2010-11	877.2
7	Antoine Carr	1984-85	876.4
8	Keon Clark	1998-99	876.3
9	Stromile Swift	2002-03	875.0
10	Terry Mills	1990-91	874.0

Baseline Basic Stats

MPG	PTS	AST	REB	BLK	STL
20.3	7.1	1.1	5.2	1.0	0.7

Advanced Metrics

USG%	3PTA/FGA	FTA/FGA	TS%	eFG%	3PT%
15.7	0.061	0.290	0.607	0.583	0.171

AST%	TOV%	OREB%	DREB%	STL%	BLK%
12.9	16.0	9.2	19.0	2.0	4.1

PER	ORTG	DRTG	WS/48	VOL	
17.87	118.7	102.9	0.174	0.478	

- Missed a month of his rookie season due to left ankle inflammation
- A fringe rotation player for Golden State last season
- Very low usage player that scored efficiently on close range shots as a rim runner, excels as a cutter
- Good passing big man, can be a little turnover prone, effective offensive rebounder
- Energetic interior defender that can rebound and block shots at a high rate, uses active hands to get steals
- Solid position defender that can defend interior players and occasionally switch onto perimeter players

Jonas Jerebko

	Height	Weight	Cap #	Years Left
	6'10"	231	$1.513M	0

Similar at Age 30

		Season	SIMsc
1	Austin Croshere	2005-06	932.7
2	Pete Chilcutt	1998-99	932.2
3	Matt Bonner	2010-11	929.0
4	Terry Mills	1997-98	928.8
5	Walter McCarty	2004-05	917.9
6	Vladimir Radmanovic	2010-11	914.4
7	David Wood	1994-95	913.8
8	Al Harrington	2010-11	913.3
9	Dennis Scott	1998-99	912.1
10	Tim Thomas	2007-08	908.7

Baseline Basic Stats

MPG	PTS	AST	REB	BLK	STL
18.3	6.1	1.0	3.2	0.3	0.5

Advanced Metrics

USG%	3PTA/FGA	FTA/FGA	TS%	eFG%	3PT%
14.4	0.472	0.171	0.551	0.528	0.381

AST%	TOV%	OREB%	DREB%	STL%	BLK%
7.8	10.3	4.9	17.5	1.2	1.1

PER	ORTG	DRTG	WS/48	VOL
11.44	110.9	106.1	0.105	0.302

- Had a bounce-back season as a regular rotational player for Utah at age 30
- Low volume spot-up shooter, made 41.4% of his threes last season
- Historically has been a league average three-point shooter for his career
- Most effective in spot-up situations and was above average as a cutter last season
- Solid stay-at-home on-ball defender against fours, good defensive rebounder

Quinn Cook

	Height	Weight	Cap #	Years Left
	6'2"	184	$1.545M	0

Similar at Age 24

		Season	SIMsc
1	Trey Burke	2016-17	920.5
2	Bobby Brown	2008-09	917.2
3	Jimmer Fredette	2013-14	914.4
4	Travis Diener	2006-07	914.1
5	Patty Mills	2012-13	913.1
6	Travis Mays	1992-93	912.6
7	Chris Quinn	2007-08	912.1
8	Ronnie Price	2007-08	911.8
9	A.J. Price	2010-11	910.2
10	Ray McCallum	2015-16	909.3

Baseline Basic Stats

MPG	PTS	AST	REB	BLK	STL
18.2	7.0	2.4	1.7	0.1	0.6

Advanced Metrics

USG%	3PTA/FGA	FTA/FGA	TS%	eFG%	3PT%
18.8	0.439	0.123	0.555	0.533	0.396

AST%	TOV%	OREB%	DREB%	STL%	BLK%
22.6	12.1	1.6	9.0	1.3	0.2

PER	ORTG	DRTG	WS/48	VOL
13.52	109.8	112.1	0.085	0.405

- Spent most of last season playing on a two-way contract, played well as a fill-in in the second half
- Was signed to the active roster in April, got some playing time in the playoffs
- Played in a low volume role, made 44.2% of his threes, showed decent playmaking skills
- Effective last season as a spot-up shooter that could run off screens
- Good pick-and-roll ball handler in a limited number of possessions
- Not especially quick and doesn't have much length, can be targeted on defense
- Passable position defender if he's hidden in favorable matchups, good defensive rebounder for his size

Damian Jones

	Height	Weight	Cap #	Years Left
	7'0"	245	$1.545M	Team Option

Similar at Age 22

		Season	SIMsc
1	Mike Brittain	1985-86	919.2
2	Bill Wennington	1985-86	915.0
3	Michael Bradley	2001-02	914.6
4	Jan Vesely	2012-13	912.7
5	Hilton Armstrong	2006-07	910.2
6	Gary Leonard	1989-90	909.1
7	Jelani McCoy	1999-00	899.7
8	Andrew Lang	1988-89	895.5
9	Travis Knight	1996-97	894.4
10	George Zidek	1995-96	890.8

Baseline Basic Stats

MPG	PTS	AST	REB	BLK	STL
13.7	4.1	0.5	3.5	0.6	0.4

Advanced Metrics

USG%	3PTA/FGA	FTA/FGA	TS%	eFG%	3PT%
15.1	0.000	0.311	0.514	0.505	0.173

AST%	TOV%	OREB%	DREB%	STL%	BLK%
4.6	17.0	10.2	16.3	1.2	3.2

PER	ORTG	DRTG	WS/48	VOL	
10.40	99.3	105.9	0.062	0.271	

- Seldomly played in two seasons, only has played 174 minutes total in his career
- Spent most of the last two years in the G-League with Santa Cruz
- In the G-League, he's a low volume rim runner that scores efficiently on close range shots
- Also draws fouls at a high rate and will crash the offensive glass
- Free throw shooting improved in his second year in the G-League
- Shot almost 70% on free throws last season after being below 50% the season before
- Has some potential as a rim protector, very good shot blocker, solid defensive rebounder

Jacob Evans

	Height	Weight	Cap #	Years Left
	6'6"	210	$1.644M	1 + 2 TO

Baseline Basic Stats

MPG	PTS	AST	REB	BLK	STL
10.9	3.5	0.9	1.4	0.1	0.4

Advanced Metrics

USG%	3PTA/FGA	FTA/FGA	TS%	eFG%	3PT%
17.4	0.262	0.220	0.478	0.441	0.282

AST%	TOV%	OREB%	DREB%	STL%	BLK%
12.1	13.8	4.3	10.8	1.7	1.0

PER	ORTG	DRTG	WS/48	VOL
10.09	98.6	107.0	0.048	N/A

- Drafted by Golden State in the first round with the 28th overall pick
- Not particularly effective at Summer League
- Struggled to adapt to a lower usage role, mainly used as a spot-up shooter, shot below 30% from the field in Las Vegas
- Flashed potential on the defensive end, very aggressive to contest shots, Block Percentage was very high in Las Vegas and Sacramento
- Solid on the ball as a stay-at-home position defender, fairly good defensive rebounding wing

HOUSTON ROCKETS

Last Season: 65 – 17, Lost Western Conference Finals to Golden State (3 – 4)

Offensive Rating: 114.7, 1st in NBA   Defensive Rating: 106.1, 6th in NBA

Primary Executive: Daryl Morey, General Manager   Head Coach: Mike D'Antoni

Key Roster Changes

Subtractions
Chinanu Onuaku, trade
Ryan Anderson, trade
Luc Mbah a Moute, free agency
Trevor Ariza, free agency
Tarik Black, free agency
Joe Johnson, free agency
Aaron Jackson, waived

Additions
Vincent Edwards, draft
Isaiah Hartenstein, signed 2017 draft pick
Gary Clark, rookie free agent
Marquese Chriss, trade
Brandon Knight, trade
James Ennis, free agency
Michael Carter-Williams, free agency
Carmelo Anthony, free agency

RAFER Projected Win Total: 53.9

Projected Best Five-Man Unit
1. Chris Paul
2. James Harden
3. James Ennis
4. P.J. Tucker
5. Clint Capela

Other Rotation Players
Eric Gordon
Carmelo Anthony
Gerald Green
Nene
Marquese Chriss

Remaining Roster

- Michael Carter-Williams
- Zhou Qi
- Brandon Knight
- Vincent Edwards
- Isaiah Hartenstein
- Gary Clark, 24, 6'8", 225, Cincinnati (Two-Way)
- Bruno Caboclo, 23, 6'9", 218, Brazil (Exhibit 10)
- Rob Gray, 24, 6'1", 185, Houston (Exhibit 10)

Season Forecast

With more than half of the Houston Rockets' roster from last season's playoff hitting the free agent market, it was expected that some changes were in order. Fortunately for Houston, they were able to keep their core intact by re-signing Chris Paul and Clint Capela to multi-year deals. However, the Rockets had to bring in some new complementary pieces because Trevor Ariza and Luc Mbah a Moute both elected to sign elsewhere. On the positive side, James Ennis could provide the Rockets with value similar to Ariza, except that Ennis is younger and will make a fraction of what is Ariza is being paid by Phoenix. On the other hand, the addition of Carmelo Anthony essentially in place of Mbah a Moute could potentially muddle up Houston's rotation because he's an aging former All-Star that has to adjust to a reduced role. As a result, Houston's chemistry could be negatively impacted, and the team could see a drop-off in their win total. However, they still have a pretty talented roster that will allow them to finish near the top of the Western Conference standings, but they're still a notch below Golden State.

The incorporation of Anthony into the rotation is Houston's main concern because it could possibly create problems for them on both ends. He fits their offensive scheme a little bit because Houston shoots more threes than any team in the league by a sizeable margin and Anthony is a willing three-point shooter that shoots around a league average percentage. However, Anthony's preferred isolation-heavy style clashes with Houston's established offensive system. After all, in the past two seasons, the Rockets have had success with lower volume, catch-and-shoot types on the wings to complement James Harden and Paul because they would either take the open shot or quickly move the ball elsewhere. Anthony did play more of a spot-up role in Oklahoma City, but he still ended a lot of his possessions with an isolation. If he maintains this tendency, it could cause problems for the Rockets because they would be trading off good offensive options like an open shot or ball movement to find a better look for a more inefficient option such as an isolation from a declining former All-Star on a systemic basis, which could hurt the team's overall efficiency. To counter this potential issue, the Rockets will have to either creatively stagger the minutes of their stars to allow Anthony to play more with the second unit or he'll have to fully commit to being effective in a lower usage role. From there, Anthony's presence in the rotation could negatively impact the team's defense because he might be taking minutes from better defensive options like Ennis or P.J. Tucker. This is a concern because head coach, Mike D'Antoni has historically played with a short rotation and if Anthony plays a starter's workload, it would come at the expense of Ennis or Tucker or possibly both of them. As a result, it could cost the team a few more points per game because they are simply putting a worse defender on the floor on a regular basis. In the Rockets' quest to challenge Golden State, Houston took a sizeable risk to give them a better chance to compete for a championship. If Anthony fits in with the Rockets better than he did with Oklahoma City, the risk could pay off and Houston would have a chance to win the title. However, if Anthony falls in line with his historical tendencies and behavior, the Rockets will still be one of the league's better teams, but their performance will likely be much worse than last season.

Veterans

James Harden

	Height	Weight	Cap #	Years Left
	6'5"	220	$30.421M	3 + PO

	Similar at Age	**28**	
		Season	**SIMsc**
1	Dwyane Wade	2009-10	883.3
2	Paul Pierce	2005-06	866.7
3	Kobe Bryant	2006-07	856.3
4	Vince Carter	2004-05	850.0
5	Deron Williams	2012-13	845.1
6	Magic Johnson*	1987-88	844.5
7	Mitch Richmond*	1993-94	840.7
8	Ray Allen*	2003-04	836.8
9	Caron Butler	2008-09	834.7
10	Jerry Stackhouse	2002-03	833.4

Baseline Basic Stats

MPG	PTS	AST	REB	BLK	STL
36.8	24.8	6.7	5.8	0.6	1.5

Advanced Metrics

USG%	3PTA/FGA	FTA/FGA	TS%	eFG%	3PT%
31.9	0.424	0.481	0.598	0.522	0.355

AST%	TOV%	OREB%	DREB%	STL%	BLK%
38.0	14.9	2.8	15.9	2.2	1.4

PER	ORTG	DRTG	WS/48	VOL	
26.10	117.2	104.7	0.226	0.185	

- Reigning NBA MVP, has led the NBA in Win Shares in three of the last four years
- Led the NBA in Usage Percentage last season, dynamic playmaker, extremely high Assist Percentage, excellent as a pick-and-roll handler
- Scores efficiently by drawing fouls at a very rate, takes a lot of threes and makes them at around a league average rate
- The NBA's most isolation heavy player, scored the most points in isolation situations with a high level of efficiency last season
- Decent position defender if he's hidden in favorable matchups, consistently gets steals at an above average rate, solid rebounding guard

Chris Paul

	Height	Weight	Cap #	Years Left
	6'0"	175	$35.654M	3

Similar at Age 32

		Season	SIMsc
1	Tim Hardaway	1998-99	904.9
2	Mark Price	1996-97	902.9
3	Darrell Armstrong	2000-01	902.4
4	Mo Williams	2014-15	894.4
5	J.J. Barea	2016-17	892.0
6	Bobby Jackson	2005-06	877.5
7	Mookie Blaylock	1999-00	874.6
8	Greg Anthony	1999-00	868.2
9	Isiah Thomas*	1993-94	868.0
10	Rafer Alston	2008-09	866.6

Baseline Basic Stats

MPG	PTS	AST	REB	BLK	STL
32.9	16.3	7.4	3.7	0.1	1.5

Advanced Metrics

USG%	3PTA/FGA	FTA/FGA	TS%	eFG%	3PT%
24.0	0.473	0.251	0.571	0.523	0.367

AST%	TOV%	OREB%	DREB%	STL%	BLK%
41.8	14.2	2.2	13.8	2.4	0.4

PER	ORTG	DRTG	WS/48	VOL	
21.76	117.8	103.8	0.200	0.410	

- All-Star level point guard entering his age-33 season
- Missed games last season due to injuries to his hamstring, groin, knee, hip and left leg
- Elite playmaker, scores efficiently in a fairly high usage role, excellent pick-and-roll ball handler
- Good three-point and mid-range shooter, shoots a high percentage at the rim
- Driving less frequently, more reliant on his jumper at this stage
- Very good in isolation situations and as a spot-up shooter
- Good on-ball defensive point guard, great rebounder for his size, posted the lowest Steal Percentage of his career

Clint Capela

	Height	Weight	Cap #	Years Left
	6'10"	245	$15.293M	4

Similar at Age 23

		Season	SIMsc
1	Samuel Dalembert	2004-05	911.7
2	Derrick Favors	2014-15	910.4
3	Ed Davis	2012-13	907.3
4	Jonas Valanciunas	2015-16	905.4
5	Emeka Okafor	2005-06	900.5
6	Herb Williams	1981-82	900.1
7	DeAndre Jordan	2011-12	899.5
8	Josh Boone	2007-08	899.4
9	John Henson	2013-14	893.9
10	Richaun Holmes	2016-17	893.8

Baseline Basic Stats

MPG	PTS	AST	REB	BLK	STL
28.9	12.4	1.2	9.3	1.7	0.8

Advanced Metrics

USG%	3PTA/FGA	FTA/FGA	TS%	eFG%	3PT%
18.9	0.002	0.374	0.623	0.616	0.056

AST%	TOV%	OREB%	DREB%	STL%	BLK%
6.7	12.8	11.7	27.5	1.3	4.6

PER	ORTG	DRTG	WS/48	VOL
21.83	121.0	103.1	0.203	0.253

- Had career best season in his fourth year in the NBA
- Established himself one of the league's best rim protectors, excellent shot blocker and rebounder
- Demonstrated enough mobility to passably defend on the perimeter in a switch situation
- Strictly a rim running big man, scored efficiently on close range shots in a low volume role
- 2nd in the NBA in Points per Game as a roll man, ranked by the NBA in the 91st percentile on a per-possession basis
- Improving as a free throw shooter, but his percentages are still below 60%

Eric Gordon

	Height	Weight	Cap #	Years Left
	6'3"	222	$13.500M	1

Similar at Age 29

	Player	Season	SIMsc
1	Randy Foye	2012-13	921.3
2	Wesley Matthews	2015-16	902.1
3	Gary Neal	2013-14	898.3
4	Voshon Lenard	2002-03	894.0
5	Arron Afflalo	2014-15	892.1
6	J.R. Smith	2014-15	890.6
7	Cuttino Mobley	2004-05	886.7
8	Jason Richardson	2009-10	885.7
9	Charlie Bell	2008-09	881.9
10	Ben Gordon	2012-13	881.5

Baseline Basic Stats

MPG	PTS	AST	REB	BLK	STL
30.3	12.9	2.3	2.9	0.2	0.8

Advanced Metrics

USG%	3PTA/FGA	FTA/FGA	TS%	eFG%	3PT%
21.0	0.553	0.205	0.550	0.514	0.364

AST%	TOV%	OREB%	DREB%	STL%	BLK%
11.5	10.2	1.4	8.3	1.2	0.9

PER	ORTG	DRTG	WS/48	VOL	
12.89	107.1	109.6	0.086	0.223	

- One of the NBA best sixth men, overall production still consistent with his career averages
- High volume scoring guard, efficient shooter that relies on making threes at an above average percentage
- Very good off the ball as a spot-up shooter that can run off screens
- Got to the basket a little more last season, drew more fouls, decent passing skills, rarely turns the ball over
- Effective with the ball in hands as an isolation scorer and pick-and-roll ball handler
- Solid on-ball position defender that can guard multiple positions

P.J. Tucker

	Height	Weight	Cap #	Years Left
	6'5"	225	$7.970M	2

Similar at Age 32

		Season	SIMsc
1	Dan Majerle	1997-98	911.4
2	Alan Anderson	2014-15	903.6
3	Shane Battier	2010-11	897.0
4	James Posey	2008-09	896.0
5	Bryon Russell	2002-03	891.1
6	Thabo Sefolosha	2016-17	888.3
7	Maurice Evans	2010-11	888.3
8	Jud Buechler	2000-01	887.9
9	Ime Udoka	2009-10	887.1
10	Rick Fox	2001-02	882.0

Baseline Basic Stats

MPG	PTS	AST	REB	BLK	STL
22.5	5.8	1.4	3.6	0.2	0.8

Advanced Metrics

USG%	3PTA/FGA	FTA/FGA	TS%	eFG%	3PT%
11.4	0.603	0.166	0.513	0.489	0.335

AST%	TOV%	OREB%	DREB%	STL%	BLK%
7.6	12.7	4.2	16.3	1.8	0.8

PER	ORTG	DRTG	WS/48	VOL	
9.09	105.4	106.3	0.079	0.333	

- Extremely durable player, has only missed six games in the last five seasons
- Entering his age-33 season, overall production has been steadily declining for about five years
- Very low volume spot-up shooter that shoots around league average on threes in general
- Much better at corner threes, 65.5% of his three-point attempts were in the corners, made 39.9% of them
- Solid on-ball defender that can guard multiple positions
- Better at handling wing players than interior players, good defensive rebounder

Carmelo Anthony

	Height	Weight	Cap #	Years Left
	6'8"	230	$2.394M	0

Similar at Age 33

		Season	SIMsc
1	Joe Johnson	2014-15	918.4
2	Antawn Jamison	2009-10	917.8
3	Vince Carter	2009-10	914.9
4	Mike Dunleavy, Jr.	2013-14	903.3
5	Paul Pierce	2010-11	902.6
6	Glen Rice	2000-01	901.1
7	Clifford Robinson	1999-00	898.5
8	Sam Perkins	1994-95	897.0
9	David West	2013-14	893.4
10	Dan Issel*	1981-82	892.6

Baseline Basic Stats

MPG	PTS	AST	REB	BLK	STL
31.9	15.1	2.3	5.5	0.4	0.8

Advanced Metrics

USG%	3PTA/FGA	FTA/FGA	TS%	eFG%	3PT%
22.8	0.370	0.207	0.509	0.477	0.352

AST%	TOV%	OREB%	DREB%	STL%	BLK%
10.0	9.2	3.6	16.2	1.2	1.3

PER	ORTG	DRTG	WS/48	VOL	
13.85	104.0	108.7	0.085	0.455	

- Entering his age-34 season, overall production has been declining for the last six seasons
- Struggled to adapt to a lower usage offensive role in Oklahoma City last season
- Shooting efficiency and effectiveness in isolation situations decreased dramatically
- No longer getting to the rim as frequently, took a lot of inefficient long twos
- Taking more threes in the last two seasons, about a league average three-point shooter right now
- Better in off ball situations as a spot-up shooter and cutter, could run off screens in a small sample of possessions
- Below average defensively overall, passable position defender if hidden in favorable matchups, solid defensive rebounder

James Ennis

	Height	Weight	Cap #	Years Left
	6'7"	210	$1.621M	Player Option

Similar at Age <u>27</u>

		Season	SIMsc
1	Eric Piatkowski	1997-98	948.1
2	Chris Douglas-Roberts	2013-14	943.9
3	Bobby Simmons	2007-08	940.1
4	Kyle Korver	2008-09	938.9
5	Chase Budinger	2015-16	933.6
6	Matt Carroll	2007-08	928.3
7	DeMarre Carroll	2013-14	925.0
8	Ira Newble	2001-02	922.8
9	Wesley Johnson	2014-15	918.0
10	John Salmons	2006-07	917.7

Baseline Basic Stats

MPG	PTS	AST	REB	BLK	STL
23.1	8.2	1.2	3.1	0.3	0.7

Advanced Metrics

USG%	3PTA/FGA	FTA/FGA	TS%	eFG%	3PT%
15.3	0.474	0.251	0.573	0.536	0.380

AST%	TOV%	OREB%	DREB%	STL%	BLK%
7.7	11.5	4.2	11.9	1.6	1.0

PER	ORTG	DRTG	WS/48	VOL
12.12	111.7	109.1	0.103	0.449

- Solid rotational wing player in his prime years, production is consistent with his career averages
- High scoring efficiency in a very low volume role, almost a league average three-point shooter for his career
- One of the best cutters in the league last season, ranked in the 97th percentile last year
- Draws more fouls than most low volume wing players, shot 71.6% on shots inside of three feet last season
- Very good on-ball wing defender, solid rebounder

Gerald Green

	Height	Weight	Cap #	Years Left
	6'8"	200	$1.513M	0

Similar at Age 32

		Season	SIMsc
1	Rod Higgins	1991-92	912.9
2	Sean Elliott	2000-01	905.6
3	Morris Peterson	2009-10	902.6
4	Matt Bullard	1999-00	897.9
5	Caron Butler	2012-13	896.9
6	Rasual Butler	2011-12	892.1
7	Francisco Garcia	2013-14	891.2
8	Wesley Person	2003-04	887.8
9	Roger Mason	2012-13	887.7
10	James Posey	2008-09	885.1

Baseline Basic Stats

MPG	PTS	AST	REB	BLK	STL
18.6	7.4	1.0	2.3	0.2	0.5

Advanced Metrics

USG%	3PTA/FGA	FTA/FGA	TS%	eFG%	3PT%
18.6	0.626	0.159	0.554	0.526	0.361

AST%	TOV%	OREB%	DREB%	STL%	BLK%
6.9	8.3	2.1	12.8	1.4	1.1

PER	ORTG	DRTG	WS/48	VOL
12.34	108.3	108.6	0.091	0.601

- Joined Houston mid-season, production last season was higher than his career averages
- Effective as a fairly high usage scorer off the bench
- Good as a pick-and-roll ball handler, above average in a small sample of isolation situations
- Took spot-up threes in much greater volume
- Threes accounted for more than 72% of his field goal attempts and he made almost 37% of them
- Solid on-ball defending wing, more of a stay-at-home defender, good defensive rebounder

Nene

	Height	Weight	Cap #	Years Left
	6'11"	260	$3.651M	1

Similar at Age **35**

		Season	SIMsc
1	Bob Lanier*	1983-84	909.2
2	Christian Laettner	2004-05	891.9
3	Joe Kleine	1996-97	873.7
4	Scott Williams	2003-04	869.1
5	Danny Schayes	1994-95	865.3
6	Danny Manning	2001-02	864.8
7	Kenyon Martin	2012-13	863.6
8	Juwan Howard	2008-09	863.1
9	Herb Williams	1993-94	862.9
10	Erick Dampier	2010-11	859.8

Baseline Basic Stats

MPG	PTS	AST	REB	BLK	STL
19.9	8.4	1.5	4.6	0.6	0.7

Advanced Metrics

USG%	3PTA/FGA	FTA/FGA	TS%	eFG%	3PT%
18.5	0.007	0.433	0.585	0.555	0.106

AST%	TOV%	OREB%	DREB%	STL%	BLK%
9.9	14.8	8.2	18.5	1.7	2.0

PER	ORTG	DRTG	WS/48	VOL
15.62	111.4	103.6	0.148	0.637

- Still effective at an advanced age, missed games last season due to injuries to his Achilles, ankle, foot, shoulder, knee, back and cornea
- Efficient scorer in a low volume role, good roll man, still a very good post-up player
- Also draws fouls at a high rate, decent passing big man
- Uses sound positioning to play effective interior defense, good rebounder
- Limited rim protector, not the shot blocker he once was, lacks mobility due to his advanced age, can only serve as a backup

Marquese Chriss

	Height	Weight	Cap #	Years Left
	6'10"	233	$3.206M	Team Option

Similar at Age 20

		Season	SIMsc
1	Trey Lyles	2015-16	915.3
2	Ryan Anderson	2008-09	914.5
3	Eddie Griffin	2002-03	904.3
4	Aaron Gordon	2015-16	901.3
5	Andray Blatche	2006-07	898.7
6	Tim Thomas	1997-98	897.9
7	Domantas Sabonis	2016-17	897.4
8	Rudy Gay	2006-07	890.7
9	Derrick Favors	2011-12	890.2
10	Rashard Lewis	1999-00	887.2

Baseline Basic Stats

MPG	PTS	AST	REB	BLK	STL
24.4	10.6	1.3	5.2	0.7	0.8

Advanced Metrics

USG%	3PTA/FGA	FTA/FGA	TS%	eFG%	3PT%
20.7	0.332	0.276	0.542	0.511	0.339

AST%	TOV%	OREB%	DREB%	STL%	BLK%
8.4	13.1	5.8	18.0	1.6	2.5

PER	ORTG	DRTG	WS/48	VOL	
14.59	104.2	108.0	0.082	0.356	

- Production tapered off in his second season, was a starter for most of his two-year career with Phoenix
- Struggled to find a role in Phoenix, most effective around the basket as a rim runner
- Has shot almost 62% on shots inside of three feet for his career
- Tried to play a stretch role, below break-even three-point shooter for his career, percentage is more respectable from the corners
- Has potential as a rim protector, good shot blocker and defensive rebounder
- Undisciplined position defender, highly foul prone, below average as an on-ball defender

Michael Carter-Williams

	Height	Weight	Cap #	Years Left
	6'6"	185	$1.757M	0

Similar at Age 26

		Season	SIMsc
1	Pete Myers	1989-90	907.9
2	Pace Mannion	1986-87	907.6
3	Brian Shaw	1992-93	906.7
4	Craig Ehlo	1987-88	906.7
5	Anthony Bowie	1989-90	906.1
6	Darrell Walker	1987-88	900.7
7	Delonte West	2009-10	896.1
8	Justin Holiday	2015-16	895.5
9	Ron Harper	1989-90	895.3
10	Nando De Colo	2013-14	894.9

Baseline Basic Stats

MPG	PTS	AST	REB	BLK	STL
24.4	9.0	3.3	3.7	0.3	1.1

Advanced Metrics

USG%	3PTA/FGA	FTA/FGA	TS%	eFG%	3PT%
18.3	0.260	0.283	0.498	0.446	0.319

AST%	TOV%	OREB%	DREB%	STL%	BLK%
21.3	15.7	4.0	14.1	2.3	1.4

PER	ORTG	DRTG	WS/48	VOL
13.30	102.6	106.9	0.033	0.476

- Has missed significant parts of the last three seasons due to injuries to his left knee, left hip, and left shoulder
- Good playmaking guard, somewhat turnover prone
- Does not shoot efficiently, struggles to make shots outside of three feet
- Drove more frequently in Charlotte last season, got to the free throw line at a high rate, shot a career best 82% on free throws
- Only effective in isolation situations against a mismatch
- More of a help defender, good Steal and Block Percentages for his career, solid rebounder
- Defends wings and small guards, slightly below average at guarding both on the ball

Brandon Knight

	Height	Weight	Cap #	Years Left
	6'3"	189	$14.631M	1

	Similar at Age	26	
		Season	SIMsc
1	Ben Gordon	2009-10	944.7
2	Derrick Rose	2014-15	939.9
3	Sam Cassell	1995-96	936.6
4	Ramon Sessions	2012-13	934.9
5	Reggie Jackson	2016-17	932.2
6	Otis Birdsong	1981-82	922.5
7	Terry Dehere	1997-98	920.4
8	Jamal Crawford	2006-07	919.0
9	Leandro Barbosa	2008-09	918.7
10	Devin Harris	2009-10	918.4

Baseline Basic Stats

MPG	PTS	AST	REB	BLK	STL
25.8	12.2	3.5	2.4	0.2	0.8

Advanced Metrics

USG%	3PTA/FGA	FTA/FGA	TS%	eFG%	3PT%
24.0	0.287	0.259	0.519	0.468	0.347

AST%	TOV%	OREB%	DREB%	STL%	BLK%
22.3	13.8	2.1	8.8	1.4	0.6

PER	ORTG	DRTG	WS/48	VOL	
13.98	103.4	111.9	0.054	0.390	

- Missed all of last season while recovering from surgery to repair a torn ACL in his left knee
- Production was declining in the previous seasons when he was healthy
- Played out of position as a two-guard in Phoenix, Assist Percentage declined as a result
- Solid playmaker in the years where he mainly played as a point guard
- Could get to the rim to either finish shots inside or draw fouls, has been inconsistent as a shooter
- Below average from mid-range, hovering around break-even as a three-point shooter in his past two healthy seasons
- Tasked to defend both guard spots in Phoenix, below average on-ball defender against either position, needs to be hidden in favorable matchups

Zhou Qi

	Height	Weight	Cap #	Years Left
	7'1"	210	$1.378M	2

Similar at Age 22

		Season	SIMsc
1	Keith Closs	1998-99	795.2
2	Jonathan Bender	2002-03	793.4
3	JaVale McGee	2009-10	783.0
4	Quincy Miller	2014-15	782.5
5	Hassan Whiteside	2011-12	780.9
6	Nazr Mohammed	1999-00	779.3
7	Elden Campbell	1990-91	773.6
8	Jim McIlvaine	1994-95	773.5
9	Shawne Williams	2008-09	769.8
10	Steven Hunter	2003-04	767.4

Baseline Basic Stats

MPG	PTS	AST	REB	BLK	STL
18.1	5.8	0.6	4.1	1.3	0.4

Advanced Metrics

USG%	3PTA/FGA	FTA/FGA	TS%	eFG%	3PT%
15.7	0.365	0.382	0.422	0.369	0.235

AST%	TOV%	OREB%	DREB%	STL%	BLK%
4.1	17.6	6.3	16.2	1.0	6.9

PER	ORTG	DRTG	WS/48	VOL
8.12	83.4	104.2	-0.014	0.897

- Rarely played in his rookie season, spent most of the year with Rio Grande Valley in the G-League
- Played a low usage stretch big role in the G-League, shot a break-even percentage on threes, decent at drawing fouls, shot 63.6% on two-point shots
- Shooting stroke may still be inconsistent, shot below 60% from the free throw line
- Blocked shots at a high rate, solid rebounder, middling position defender due to his relatively thin frame

Isaiah Hartenstein

	Height	Weight	Cap #	Years Left
	7'0"	249	$0.838M	2

Baseline Basic Stats

MPG	PTS	AST	REB	BLK	STL
16.3	5.2	0.6	4.3	0.9	0.4

Advanced Metrics

USG%	3PTA/FGA	FTA/FGA	TS%	eFG%	3PT%
15.4	0.095	0.302	0.536	0.510	0.355

AST%	TOV%	OREB%	DREB%	STL%	BLK%
7.9	16.2	12.8	21.6	1.3	4.4

PER	ORTG	DRTG	WS/48	VOL	
14.82	112.4	109.0	0.093	0.573	

- Drafted by Houston in 2017 in the second round with the 43rd overall pick
- Played last season in the G-League with Rio Grande Valley, projection uses translated G-League stats
- Very effective on offense, scored efficiently by shooting over 61% on two-pointers, got to the free throw line at a high rate
- Also flashed some stretch potential by shooting an above break-even percentage on threes, excellent at crashing the offensive boards
- Showed some promise on defense, good shot blocker and defensive rebounder, still needs to improve his position defense

Vincent Edwards

	Height	Weight	Cap #	Years Left
	6'8"	225	$0.838M	0

Baseline Basic Stats

MPG	PTS	AST	REB	BLK	STL
19.3	6.1	1.4	3.0	0.2	0.6

Advanced Metrics

USG%	3PTA/FGA	FTA/FGA	TS%	eFG%	3PT%
15.7	0.354	0.193	0.524	0.494	0.354

AST%	TOV%	OREB%	DREB%	STL%	BLK%
11.2	13.1	4.3	13.7	1.7	0.9

PER	ORTG	DRTG	WS/48	VOL
11.51	104.7	108.4	0.033	N/A

- Drafted by Utah with the 52nd overall pick, then traded to Houston
- Not especially effective in his minutes at Summer League, could use additional seasoning in the G-League
- Played in a lower volume, catch-and-shoot role, struggled to make shots
- Only shot around 21% on threes and 35% from the field
- Decent as a stay-at-home on-ball defending wing, rebounded well at the defensive end

OKLAHOMA CITY THUNDER

Last Season: 48 – 34, Lost 1st Round to Utah (2 – 4)

Offensive Rating: 110.7, 7th in NBA   Defensive Rating: 107.2, 9th in NBA

Primary Executive: Sam Presti, Executive Vice President & General Manager

Head Coach: Billy Donovan

Key Roster Changes

Subtractions
Carmelo Anthony, trade
Dakari Johnson, trade
Corey Brewer, free agency
Josh Huestis, free agency
Kyle Singler, waived

Additions
Hamidou Diallo, draft
Dennis Schroder, trade
Timothe Luwawu-Cabarrot, trade
Abdel Nader, trade
Nerlens Noel, free agency

RAFER Projected Win Total: 46.4

Projected Best Five-Man Unit
1.   Russell Westbrook
2.   Paul George
3.   Jerami Grant
4.   Andre Roberson
5.   Steven Adams

Other Rotation Players
Dennis Schroder
Patrick Patterson
Nerlens Noel
Alex Abrines
Timothe Luwawu-Cabarrot
Raymond Felton

Remaining Roster

- Terrance Ferguson
- Abdel Nader
- Hamidou Diallo
- Deonte Burton, 25, 6'5", 250, Iowa State (Two-Way)
- Tyler Davis, 21, 6'10", 266, Texas A&M (Two-Way)
- Donte Grantham, 23, 6'8", 215, Clemson (Exhibit 10)

Season Forecast

The Oklahoma City Thunder's gamble to trade for Paul George paid off this summer when he was re-signed to a four-year maximum contract, leaving the team's primary core intact for the next few years. After all, the Thunder also has Russell Westbrook and Steven Adams locked up to multi-year deals. From there, Oklahoma City made some tweaks to the rotation by picking up Nerlens Noel in free agency and trading Carmelo Anthony for Dennis Schroder and Timothe Luwawu-Cabarrot. With these moves, the Thunder appears to have a more clearly defined identity as a high energy, versatile and athletic defensive minded team, which could keep them in the playoff picture in the Western Conference and allow them to finish near the top of the conference standings.

The Thunder have had a top ten ranked defense for the last two seasons, which is impressive given that they had to find ways to hide key rotation players like Enes Kanter and Carmelo Anthony for large stretches of game action. This year, they may not need to do that as much because most of the players in the team's expected primary rotation are solid individual defenders with Schroder being an exception. However, he's expected to be a backup, so he might not need to play critical late game minutes. For the most part, Oklahoma City can play a more aggressive brand of high pressure defense that can really leverage the team's ability to create turnovers. By replacing Anthony's minutes with players like Jerami Grant or Luwawu-Cabarrot, the Thunder can actively switch screens and match up to different types of lineups. Also, Noel gives them another rim protector that adds the extra dimension of mobility if opponents try to go small to take Adams off the floor. If everyone in their rotation stays healthy, Oklahoma City should be one of the best defensive teams in the league this coming season. An improved and a more aggressive defense should make the team's offense better because the added athleticism should result in more transition opportunities. In the 2016-17 season, Oklahoma City was one of the league's best transition teams, but they had to slow their offense down to accommodate Anthony. The addition of George last season made their half-court offense better, but they lost a major strength when they slowed the team down. Now that they will infuse some younger and more athletic players into the rotation, they can potentially recapture their success in transition to go along with the individual skills of their main stars, Westbrook and George. If this happens, the team's offense could improve slightly even though they still don't have a lot of outside shooting around their two All-Stars. In general, Oklahoma City has a chance to be an improved team as a whole. They will likely be an excellent defensive team that generates turnovers and forces more misses than they did last year. If they regain their ability to be an explosive transition offense, then they could possibly compete with Houston to be the Western Conference's second seed. Otherwise, if their offense is similar to last year, then they will be a solid playoff team that's capable of reaching the second round.

Veterans

Russell Westbrook

	Height	Weight	Cap #	Years Left
	6'3"	187	$35.350M	3 + PO

Similar at Age 29

		Season	SIMsc
1	Rod Strickland	1995-96	859.3
2	Jeff Hornacek	1992-93	857.8
3	Jason Kidd*	2002-03	856.5
4	Derek Harper	1990-91	848.7
5	Gary Payton*	1997-98	844.1
6	Kobe Bryant	2007-08	838.7
7	Monta Ellis	2014-15	838.6
8	Ray Williams	1983-84	835.0
9	Allen Iverson*	2004-05	835.0
10	Jay Humphries	1991-92	833.5

Baseline Basic Stats

MPG	PTS	AST	REB	BLK	STL
35.2	20.3	7.7	5.2	0.3	1.7

Advanced Metrics

USG%	3PTA/FGA	FTA/FGA	TS%	eFG%	3PT%
31.7	0.215	0.355	0.528	0.472	0.305

AST%	TOV%	OREB%	DREB%	STL%	BLK%
43.7	15.5	4.6	19.7	2.4	0.7

PER	ORTG	DRTG	WS/48	VOL
23.36	108.6	104.3	0.163	0.348

- One of the top point guards in the NBA, has been an All-Star in seven of the last eight seasons
- Very durable over the last three seasons, has only missed 5 games in that span
- Extremely high usage, very ball dominant, led the NBA in Time of Possession last season
- Heavy score-first mindset, but has led the NBA in Assist Percentage in each of the last two seasons
- Efficient slashing guard, finishes above the rim, draws fouls at a high rate, below average outside shooter
- Active help defender, excellent rebounding point guard, gets steals at a high rate
- Plays solid position defense, but can gamble a bit too much

Paul George

	Height	Weight	Cap #	Years Left
	6'8"	210	$30.561M	2 + PO

Similar at Age 27

		Season	SIMsc
1	Danny Granger	2010-11	924.2
2	Stephen Jackson	2005-06	922.5
3	Jalen Rose	1999-00	921.5
4	J.R. Smith	2012-13	916.4
5	Sean Elliott	1995-96	915.2
6	Jason Richardson	2007-08	912.6
7	Glen Rice	1994-95	912.3
8	Clyde Drexler*	1989-90	908.6
9	James Posey	2003-04	907.7
10	Ray Allen*	2002-03	906.3

Baseline Basic Stats

MPG	PTS	AST	REB	BLK	STL
35.6	19.5	3.8	5.4	0.5	1.3

Advanced Metrics

USG%	3PTA/FGA	FTA/FGA	TS%	eFG%	3PT%
25.8	0.399	0.302	0.563	0.512	0.391

AST%	TOV%	OREB%	DREB%	STL%	BLK%
17.6	12.5	3.2	14.5	2.2	1.0

PER	ORTG	DRTG	WS/48	VOL	
18.57	110.4	107.2	0.134	0.353	

- One of the best two-way wing players in the league, production still consistent with his career averages
- Efficient scorer in a fairly high volume role, very good three-point shooter, some playmaking skills
- Effective driver that will finish shots inside at a high percentage or draw fouls, prone to taking a lot of inefficient long twos
- Good with the ball as an isolation scorer and pick-and-roll ball handler
- Very good off the ball as a spot-up shooter and cutter that can also come off screens
- Good on-ball defending wing player, uses active hands to play passing lanes and get steals at a high rate

Steven Adams

	Height	Weight	Cap #	Years Left
	7'0"	**250**	**$24.157M**	**2**

Similar at Age **24**

		Season	SIMsc
1	Cody Zeller	2016-17	919.1
2	DeAndre Jordan	2012-13	906.7
3	Tyler Zeller	2013-14	904.8
4	Mike Gminski	1983-84	903.0
5	Dale Davis	1993-94	902.8
6	Paul Mokeski	1980-81	895.8
7	Matt Geiger	1993-94	894.5
8	Dave Corzine	1980-81	893.7
9	Jamaal Magloire	2002-03	893.1
10	Nene Hilario	2006-07	891.2

Baseline Basic Stats

MPG	PTS	AST	REB	BLK	STL
29.5	11.0	1.2	8.1	1.3	0.7

Advanced Metrics

USG%	3PTA/FGA	FTA/FGA	TS%	eFG%	3PT%
16.7	0.002	0.394	0.600	0.584	0.081

AST%	TOV%	OREB%	DREB%	STL%	BLK%
6.3	13.1	13.0	17.5	1.4	2.9

PER	ORTG	DRTG	WS/48	VOL	
18.51	119.4	106.0	0.160	0.149	

- Entering his prime years, had a career best season in his fifth year in the NBA
- Low usage big man, shoots efficiently mainly due to his excellent rim running skills
- Showed an improved post-up game, draws fouls at a high rate, but still a below 60% free throw shooter
- Excellent offensive rebounder, defensive rebound rate has gradually decreased over the last four seasons
- Very good rim protector despite being only an above average shot blocker, limited lateral mobility

Andre Roberson

	Height	Weight	Cap #	Years Left
	6'7"	210	$10.000M	1

Similar at Age 26

		Season	SIMsc
1	James Ennis	2016-17	901.8
2	Ryan Bowen	2001-02	899.9
3	Thabo Sefolosha	2010-11	893.5
4	Wesley Johnson	2013-14	886.3
5	Harold Pressley	1989-90	886.0
6	Eddie Robinson	2002-03	882.9
7	Alonzo Gee	2013-14	882.0
8	Jud Buechler	1994-95	880.2
9	Darvin Ham	1999-00	878.3
10	Danny Vranes	1984-85	877.2

Baseline Basic Stats

MPG	PTS	AST	REB	BLK	STL
21.6	6.4	1.1	3.4	0.5	0.8

Advanced Metrics

USG%	3PTA/FGA	FTA/FGA	TS%	eFG%	3PT%
12.0	0.321	0.223	0.536	0.529	0.311

AST%	TOV%	OREB%	DREB%	STL%	BLK%
6.8	11.9	5.8	11.6	1.9	2.3

PER	ORTG	DRTG	WS/48	VOL	
11.08	110.6	106.9	0.099	0.427	

- Missed the second half of last season due to a torn patellar tendon in his left knee
- Extremely low usage offensive player, can only score on shots inside of three feet
- No jump shot, career Free Throw Percentage is below 50%
- Not effective in any half-court offensive situation last season
- Excellent on-ball wing defender, active as a help defender
- Solid rebounder that gets steals at a good rate, posted the highest Block Percentage in his career last season

Dennis Schroder

	Height	Weight	Cap #	Years Left
	6'1"	168	$15.500M	2

Similar at Age 24

		Season	SIMsc
1	Brandon Jennings	2013-14	924.4
2	Kemba Walker	2014-15	918.2
3	Mo Williams	2006-07	917.9
4	Kyrie Irving	2016-17	916.5
5	Nick Van Exel	1995-96	914.7
6	Kenny Anderson	1994-95	912.3
7	Kelvin Ransey	1982-83	912.0
8	Larry Drew	1982-83	911.4
9	Mahmoud Abdul-Rauf	1993-94	908.8
10	Tony Parker	2006-07	907.2

Baseline Basic Stats

MPG	PTS	AST	REB	BLK	STL
32.1	16.8	6.0	2.8	0.2	1.2

Advanced Metrics

USG%	3PTA/FGA	FTA/FGA	TS%	eFG%	3PT%
26.9	0.265	0.247	0.531	0.484	0.337

AST%	TOV%	OREB%	DREB%	STL%	BLK%
34.8	13.4	2.0	8.6	1.7	0.4

PER	ORTG	DRTG	WS/48	VOL	
17.68	107.4	109.9	0.093	0.299	

- Posted the highest PER of his career in his fifth season, will have to adjust to a backup role in Oklahoma City
- Good playmaker, cut his Turnover Percentage significantly
- Played a very high usage role in Atlanta, excelled as a slasher and mid-range shooter, below break-even as a three-point shooter
- Mainly effective with the ball in his hands in isolation situations and as a pick-and-roll ball handler
- Below average in almost every off-ball offensive situation last season
- Below average on-ball defender, doesn't get steals either

Jerami Grant

	Height	Weight	Cap #	Years Left
	6'8"	210	$8.654M	1 + PO

Similar at Age 23

		Season	SIMsc
1	Maurice Harkless	2016-17	910.0
2	Harrison Barnes	2015-16	899.1
3	Josh Childress	2006-07	898.7
4	Cliff Levingston	1983-84	891.3
5	Amir Johnson	2010-11	890.7
6	Antoine Wright	2007-08	885.4
7	Sam Williams	1982-83	881.8
8	Wilson Chandler	2010-11	881.7
9	Brandon Rush	2008-09	881.2
10	Roy Hinson	1984-85	880.9

Baseline Basic Stats

MPG	PTS	AST	REB	BLK	STL
24.6	9.4	1.1	4.3	0.8	0.7

Advanced Metrics

USG%	3PTA/FGA	FTA/FGA	TS%	eFG%	3PT%
16.6	0.237	0.397	0.575	0.538	0.346

AST%	TOV%	OREB%	DREB%	STL%	BLK%
6.2	10.5	5.2	13.9	1.3	3.1

PER	ORTG	DRTG	WS/48	VOL	
14.33	113.9	107.6	0.125	0.426	

- Dramatically improved in his fourth year in the NBA, had a career best season last year at age 23

- Played in a low volume role, excelled as a cutter, draws fouls at a very high rate

- Effective as a roll man, good at posting up smaller perimeter players

- Outside shot is inconsistent, Three-Point Percentage dropped significantly from the year before, now below break-even

- Good on-ball defender that can guard multiple positions, good rebounder, excellent shot blocker

Patrick Patterson

	Height	Weight	Cap #	Years Left
	6'9"	235	$5.452M	Player Option

Similar at Age 28

		Season	SIMsc
1	Marvin Williams	2014-15	946.1
2	Shawne Williams	2014-15	929.1
3	Brian Scalabrine	2006-07	922.3
4	Scott Padgett	2004-05	922.1
5	Walter McCarty	2002-03	918.5
6	Anthony Tolliver	2013-14	915.2
7	Dante Cunningham	2015-16	914.5
8	Mirza Teletovic	2013-14	913.4
9	Vladimir Radmanovic	2008-09	911.6
10	Ersan Ilyasova	2015-16	906.7

Baseline Basic Stats

MPG	PTS	AST	REB	BLK	STL
20.5	6.5	1.0	3.6	0.3	0.5

Advanced Metrics

USG%	3PTA/FGA	FTA/FGA	TS%	eFG%	3PT%
12.7	0.685	0.161	0.557	0.532	0.384

AST%	TOV%	OREB%	DREB%	STL%	BLK%
6.6	9.7	3.7	15.5	1.5	1.3

PER	ORTG	DRTG	WS/48	VOL	
10.81	113.0	107.3	0.093	0.255	

- Durable part of Oklahoma City's rotation last season, played all 82 games
- Production down overall, but consistent with his performance over the last three seasons
- Extremely low volume spot-up shooter, excellent career corner three-point shooter with a percentage of 39.9%
- Has consistently shot an above average three-point percentage in each of the six seasons
- Still effective at posting up smaller perimeter players
- Decent stay-at-home on-ball defender, solid on the defensive boards

Nerlens Noel

	Height	Weight	Cap #	Years Left
	6'11"	228	$1.757M	Player Option

Similar at Age 23

		Season	SIMsc
1	Jan Vesely	2013-14	905.2
2	Larry Micheaux	1983-84	899.0
3	Tony Battie	1999-00	898.5
4	Terry Mills	1990-91	895.7
5	Ed Davis	2012-13	892.8
6	Lucas Nogueira	2015-16	890.6
7	Joakim Noah	2008-09	886.2
8	Granville Waiters	1983-84	885.5
9	Cole Aldrich	2011-12	884.3
10	Scott Williams	1991-92	883.9

Baseline Basic Stats

MPG	PTS	AST	REB	BLK	STL
20.2	7.2	0.9	6.0	1.0	0.6

Advanced Metrics

USG%	3PTA/FGA	FTA/FGA	TS%	eFG%	3PT%
16.5	0.010	0.333	0.566	0.530	0.065

AST%	TOV%	OREB%	DREB%	STL%	BLK%
7.2	14.3	11.1	24.2	2.2	3.7

PER	ORTG	DRTG	WS/48	VOL
17.52	113.3	102.0	0.155	0.513

- Missed most of last season while recovering from a thumb injury
- Also suspended for 5 games for violating the NBA's anti-drug program
- Very low volume offensive player, strictly a rim runner that scores on close range shots
- Mainly effective last season as a cutter, will crash the offensive glass and draw fouls
- Solid rim protector, excellent shot blocker and defensive rebounder
- Thin frame makes him vulnerable in post defense

Timothe Luwawu-Cabarrot

	Height	Weight	Cap #	Years Left
	6'6"	205	$1.545M	Team Option

Similar at Age 22

	Season	SIMsc
1	Nik Stauskas	2015-16	939.5
2	Darrun Hilliard	2015-16	932.6
3	James Anderson	2011-12	928.3
4	Tony Snell	2013-14	926.2
5	Chris Carr	1996-97	924.7
6	Kyle Korver	2003-04	922.6
7	Tim Hardaway, Jr.	2014-15	920.8
8	Daequan Cook	2009-10	916.6
9	Bill Walker	2009-10	916.3
10	Doron Lamb	2013-14	916.2

Baseline Basic Stats

MPG	PTS	AST	REB	BLK	STL
21.4	8.4	1.5	2.5	0.2	0.6

Advanced Metrics

USG%	3PTA/FGA	FTA/FGA	TS%	eFG%	3PT%
18.2	0.469	0.247	0.538	0.495	0.348

AST%	TOV%	OREB%	DREB%	STL%	BLK%
11.1	12.2	2.3	10.0	1.3	0.7

PER	ORTG	DRTG	WS/48	VOL
10.37	104.5	110.3	0.063	0.420

- Fell out of the rotation in Philadelphia, missed games due to patellar tendinitis in his right knee
- Low volume spot-up shooter, excelled as a cutter
- Three-Point Percentage improved to break-even last season
- Better at shooting threes in the corners than above the break
- Solid stay-at-home on-ball wing defender, good at using length to contest shots

Alex Abrines

	Height	Weight	Cap #	Years Left
	6'6"	190	$5.455M	0

Similar at Age **24**

		Season	SIMsc
1	Chris Johnson	2014-15	915.6
2	Terrence Ross	2015-16	913.9
3	Eric Washington	1998-99	907.2
4	Sasha Vujacic	2008-09	903.0
5	Daequan Cook	2011-12	902.0
6	Rudy Fernandez	2009-10	900.6
7	J.J. Redick	2008-09	891.4
8	Rodney Carney	2008-09	890.1
9	Bill Walker	2011-12	889.0
10	Quincy Pondexter	2012-13	888.0

Baseline Basic Stats

MPG	PTS	AST	REB	BLK	STL
17.8	6.5	1.1	2.1	0.2	0.6

Advanced Metrics

USG%	3PTA/FGA	FTA/FGA	TS%	eFG%	3PT%
16.2	0.656	0.157	0.544	0.513	0.369

AST%	TOV%	OREB%	DREB%	STL%	BLK%
7.7	9.2	1.9	10.4	1.7	0.8

PER	ORTG	DRTG	WS/48	VOL	
10.45	109.0	109.8	0.097	0.400	

- Shooting specialist that's been a regular part of Oklahoma City's rotation for the last two seasons
- Low usage offensive player, has shot threes at a 38% rate in each of the last two seasons
- Mainly used in a spot-up role, above average at shooting off screens
- Improved his ability to finish shots inside of three feet last season
- Below average on-ball defender, decent position defender if he's hidden in favorable matchups

Raymond Felton

	Height	Weight	Cap #	Years Left
	6'1"	198	$1.513M	0

Similar at Age 33

		Season	SIMsc
1	Mike James	2008-09	932.0
2	Derek Fisher	2007-08	929.1
3	Bobby Jackson	2006-07	917.3
4	Nick Van Exel	2004-05	914.4
5	Kirk Hinrich	2013-14	913.9
6	David Wesley	2003-04	913.6
7	Terry Porter	1996-97	911.3
8	Rafer Alston	2009-10	908.8
9	Mo Williams	2015-16	904.7
10	Anthony Johnson	2007-08	902.9

Baseline Basic Stats

MPG	PTS	AST	REB	BLK	STL
23.2	8.2	2.7	2.3	0.1	0.8

Advanced Metrics

USG%	3PTA/FGA	FTA/FGA	TS%	eFG%	3PT%
17.3	0.404	0.165	0.511	0.483	0.357

AST%	TOV%	OREB%	DREB%	STL%	BLK%
17.7	12.5	1.9	10.3	1.9	0.7

PER	ORTG	DRTG	WS/48	VOL	
11.86	105.4	107.5	0.082	0.415	

- Durable over the last three seasons, has only missed four games
- Had his best season in five years, production still down from his career averages
- Decent playmaker that limits turnovers, almost strictly a jump shooter at this stage
- Still had effectiveness as a pick-and-roll ball handler last season
- Historically a below break-even three-point shooter, takes mid-range shots with great frequency, below average at making them
- Solid at defending both guard spots last season, better at handling two guards than point guards, good defensive rebounding point guard

Terrance Ferguson

	Height	Weight	Cap #	Years Left
	6'7"	184	$2.119M	2 Team Options

Similar at Age **19**

		Season	SIMsc
1	Rashad Vaughn	2015-16	879.0
2	Derrick Jones	2016-17	858.8
3	Martell Webster	2005-06	853.8
4	Dante Exum	2014-15	844.3
5	James Young	2014-15	822.0

Baseline Basic Stats

MPG	PTS	AST	REB	BLK	STL
19.8	6.8	1.1	2.5	0.2	0.6

Advanced Metrics

USG%	3PTA/FGA	FTA/FGA	TS%	eFG%	3PT%
13.4	0.571	0.138	0.580	0.559	0.388

AST%	TOV%	OREB%	DREB%	STL%	BLK%
6.5	8.8	2.2	9.3	1.8	1.0

PER	ORTG	DRTG	WS/48	VOL
10.55	115.4	110.1	0.104	0.447

- On the fringes of Oklahoma City's rotation as a 19-year old rookie
- Hard to find comparables because not many 19-year old players entered the NBA with Ferguson's body type
- Played an extremely low volume role, dynamic finisher in transition, break-even three-point shooter
- May be better in motion than as a stationary player
- Good at coming off screens and cutting in a very small sample of possessions
- Decent on-ball defending wing player, more of a stay-at-home defender at this stage

Abdel Nader

	Height	Weight	Cap #	Years Left
	6'6"	230	$1.378M	1 + TO

Similar at Age 24

		Season	SIMsc
1	Lazar Hayward	2010-11	936.0
2	Cartier Martin	2008-09	920.3
3	Jeffery Taylor	2013-14	916.5
4	Anthony Parker	1999-00	916.1
5	Jumaine Jones	2003-04	912.9
6	Donny Marshall	1996-97	911.0
7	Orlando Johnson	2013-14	910.5
8	Chase Budinger	2012-13	909.6
9	Carlos Delfino	2006-07	906.0
10	Dahntay Jones	2004-05	902.7

Baseline Basic Stats

MPG	PTS	AST	REB	BLK	STL
18.2	6.3	1.0	3.0	0.2	0.5

Advanced Metrics

USG%	3PTA/FGA	FTA/FGA	TS%	eFG%	3PT%
17.0	0.441	0.252	0.496	0.463	0.359

AST%	TOV%	OREB%	DREB%	STL%	BLK%
8.3	13.8	3.7	14.3	1.4	1.0

PER	ORTG	DRTG	WS/48	VOL	
9.00	97.0	107.5	0.040	0.437	

- Limited playing time off the bench with Boston last season as a rookie, played 522 minutes
- Primarily a defensive specialist, solid on-ball defender, good at using length to contest shots
- Good defensive rebounding wing player
- Struggled to shoot efficiently in a low volume, spot-up role
- Made threes at an above break-even rate, shot a very low percentage on two-point shots, had difficulties finishing shots inside of three feet
- Below average in most offensive situations, above average at shooting off screens last season

Hamidou Diallo

	Height	Weight	Cap #	Years Left
	6'5"	198	$0.838M	2

Baseline Basic Stats

MPG	PTS	AST	REB	BLK	STL
11.5	4.2	0.8	1.5	0.2	0.3

Advanced Metrics

USG%	3PTA/FGA	FTA/FGA	TS%	eFG%	3PT%
17.0	0.208	0.290	0.499	0.446	0.316

AST%	TOV%	OREB%	DREB%	STL%	BLK%
9.7	13.0	5.6	12.2	1.7	1.0

PER	ORTG	DRTG	WS/48	VOL	
10.92	102.5	108.8	0.056	N/A	

- Drafted by Brooklyn with the 45th overall pick, then traded to Oklahoma City
- Good overall performance at Summer League
- Played with a heavy scoring mindset, able to slash to the rim to finish shots inside, was 4-for-9 on threes
- Shooting stroke may be somewhat inconsistent, only 10-for-18 at the free throw line
- Didn't really look to make plays for others, only two assists in 95 total minutes
- Solid defensively, has potential to defend both guard spots, rebounded well, got steals at a high rate

MINNESOTA TIMBERWOLVES

<u>Last Season</u>: 47 – 35, Lost 1st Round to Houston (1 – 4)

<u>Offensive Rating</u>: 113.4, 4th in NBA   <u>Defensive Rating</u>: 111.1, 27th in NBA

<u>Primary Executive</u>: Tom Thibodeau, President of Basketball Operations

<u>Head Coach</u>: Tom Thibodeau

Key Roster Changes

<u>Subtractions</u>	<u>Additions</u>
Jamal Crawford, free agency	Josh Okogie, draft
Aaron Brooks, free agency	Keita Bates-Diop, draft
Nemanja Bjelica, free agency	Anthony Tolliver, free agency
Marcus Georges-Hunt, free agency	James Nunnally, free agency
Amile Jefferson, free agency	Luol Deng, free agency
Cole Aldrich, waived	

RAFER Projected Win Total: 46.3

<u>Projected Best Five-Man Unit</u>	<u>Other Rotation Players</u>
1. Tyus Jones	Andrew Wiggins
2. Jeff Teague	Gorgui Dieng
3. Jimmy Butler	Anthony Tolliver
4. Taj Gibson	James Nunnally
5. Karl-Anthony Towns	Derrick Rose

Remaining Roster

- Luol Deng
- Justin Patton
- Josh Okogie
- Keita Bates-Diop
- C.J. Williams, 28, 6'5", 225, NC State (Two-Way)
- Jared Terrell, 23, 6'3", 215, Rhode Island (Two-Way)

Season Forecast

The Minnesota Timberwolves used up most of their cap space last season, so they could only make a few small moves like picking up Anthony Tolliver from Detroit and James Nunnally from Europe to tweak their rotation. Their primary starting five from last year is still intact, so they should be close to the same team that they were before Jimmy Butler got hurt in late February. However, the margin for error is razor thin because head coach, Tom Thibodeau tends to ride his main players, last year was no different, and they have very little depth on the bench. Therefore, their rotation would change dramatically in the case of an injury and the team's performance would likely suffer as a result. If one of the team's recent draft picks emerges as a rotation player, it could do wonders to lengthen out the rotation and possibly keep their starters fresh for the playoffs. If Minnesota's main players are healthy all season long, they should be a solid playoff team in the Western Conference. On the other hand, if they get any kind of unlucky injury break, the Timberwolves probably don't have enough depth or balance to sustain a big loss to their lineup and they would likely miss the playoffs.

The main concern for the Timberwolves is going to be their defense. Even though they got a significant talent upgrade last summer, the team was still one of the worst per-possession defensive teams in the league last season. One of the primary reasons for Minnesota's lack of success on defense is that they employ a very traditional lineup with a small guard and two interior players a vast majority of the time. Because opponents are straying from this type of lineup in favor of ones that are more versatile and perimeter oriented, opposing offenses have an easier time of finding exploitable matchups. It also doesn't help matters that their best offensive big man, Karl-Anthony Towns has not really established himself as a reliable rim protector, so opponents get a lot of makeable easy shots around the rim. Stylistically, it's unlikely that Thibodeau would creatively manipulate his lineups to increase the team's defensive versatility because he hasn't really done so in the past. Therefore, any improvement from Minnesota's defense is likely to be mildly incremental at best. Tolliver gives them an extra interior player that has been effective at defending on the perimeter in his prior stops and Nunnally is solid enough on the ball to spell Andrew Wiggins for brief stretches. With these additions, the Timberwolves might get a few extra stops on defense to help out their offense. Aesthetically, Minnesota's offense is not always pleasing to watch due to its slow, grinding pace and a lack of ball movement, but it has been highly effective for the last two seasons. This is mainly due to the individual skills of Towns and Butler, but also because the team has been one of the league's best at drawing fouls, making free throws and crashing the offensive boards. With the same personnel in place, Minnesota should expect the same level of offensive performance with a possible uptick in their three-point shooting, now with Nunnally and Tolliver in the rotation. Overall, Minnesota's success is going to largely depend on the overall health of its primary players because they have to a maintain a sizeable workload for a long 82-game season. If everything breaks right and their top players stay healthy, the Timberwolves could be a top-five seed in the West this coming season. Otherwise, they could miss the playoffs and be forced to explore some major changes to help them sustain their quality of play over a long season.

Veterans

Karl-Anthony Towns

	Height	Weight	Cap #	Years Left
	7'0"	244	$7.839M	0

Similar at Age **22**

		Season	SIMsc
1	Dirk Nowitzki	2000-01	912.5
2	LaMarcus Aldridge	2007-08	899.4
3	Tim Duncan	1998-99	890.4
4	Pau Gasol	2002-03	888.2
5	Brook Lopez	2010-11	885.5
6	Nenad Krstic	2005-06	879.5
7	Amar'e Stoudemire	2004-05	878.5
8	Joe Barry Carroll	1980-81	877.4
9	Al Horford	2008-09	875.9
10	Blake Griffin	2011-12	875.3

Baseline Basic Stats

MPG	PTS	AST	REB	BLK	STL
35.0	19.0	2.3	9.1	1.3	0.8

Advanced Metrics

USG%	3PTA/FGA	FTA/FGA	TS%	eFG%	3PT%
24.6	0.175	0.331	0.609	0.561	0.424

AST%	TOV%	OREB%	DREB%	STL%	BLK%
12.1	10.6	8.5	25.6	1.2	2.9

PER	ORTG	DRTG	WS/48	VOL	
23.93	120.3	105.0	0.218	0.404	

- One of the most productive big men in the league, made his first appearance on an All-NBA team
- Extremely durable, hasn't missed a game in three seasons
- Excellent post-up player, highly efficient scorer at the rim, draws fouls, good three-point shooter
- Solid passing big man, good offensive rebounder
- Effective in virtually every relevant offensive situation for big men
- Grabs defensive rebounds and can block shots, can be out of position a lot leading to easy baskets inside
- Below average as an on-ball defender, highly foul prone, led the NBA in total personal fouls last season

Jimmy Butler

	Height	Weight	Cap #	Years Left
	6'7"	220	$20.446M	Player Option

Similar at Age 28

		Season	SIMsc
1	Caron Butler	2008-09	945.5
2	Clyde Drexler*	1990-91	924.2
3	Rudy Gay	2014-15	919.1
4	Vince Carter	2004-05	914.2
5	Manu Ginobili	2005-06	914.1
6	Michael Redd	2007-08	911.8
7	Jerry Stackhouse	2002-03	911.8
8	Richard Jefferson	2008-09	909.1
9	Luol Deng	2013-14	908.3
10	Michael Finley	2001-02	906.0

Baseline Basic Stats

MPG	PTS	AST	REB	BLK	STL
35.1	19.6	3.8	5.5	0.5	1.3

Advanced Metrics

USG%	3PTA/FGA	FTA/FGA	TS%	eFG%	3PT%
24.7	0.244	0.415	0.568	0.498	0.348

AST%	TOV%	OREB%	DREB%	STL%	BLK%
19.6	10.3	4.3	13.4	2.2	1.0

PER	ORTG	DRTG	WS/48	VOL	
20.91	115.7	107.1	0.168	0.429	

- Coming off his fourth straight All-Star appearance, still in his prime
- Missed more than a month last season due to an injury to the meniscus in his right knee
- On offense, slashing, high volume wing that can finish at the rim, get to the foul line at a high rate
- Good playmaker that rarely turns the ball over, makes threes at an above break-even rate
- Very effective in virtually every offensive situation last season
- Excellent on-ball defending wing, gets steals at a high rate, good rebounder

Andrew Wiggins

	Height	Weight	Cap #	Years Left
	6'8"	199	$25.250M	4

Similar at Age 22

		Season	SIMsc
1	Rudy Gay	2008-09	920.6
2	Gordon Hayward	2012-13	915.1
3	Klay Thompson	2012-13	909.9
4	Tobias Harris	2014-15	908.1
5	Sean Elliott	1990-91	906.1
6	Nicolas Batum	2010-11	904.9
7	Adam Morrison	2006-07	904.5
8	Dennis Scott	1990-91	902.1
9	DeMar DeRozan	2011-12	900.1
10	Luol Deng	2007-08	898.2

Baseline Basic Stats

MPG	PTS	AST	REB	BLK	STL
35.4	18.1	2.5	4.9	0.5	1.1

Advanced Metrics

USG%	3PTA/FGA	FTA/FGA	TS%	eFG%	3PT%
24.3	0.216	0.285	0.532	0.493	0.351

AST%	TOV%	OREB%	DREB%	STL%	BLK%
11.0	9.7	3.6	10.9	1.6	1.2

PER	ORTG	DRTG	WS/48	VOL	
15.52	106.5	111.3	0.078	0.323	

- Extremely durable, has only missed one game in four seasons, has averaged over 36 minutes per game for his career
- Struggled to adapt to a lower volume role, had to become more of a jump shooter, driving less frequently
- Excellent finisher inside, good at cutting to the rim but doesn't do it very often
- Takes too many mid-range shots and shoots them at a below average percentage
- Below break-even three-point shooter, seldomly looks to make plays for others
- Good post-up wing player despite not a lot of post touches
- Decent overall defender, better at defending jump shots, can be vulnerable against the drive
- Can use length and athleticism to contest shots, solid rebounding wing player

Taj Gibson

	Height	Weight	Cap #	Years Left
	6'9"	225	$14.000M	0

Similar at Age <u>32</u>

		Season	SIMsc
1	Joe Smith	2007-08	919.9
2	Otis Thorpe	1994-95	919.8
3	Kurt Thomas	2004-05	918.4
4	Dean Garrett	1998-99	917.2
5	Horace Grant	1997-98	916.6
6	Tony Battie	2008-09	915.2
7	Kenyon Martin	2009-10	915.2
8	Mikki Moore	2007-08	914.5
9	Dale Davis	2001-02	914.5
10	Armen Gilliam	1996-97	913.3

Baseline Basic Stats

MPG	PTS	AST	REB	BLK	STL
27.8	9.8	1.4	6.9	0.7	0.7

Advanced Metrics

USG%	3PTA/FGA	FTA/FGA	TS%	eFG%	3PT%
15.9	0.040	0.268	0.555	0.521	0.219

AST%	TOV%	OREB%	DREB%	STL%	BLK%
7.2	11.9	8.7	18.6	1.2	1.9

PER	ORTG	DRTG	WS/48	VOL
14.40	113.0	106.9	0.117	0.395

- Production has been consistent with his career averages for the last five seasons despite the fact that he is in early 30s
- Mainly a low volume rim runner that will draw fouls, has historically been an above average mid-range shooter
- Most effective as a roll man and post-up player last season
- Solid position defender, better at defending inside than out on the perimeter
- Good overall rebounder, not as active on the offensive boards as he once was
- Shot blocking rates have been steadily declining for the last five seasons

Jeff Teague

	Height	Weight	Cap #	Years Left
	6'2"	180	$19.000M	Player Option

Similar at Age 29

		Season	SIMsc
1	Luke Ridnour	2010-11	938.3
2	Stephon Marbury	2006-07	936.9
3	Mike Conley	2016-17	935.4
4	Eddie Johnson	1984-85	929.3
5	Goran Dragic	2015-16	927.5
6	Jay Humphries	1991-92	925.2
7	Rafer Alston	2005-06	925.0
8	Jeff Hornacek	1992-93	923.9
9	Kevin Johnson	1995-96	921.0
10	Scott Skiles	1993-94	918.9

Baseline Basic Stats

MPG	PTS	AST	REB	BLK	STL
31.6	14.6	5.5	2.9	0.2	1.2

Advanced Metrics

USG%	3PTA/FGA	FTA/FGA	TS%	eFG%	3PT%
21.7	0.283	0.320	0.549	0.492	0.363

AST%	TOV%	OREB%	DREB%	STL%	BLK%
29.0	15.1	1.6	9.2	1.9	0.7

PER	ORTG	DRTG	WS/48	VOL	
16.55	110.1	109.6	0.113	0.348	

- Entering his age-30 season, production slightly down from his career averages
- Got to the rim less frequently as a result of sharing the court with mostly inside players, drew fewer fouls
- Shot efficiently, slightly above average as a mid-range and three-point shooter
- Solid playmaker, but somewhat turnover prone
- Effective as a pick-and-roll ball handler and isolation player, but got fewer touches
- Below average on-ball defender, can be targeted on defense
- Steal Percentage has been below his career average for the last three seasons

Gorgui Dieng

	Height	Weight	Cap #	Years Left
	6'11"	245	$15.171M	2

Similar at Age 28

		Season	SIMsc
1	Brad Miller	2004-05	932.6
2	Marcin Gortat	2012-13	925.9
3	Raef LaFrentz	2004-05	919.7
4	Andrew Lang	1994-95	918.8
5	P.J. Brown	1997-98	918.0
6	Jason Thompson	2014-15	917.7
7	Matt Geiger	1997-98	917.2
8	LaSalle Thompson	1989-90	917.1
9	Dave Corzine	1984-85	916.2
10	Cherokee Parks	2000-01	916.2

Baseline Basic Stats

MPG	PTS	AST	REB	BLK	STL
26.6	9.5	1.5	6.8	0.9	0.7

Advanced Metrics

USG%	3PTA/FGA	FTA/FGA	TS%	eFG%	3PT%
15.9	0.114	0.278	0.545	0.505	0.365

AST%	TOV%	OREB%	DREB%	STL%	BLK%
8.4	13.8	8.0	21.7	1.5	2.6

PER	ORTG	DRTG	WS/48	VOL
13.93	109.3	107.1	0.102	0.350

- Very durable big man, has only missed three games in the last three seasons
- Playing time severely reduced after the addition of Taj Gibson
- Per-minute production increased a bit over the season before
- Low usage big man that's straying further away from the basket
- Shot attempts inside of three feet have decreased every year for the last five seasons
- Still efficient at scoring, has turned into a good mid-range shooter
- Can occasionally make threes, but he's been below break-even for his career
- Good rebounder on both ends, below average overall defender, has trouble defending on the ball
- Subpar rim protector despite decent shot blocking rates
- Block Percentage has decreased in each of his five seasons

Anthony Tolliver

	Height	Weight	Cap #	Years Left
	6'8"	240	$5.750M	0

Similar at Age 32

		Season	SIMsc
1	Matt Bonner	2012-13	906.7
2	Mike Miller	2012-13	895.0
3	James Posey	2008-09	890.9
4	Channing Frye	2015-16	889.0
5	Mike Dunleavy, Jr.	2012-13	888.7
6	LaPhonso Ellis	2002-03	882.5
7	Terry Mills	1999-00	881.6
8	Alan Anderson	2014-15	879.1
9	Shane Battier	2010-11	875.8
10	Austin Croshere	2007-08	872.9

Baseline Basic Stats

MPG	PTS	AST	REB	BLK	STL
18.5	6.1	1.0	2.9	0.3	0.4

Advanced Metrics

USG%	3PTA/FGA	FTA/FGA	TS%	eFG%	3PT%
14.0	0.730	0.210	0.589	0.564	0.381

AST%	TOV%	OREB%	DREB%	STL%	BLK%
7.6	10.8	2.9	14.3	1.0	1.2

PER	ORTG	DRTG	WS/48	VOL
11.29	114.0	109.8	0.104	0.332

- Journeyman rotational four, had a career best season at age 32 in Detroit last year
- Historically a very low usage offensive player, has mostly been a spot-up shooter for the last six seasons
- Shot extremely well last year, made 43.6% of his threes
- Pretty good three-point shooter throughout his career with a percentage 37.6%
- Effective in a small sample of possessions as the screener in pick-and-roll situations
- Solid position defender, most comfortable defending fours, decent on the defensive boards

Tyus Jones

	Height	**Weight**	**Cap #**	**Years Left**
	6'2"	195	$2.444M	0

Similar at Age 21

		Season	SIMsc
1	Devin Harris	2004-05	910.1
2	Jay Williams	2002-03	893.7
3	Cameron Payne	2015-16	892.0
4	William Avery	2000-01	889.6
5	Daniel Gibson	2007-08	889.5
6	Reggie Jackson	2011-12	885.6
7	Cory Joseph	2012-13	884.5
8	Leandro Barbosa	2003-04	883.1
9	Eric Bledsoe	2010-11	882.6
10	Chauncey Billups	1997-98	882.4

Baseline Basic Stats

MPG	PTS	AST	REB	BLK	STL
20.7	7.5	3.4	2.1	0.1	1.0

Advanced Metrics

USG%	3PTA/FGA	FTA/FGA	TS%	eFG%	3PT%
15.5	0.264	0.289	0.531	0.485	0.331

AST%	TOV%	OREB%	DREB%	STL%	BLK%
26.2	15.7	1.9	8.9	2.6	0.4

PER	ORTG	DRTG	WS/48	VOL	
13.45	112.1	109.4	0.101	0.356	

- Has improved in each of his three seasons, became a regular rotation player for the first time last season
- Decent playmaker, cut down on his turnovers, most effective as a pick-and-roll ball handler
- Shot much more efficiently last season in a very low usage role
- Has become a good mid-range shooter, above break-even as a three-point shooter
- Improved his ability to finish shots around the rim by being a good cutter
- Below average on-ball defender, solid defensive rebounder for his size
- Get steals at a high rate, Steal Percentage has increased in each of his three seasons

Derrick Rose

	Height	Weight	Cap #	Years Left
	6'3"	190	$1.513M	0

Similar at Age 29

		Season	SIMsc
1	Doug Overton	1998-99	934.3
2	Andrew Toney	1986-87	925.1
3	Ben Gordon	2012-13	914.9
4	Sidney Moncrief	1986-87	907.6
5	Ramon Sessions	2015-16	905.6
6	Darrell Griffith	1987-88	904.4
7	Joe Dumars*	1992-93	904.4
8	Quintin Dailey	1989-90	902.9
9	Otis Birdsong	1984-85	902.7
10	Brian Winters	1981-82	901.7

Baseline Basic Stats

MPG	PTS	AST	REB	BLK	STL
27.5	13.5	3.1	2.4	0.2	0.9

Advanced Metrics

USG%	3PTA/FGA	FTA/FGA	TS%	eFG%	3PT%
23.4	0.164	0.238	0.518	0.473	0.302

AST%	TOV%	OREB%	DREB%	STL%	BLK%
17.4	12.8	3.0	7.0	1.3	0.6

PER	ORTG	DRTG	WS/48	VOL	
13.64	103.2	113.0	0.040	0.580	

- Past injuries have put him in a highly diminished state
- Playing time last season was limited due to a sprained ankle and ineffectiveness
- Struggles to score efficiently, can only score inside of three feet
- Draws fewer fouls, shoots a low percentage on any kind jump shot
- Playmaking skills have declined, Assist Percentage has sharply decreased in each of the last four seasons
- Below average on-ball defender, needs to be hidden in favorable matchups

Luol Deng

	Height	Weight	Cap #	Years Left
	6'8"	220	$18.000M	1

Similar at Age 32

		Season	SIMsc
1	Duane Ferrell	1997-98	858.9
2	Gerald Wallace	2014-15	856.3
3	George Lynch	2002-03	856.2
4	Adrian Griffin	2006-07	854.0
5	Luke Walton	2012-13	853.8
6	Ryan Bowen	2007-08	853.5
7	Devean George	2009-10	850.5
8	Shandon Anderson	2005-06	848.8
9	John Salmons	2011-12	843.7
10	Damien Wilkins	2011-12	843.2

Baseline Basic Stats

MPG	PTS	AST	REB	BLK	STL
19.1	6.0	1.3	2.6	0.2	0.6

Advanced Metrics

USG%	3PTA/FGA	FTA/FGA	TS%	eFG%	3PT%
13.5	0.267	0.154	0.535	0.511	0.262

AST%	TOV%	OREB%	DREB%	STL%	BLK%
10.4	17.8	3.2	8.8	2.0	0.6

PER	ORTG	DRTG	WS/48	VOL	
10.30	100.8	109.0	0.060	0.869	

- Only played 13 minutes last season, unclear if he was injured
- Production has severely declined over the last two seasons
- Struggled to adapt to a lower volume role, doesn't get to the rim as often
- Below break-even three-point shooter for his career, middling playmaking skills
- Most effective at cutting to the basket in 2016-17
- When healthy, solid on-ball wing defender, fairly good defensive rebounder
- May be physically diminished due to past injuries and heavy wear and tear on his body

Justin Patton

	Height	Weight	Cap #	Years Left
	6'11"	229	$2.668M	2 Team Options

	Similar at Age	**20**	
		Season	SIMsc
1	Byron Mullens	2009-10	630.0
2	Quincy Miller	2012-13	609.4
3	Josh McRoberts	2007-08	596.3
4	Alexis Ajinca	2008-09	587.1
5	Chris McCullough	2015-16	586.2
6	Bruno Sundov	2000-01	585.5
7	Cliff Alexander	2015-16	581.8
8	Nikoloz Tskitishvili	2003-04	575.7
9	Skal Labissiere	2016-17	571.9
10	Chris Wilcox	2002-03	567.3

Baseline Basic Stats

MPG	PTS	AST	REB	BLK	STL
15.2	5.0	0.7	3.2	0.3	0.4

Advanced Metrics

USG%	3PTA/FGA	FTA/FGA	TS%	eFG%	3PT%
22.3	0.327	0.196	0.670	0.657	0.329

AST%	TOV%	OREB%	DREB%	STL%	BLK%
6.5	9.3	4.9	8.9	4.6	1.4

PER	ORTG	DRTG	WS/48	VOL	
17.43	133.8	106.1	0.135	0.184	

- Only played four minutes in his rookie season, spent most of the year in the G-League with Iowa
- Currently recovering from multiple foot surgeries
- Played in a higher volume stretch big role in the G-League, good shooter from mid-range, but still below break-even as a three-point shooter
- Showed some passing skills, but was a bit turnover prone
- Active help defender that blocks shots and gets steals at a high rate
- On-ball defense needs work, sacrifices position to go for blocks, middling as a defensive rebounder

Newcomers

James Nunnally

		Height	**Weight**	**Cap #**	**Years Left**
		6'7"	205	$1.349M	1

Baseline Basic Stats

MPG	PTS	AST	REB	BLK	STL
21.1	8.2	1.3	2.5	0.2	0.6

Advanced Metrics

USG%	3PTA/FGA	FTA/FGA	TS%	eFG%	3PT%
17.3	0.563	0.173	0.631	0.604	0.469

AST%	TOV%	OREB%	DREB%	STL%	BLK%
10.8	12.8	2.5	11.4	1.6	0.8

PER	ORTG	DRTG	WS/48	VOL
11.46	116.6	117.8	0.076	0.678

- Played last season with Fenerbahce in Turkey, projection uses translated EuroLeague stats
- Expected to play a lower volume role this coming season
- Has been excellent three-point shooter for Fenerbahce, made threes at a 52% rate over the last two seasons
- Decent playmaking wing player, a little bit turnover prone
- Above average on-ball defender, solid rebounding wing player

Josh Okogie

	Height	Weight	Cap #	Years Left
	6'4"	213	$2.161M	1 + 2 TO

Baseline Basic Stats

MPG	PTS	AST	REB	BLK	STL
11.1	3.8	0.5	1.6	0.2	0.3

Advanced Metrics

USG%	3PTA/FGA	FTA/FGA	TS%	eFG%	3PT%
19.4	0.191	0.292	0.461	0.420	0.271

AST%	TOV%	OREB%	DREB%	STL%	BLK%
7.7	14.0	5.5	11.4	1.5	1.1

PER	ORTG	DRTG	WS/48	VOL
8.60	92.6	108.6	0.005	N/A

- Drafted by Minnesota in the first round with the 20th overall pick
- Performance at Summer League produced mixed results
- Flashed great defensive potential, aggressive on-ball defender that could guard multiple positions
- Very active help defender that got steals and blocks at a high rate without fouling, good defensive rebounder
- On offense, got to the foul line at a high rate, but really struggled to shoot efficiently
- Shot under 30% from the field and under 16% from the three-point line, a bit turnover prone

Keita Bates-Diop

	Height	Weight	Cap #	Years Left
	6'7"	235	$0.838M	1 + TO

Baseline Basic Stats

MPG	PTS	AST	REB	BLK	STL
10.5	3.4	0.5	2.0	0.2	0.3

Advanced Metrics

USG%	3PTA/FGA	FTA/FGA	TS%	eFG%	3PT%
16.3	0.228	0.163	0.465	0.444	0.270

AST%	TOV%	OREB%	DREB%	STL%	BLK%
7.9	10.5	6.1	17.0	1.4	1.6

PER	ORTG	DRTG	WS/48	VOL
10.41	97.0	105.2	0.054	N/A

- Drafted by Minnesota in the second round with the 48th overall pick
- Solid showing at Summer League in July
- Strong potential as a defender that could guard multiple positions, used great length to contest shots
- Good help defender, grabbed defensive rebounds, blocked shots and got steals at a high rate without fouling
- Scored in volume on offense, but wasn't especially efficient
- Shot over 50% on two-pointers, but made less than 25% of his threes, also highly turnover prone

UTAH JAZZ

Last Season: 48 – 34, Lost 2nd Round to Houston (1 – 4)

Offensive Rating: 108.4, 16th in NBA

Defensive Rating: 103.9, 2nd in NBA

Primary Executive: Dennis Lindsey, General Manager

Head Coach: Quin Snyder

Key Roster Changes

Subtractions
Jonas Jerebko, waived
David Stockton, waived

Additions
Grayson Allen, draft

RAFER Projected Win Total: 44.9

Projected Best Five-Man Unit
1. Ricky Rubio
2. Donovan Mitchell
3. Joe Ingles
4. Thabo Sefolosha
5. Rudy Gobert

Other Rotation Players
Derrick Favors
Jae Crowder
Dante Exum
Alec Burks
Royce O'Neale
Grayson Allen

Remaining Roster

- Ekpe Udoh
- Raul Neto
- Georges Niang
- Tony Bradley
- Naz Mitrou-Long, 25, 6'4", 209, Iowa State (Two-Way)
- Tyler Cavanaugh, 24, 6'9", 239, George Washington (Two-Way)
- Jairus Lyles, 22, 6'2", 175, Maryland - Baltimore County (Exhibit 10)
- Isaac Haas, 23, 7'2", 290, Purdue (Exhibit 10)
- Trey Lewis, 26, 6'2", 185, Louisville (Exhibit 10)

Season Forecast

The Utah Jazz are basically running back the same roster from last season, as they only really switched out Jonas Jerebko for rookie Grayson Allen. The rest of their roster is intact and mostly consists of players in their 20s, so the results should be similar to last season. There is some room for a little bit of internal growth because Donovan Mitchell is heading into his second year after an excellent rookie season. Even if things stay the same, Utah should be a solid playoff team in the West because they have been one of the league's best defensive teams for the last three seasons and the continuity of their roster should help them be a little more efficient on offense. However, the increased competition in the Western Conference could push them down to a middle seed, which hurts their chances of advancing far in the playoffs. In all probability, the Jazz will be good enough to get out of the first round, but not get much further than that.

Utah projects to once again be one of the NBA's defensive teams. Historically, their performance on this end is due to the elite rim protecting skills of Rudy Gobert, the league's reigning Defensive Player of the Year. However, the Jazz were able to maintain their proficiency on defense in the games when he was out due to injuries to his leg and knee by sliding Derrick Favors down to the five and playing lineups that featured players with greater versatility that could defend multiple positions. As a result, Utah was better equipped to handle different kinds of lineups. This year, they will get Thabo Sefolosha back from injury and they will get a full season from Jae Crowder. Therefore, they could be better because they would have more quality wing defenders to roll at the league's best perimeter scorers to potentially wear them down and keep them in check. Offensively, it's uncertain if there's much room for Utah to grow because they only really have one reliable shot creator in Mitchell. The rest of the players in their rotation all have their limitations on offense, so most of the offensive responsibility is going to fall on Mitchell's shoulders. If he improves his shooting efficiency and playmaking skills, Utah's offense could go up a notch. Otherwise, the Jazz will still have an average offensive unit. Generally speaking, the Utah Jazz should be a good team that will rely heavily on an elite defense and an offense that will grind out enough points to win games. Most likely, they will reach the second round of the playoffs, but they probably won't go much further than this because they simply do not have the offensive firepower to match up with either Golden State or Houston.

Veterans

Rudy Gobert

	Height	Weight	Cap #	Years Left
	7'1"	220	$23.492M	2

Similar at Age 25

		Season	SIMsc
1	Tyson Chandler	2007-08	884.5
2	Keon Clark	2000-01	881.2
3	Joel Przybilla	2004-05	875.9
4	Marcus Camby	1999-00	873.3
5	John Salley	1989-90	869.9
6	Dale Davis	1994-95	869.8
7	Antonio Davis	1993-94	868.1
8	Hot Rod Williams	1987-88	865.1
9	Theo Ratliff	1998-99	863.0
10	Steven Hunter	2006-07	862.3

Baseline Basic Stats

MPG	PTS	AST	REB	BLK	STL
29.4	10.1	1.1	8.9	2.1	0.7

Advanced Metrics

USG%	3PTA/FGA	FTA/FGA	TS%	eFG%	3PT%
16.1	0.002	0.603	0.619	0.591	0.032

AST%	TOV%	OREB%	DREB%	STL%	BLK%
6.2	15.8	11.2	25.2	1.1	5.4

PER	ORTG	DRTG	WS/48	VOL
18.94	118.1	100.0	0.187	0.272

- Won Defensive Player of the Year last season, missed almost two months due to injuries to his right leg and left knee
- Elite rim protector, excellent shot blocker and defensive rebounder
- Can be vulnerable against guards on switches
- Strictly a low volume rim runner that scores on cuts and rolls to the rim
- Has shot over 70% on shots inside of three feet for his career
- Excellent at getting at second chance opportunities on the offensive boards
- Doesn't post up very much, was only about average in a small sample of possessions

Donovan Mitchell

	Height	Weight	Cap #	Years Left
	6'3"	211	$3.111M	2 Team Options

Similar at Age 21

		Season	SIMsc
1	Bradley Beal	2014-15	922.4
2	O.J. Mayo	2008-09	917.9
3	Ben Gordon	2004-05	912.5
4	Dion Waiters	2012-13	910.1
5	Gary Harris	2015-16	895.1
6	Kyrie Irving	2013-14	894.8
7	Ray Allen*	1996-97	894.3
8	Deron Williams	2005-06	894.2
9	Victor Oladipo	2013-14	891.7
10	Chauncey Billups	1997-98	891.1

Baseline Basic Stats

MPG	PTS	AST	REB	BLK	STL
33.9	18.7	3.5	3.5	0.3	1.1

Advanced Metrics

USG%	3PTA/FGA	FTA/FGA	TS%	eFG%	3PT%
25.6	0.267	0.249	0.545	0.506	0.352

AST%	TOV%	OREB%	DREB%	STL%	BLK%
18.9	12.8	2.2	9.3	2.0	0.7

PER	ORTG	DRTG	WS/48	VOL
15.80	105.6	107.5	0.100	0.292

- Runner-up in the Rookie of the Year voting in his age-21 season
- Dynamic high volume scoring guard with decent playmaking skills
- Relies on slashing to the rim to get high percentage shots inside of three feet or draw fouls
- Has an effective enough outside shot to keep defenders honest, almost average from mid-range, slightly above break-even from the three-point line
- Above average or better in virtually every offensive situation
- Plays solid on-ball defense, can defend both guard spots
- Posts an above average Steal Percentage, good rebounder for his size

Joe Ingles

	Height	Weight	Cap #	Years Left
	6'8"	216	$13.045M	2

Similar at Age 30

	Player	Season	SIMsc
1	Kyle Korver	2011-12	914.0
2	James Posey	2006-07	911.3
3	DeMarre Carroll	2016-17	909.2
4	Jared Dudley	2015-16	905.5
5	Boris Diaw	2012-13	897.3
6	Morris Peterson	2007-08	896.3
7	Chuck Person	1994-95	895.1
8	Trevor Ariza	2015-16	892.6
9	Shane Battier	2008-09	892.0
10	Dan Majerle	1995-96	890.5

Baseline Basic Stats

MPG	PTS	AST	REB	BLK	STL
27.2	9.1	2.3	4.1	0.3	0.9

Advanced Metrics

USG%	3PTA/FGA	FTA/FGA	TS%	eFG%	3PT%
15.1	0.644	0.161	0.611	0.591	0.427

AST%	TOV%	OREB%	DREB%	STL%	BLK%
16.8	16.2	1.5	15.3	1.7	0.7

PER	ORTG	DRTG	WS/48	VOL
13.00	112.7	105.9	0.117	0.274

- Has improved in each of his four seasons in the league
- Extremely durable, has only missed four games in four seasons
- Increased his efficiency each season in a very low volume role by almost eliminating the long two from his shot selection
- Has become one of the NBA's best three-point shooters
- Finished in the top five in Three-Point Percentage in each of the last two seasons with a percentage over 44%
- Mainly effective as a spot-up shooter, but can also run off screens and cut to the basket
- Passing has gradually gotten better over the last three seasons, but still a little turnover prone
- Solid position defender despite having less than ideal athletic tools, effective on the defensive glass

Ricky Rubio

	Height	Weight	Cap #	Years Left
	6'4"	180	$14.975M	0

Similar at Age 27

		Season	SIMsc
1	Derek Harper	1988-89	917.0
2	Scott Skiles	1991-92	915.2
3	Doc Rivers	1988-89	914.6
4	Kirk Hinrich	2007-08	913.6
5	Goran Dragic	2013-14	911.3
6	Terry Porter	1990-91	911.3
7	Vernon Maxwell	1992-93	908.9
8	Luke Ridnour	2008-09	907.5
9	Micheal Williams	1993-94	906.8
10	Sleepy Floyd	1987-88	906.3

Baseline Basic Stats

MPG	PTS	AST	REB	BLK	STL
32.5	14.3	6.6	3.5	0.2	1.5

Advanced Metrics

USG%	3PTA/FGA	FTA/FGA	TS%	eFG%	3PT%
20.5	0.321	0.325	0.540	0.482	0.352

AST%	TOV%	OREB%	DREB%	STL%	BLK%
31.6	17.6	2.6	11.8	2.4	0.4

PER	ORTG	DRTG	WS/48	VOL	
16.06	109.5	106.8	0.119	0.316	

- Solid season at age 27, production slightly down but still consistent with his career averages
- Took on a higher usage role, maintained his shooting efficiency
- More of a jump shooter, drew fewer fouls
- Shot an above break-even three-point percentage for the first time since his rookie year
- Not the same heavy pass-first point guard that was in Minnesota, good playmaker, posted lowest Turnover Percentage of his career
- Good help defender, gets steals and defensive rebounds at a high rate, below average as an on-ball defender

Derrick Favors

	Height	Weight	Cap #	Years Left
	6'10"	246	$16.900M	1

Similar at Age 26

		Season	SIMsc
1	Clemon Johnson	1982-83	941.5
2	Jordan Hill	2013-14	925.8
3	Jason Thompson	2012-13	923.9
4	Al Horford	2012-13	923.4
5	Amar'e Stoudemire	2008-09	918.7
6	Marcin Gortat	2010-11	916.9
7	Gustavo Ayon	2011-12	914.0
8	Jim Petersen	1988-89	910.9
9	Drew Gooden	2007-08	910.1
10	LaSalle Thompson	1987-88	910.0

Baseline Basic Stats

MPG	PTS	AST	REB	BLK	STL
26.5	11.4	1.5	7.0	0.9	0.7

Advanced Metrics

USG%	3PTA/FGA	FTA/FGA	TS%	eFG%	3PT%
19.6	0.055	0.288	0.555	0.526	0.281

AST%	TOV%	OREB%	DREB%	STL%	BLK%
8.5	11.6	9.3	19.9	1.4	2.8

PER	ORTG	DRTG	WS/48	VOL	
17.16	111.2	104.8	0.133	0.451	

- Had a bounce back year last season after his production was down the season before
- Very good rim protector, good shot blocker, rebounder and interior position defender
- Displayed better mobility, allowing him to be competent at defending out on the perimeter
- Primarily a low volume, high efficiency rim runner that scores as a roll man and cutter
- Effective offensive rebounder that scores on second chance opportunities
- Improved his mid-range shot to shoot a slightly above average percentage
- Posted the lowest Turnover Percentage of his career

Jae Crowder

	Height	Weight	Cap #	Years Left
	6'7"	240	$7.306M	1

Similar at Age <u>27</u>

		Season	SIMsc
1	Ryan Gomes	2009-10	939.4
2	Carlos Delfino	2009-10	926.2
3	Morris Peterson	2004-05	925.0
4	Jared Dudley	2012-13	924.8
5	Eric Piatkowski	1997-98	919.7
6	Mike Scott	2015-16	919.2
7	Al Harrington	2007-08	914.0
8	Kyle Korver	2008-09	913.8
9	Marvin Williams	2013-14	912.4
10	Bryon Russell	1997-98	911.8

Baseline Basic Stats

MPG	PTS	AST	REB	BLK	STL
25.7	10.1	1.5	3.8	0.3	0.8

Advanced Metrics

USG%	3PTA/FGA	FTA/FGA	TS%	eFG%	3PT%
17.6	0.526	0.222	0.549	0.513	0.361

AST%	TOV%	OREB%	DREB%	STL%	BLK%
8.7	9.7	3.0	13.7	1.5	0.8

PER	ORTG	DRTG	WS/48	VOL	
12.50	108.9	108.7	0.094	0.474	

- Production has been declining over the last three seasons, struggled in the playoffs last season
- Athleticism may be diminishing, dunking at a much lower rate
- Only three dunks last season compared to 13 the season before
- Low volume spot-up shooter, free throw attempt rate is decreasing
- Three-point percentage has been inconsistent overall
- Still a good three-point shooter in the corners, good at coming off screens
- Good on-ball defender, more of a position defender over the last two seasons, solid defensive rebounder

Thabo Sefolosha

	Height	Weight	Cap #	Years Left
	6'5"	215	$5.250M	0

Similar at Age 33

		Season	SIMsc
1	Mitchell Butler	2003-04	890.7
2	Bryon Russell	2003-04	888.2
3	Ira Newble	2007-08	886.7
4	Tyrone Corbin	1995-96	885.3
5	Tony Allen	2014-15	884.7
6	Anthony Parker	2008-09	881.9
7	Caron Butler	2013-14	880.6
8	Damien Wilkins	2012-13	880.1
9	Stacey Augmon	2001-02	879.9
10	Maurice Evans	2011-12	879.6

Baseline Basic Stats

MPG	PTS	AST	REB	BLK	STL
22.1	6.4	1.5	3.5	0.2	1.0

Advanced Metrics

USG%	3PTA/FGA	FTA/FGA	TS%	eFG%	3PT%
14.1	0.394	0.202	0.547	0.521	0.370

AST%	TOV%	OREB%	DREB%	STL%	BLK%
8.7	11.7	4.0	15.5	2.7	1.1

PER	ORTG	DRTG	WS/48	VOL	
12.59	109.2	102.7	0.121	0.469	

- Missed most of last season due to a knee injury that required surgery
- Was having career best season at age 33 before injuring his knee in January
- Good on-ball wing defender, solid defensive rebounder
- Posted the highest Steal Percentage of his career last season
- Utilized as a low volume spot-up shooter, very good overall three-point shooter last season
- Has been a good corner three-point shooter throughout his career, even with some fluctuating percentages
- Was one of the league's best cutters last season finishing in the 90th percentile on plays that ended with a cut

Dante Exum

	Height	Weight	Cap #	Years Left
	6'6'	190	$9.600M	2

Similar at Age 22

		Season	SIMsc
1	Tony Dumas	1994-95	930.0
2	Jordan Clarkson	2014-15	919.8
3	Nick Young	2007-08	914.3
4	Corey Benjamin	2000-01	913.8
5	Manny Harris	2011-12	911.9
6	Evan Fournier	2014-15	910.8
7	Jamal Crawford	2002-03	909.0
8	Marco Belinelli	2008-09	906.5
9	Tate George	1990-91	904.9
10	Steve Smith	1991-92	903.6

Baseline Basic Stats

MPG	PTS	AST	REB	BLK	STL
21.6	9.5	2.4	2.3	0.2	0.7

Advanced Metrics

USG%	3PTA/FGA	FTA/FGA	TS%	eFG%	3PT%
21.4	0.296	0.270	0.535	0.491	0.327

AST%	TOV%	OREB%	DREB%	STL%	BLK%
20.4	13.8	2.5	9.6	1.6	0.9

PER	ORTG	DRTG	WS/48	VOL
13.90	105.9	108.8	0.085	0.478

- Missed most of last season due to a separated left shoulder
- Missed all of 2015-16 due to a torn ACL in his left knee
- Showed significant improvement in a small sample of minutes last season
- Scored efficiently by focusing on slashing to the rim to make high percentage shots inside or draw fouls
- Taking fewer outside shots, three-point percentage has decreased each season
- Dramatically improved as a playmaker
- More than doubled his Assist Percentage from the 2016-17 season
- Only effective in situations with the ball in his hands as a pick-and-roll ball handler and in isolation situations
- Below average in virtually every situation off the ball
- Solid on-ball defender that can defend both guard spots, above average rebounding guard

Alec Burks

	Height	Weight	Cap #	Years Left
	6'6"	195	$11.537M	0

	Similar at Age	**26**	
		Season	**SIMsc**
1	Marquis Daniels	2006-07	921.3
2	Jonathon Simmons	2015-16	920.5
3	Jeff Lamp	1985-86	915.6
4	Alexey Shved	2014-15	915.5
5	Nick Young	2011-12	910.8
6	Tracy Moore	1991-92	910.4
7	Brandon Roy	2010-11	910.3
8	Gary Forbes	2011-12	910.2
9	Bob Hansen	1986-87	909.9
10	Sasha Vujacic	2010-11	908.5

Baseline Basic Stats

MPG	PTS	AST	REB	BLK	STL
23.6	11.0	1.7	2.6	0.2	0.7

Advanced Metrics

USG%	3PTA/FGA	FTA/FGA	TS%	eFG%	3PT%
22.4	0.322	0.283	0.530	0.479	0.358

AST%	TOV%	OREB%	DREB%	STL%	BLK%
11.2	10.7	2.5	13.3	1.6	0.6

PER	ORTG	DRTG	WS/48	VOL
13.51	104.4	108.3	0.082	0.460

- Stayed healthy last season, but missed games in the two previous seasons due to a broken leg along with injuries to his knee and ankle that both required surgery
- Moderate volume guard that gets to the rim and draws fouls by using above average isolation skills and by being a good cutter
- An above break-even three-point shooter for his career, but his percentages have been inconsistent on a year-to-year basis
- Fairly good on-ball wing defender, posted the highest Steal Percentage of his career last season, good defensive rebounding wing

Royce O'Neale

	Height	Weight	Cap #	Years Left
	6'6"	215	$1.378M	1

Similar at Age 24

		Season	SIMsc
1	James Ennis	2014-15	926.5
2	Solomon Hill	2015-16	924.3
3	Carlos Delfino	2006-07	924.2
4	James Anderson	2013-14	921.5
5	Quincy Pondexter	2012-13	920.5
6	Martell Webster	2010-11	917.4
7	John Salmons	2003-04	916.8
8	Bill Walker	2011-12	916.6
9	Antoine Wright	2008-09	914.9
10	Eric Piatkowski	1994-95	913.5

Baseline Basic Stats

MPG	PTS	AST	REB	BLK	STL
22.7	7.6	1.7	3.2	0.3	0.8

Advanced Metrics

USG%	3PTA/FGA	FTA/FGA	TS%	eFG%	3PT%
15.9	0.442	0.252	0.537	0.496	0.354

AST%	TOV%	OREB%	DREB%	STL%	BLK%
12.6	13.0	2.9	16.5	1.7	1.0

PER	ORTG	DRTG	WS/48	VOL	
11.72	106.2	106.4	0.090	0.477	

- Regular part of Utah's rotation as a rookie, moderately effective in the playoffs
- Primarily a low volume spot-up shooter with some passing skills
- Excellent cutter that will draw fouls
- Rated by the NBA as the one of the best per-possession cutters in the league, ranked in the 99th percentile
- Almost league average as an overall three-point shooter, much better in the corners, made 41.1% of his corner threes
- Good on-ball wing defender that contests shots, excellent defensive rebounding wing player

Ekpe Udoh

	Height	Weight	Cap #	Years Left
	6'10"	240	$3.360M	0

Similar at Age 30

		Season	SIMsc
1	Joel Anthony	2012-13	878.9
2	Clemon Johnson	1986-87	861.9
3	Ronny Turiaf	2012-13	855.5
4	Jared Jeffries	2011-12	855.4
5	Chris Andersen	2008-09	854.5
6	Dan Gadzuric	2008-09	848.8
7	Adonal Foyle	2005-06	845.9
8	Brandon Bass	2015-16	844.2
9	Theo Ratliff	2003-04	843.9
10	Calvin Booth	2006-07	843.7

Baseline Basic Stats

MPG	PTS	AST	REB	BLK	STL
14.4	2.9	0.4	3.3	0.9	0.3

Advanced Metrics

USG%	3PTA/FGA	FTA/FGA	TS%	eFG%	3PT%
9.4	0.005	0.460	0.540	0.496	-0.013

AST%	TOV%	OREB%	DREB%	STL%	BLK%
6.2	14.9	9.1	14.9	1.7	5.6

PER	ORTG	DRTG	WS/48	VOL
12.01	116.4	101.7	0.129	0.467

- A fringe rotation player for Utah last season after spending the previous two years in Turkey
- Had the best season of his career last season at age 30
- Mainly used as a very low usage rim runner that scored from inside three feet and drew fouls at a high rate
- Shot blocking specialist on defense, posted the highest Block Percentage of his career last season, solid rim protector
- Struggles to defend on the ball, sacrifices positioning to go for blocks, below average defensive rebounder

Raul Neto

	Height	Weight	Cap #	Years Left
	6'1"	179	$2.150M	1

Similar at Age 25

		Season	SIMsc
1	Anthony Goldwire	1996-97	930.4
2	Bimbo Coles	1993-94	928.3
3	Shawn Respert	1997-98	925.6
4	A.J. Price	2011-12	925.2
5	Shabazz Napier	2016-17	923.7
6	George Hill	2011-12	923.5
7	Ronnie Price	2008-09	923.1
8	Vonteego Cummings	2001-02	921.2
9	Chris Quinn	2008-09	919.7
10	Mike Evans	1980-81	918.2

Baseline Basic Stats

MPG	PTS	AST	REB	BLK	STL
20.7	7.8	3.0	2.0	0.1	0.8

Advanced Metrics

USG%	3PTA/FGA	FTA/FGA	TS%	eFG%	3PT%
18.3	0.319	0.181	0.525	0.495	0.367

AST%	TOV%	OREB%	DREB%	STL%	BLK%
21.8	14.6	1.6	8.8	1.9	0.6

PER	ORTG	DRTG	WS/48	VOL	
12.40	104.7	107.7	0.085	0.383	

- Fallen out of the rotation in the last two seasons
- Also missed games due to a hamstring injury, a fractured wrist and a concussion
- Has improved his per-minute production in each of his three seasons
- Low volume point guard with decent playmaking skills, but is somewhat turnover prone
- Good three-point shooter over his career, percentages have fluctuated from year-to-year
- Shoots a high percentage on shots inside three feet, drew fouls at a much higher rate last season
- Effective defender when hidden in favorable matchups, gets steals, solid rebounder for his size

Tony Bradley

	Height	Weight	Cap #	Years Left
	6'11"	240	$1.680M	2 Team Options

Similar at Age 20

		Season	SIMsc
1	Stephen Zimmerman	2016-17	830.5
2	Bobby Portis	2015-16	825.8
3	Brandon Bass	2005-06	813.6
4	Nikoloz Tskitishvili	2003-04	810.2
5	Henry Ellenson	2016-17	809.3
6	Cheick Diallo	2016-17	800.2
7	Yi Jianlian	2007-08	797.8
8	Noah Vonleh	2015-16	792.2
9	Trey Lyles	2015-16	791.7
10	Maciej Lampe	2005-06	791.4

Baseline Basic Stats

MPG	PTS	AST	REB	BLK	STL
14.6	5.4	0.6	3.9	0.5	0.3

Advanced Metrics

USG%	3PTA/FGA	FTA/FGA	TS%	eFG%	3PT%
17.3	0.150	0.211	0.485	0.447	0.215

AST%	TOV%	OREB%	DREB%	STL%	BLK%
6.4	6.9	10.7	22.2	0.8	1.3

PER	ORTG	DRTG	WS/48	VOL	
13.24	107.2	107.0	0.102	0.711	

- Only played 29 minutes in the NBA as a rookie
- Spent most of last season with the Salt Lake City Stars in the G-League
- Played a moderate volume role on offense in the G-League, mainly did his damage inside
- Shot over 58% from the field, flashed mid-range potential by making over 81% of his free throws
- Very good rebounder on both ends, active help defender that got steals and blocked shots at a high rate, position defense may still need work

Georges Niang

	Height	Weight	Cap #	Years Left
	6'8"	230	$1.513M	2

Similar at Age 24

		Season	SIMsc
1	Chris Singleton	2013-14	896.5
2	Donny Marshall	1996-97	886.8
3	Wilson Chandler	2011-12	879.3
4	Frank Kornet	1990-91	875.4
5	John Williams	1990-91	875.0
6	Craig Brackins	2011-12	866.5
7	Jarvis Hayes	2005-06	865.6
8	Brian Evans	1997-98	865.6
9	Cleanthony Early	2015-16	865.2
10	Luke Walton	2004-05	865.2

Baseline Basic Stats

MPG	PTS	AST	REB	BLK	STL
20.1	7.9	1.5	3.7	0.3	0.6

Advanced Metrics

USG%	3PTA/FGA	FTA/FGA	TS%	eFG%	3PT%
19.4	0.268	0.177	0.458	0.427	0.221

AST%	TOV%	OREB%	DREB%	STL%	BLK%
11.4	13.1	6.4	18.0	1.9	0.6

PER	ORTG	DRTG	WS/48	VOL
10.74	94.7	105.7	0.033	0.571

- Played on a two-way contract with Utah last season

- Spent most of the season in the G-League with two different teams

- Effective in a moderate volume offensive role, displayed good passing skills, but was somewhat turnover prone

- Much more efficient as a shooter, more jump shot dependent, made 45.9% of his threes last season

- Middling to below average as a position defender, solid defensive rebounder

Newcomers

Grayson Allen

	Height	Weight	Cap #	Years Left
	6'5"	205	$2.074M	1 + 2 TO

Baseline Basic Stats

MPG	PTS	AST	REB	BLK	STL
20.2	8.5	2.5	2.4	0.2	0.7

Advanced Metrics

USG%	3PTA/FGA	FTA/FGA	TS%	eFG%	3PT%
21.2	0.316	0.252	0.523	0.481	0.366

AST%	TOV%	OREB%	DREB%	STL%	BLK%
20.3	15.0	2.8	10.6	1.8	0.6

PER	ORTG	DRTG	WS/48	VOL
13.39	103.0	108.9	0.048	N/A

- Drafted by Utah in the first round with the 21st overall pick
- Strong performance in the Las Vegas Summer League
- Pesky, aggressive on-ball defender, used active hands to get steals at a high rate, rebounded very well
- Displayed very good playmaking and ball control skills
- Scored in volume, but struggled to make shots efficiently, shot below 40% from the field and below 25% on threes in Las Vegas

SAN ANTONIO SPURS

Last Season: 47 – 35, Lost 1st Round to Golden State (1 – 4)

Offensive Rating: 107.9, 17th in NBA   Defensive Rating: 104.8, 3rd in NBA

Primary Executive: R.C. Buford, President of Sports Franchises for Spurs Sports and Entertainment

Head Coach: Gregg Popovich

Key Roster Changes

Subtractions
Kawhi Leonard, trade
Danny Green, trade
Tony Parker, free agency
Kyle Anderson, free agency
Joffrey Lauvergne, free agency
Brandon Paul, waived
Manu Ginobili, retired

Additions
Lonnie Walker IV, draft
Chimezie Metu, draft
DeMar DeRozan, trade
Jakob Poeltl, trade
Marco Belinelli, free agency
Dante Cunningham, free agency
Quincy Pondexter, free agency

RAFER Projected Win Total: 44.6

Projected Best Five-Man Unit
1. Patty Mills
2. DeMar DeRozan
3. Rudy Gay
4. LaMarcus Aldridge
5. Jakob Poeltl

Other Rotation Players
Pau Gasol
Dejounte Murray
Marco Belinelli
Derrick White
Davis Bertans

Remaining Roster

- Dante Cunningham
- Bryn Forbes
- Quincy Pondexter
- Lonnie Walker IV
- Chimezie Metu
- Josh Huestis, 27, 6'7", 230, Stanford (Exhibit 10)

Season Forecast

The San Antonio Spurs' offseason didn't get off to a great start when Kawhi Leonard made it public that he wished to be traded elsewhere. Initially, the Spurs didn't give in to Leonard's trade demands, but then they worked out a deal with Toronto to get back an All-Star in DeMar DeRozan, a promising young center in Jakob Poeltl and a draft pick in return for Leonard and Danny Green. By receiving a player like DeRozan to replace Leonard, it allows the Spurs to continue to be competitive in a very tough Western Conference. The team made the playoffs with Leonard missing most of the season last year, so a full season with an All-Star like DeRozan combined with the existing talent on their roster should allow them to be a solid playoff team this coming season.

Despite not having Leonard in the lineup, the Spurs were one of the league's best defensive teams last season. It was impressive considering that they had no real standout individual defender in their regular rotation. San Antonio relied on a methodical rotation scheme to force their opponents to either go to their secondary options or steer the ball into the inefficient parts of the floor. Most likely, they will keep using the same scheme because most of the team's rotation from last season is intact, except that they will add a solid defender in DeRozan and a very good rim protecting big man in Poeltl. Poeltl could give the Spurs' defense a boost if he's deployed properly. Mainly, if he can match up with another big body center, his shot blocking skills should keep opponents out of the paint and possibly his presence would allow the team's perimeter defenders to be a little more aggressive to create more turnovers. In addition to the players that they received in the trade, the defense could get a boost with infusion of youth and athleticism to their rotation. In particular, by letting Tony Parker go, they are subbing out an aging veteran with a younger, longer athlete in 2017 first round pick, Derrick White. Therefore, the increased level of athleticism could improve their perimeter defense a little bit. Offensively, the Spurs should be improved because they now have a shot creator in DeRozan to go along with All-Star LaMarcus Aldridge. Right now, DeRozan is not quite the offensive player that Leonard was when he was healthy in 2016-17. However, there is a chance the Spurs' coaching staff, famed shooting guru, Chip Engelland in particular, could unlock some additional production from DeRozan by working with him to improve his outside shooting. If that happens, San Antonio could be one of the best teams in the Western Conference next season. Otherwise, if DeRozan stays as is, the Spurs improve, but they only will be above average on offense. They still may struggle to make enough outside shots to provide space for Aldridge inside, although they did add Marco Belinelli to address some of their outside shooting issues. If the latter scenario were to occur, then San Antonio would still be a solid playoff in the West that could win a round in the playoffs but wouldn't be likely to advance further than that.

Veterans

DeMar DeRozan

	Height	Weight	Cap #	Years Left
	6'7"	220	$27.740M	1 + PO

Similar at Age **28**

		Season	SIMsc
1	Jerry Stackhouse	2002-03	940.8
2	Vince Carter	2004-05	938.3
3	Michael Redd	2007-08	938.1
4	Caron Butler	2008-09	930.1
5	Glenn Robinson	2000-01	924.9
6	Richard Jefferson	2008-09	924.5
7	Joe Johnson	2009-10	924.5
8	Michael Finley	2001-02	922.0
9	Rudy Gay	2014-15	918.8
10	Tracy McGrady*	2007-08	918.5

Baseline Basic Stats

MPG	PTS	AST	REB	BLK	STL
36.3	21.5	3.6	5.1	0.4	1.1

Advanced Metrics

USG%	3PTA/FGA	FTA/FGA	TS%	eFG%	3PT%
27.9	0.203	0.355	0.548	0.486	0.331

AST%	TOV%	OREB%	DREB%	STL%	BLK%
19.5	9.8	3.2	11.8	1.5	0.7

PER	ORTG	DRTG	WS/48	VOL	
19.74	111.3	108.6	0.143	0.262	

- All-Star wing player in his prime
- Elite production in the regular season, but performance is significantly worse in the playoffs
- Good isolation scorer that gets to the rim and draws fouls, good mid-range shooter
- Playmaking skills continue to improve, Assist Percentage has steadily increased in almost every season
- Historically has been a below break-even three-point shooter overall, much better in the corners than above the break, solid corner Three-Point Percentage of 36.8% for his career
- Solid on-ball wing defender, more of a stay-at-home type, decent rebounding wing player

LaMarcus Aldridge

	Height	Weight	Cap #	Years Left
	6'11"	240	$22.347M	2

Similar at Age 32

	Player	Season	SIMsc
1	Tim Duncan	2008-09	913.8
2	Dirk Nowitzki	2010-11	910.8
3	David West	2012-13	910.1
4	Derrick Coleman	1999-00	897.4
5	Patrick Ewing*	1994-95	891.9
6	Robert Parish*	1985-86	889.8
7	Herb Williams	1990-91	889.1
8	Tom Chambers	1991-92	885.3
9	Chris Webber	2005-06	885.2
10	Joe Smith	2007-08	884.3

Baseline Basic Stats

MPG	PTS	AST	REB	BLK	STL
32.6	18.7	2.5	8.5	1.1	0.7

Advanced Metrics

USG%	3PTA/FGA	FTA/FGA	TS%	eFG%	3PT%
25.8	0.061	0.278	0.549	0.503	0.310

AST%	TOV%	OREB%	DREB%	STL%	BLK%
12.4	8.2	8.6	20.2	0.9	2.8

PER	ORTG	DRTG	WS/48	VOL	
21.50	113.3	103.2	0.167	0.000	

- Made six All-Star teams in the last seven years, had a career best season at age 32
- Good post-up big man that's very efficient inside and will draw fouls, has solid passing skills
- Very good mid-range shooter, can occasionally hit threes but his percentages have been below break-even for his career
- Solid rebounder at both ends, went to the offensive boards with greater frequency last season
- Effective position defender and rim protector
- Shot blocking rates have been much higher with the Spurs than they were in Portland

Pau Gasol

	Height	Weight	Cap #	Years Left
	7'0"	227	$16.000M	1

Similar at Age 37

		Season	SIMsc
1	Patrick Ewing*	1999-00	898.9
2	Tim Duncan	2013-14	894.3
3	Kareem Abdul-Jabbar*	1984-85	878.6
4	Robert Parish*	1990-91	875.4
5	Kevin Willis	1999-00	863.5
6	Elvin Hayes*	1982-83	862.9
7	P.J. Brown	2006-07	862.9
8	Dirk Nowitzki	2015-16	861.4
9	Kevin Garnett	2013-14	857.7
10	David Robinson*	2002-03	857.1

Baseline Basic Stats

MPG	PTS	AST	REB	BLK	STL
26.7	12.6	1.9	8.0	1.2	0.6

Advanced Metrics

USG%	3PTA/FGA	FTA/FGA	TS%	eFG%	3PT%
22.1	0.106	0.308	0.535	0.493	0.424

AST%	TOV%	OREB%	DREB%	STL%	BLK%
16.8	12.3	8.1	27.6	1.1	3.6

PER	ORTG	DRTG	WS/48	VOL
19.49	109.6	102.1	0.140	0.407

- Has been in a gradual decline stage over the last four seasons
- Still a productive big man entering his age-38 season
- Not quite the post-up player he once was, above average roll man
- Excellent passing big man, has become a league average three-point shooter
- Very good rim protector, shot blocking rates are still consistent with his career averages
- Excellent defensive rebounder, struggles defending on the ball due to a lack of mobility

Rudy Gay

	Height	Weight	Cap #	Years Left
	6'9"	220	$10.087M	0

Similar at Age 31

		Season	SIMsc
1	Danny Manning	1997-98	913.6
2	Orlando Woolridge	1990-91	907.4
3	Bob McAdoo*	1982-83	906.7
4	Chris Bosh	2015-16	905.9
5	Andrei Kirilenko	2012-13	905.8
6	Tony Massenburg	1998-99	902.4
7	Al Harrington	2011-12	901.9
8	Clifford Robinson	1997-98	900.7
9	Glenn Robinson	2003-04	900.3
10	Paul Millsap	2016-17	898.0

Baseline Basic Stats

MPG	PTS	AST	REB	BLK	STL
24.8	12.4	1.6	4.4	0.6	0.8

Advanced Metrics

USG%	3PTA/FGA	FTA/FGA	TS%	eFG%	3PT%
23.3	0.205	0.331	0.545	0.500	0.367

AST%	TOV%	OREB%	DREB%	STL%	BLK%
10.7	12.3	5.2	15.8	1.7	2.2

PER	ORTG	DRTG	WS/48	VOL
16.31	105.9	104.9	0.059	0.404

- Missed two months last season due to bursitis in his right heel
- Missed the second half of the 2016-17 season due to torn left Achilles tendon
- Solid isolation scorer that will get to the rim and draw fouls, good mid-range shooter
- Inconsistent as a three-point shooter, above break-even on threes for his career, historically better in the corners
- Solid on-ball defender that can guard multiple positions
- Shot blocking rates have increased in each of the last four seasons, good defensive rebounder

Dejounte Murray

	Height	Weight	Cap #	Years Left
	6'5"	170	$1.545M	Team Option

Similar at Age 21

		Season	SIMsc
1	Shaun Livingston	2006-07	892.0
2	Manny Harris	2010-11	889.6
3	Elfrid Payton	2015-16	887.6
4	Javaris Crittenton	2008-09	881.5
5	Alec Burks	2012-13	879.2
6	Smush Parker	2002-03	878.5
7	Larry Hughes	1999-00	878.2
8	Monta Ellis	2006-07	875.0
9	Archie Goodwin	2015-16	874.3
10	Sergio Rodriguez	2007-08	873.3

Baseline Basic Stats

MPG	PTS	AST	REB	BLK	STL
24.6	11.3	2.8	3.4	0.3	1.0

Advanced Metrics

USG%	3PTA/FGA	FTA/FGA	TS%	eFG%	3PT%
21.5	0.118	0.284	0.508	0.467	0.300

AST%	TOV%	OREB%	DREB%	STL%	BLK%
20.0	16.1	4.3	14.4	2.2	1.0

PER	ORTG	DRTG	WS/48	VOL	
13.74	101.7	107.0	0.034	0.630	

- Greatly improved in his second season, became a regular in San Antonio's rotation
- Decent playmaker, but turnover prone, struggled to shoot efficiently
- Mainly looks to slash to the rim for high percentage close range shots or to draw fouls, had difficulty making shots outside of three feet
- Below average effectiveness in virtually every half-court offensive situation
- Capable of defending both guard spots, better at handling wing players
- Gets steals at a high rate, uses length to contest shots, good rebounding guard

Patty Mills

	Height	Weight	Cap #	Years Left
	6'0"	185	$12.429M	2

Similar at Age 29

		Season	SIMsc
1	D.J. Augustin	2016-17	936.1
2	Tony Delk	2002-03	934.6
3	Mo Williams	2011-12	932.6
4	Brian Roberts	2014-15	928.3
5	Eddie House	2007-08	928.2
6	Pooh Richardson	1995-96	924.0
7	Jason Williams	2004-05	917.9
8	Chris Duhon	2011-12	914.2
9	Chris Whitney	2000-01	911.3
10	Darren Collison	2016-17	910.8

Baseline Basic Stats

MPG	PTS	AST	REB	BLK	STL
25.9	10.2	3.7	2.2	0.1	0.8

Advanced Metrics

USG%	3PTA/FGA	FTA/FGA	TS%	eFG%	3PT%
18.5	0.503	0.174	0.546	0.514	0.380

AST%	TOV%	OREB%	DREB%	STL%	BLK%
20.5	12.8	1.5	7.6	1.6	0.3

PER	ORTG	DRTG	WS/48	VOL	
13.08	109.1	109.1	0.101	0.298	

- Entering his age-30 season, possibly over-extended last season with a starter's workload, per-minute production was down
- Good overall three-point shooter, excellent in the corners
- Mainly effective as a spot-up shooter that can also come off screens
- Can use the threat of his shot to get by defenders to draw fouls, but not getting to the rim as often
- Decent playmaker, Assist Percentage decreased significantly last season
- Adequate position defender, has difficulties on defense due to his small size

Marco Belinelli

	Height	Weight	Cap #	Years Left
	6'5"	192	$6.154M	1

Similar at Age 31

		Season	SIMsc
1	J.J. Redick	2015-16	935.5
2	Lucious Harris	2001-02	932.1
3	Rex Chapman	1998-99	927.4
4	Wesley Person	2002-03	926.1
5	Roger Mason	2011-12	923.4
6	Byron Scott	1992-93	919.9
7	Courtney Lee	2016-17	918.7
8	Dell Curry	1995-96	915.4
9	John Long	1987-88	915.0
10	Jon Barry	2000-01	912.3

Baseline Basic Stats

MPG	PTS	AST	REB	BLK	STL
25.8	11.1	2.1	2.4	0.2	0.7

Advanced Metrics

USG%	3PTA/FGA	FTA/FGA	TS%	eFG%	3PT%
19.7	0.442	0.225	0.562	0.518	0.381

AST%	TOV%	OREB%	DREB%	STL%	BLK%
12.8	10.3	1.3	8.7	1.4	0.5

PER	ORTG	DRTG	WS/48	VOL	
13.47	109.1	109.9	0.094	0.294	

- Productive rotational shooting specialist for Atlanta and Philadelphia last season
- Good overall three-point shooter, excellent at coming off screens
- Career 42.0% three-point shooter from the corners, above average passing skills
- Effective in a small sample of possessions as a pick-and-roll ball handler last season
- Decent position defender if hidden in favorable matchups

Jakob Poeltl

	Height	Weight	Cap #	Years Left
	7'0"	248	$2.947M	Team Option

Similar at Age 22

		Season	SIMsc
1	Travis Knight	1996-97	942.2
2	Steven Adams	2015-16	934.4
3	Willie Cauley-Stein	2015-16	930.2
4	Kosta Koufos	2011-12	927.0
5	Duane Causwell	1990-91	918.3
6	Greg Smith	2012-13	910.6
7	Jelani McCoy	1999-00	909.4
8	Andrew Lang	1988-89	904.6
9	Jon Koncak	1985-86	901.2
10	Hilton Armstrong	2006-07	898.8

Baseline Basic Stats

MPG	PTS	AST	REB	BLK	STL
21.1	6.7	0.7	5.5	1.2	0.5

Advanced Metrics

USG%	3PTA/FGA	FTA/FGA	TS%	eFG%	3PT%
14.2	0.009	0.313	0.604	0.592	0.290

AST%	TOV%	OREB%	DREB%	STL%	BLK%
5.0	15.9	11.2	17.4	1.4	4.3

PER	ORTG	DRTG	WS/48	VOL
15.23	116.0	105.1	0.144	0.341

- Improved in his second season in the NBA, became a regular part of Toronto's rotation
- Good rim protector, developed into an excellent shot blocker
- Decent defensive rebounder, sacrifices positioning to go for blocks
- Strictly a low volume rim runner that scores inside of three feet
- Good offensive rebounder, somewhat turnover prone
- Primarily effective as a roll man and cutter
- Good at running the floor in transition despite his lumbering foot speed

Derrick White

	Height	Weight	Cap #	Years Left
	6'5"	190	$1.667M	2 Team Options

Similar at Age 23

		Season	SIMsc
1	Garrett Temple	2009-10	888.9
2	Tyler Johnson	2015-16	884.2
3	Delon Wright	2015-16	880.6
4	Bryce Dejean-Jones	2015-16	878.5
5	K.J. McDaniels	2016-17	871.6
6	Kelenna Azubuike	2006-07	870.4
7	Spencer Dinwiddie	2016-17	870.2
8	Jeremy Lamb	2015-16	866.0
9	Ben McLemore	2016-17	865.1
10	Marco Belinelli	2009-10	864.8

Baseline Basic Stats

MPG	PTS	AST	REB	BLK	STL
21.3	8.6	2.0	3.0	0.4	0.7

Advanced Metrics

USG%	3PTA/FGA	FTA/FGA	TS%	eFG%	3PT%
18.2	0.444	0.386	0.592	0.555	0.479

AST%	TOV%	OREB%	DREB%	STL%	BLK%
13.6	11.0	3.2	15.4	1.6	1.5

PER	ORTG	DRTG	WS/48	VOL
15.64	116.5	106.4	0.146	0.711

- Played only 139 minutes for San Antonio, spent most of the season with Austin in the G-League
- Was one of the best players in the G-League last season, ranked 5th in PER
- Excelled in a high usage role, solid playmaker, efficient scorer
- Relied on getting to the rim to finish inside or draw fouls, around average as a mid-range shooter
- Below break-even on threes in the G-League, was 8-for-13 on threes in the NBA
- Can defend both guard spots, effective defender in the NBA in a very small sample size
- Active help defender that could rotate for blocks, get steals at a high rate, good rebounding guard

Davis Bertans

	Height	Weight	Cap #	Years Left
	6'10"	210	$7.000M	1

Similar at Age 25

		Season	SIMsc
1	DerMarr Johnson	2005-06	932.0
2	Steve Novak	2008-09	918.5
3	Matt Bullard	1992-93	914.2
4	Nikola Mirotic	2016-17	902.0
5	Travis Outlaw	2009-10	893.7
6	Luke Babbitt	2014-15	889.4
7	Rodney Carney	2009-10	888.1
8	Sam Mack	1995-96	886.8
9	Vladimir Radmanovic	2005-06	885.8
10	Chase Budinger	2013-14	884.3

Baseline Basic Stats

MPG	PTS	AST	REB	BLK	STL
18.2	6.8	0.9	2.6	0.4	0.5

Advanced Metrics

USG%	3PTA/FGA	FTA/FGA	TS%	eFG%	3PT%
17.0	0.610	0.154	0.559	0.536	0.373

AST%	TOV%	OREB%	DREB%	STL%	BLK%
8.5	9.6	2.6	12.9	1.3	1.8

PER	ORTG	DRTG	WS/48	VOL
12.50	109.2	107.0	0.101	0.401

- Improved slightly in his second season, became a regular part of San Antonio's rotation last season
- Low volume three-point specialist, almost 70% of his shots are threes
- Good three-point shooter overall, extremely good in the corners
- Made 49.3% of his corner threes over the last two seasons
- Mainly a spot-up shooter, can also come off screens and play as a screener in pick-and-roll situations, good cutter as well
- Solid defensively, good position defender
- Provides some rim protection, decent shot blocker, below average rebounding big man

Dante Cunningham

	Height	Weight	Cap #	Years Left
	6'8"	230	$2.487M	0

Similar at Age 30

		Season	SIMsc
1	Luc Mbah a Moute	2016-17	926.4
2	Anthony Tolliver	2015-16	924.7
3	Dennis Scott	1998-99	921.6
4	Shane Battier	2008-09	910.3
5	James Jones	2010-11	906.2
6	Matt Bonner	2010-11	906.1
7	Mike Dunleavy, Jr.	2010-11	905.0
8	Marvin Williams	2016-17	903.9
9	Jud Buechler	1998-99	903.8
10	Morris Peterson	2007-08	903.5

Baseline Basic Stats

MPG	PTS	AST	REB	BLK	STL
21.4	6.6	1.1	3.3	0.4	0.6

Advanced Metrics

USG%	3PTA/FGA	FTA/FGA	TS%	eFG%	3PT%
12.4	0.518	0.162	0.565	0.550	0.374

AST%	TOV%	OREB%	DREB%	STL%	BLK%
6.0	9.0	4.1	14.1	1.3	1.5

PER	ORTG	DRTG	WS/48	VOL
11.00	112.6	108.8	0.090	0.325

- Overall production has been down for the last four seasons
- Play improved when he was traded to Brooklyn last season
- Low volume spot-up shooter with an average ability to cut to the rim
- Break-even three-point shooter overall for his career, much better in the corners
- Can passably defend multiple positions, but may need to be hidden in favorable matchups at this stage of his career
- Not as active in help defense like he was in years past, steals and blocks rates are down, decent defensive rebounder

Bryn Forbes

	Height	Weight	Cap #	Years Left
	6'3"	190	$1.513M	1

Similar at Age 24

		Season	SIMsc
1	J.J. Redick	2008-09	928.4
2	Rex Walters	1994-95	925.9
3	Damon Jones	2000-01	916.6
4	E'Twaun Moore	2013-14	916.1
5	Wayne Ellington	2011-12	912.7
6	Marco Belinelli	2010-11	910.5
7	Trajan Langdon	2000-01	908.1
8	Ray McCallum	2015-16	906.3
9	Steve Blake	2004-05	904.9
10	Khalid Reeves	1996-97	900.9

Baseline Basic Stats

MPG	PTS	AST	REB	BLK	STL
20.1	7.3	2.0	1.7	0.1	0.5

Advanced Metrics

USG%	3PTA/FGA	FTA/FGA	TS%	eFG%	3PT%
17.2	0.479	0.167	0.526	0.498	0.375

AST%	TOV%	OREB%	DREB%	STL%	BLK%
14.6	9.4	1.1	8.2	1.1	0.2

PER	ORTG	DRTG	WS/48	VOL
10.76	107.0	110.4	0.078	0.391

- Slightly improved in his second season, became a regular rotation player for San Antonio last season
- Low volume shooting specialist that rarely turned the ball over, very good at coming off screens
- Shot 39% on all threes last season, made 50% of his corner threes
- Had effectiveness as a pick-and-roll ball handler last season
- Was hidden in favorable matchups, played solid position defense against his assigned matchup

Quincy Pondexter

	Height	Weight	Cap #	Years Left
	6'7"	220	$1.513M	0

Similar at Age 29

		Season	SIMsc
1	Bobby Simmons	2009-10	913.1
2	Sam Mack	1999-00	907.8
3	Damien Wilkins	2008-09	900.9
4	Mark Jones	2004-05	894.3
5	Devean George	2006-07	890.7
6	Cartier Martin	2013-14	890.1
7	David Benoit	1997-98	885.3
8	Tracy Murray	2000-01	884.8
9	Eric Williams	2001-02	883.8
10	Juaquin Hawkins	2002-03	882.9

Baseline Basic Stats

MPG	PTS	AST	REB	BLK	STL
18.3	5.4	1.0	2.9	0.3	0.6

Advanced Metrics

USG%	3PTA/FGA	FTA/FGA	TS%	eFG%	3PT%
14.1	0.437	0.257	0.465	0.414	0.241

AST%	TOV%	OREB%	DREB%	STL%	BLK%
7.2	13.3	4.9	12.6	1.8	1.0

PER	ORTG	DRTG	WS/48	VOL	
7.79	95.6	109.2	0.025	0.269	

- Played sparingly for Chicago last season after missing the previous two seasons while recovering from surgery to repair cartilage damage in his left knee
- Struggled to regain the effectiveness from his healthy seasons
- In a limited number of possessions, could cut to the rim and draw fouls, had trouble finishing due to his diminishing athleticism
- Had great difficulties with his shooting, True Shooting Percentage was below 40%
- Shot less than 30% from the field in a small sample of field goal attempts
- Still a solid on-ball wing defender despite his knee injury
- Posted a career high Steal Percentage in a small sample of minutes, good defensive rebounder

Newcomers

Lonnie Walker IV	Height	Weight	Cap #	Years Left
	6'5"	204	$2.357M	1 + 2 TO

Baseline Basic Stats

MPG	PTS	AST	REB	BLK	STL
10.1	3.5	0.7	1.1	0.1	0.3

Advanced Metrics

USG%	3PTA/FGA	FTA/FGA	TS%	eFG%	3PT%
19.3	0.435	0.164	0.449	0.421	0.298

AST%	TOV%	OREB%	DREB%	STL%	BLK%
10.2	10.9	2.8	9.6	1.4	0.7

PER	ORTG	DRTG	WS/48	VOL
8.08	92.5	109.2	0.004	N/A

- Drafted by San Antonio in the first round with the 18th pick
- Ineffective performance in the Las Vegas and Salt Lake City Summer Leagues
- Flashed potential defensively, capable of defending both guard spots
- Active help defender that got steals and rebounded at a high rate
- Needs to work on position defense, tended to gamble quite a bit
- Played a high usage scoring role, didn't look to pass very often
- Scored in volume, but did not shoot efficiently, True Shooting Percentage below 40%
- Shot below 35% from the field and below 30% on threes, took a lot of jump shots, drew fouls at a low rate

Chimezie Metu

	Height	Weight	Cap #	Years Left
	6'11"	225	$3.382M	2

Baseline Basic Stats

MPG	PTS	AST	REB	BLK	STL
11.8	3.9	0.5	2.5	0.4	0.3

Advanced Metrics

USG%	3PTA/FGA	FTA/FGA	TS%	eFG%	3PT%
17.1	0.099	0.325	0.502	0.469	0.184

AST%	TOV%	OREB%	DREB%	STL%	BLK%
6.9	13.0	9.4	15.4	1.4	2.7

PER	ORTG	DRTG	WS/48	VOL	
12.55	102.1	107.8	0.035	N/A	

- Drafted by San Antonio in the second round with the 49th overall pick
- Strong overall showing in Summer League, better in Salt Lake City than in Vegas
- Good offensively as a mid-range shooter, went 25-for-44 on two-point shots over both Summer Leagues
- More of a catch-and-shoot player in Salt Lake City, passed more in Vegas, but also turned the ball over more
- Good rebounder on both ends, much better on the offensive boards
- Decent interior defender that can use his length to contest or block shots
- Salary is more in line with a first round pick, may play more for San Antonio than initially expected this season

NEW ORLEANS PELICANS

<u>Last Season</u>: 48 – 34, Lost 2nd Round to Golden State (1 – 4)

<u>Offensive Rating</u>: 109.6, 10th in NBA   <u>Defensive Rating</u>: 108.3, 14th in NBA

<u>Primary Executive</u>: Dell Demps, Senior Vice President of Basketball Operations/General Manager

<u>Head Coach</u>: Alvin Gentry

Key Roster Changes

Subtractions
DeMarcus Cousins, free agency
Rajon Rondo, free agency
Jordan Crawford, free agency
DeAndre Liggins, waived

Additions
Elfrid Payton, free agency
Julius Randle, free agency
Troy Williams, free agency
Jahlil Okafor, free agency

RAFER Projected Win Total: 44.3

Projected Best Five-Man Unit
1. Jrue Holiday
2. E'Twaun Moore
3. Darius Miller
4. Julius Randle
5. Anthony Davis

Other Rotation Players
Nikola Mirotic
Elfrid Payton
Ian Clark

Remaining Roster

- Solomon Hill
- Emeka Okafor
- Cheick Diallo
- Alexis Ajinca
- Frank Jackson
- Jahlil Okafor
- Troy Williams
- Darius Morris
- Kenrich Williams, 24, 6'7", 210, TCU (Two-Way)
- Trevon Bluiett, 24, 6'6", 198, Xavier (Two-Way)

Season Forecast

After having success with DeMarcus Cousins out of the lineup due to his Achilles injury last season, the New Orleans Pelicans deemed that he was expendable, and they elected to let him go to Golden State in free agency. To fill the holes in the rotation left by Cousins and also Rajon Rondo, New Orleans signed a couple of younger options in Julius Randle and Elfrid Payton to serve as replacements. As of now, the Pelicans have the same level of talent as they had last season, but the new incoming players are still relatively untested in playoff type games because both Randle and Payton have never played for a winning team. Therefore, fitting these two into the rotation is going to be critical for New Orleans. If they adapt to their roles, the Pelicans could continue their success from the second half of last season and compete for a top four seed. Otherwise, they will simply be a solid playoff team in the Western Conference, landing one of the lower seeds.

The Pelicans were successful last season because they were a very good offensive team all year long mainly due to the individual brilliance of Anthony Davis. Davis had an MVP-caliber season and basically carried the team when Cousins was out. Davis' presence along with some steady play from Jrue Holiday allowed the complementary players to fit into their role and provide production when they were needed. The new additions of Randle and Payton could allow them to sustain the losses to Cousins and Rondo because they are essentially younger variations of the players that they are replacing. Randle isn't nearly as productive as Cousins has been throughout his career, but stylistically Randle can make up some of the value lost by Cousins' departure. Specifically, he gives them a strong, hard driving big man that can handle the ball and make plays for others. As a result, the Pelicans can still use some of the same actions to generate offense with Davis and Randle that they did earlier last season with Davis and Cousins, with the exception that Randle isn't nearly good of an outside shooter as Cousins is. As for Payton, he's an athletic, playmaking point guard like Rondo, but he might have some more upside because he showed signs that he was improving as a shooter. Last season, Payton was an above average three-point shooter in Orlando, but then after he was traded to Phoenix, his percentages cratered, and he wasn't as effective. If Payton can recapture his shooting from the first half of last season, the Pelicans could improve on offense because they would have another shooter to space the floor for Davis. Otherwise, he'll fill Rondo's role as an additional facilitator to help the others get more open looks. On the other side of the ball, there could be some concerns because the two main new additions haven't established themselves as positive defensive contributors in their previous stops. Going from Cousins to Randle is not nearly as a big of a concern because Cousins was only about middling as an overall defender. However, the switch from Rondo to Payton could have a negative impact because the team is replacing a good defensive player for one that has historically been below average overall. This could cost New Orleans them a couple of wins due to an incremental defensive drop-off, unless the coaching staff works with Payton to improve as a defender. In general, New Orleans should be around the same team that they were last season with a good offense and about an average defense. This should be good enough for them to earn a playoff spot in the Western Conference, but they may only be talented enough to win a round in the playoffs at the most.

Veterans

Anthony Davis

	Height	Weight	Cap #	Years Left
	6'10"	220	$25.434M	2

Similar at Age 24

		Season	SIMsc
1	Antonio McDyess	1998-99	902.4
2	Jermaine O'Neal	2002-03	901.7
3	Kevin Garnett	2000-01	896.7
4	Chris Bosh	2008-09	891.6
5	Keith Van Horn	1999-00	880.7
6	Alonzo Mourning*	1994-95	872.9
7	Pervis Ellison	1991-92	872.8
8	Shawn Kemp	1993-94	872.6
9	Serge Ibaka	2013-14	872.1
10	Derrick Coleman	1991-92	871.5

Baseline Basic Stats

MPG	PTS	AST	REB	BLK	STL
36.5	21.7	3.0	10.1	1.6	1.1

Advanced Metrics

USG%	3PTA/FGA	FTA/FGA	TS%	eFG%	3PT%
29.1	0.097	0.401	0.578	0.520	0.317

AST%	TOV%	OREB%	DREB%	STL%	BLK%
13.3	9.6	7.3	25.2	1.7	4.1

PER	ORTG	DRTG	WS/48	VOL
25.91	114.2	102.3	0.205	0.247

- Posted an MVP-caliber season at age 24, has made the last five All-Star teams
- Efficient high volume scorer that's good on post-ups and on rolls to the rim, draws fouls at a high rate
- Excellent cutter and very good at running the floor to finish plays in transition
- Solid mid-range shooter throughout his career, has expanded his range to the three-point line
- Shot an above break-even percentage on threes for the first time last season, solid passing big man
- Excellent rim protector, one of the best shot blockers in the league, led the NBA in Blocks per Game
- Solid on-ball defender that can guard quicker players in space, good rebounder on both ends

Jrue Holiday

	Height	Weight	Cap #	Years Left
	6'3"	180	$26.161M	2 + PO

	Similar at Age	27	
		Season	SIMsc
1	Goran Dragic	2013-14	942.5
2	Mike Conley	2014-15	934.7
3	John Starks	1992-93	934.5
4	Jeff Teague	2015-16	930.2
5	Kirk Hinrich	2007-08	924.8
6	Monta Ellis	2012-13	922.1
7	Derek Harper	1988-89	920.4
8	Byron Scott	1988-89	915.9
9	Jason Terry	2004-05	915.1
10	Gary Payton*	1995-96	911.6

Baseline Basic Stats

MPG	PTS	AST	REB	BLK	STL
32.7	15.5	5.3	3.1	0.2	1.3

Advanced Metrics

USG%	3PTA/FGA	FTA/FGA	TS%	eFG%	3PT%
22.4	0.321	0.232	0.549	0.514	0.351

AST%	TOV%	OREB%	DREB%	STL%	BLK%
27.8	14.0	2.1	9.8	2.0	1.0

PER	ORTG	DRTG	WS/48	VOL
16.75	109.1	108.8	0.109	0.284

- Highly productive in his age-27 season, performance improved slightly in the playoffs
- Good pick-and-roll ball handler, very good playmaker that limits turnovers
- Assist Percentage went down because he often shared the floor with Rajon Rondo, who took assist opportunities away
- Had the most efficient shooting season of his career, got to the rim more and shot really well from mid-range
- Three-point percentage fell to about break-even, historically he's been around league average
- Solid on-ball defender that can defend both guard spots
- Gets steals, but Steal Percentage has been slowly declining for the last five seasons, solid rebounding point guard

E'Twaun Moore

	Height	Weight	Cap #	Years Left
	6'4"	191	$8.809M	1

Similar at Age 28

		Season	SIMsc
1	Vinny Del Negro	1994-95	940.9
2	Rex Chapman	1995-96	931.7
3	Courtney Lee	2013-14	929.8
4	Wesley Person	1999-00	927.4
5	Hubert Davis	1998-99	926.8
6	Byron Scott	1989-90	925.9
7	Keyon Dooling	2008-09	914.9
8	Trent Tucker	1987-88	913.0
9	Cuttino Mobley	2003-04	912.0
10	Wayne Ellington	2015-16	911.7

Baseline Basic Stats

MPG	PTS	AST	REB	BLK	STL
26.4	10.5	2.3	2.5	0.2	0.8

Advanced Metrics

USG%	3PTA/FGA	FTA/FGA	TS%	eFG%	3PT%
17.0	0.398	0.133	0.553	0.531	0.395

AST%	TOV%	OREB%	DREB%	STL%	BLK%
12.5	10.5	2.0	8.3	1.5	0.7

PER	ORTG	DRTG	WS/48	VOL
12.02	107.8	109.9	0.078	0.317

- Became a regular starter for New Orleans for the first time last year in his age-28 season
- Low volume shooter that can make spot-up jumpers and run off screens, very good cutter as well
- Good three-point shooter throughout his career, shot 42.5% on threes last season
- Effective scorer on a small sample of isolation possessions
- Good stay-at-home on-ball wing defender despite being a bit undersized

Nikola Mirotic

	Height	Weight	Cap #	Years Left
	6'10"	220	$12.500M	0

Similar at Age 26

		Season	SIMsc
1	Danilo Gallinari	2014-15	930.2
2	Jon Leuer	2015-16	918.1
3	Charlie Villanueva	2010-11	915.6
4	Bostjan Nachbar	2006-07	915.5
5	Keith Van Horn	2001-02	908.3
6	Wilson Chandler	2013-14	904.2
7	Al-Farouq Aminu	2016-17	901.9
8	Dennis Scott	1994-95	899.9
9	Robert Covington	2016-17	899.2
10	Earl Clark	2013-14	895.9

Baseline Basic Stats

MPG	PTS	AST	REB	BLK	STL
28.7	13.0	1.6	5.7	0.5	0.8

Advanced Metrics

USG%	3PTA/FGA	FTA/FGA	TS%	eFG%	3PT%
21.1	0.485	0.225	0.559	0.521	0.368

AST%	TOV%	OREB%	DREB%	STL%	BLK%
8.9	9.8	4.5	20.2	1.5	1.7

PER	ORTG	DRTG	WS/48	VOL	
16.07	109.2	106.7	0.113	0.303	

- Had a torrid start in Chicago last season, cooled off a bit after being traded to New Orleans
- Had best his season in the NBA at age-26
- Posted the highest True Shooting Percentage of his career
- Made spot-up jumpers in high volume and at a high percentage
- Shot almost 38% on threes overall last season
- Three-Point Percentage in the corners has been over 40% in each of the last three seasons
- Very good in a small sample of isolations, ranked in the 92nd percentile by the NBA in per-possession isolations
- Decent position defender if he's hidden in favorable matchups, good defensive rebounder, can block shots on occasion

Julius Randle

	Height	Weight	Cap #	Years Left
	6'9"	250	$8.641M	Player Option

Similar at Age **23**

		Season	SIMsc
1	Carlos Boozer	2004-05	944.1
2	Brian Grant	1995-96	934.4
3	Blake Griffin	2012-13	922.8
4	Gary Trent	1997-98	919.0
5	Karl Malone*	1986-87	917.0
6	Jeff Ruland	1981-82	915.4
7	Sean Rooks	1992-93	913.9
8	Wayman Tisdale	1987-88	911.5
9	Victor Alexander	1992-93	907.1
10	Maurice Taylor	1999-00	906.8

Baseline Basic Stats

MPG	PTS	AST	REB	BLK	STL
29.8	15.5	2.1	7.6	0.7	0.8

Advanced Metrics

USG%	3PTA/FGA	FTA/FGA	TS%	eFG%	3PT%
24.1	0.045	0.399	0.575	0.532	0.257

AST%	TOV%	OREB%	DREB%	STL%	BLK%
14.9	14.3	8.1	21.8	1.1	1.5

PER	ORTG	DRTG	WS/48	VOL	
18.89	110.3	107.0	0.134	0.401	

- Has continued to improve over the last three seasons, had his best season in his fourth year in the NBA

- Very good pick-and-roll player, primarily used as the screener

- Has developed his playmaking skills to be effective as the ball handler

- In a small sample of possessions as the pick-and-roll ball handler, he was ranked in the 94th percentile by the NBA

- Aggressive to cut and drive inside, great finisher, will draw fouls and score off put-backs

- Good overall rebounder, below average defender, struggles with position defense and has limited rim protection skills

Elfrid Payton

	Height	Weight	Cap #	Years Left
	6'4"	185	$2.700M	0

Similar at Age **23**

		Season	SIMsc
1	Vernon Maxwell	1988-89	927.7
2	Larry Hughes	2001-02	924.0
3	Rex Chapman	1990-91	916.1
4	Delonte West	2006-07	915.6
5	Michael Carter-Williams	2014-15	914.2
6	Jrue Holiday	2013-14	914.0
7	Mark Jackson	1988-89	910.0
8	Vinny Del Negro	1989-90	910.0
9	Vonteego Cummings	1999-00	909.3
10	Goran Dragic	2009-10	907.9

Baseline Basic Stats

MPG	PTS	AST	REB	BLK	STL
28.7	12.6	4.9	3.2	0.3	1.3

Advanced Metrics

USG%	3PTA/FGA	FTA/FGA	TS%	eFG%	3PT%
22.1	0.210	0.272	0.531	0.495	0.327

AST%	TOV%	OREB%	DREB%	STL%	BLK%
31.3	15.7	3.2	11.2	2.2	0.9

PER	ORTG	DRTG	WS/48	VOL
16.84	106.9	109.0	0.094	0.296

- Productive in his fourth NBA season, missed games due to a sore left hamstring and left knee injury
- Great playmaker, but a little turnover prone
- Most effective at using quickness to get to the rim in isolation situations, solid pick-and-roll ball handler
- Posted his highest True Shooting Percentage, shot over 67% on shots inside of three feet
- Shots threes at a 37.3% rate in Orlando last season, Three-Point Percentage severely dropped in Phoenix
- Can get steals, good rebounding guard, below average on-ball defender throughout his career

Darius Miller

	Height	Weight	Cap #	Years Left
	6'8"	235	$2.205M	0

Similar at Age **27**

		Season	SIMsc
1	Patrick Patterson	2016-17	914.0
2	James Jones	2007-08	911.6
3	Luke Babbitt	2016-17	907.5
4	Anthony Tolliver	2012-13	906.7
5	Martell Webster	2013-14	902.9
6	Mike Scott	2015-16	888.0
7	Jason Kapono	2008-09	887.4
8	Dennis Scott	1995-96	882.8
9	Lance Thomas	2015-16	880.1
10	Vladimir Radmanovic	2007-08	875.0

Baseline Basic Stats

MPG	PTS	AST	REB	BLK	STL
17.1	4.9	0.7	2.5	0.2	0.4

Advanced Metrics

USG%	3PTA/FGA	FTA/FGA	TS%	eFG%	3PT%
12.6	0.783	0.169	0.575	0.551	0.388

AST%	TOV%	OREB%	DREB%	STL%	BLK%
6.6	9.2	2.1	10.7	0.9	0.8

PER	ORTG	DRTG	WS/48	VOL	
9.27	113.3	110.8	0.084	0.200	

- Became a regular in New Orleans' rotation after spending the previous two seasons in Germany
- Effective as a low volume spot-up shooter, ranked in 93rd percentile by the NBA on spot-ups last season
- Above average at running off screens, very good overall three-point shooter, shot 41.1% on threes last season
- Solid in a small sample of possessions as a pick-and-roll ball handler
- Good stay-at-home on-ball defender that can guard multiple positions

Ian Clark

	Height	Weight	Cap #	Years Left
	6'3"	175	$1.513M	0

Similar at Age 26

		Season	SIMsc
1	Steve Kerr	1991-92	929.0
2	A.J. Price	2012-13	928.8
3	James Robinson	1996-97	925.7
4	Damon Jones	2002-03	924.2
5	E'Twaun Moore	2015-16	923.9
6	Rex Walters	1996-97	919.6
7	Avery Bradley	2016-17	919.2
8	Norris Cole	2014-15	918.4
9	Luther Head	2008-09	917.8
10	Mike Penberthy	2000-01	916.6

Baseline Basic Stats

MPG	PTS	AST	REB	BLK	STL
23.1	9.5	2.6	2.1	0.1	0.7

Advanced Metrics

USG%	3PTA/FGA	FTA/FGA	TS%	eFG%	3PT%
18.9	0.374	0.144	0.543	0.519	0.371

AST%	TOV%	OREB%	DREB%	STL%	BLK%
15.2	11.7	1.6	8.6	1.4	0.5

PER	ORTG	DRTG	WS/48	VOL	
12.15	105.6	110.4	0.064	0.372	

- Had a down year in his first season with New Orleans after spending the previous two years with Golden State
- Largely used as a low volume spot-up shooter, struggled to make shots, Three-Point Percentage fell to below break-even overall
- Shot much better in the corners, was most effective as a score-first, pick-and-roll ball handler
- Very effective at running off screens in his prior stop in Golden State, was not used in this situation in New Orleans
- Offered little value on the defensive end, below average on the ball
- Did not get steals, fairly solid defensive rebounder

Solomon Hill

	Height	Weight	Cap #	Years Left
	6'7"	220	$12.753M	1

Similar at Age 26

		Season	SIMsc
1	Sam Mack	1996-97	930.7
2	Scott Burrell	1996-97	926.6
3	Cartier Martin	2010-11	918.3
4	Alonzo Gee	2013-14	917.9
5	James Anderson	2015-16	909.3
6	Sasha Pavlovic	2009-10	908.8
7	Chase Budinger	2014-15	904.6
8	Kasib Powell	2007-08	903.1
9	James Ennis	2016-17	900.7
10	Luke Jackson	2007-08	899.7

Baseline Basic Stats

MPG	PTS	AST	REB	BLK	STL
19.4	6.3	1.3	2.7	0.2	0.6

Advanced Metrics

USG%	3PTA/FGA	FTA/FGA	TS%	eFG%	3PT%
14.2	0.478	0.219	0.486	0.454	0.326

AST%	TOV%	OREB%	DREB%	STL%	BLK%
11.3	13.5	4.1	12.4	1.6	0.8

PER	ORTG	DRTG	WS/48	VOL	
9.52	101.5	109.6	0.061	0.496	

- Missed most of last season due to a torn left hamstring
- Historically a lower volume offensive player that has been an above average spot-up shooter and cutter
- For his career, three-point shooting is slightly below break-even, shoots much better in the corners
- Historically has had some difficulty finishing shots inside of three feet
- Fairly good, stay-at-home on-ball wing defender when healthy, solid defensive rebounder

Emeka Okafor

	Height	Weight	Cap #	Years Left
	6'10"	252	$2.445M	0

Similar at Age 35

		Season	SIMsc
1	Herb Williams	1993-94	890.7
2	Nazr Mohammed	2012-13	865.7
3	Wayne Cooper	1991-92	864.6
4	Chris Andersen	2013-14	864.1
5	Sean Marks	2010-11	861.6
6	Joe Kleine	1996-97	860.6
7	Rick Mahorn	1993-94	854.7
8	Ervin Johnson	2002-03	853.3
9	Dale Davis	2004-05	852.3
10	Jermaine O'Neal	2013-14	848.8

Baseline Basic Stats

MPG	PTS	AST	REB	BLK	STL
14.0	3.9	0.4	3.7	0.9	0.3

Advanced Metrics

USG%	3PTA/FGA	FTA/FGA	TS%	eFG%	3PT%
13.7	0.007	0.260	0.532	0.497	0.047

AST%	TOV%	OREB%	DREB%	STL%	BLK%
4.0	14.5	12.4	20.7	1.1	5.3

PER	ORTG	DRTG	WS/48	VOL
13.63	108.8	104.6	0.107	0.436

- Effectively came back to the NBA at age 35 after being out of the league for four years
- Provided excellent rim protection in a token starter role when he joined New Orleans
- Excellent shot blocker and overall rebounder, struggled in position defense due to a lack of mobility
- Low volume rim runner that relied on making close range shots
- Shot abnormally well from the free throw line, career Free Throw Percentage is below 60%
- He went 18-for-22 on free throws last season

Cheick Diallo

	Height	Weight	Cap #	Years Left
	6'9"	220	$1.545M	0

Similar at Age 21

		Season	SIMsc
1	Brandan Wright	2008-09	918.0
2	Donnell Harvey	2001-02	912.7
3	Darrell Arthur	2009-10	912.1
4	Kris Humphries	2006-07	910.6
5	Kenny Williams	1990-91	907.5
6	Samaki Walker	1997-98	906.3
7	Patrick Patterson	2010-11	905.5
8	Chris Wilcox	2003-04	905.5
9	Ed Davis	2010-11	896.4
10	Antonio McDyess	1995-96	890.4

Baseline Basic Stats

MPG	PTS	AST	REB	BLK	STL
18.6	7.3	0.7	4.6	0.5	0.5

Advanced Metrics

USG%	3PTA/FGA	FTA/FGA	TS%	eFG%	3PT%
18.7	0.003	0.325	0.544	0.506	0.029

AST%	TOV%	OREB%	DREB%	STL%	BLK%
5.1	11.9	9.7	21.7	1.2	2.1

PER	ORTG	DRTG	WS/48	VOL
14.64	108.1	106.0	0.109	0.297

- Fringe rotation player for New Orleans, very effective per-minute player in his two seasons in the NBA
- Primarily a low volume rim runner that scores on rolls to the rim and cuts to the basket
- Improving as a mid-range shooter, was very effective shooter from inside of 16 feet
- Good shot blocker and rebounder, undisciplined defender overall
- Struggles with on-ball defense, sacrifices position to go for blocks, commits fouls at a high rate

Troy Williams

	Height	Weight	Cap #	Years Left
	6'7"	218	$1.513M	0

Similar at Age 23

		Season	SIMsc
1	Cleanthony Early	2014-15	927.2
2	Scott Burrell	1993-94	923.2
3	Bryon Russell	1993-94	912.1
4	Jordan Hamilton	2013-14	909.0
5	James Anderson	2012-13	908.5
6	Kelenna Azubuike	2006-07	908.5
7	Rick Fox	1992-93	907.4
8	Tyrone Corbin	1985-86	906.7
9	Carlos Delfino	2005-06	906.7
10	Alan Anderson	2005-06	906.0

Baseline Basic Stats

MPG	PTS	AST	REB	BLK	STL
20.0	7.0	1.2	3.1	0.3	0.7

Advanced Metrics

USG%	3PTA/FGA	FTA/FGA	TS%	eFG%	3PT%
17.5	0.412	0.245	0.545	0.516	0.349

AST%	TOV%	OREB%	DREB%	STL%	BLK%
8.4	12.4	5.3	13.0	2.3	1.1

PER	ORTG	DRTG	WS/48	VOL
12.97	106.7	108.5	0.085	0.400

- Split time last season between Rio Grande Valley in the G-League, Houston and New York

- Struggled in a spot-up role with Houston, but was better as a finisher in transition with the Knicks

- Shot a break-even percentage on threes with New York, good offensive rebounding wing

- Got steals at a high rate, good defensive rebounder

- Below average on-ball defender, gambles too much and can get caught out of position

Jahlil Okafor

	Height	Weight	Cap #	Years Left
	6'11"	275	$1.567M	Team Option

Similar at Age 22

		Season	SIMsc
1	Byron Mullens	2011-12	906.5
2	Vitaly Potapenko	1997-98	903.9
3	Eddy Curry	2004-05	903.4
4	Robin Lopez	2010-11	903.2
5	Chris Kaman	2004-05	901.9
6	Andrew Bynum	2009-10	900.3
7	Sharone Wright	1994-95	899.0
8	Chris Mihm	2001-02	897.6
9	Sean May	2006-07	891.0
10	Mike Gminski	1981-82	890.9

Baseline Basic Stats

MPG	PTS	AST	REB	BLK	STL
24.0	10.6	0.9	6.0	1.0	0.4

Advanced Metrics

USG%	3PTA/FGA	FTA/FGA	TS%	eFG%	3PT%
21.7	0.024	0.330	0.564	0.532	0.246

AST%	TOV%	OREB%	DREB%	STL%	BLK%
7.0	13.7	7.8	18.8	0.8	3.2

PER	ORTG	DRTG	WS/48	VOL	
15.80	105.2	107.1	0.086	0.401	

- Played sparingly for Philadelphia and Brooklyn last season, only played 353 minutes last year
- Scores efficiently by finishing garbage plays inside of three feet
- Above average on rolls to the rim, middling post-up player
- Can be a liability on defense due to a lack of mobility, struggles to defend on the ball
- Decent shot blocker and rebounder, but his teams have historically defended better with him off the court

Alexis Ajinca

	Height	Weight	Cap #	Years Left
	7'0"	220	$5.285M	0

Similar at Age 29

		Season	SIMsc
1	Dino Radja	1996-97	914.5
2	Kevin Kunnert	1980-81	908.3
3	Nazr Mohammed	2006-07	907.1
4	Kurt Nimphius	1987-88	904.6
5	Lorenzen Wright	2004-05	904.1
6	Antonio McDyess	2003-04	902.5
7	Joe Barry Carroll	1987-88	899.9
8	Mikki Moore	2004-05	894.1
9	Edgar Jones	1985-86	893.6
10	Melvin Turpin	1989-90	890.8

Baseline Basic Stats

MPG	PTS	AST	REB	BLK	STL
19.5	6.7	0.8	5.4	0.6	0.5

Advanced Metrics

USG%	3PTA/FGA	FTA/FGA	TS%	eFG%	3PT%
18.2	0.011	0.241	0.506	0.477	0.093

AST%	TOV%	OREB%	DREB%	STL%	BLK%
5.7	12.9	9.7	22.6	1.3	2.7

PER	ORTG	DRTG	WS/48	VOL
13.11	100.8	104.3	0.079	0.641

- Missed all of last season due to a knee injury that required surgery
- Also missed games in the season before due to shoulder and hip injuries
- Has been a fringe rotation player in the previous four seasons when healthy
- Production was in decline in the three seasons before last season
- When healthy, used as a low volume rim runner that mainly scored on close range shots
- Below average position defender that struggles to defend on the ball, good defensive rebounder, solid shot blocker

Newcomers

Frank Jackson

	Height	Weight	Cap #	Years Left
	6'4"	202	$1.378M	1

Baseline Basic Stats

MPG	PTS	AST	REB	BLK	STL
12.1	4.2	0.9	1.4	0.1	0.3

Advanced Metrics

USG%	3PTA/FGA	FTA/FGA	TS%	eFG%	3PT%
17.3	0.312	0.218	0.489	0.450	0.322

AST%	TOV%	OREB%	DREB%	STL%	BLK%
10.1	11.5	3.0	12.2	1.6	0.7

PER	ORTG	DRTG	WS/48	VOL
10.03	99.0	109.4	0.043	N/A

- Drafted by Charlotte with the 31st overall pick in 2017, then traded to New Orleans
- Missed all of last season due to a fractured right foot
- Played very well in his only game at Las Vegas Summer League this past July
- Took on a heavy score-first mindset in a short 12 minute stint
- Got to the rim and drew fouls, scored 13 points on 7 shots, missed his only three, committed 3 turnovers
- Active on defense, got a steal, was good on the defensive glass, played decent on-ball defense

Darius Morris

		Height	Weight	2018 Cap #	Years Left
		6'4"	190	$1.621M	1

Baseline Basic Stats

MPG	PTS	AST	REB	BLK	STL
17.2	5.5	1.7	1.9	0.1	0.6

Advanced Metrics

USG%	3PTA/FGA	FTA/FGA	TS%	eFG%	3PT%
15.7	0.348	0.196	0.451	0.429	0.295

AST%	TOV%	OREB%	DREB%	STL%	BLK%
16.9	11.0	2.1	11.1	1.7	0.3

PER	ORTG	DRTG	WS/48	VOL	
10.54	90.4	93.1	0.065	0.521	

- Played parts of four seasons in the NBA between 2011 to 2015, out of the league for the last three seasons
- Spent most of last season in China with Guangdong, projection used translated Chinese CBA stats
- Low usage point guard with middling playmaking skills and struggled to shoot efficiently in his previous years in the NBA
- Played a higher volume role in China, more effective at driving to the basket to score on high percentage shots inside
- Showed better playmaking skills and an ability to control the ball
- Still not an outside shooter at this stage, below 30% on threes in China, below 60% on free throws
- Got steals at a high rate and was an effective defensive rebounder last season
- On-ball defense is still uncertain due to the lower level of competition in China
- Was slightly below average as an on-ball defender in his previous years in the NBA

LOS ANGELES LAKERS

<u>Last Season</u>: 35 – 47, Missed the Playoffs

<u>Offensive Rating</u>: 106.5, 23rd in NBA

<u>Defensive Rating</u>: 108.0, 12th in NBA

<u>Primary Executive</u>: Magic Johnson, President of Basketball Operations

<u>Head Coach</u>: Luke Walton

Key Roster Changes

Subtractions
Julius Randle, free agency
Brook Lopez, free agency
Isaiah Thomas, free agency
Channing Frye, free agency
Andre Ingram, free agency
Tyler Ennis, waived
Thomas Bryant, waived
Luol Deng, waived

Additions
Moritz Wagner, draft
Isaac Bonga, draft
Svi Mykhailiuk, draft
LeBron James, free agency
Rajon Rondo, free agency
JaVale McGee, free agency
Lance Stephenson, free agency
Michael Beasley, free agency

RAFER Projected Win Total: 44.0

Projected Best Five-Man Unit
1. Rajon Rondo
2. Kentavious Caldwell-Pope
3. Josh Hart
4. Kyle Kuzma
5. LeBron James

Other Rotation Players
Lonzo Ball
Brandon Ingram
JaVale McGee
Lance Stephenson
Michael Beasley

Remaining Roster

- Ivica Zubac
- Moritz Wagner
- Svi Mykhailiuk
- Isaac Bonga
- Travis Wear, 28, 6'10", 230, UCLA (Two-Way)
- Joel Berry, 23, 6'0", 195, North Carolina (Exhibit 10)
- Jeffrey Carroll, 24, 6'6", 220, Oklahoma State (Exhibit 10)
- Johnathan Williams, 23, 6'9", 228, Gonzaga (Exhibit 10)

Season Forecast

The Los Angeles Lakers made the biggest move of the summer by landing LeBron James on the first day of free agency. James should help the Lakers improve significantly but may be not to the extent that his previous teams did when he signed with Miami in 2010 and Cleveland in 2014, respectively. This is mainly because the Lakers took a different approach with the rest of the roster, as they didn't immediately try to deal some of their young players or assets for established veterans. Instead they signed veteran stop-gaps like Rajon Rondo, JaVale McGee, Lance Stephenson and Michael Beasley to one-year deals to preserve cap space to make a run at a major free agent next summer, where many big names will potentially be available. As for this season, James' presence should make them very competitive in a very tough Western Conference, but it could take some time for the Lakers to gel and get some of their players adjusted to new roles. Therefore, the team's record could take a hit in the early going, but they could be a dangerous team once they hit their stride. Most likely, they will make the playoffs as a middle to lower seeded team, but they would be a very tough out that's capable of pulling off an upset in the playoffs due to the individual brilliance of LeBron James.

The Lakers are probably going to lean pretty heavily on their defense to help them win games this season. Up until the trade with Cleveland last season, the Lakers were one of the better defensive teams in the league despite not having any singular standout defenders on the roster. They were able to play effective defense in the first half of last season because their rotation featured a lot of taller perimeter players, which enabled them to constantly switch screens to stay attached to opposing offensive players to force more misses. This roster allows them to play a similar style of defense with the only shorter player being Rondo and he's historically been someone that's been able to use his length to play bigger than this actual size. Therefore, the defense could improve a bit, assuming the team doesn't make a move to change the rotation. Offensively, there may be a bit of an adjustment period because there are a lot of moving parts in their rotation around James. Ideally, James works best with one additional quality high volume shot creator and shooters to fill the remaining roles. The rotation right now isn't quite constructed to provide multiple lineups to properly complement James. Brandon Ingram and Kyle Kuzma have flashed some high-end potential, but neither one has reached the level of James' previous sidekicks at this point, so it's uncertain if either could immediately fill this role. If they show some significant improvement, it could be possible for one of them to fill a high usage role around LeBron James. However, at this stage, they might be better suited to playing in complementary shooter roles. From there, they simply may not have enough shooters for them to sustain an efficient offense for a full 82-game season. As it stands, the Lakers may be a year away from being true contenders in the West. Right now, they will be significantly improved and are probably a solid playoff team in the Western Conference, but they might not have enough overall talent to beat the best teams in the league on a regular basis.

Veterans

LeBron James

	Height	Weight	Cap #	Years Left
	6'8"	240	$35.654M	2 + PO

	Similar at Age	33	
		Season	**SIMsc**
1	Karl Malone*	1996-97	876.0
2	Larry Bird*	1989-90	869.5
3	Frank Brickowski	1992-93	847.2
4	Paul Pierce	2010-11	842.2
5	Dirk Nowitzki	2011-12	833.3
6	David West	2013-14	830.6
7	Clifford Robinson	1999-00	827.7
8	Antawn Jamison	2009-10	825.0
9	Scottie Pippen*	1998-99	819.6
10	Chris Webber	2006-07	818.2

Baseline Basic Stats

MPG	PTS	AST	REB	BLK	STL
35.3	22.5	5.0	7.5	0.7	1.3

Advanced Metrics

USG%	3PTA/FGA	FTA/FGA	TS%	eFG%	3PT%
29.2	0.224	0.350	0.592	0.556	0.362

AST%	TOV%	OREB%	DREB%	STL%	BLK%
32.4	14.3	4.1	20.7	1.9	1.6

PER	ORTG	DRTG	WS/48	VOL	
25.03	114.4	106.0	0.223	0.620	

- Still the best all-around player in the NBA entering his age-34 season, continues to produce at MVP-like levels
- Projection is a bit undershot, not many reliable comparables due to his body type and high level of performance
- Projection incorporates the possibility of aging, but he so far has not shown any signs of decline
- Dynamic playmaking skills and still very efficient as a high volume scorer
- Excellent as a pick-and-roll ball handler, very good in post-ups and isolations
- Still excellent at finishing at the rim and drawing fouls, shooting more threes and making them at a league average rate
- Good help defender that can make chase-down blocks and grab defensive rebounds at a high rate
- Solid on-ball defender that can guard multiple positions, has looked to conserve energy on defense in recent years, doesn't go all out in the regular season like he did in his 20s

Brandon Ingram

	Height	Weight	Cap #	Years Left
	6'9"	190	$5.757M	1

Similar at Age 20

		Season	SIMsc
1	Harrison Barnes	2012-13	907.3
2	Rudy Gay	2006-07	899.2
3	Darius Miles	2001-02	895.1
4	Giannis Antetokounmpo	2014-15	892.4
5	Marvin Williams	2006-07	891.7
6	DerMarr Johnson	2000-01	888.5
7	Gordon Hayward	2010-11	882.1
8	Andrew Wiggins	2015-16	881.1
9	Luol Deng	2005-06	877.4
10	Rashard Lewis	1999-00	872.2

Baseline Basic Stats

MPG	PTS	AST	REB	BLK	STL
31.1	14.1	2.4	4.9	0.6	1.0

Advanced Metrics

USG%	3PTA/FGA	FTA/FGA	TS%	eFG%	3PT%
22.0	0.223	0.320	0.534	0.494	0.367

AST%	TOV%	OREB%	DREB%	STL%	BLK%
14.2	12.3	3.5	13.2	1.4	1.3

PER	ORTG	DRTG	WS/48	VOL
14.38	105.7	110.1	0.078	0.315

- Significantly improved in his second season, missed games due to a strained left hip flexor
- Increased his offensive efficiency, rated by the NBA per-possession metrics as above average or better on cuts, transition plays and spot-ups
- Improved his three-point shooting by making 39% of his threes, Assist Percentage went up significantly
- Below average in isolations, post-ups and plays as the pick-and-roll ball handler, may not be as effective at scoring off the dribble
- Solid on-ball defender that's good at using his length to shots, better at handling taller wings than smaller guards, decent defensive rebounder

Kyle Kuzma

	Height	Weight	Cap #	Years Left
	6'9"	220	$1.690M	2 Team Options

Similar at Age 22

		Season	SIMsc
1	Mike Miller	2002-03	941.8
2	Tobias Harris	2014-15	940.1
3	Peja Stojakovic	1999-00	935.2
4	Wilson Chandler	2009-10	931.1
5	Vladimir Radmanovic	2002-03	924.3
6	Dario Saric	2016-17	922.1
7	Omri Casspi	2010-11	921.5
8	Rashard Lewis	2001-02	921.1
9	Chase Budinger	2010-11	918.1
10	Jeff Green	2008-09	915.8

Baseline Basic Stats

MPG	PTS	AST	REB	BLK	STL
31.0	14.4	1.9	5.2	0.5	0.9

Advanced Metrics

USG%	3PTA/FGA	FTA/FGA	TS%	eFG%	3PT%
21.7	0.360	0.228	0.555	0.522	0.375

AST%	TOV%	OREB%	DREB%	STL%	BLK%
9.9	10.5	3.9	15.7	1.3	1.2

PER	ORTG	DRTG	WS/48	VOL
15.40	108.2	107.9	0.100	0.399

- Very productive in his rookie season, made the All-Rookie first team
- Very good on post-ups and isolations, excelled at scoring in late shot clock situations
- Fairly good outside shooter, made just over a league average percentage on threes
- Rated as below average in situations where he had to play off the ball or make plays for others
- Decent on-ball defender, better handling perimeter players than inside players, solid defensive rebounder

Lonzo Ball

	Height	Weight	Cap #	Years Left
	6'6"	190	$7.462M	2 Team Options

Similar at Age 20

		Season	SIMsc
1	Jamal Crawford	2000-01	896.1
2	Rashad Vaughn	2016-17	873.8
3	D'Angelo Russell	2016-17	872.2
4	Elfrid Payton	2014-15	853.4
5	Shaun Livingston	2005-06	853.2
6	Jordan Farmar	2006-07	843.7
7	Emmanuel Mudiay	2016-17	840.7
8	Maurice Harkless	2013-14	840.1
9	Martell Webster	2006-07	839.3
10	Marcus Smart	2014-15	837.7

Baseline Basic Stats

MPG	PTS	AST	REB	BLK	STL
26.8	11.0	4.1	3.4	0.4	1.1

Advanced Metrics

USG%	3PTA/FGA	FTA/FGA	TS%	eFG%	3PT%
20.2	0.466	0.168	0.494	0.474	0.343

AST%	TOV%	OREB%	DREB%	STL%	BLK%
27.5	16.1	3.2	13.8	2.1	1.3

PER	ORTG	DRTG	WS/48	VOL	
14.13	102.6	106.4	0.082	0.772	

- Made the All-Rookie second team, missed a chunk of the season due to a sprained knee
- Played in a low usage role, very good as a playmaker, but a little turnover prone
- Inefficient as a scorer in all situations, performed best in spot-up situations, but was still slightly below average
- Took a lot of threes, but made them at a below break-even rate
- Team was better on defense with him on the court, effective help defender that could get steals, rotate for blocks and grab defensive rebounds
- Decent as an on-ball defender, but could still use some improvement, might be able to guard multiple positions in the future

Kentavious Caldwell-Pope

	Height	Weight	Cap #	Years Left
	6'5"	205	$12.000M	0

Similar at Age 24

		Season	SIMsc
1	Courtney Lee	2009-10	954.6
2	Voshon Lenard	1997-98	947.4
3	Anthony Morrow	2009-10	938.0
4	Wesley Person	1995-96	936.3
5	James Anderson	2013-14	932.3
6	Marcus Thornton	2011-12	931.3
7	Dion Waiters	2015-16	931.2
8	Victor Oladipo	2016-17	930.4
9	Danny Green	2011-12	929.3
10	Tim Hardaway, Jr.	2016-17	927.1

Baseline Basic Stats

MPG	PTS	AST	REB	BLK	STL
27.7	11.9	1.9	3.1	0.2	1.0

Advanced Metrics

USG%	3PTA/FGA	FTA/FGA	TS%	eFG%	3PT%
18.9	0.487	0.227	0.551	0.511	0.377

AST%	TOV%	OREB%	DREB%	STL%	BLK%
11.5	9.6	2.4	11.5	1.9	0.6

PER	ORTG	DRTG	WS/48	VOL	
14.00	110.0	108.5	0.111	0.301	

- Consistent starting level wing player, had his best season in the NBA at age 24
- Filled a low usage role, most effective as a spot-up shooter, shot a career best 38.3% on threes last season
- Average at running off screens, pretty effective in a small sample of isolation possessions
- Generally an above average on-ball wing defender, gets steals at a fairly high rate
- Posted the best Defensive Rebound Percentage of his career last season

Rajon Rondo

	Height	Weight	Cap #	Years Left
	6'1"	171	$9.000M	0

Similar at Age 31

		Season	SIMsc
1	Larry Drew	1989-90	902.1
2	John Bagley	1991-92	891.7
3	Johnny Dawkins	1994-95	891.4
4	Mike Evans	1986-87	885.7
5	Mark Jackson	1996-97	884.5
6	Monta Ellis	2016-17	881.0
7	Gerald Henderson	1986-87	880.9
8	Rafer Alston	2007-08	880.6
9	Howard Eisley	2003-04	880.6
10	Allen Leavell	1988-89	878.1

Baseline Basic Stats

MPG	PTS	AST	REB	BLK	STL
27.1	8.5	6.6	3.3	0.1	1.1

Advanced Metrics

USG%	3PTA/FGA	FTA/FGA	TS%	eFG%	3PT%
16.9	0.298	0.144	0.510	0.492	0.360

AST%	TOV%	OREB%	DREB%	STL%	BLK%
38.2	21.1	2.6	12.6	2.1	0.4

PER	ORTG	DRTG	WS/48	VOL	
14.94	107.6	107.4	0.098	0.604	

- Had a bounce back season with New Orleans last year after a down year in Chicago in 2016-17
- Excellent playmaker in a low usage role, fairly turnover prone
- Very good as a pick-and-roll ball handler, got to the rim more frequently to boost his shooting efficiency
- Shot an above average percentage from mid-range and break-even on threes last season
- Still a good rebounding point guard, posted the lowest Steal Percentage of his career last season
- Decent on-ball defender, can gamble a bit too much

Josh Hart

	Height	Weight	Cap #	Years Left
	6'5"	209	$1.655M	2 Team Options

Similar at Age **22**

		Season	SIMsc
1	Casey Jacobsen	2003-04	920.9
2	Josh Richardson	2015-16	919.2
3	Iman Shumpert	2012-13	916.7
4	Caris LeVert	2016-17	913.8
5	Chris Carr	1996-97	913.8
6	Hollis Thompson	2013-14	912.5
7	Landry Fields	2010-11	908.7
8	Tony Snell	2013-14	907.7
9	Ben McLemore	2015-16	907.4
10	Allen Crabbe	2014-15	907.3

Baseline Basic Stats

MPG	PTS	AST	REB	BLK	STL
25.9	9.6	1.7	3.3	0.3	0.7

Advanced Metrics

USG%	3PTA/FGA	FTA/FGA	TS%	eFG%	3PT%
16.0	0.477	0.231	0.575	0.545	0.389

AST%	TOV%	OREB%	DREB%	STL%	BLK%
9.8	10.7	2.6	13.4	1.4	0.8

PER	ORTG	DRTG	WS/48	VOL
12.22	111.6	109.3	0.099	0.380

- Productive in a regular rotation role for the Lakers as a rookie
- Played in a very low usage role, mainly utilized as a spot-up shooter and finisher in transition with great effectiveness
- Made almost 40% of his threes overall and more than 50% of his corner threes
- Flashed some ability to run off screens in a small sample of possessions
- Ranked in the 84th percentile by the NBA at coming off screens on a per-possession basis
- Fairly solid on-ball defending wing player, good defensive rebounder

Lance Stephenson

	Height	Weight	Cap #	Years Left
	6'5"	210	$4.449M	0

Similar at Age 27

		Season	SIMsc
1	Gordan Giricek	2004-05	922.9
2	O.J. Mayo	2014-15	914.5
3	Bobby Phills	1996-97	911.9
4	Gerald Henderson	2014-15	908.3
5	Laron Profit	2004-05	907.6
6	Gary Neal	2011-12	907.6
7	Greg Minor	1998-99	906.2
8	Arron Afflalo	2012-13	904.5
9	Mitch Richmond*	1992-93	902.5
10	Bob Sura	2000-01	902.4

Baseline Basic Stats

MPG	PTS	AST	REB	BLK	STL
25.5	10.7	2.4	3.0	0.2	0.8

Advanced Metrics

USG%	3PTA/FGA	FTA/FGA	TS%	eFG%	3PT%
19.9	0.342	0.215	0.519	0.488	0.346

AST%	TOV%	OREB%	DREB%	STL%	BLK%
17.3	13.3	2.8	15.1	1.4	0.6

PER	ORTG	DRTG	WS/48	VOL
12.56	103.6	109.1	0.064	0.279

- Bounced back to a regular rotation role in Indiana after missing most of 2016-17 due to a torn groin muscle and splitting time between three different teams
- Prefers to play with the ball in his hands, but below average as a pick-and-roll ball handler and as an isolation player
- More effective last season as a cutter in limited situations and as a slightly above average spot-up shooter, has some playmaking skills
- Historically a below break-even three-point shooter overall, but has shot almost 37% on corner threes throughout his career
- Solid on-ball defending wing, good defensive rebounder
- Below average as a team defender, can have lapses when making defensive rotations

Michael Beasley

	Height	Weight	Cap #	Years Left
	6'9"	235	$3.500M	0

Similar at Age 29

		Season	SIMsc
1	Amar'e Stoudemire	2011-12	920.3
2	Drew Gooden	2010-11	912.1
3	Kris Humphries	2014-15	910.4
4	Bison Dele	1998-99	910.2
5	Ersan Ilyasova	2016-17	907.5
6	Lee Nailon	2004-05	906.3
7	David West	2009-10	905.5
8	Al Harrington	2009-10	902.2
9	Antoine Carr	1990-91	902.1
10	Luis Scola	2009-10	901.4

Baseline Basic Stats

MPG	PTS	AST	REB	BLK	STL
26.0	12.8	1.5	5.9	0.7	0.6

Advanced Metrics

USG%	3PTA/FGA	FTA/FGA	TS%	eFG%	3PT%
24.1	0.098	0.238	0.542	0.507	0.363

AST%	TOV%	OREB%	DREB%	STL%	BLK%
10.2	12.2	6.8	19.0	1.2	2.1

PER	ORTG	DRTG	WS/48	VOL
16.60	104.4	106.9	0.072	0.473

- Solid rotation player for New York after being a fringe rotation player for the previous four seasons
- Played a high usage role off the bench, effective with the ball in his hands, good on isolations and post-ups
- Solid as a roll man and a good cutter, shot almost 40% on threes in a limited number of attempts
- According to the NBA play-type metrics, he struggled in spot-up situations because he frequently turned the ball over
- Good rebounder, can occasionally block shots
- Below average defender overall, struggles to defend on the ball, has lapses when making defensive rotations

JaVale McGee

	Height	Weight	Cap #	Years Left
	7'0"	237	$1.513M	0

Similar at Age 30

		Season	SIMsc
1	Alton Lister	1988-89	885.5
2	Jason Smith	2016-17	876.9
3	Dan Gadzuric	2008-09	873.0
4	Antonio Harvey	2000-01	870.3
5	Jim Grandholm	1990-91	869.3
6	D.J. Mbenga	2010-11	867.0
7	Will Perdue	1995-96	860.9
8	Duane Causwell	1998-99	860.2
9	Samuel Dalembert	2011-12	859.5
10	Salah Mejri	2016-17	857.6

Baseline Basic Stats

MPG	PTS	AST	REB	BLK	STL
13.0	4.4	0.4	3.9	0.8	0.3

Advanced Metrics

USG%	3PTA/FGA	FTA/FGA	TS%	eFG%	3PT%
17.1	0.046	0.322	0.615	0.602	0.102

AST%	TOV%	OREB%	DREB%	STL%	BLK%
5.0	13.7	12.9	21.9	1.3	5.8

PER	ORTG	DRTG	WS/48	VOL
18.66	118.1	104.5	0.167	0.297

- Effective in a limited role in Golden State, served as a token starter for nine games in the playoffs
- Primarily a low volume rim runner, did the bulk of his scoring inside of three feet
- Over 55% of his made field goals were dunks last season
- Very good rim protector, excellent shot blocker and offensive rebounder
- Solid on the defensive boards, sometimes sacrifices positioning to go for blocks
- Has some trouble on the ball against quicker players, can have lapses when making defensive rotations

Ivica Zubac

	Height	Weight	Cap #	Years Left
	7'1"	265	$1.545M	0

	Similar at Age	**20**	
		Season	SIMsc
1	Kosta Koufos	2009-10	910.3
2	Al Jefferson	2004-05	902.4
3	Brook Lopez	2008-09	898.1
4	Kwame Brown	2002-03	896.9
5	Jackie Butler	2005-06	895.0
6	Robin Lopez	2008-09	891.2
7	Robert Swift	2005-06	890.5
8	Alex Len	2013-14	889.5
9	Enes Kanter	2012-13	888.5
10	J.J. Hickson	2008-09	887.5

Baseline Basic Stats

MPG	PTS	AST	REB	BLK	STL
18.5	6.7	0.5	5.2	0.9	0.4

Advanced Metrics

USG%	3PTA/FGA	FTA/FGA	TS%	eFG%	3PT%
18.4	0.009	0.352	0.559	0.518	0.117

AST%	TOV%	OREB%	DREB%	STL%	BLK%
5.6	14.4	9.8	21.1	1.1	3.2

PER	ORTG	DRTG	WS/48	VOL	
15.58	108.0	104.7	0.118	0.421	

- Played limited minutes for the Lakers last season, split between Los Angeles and South Bay in the G-League
- Efficient low usage rim runner, scored mostly inside of three feet, drew fouls and crashed the offensive glass
- Shown promise as a rim protector, good at contesting shots inside, solid blocks and defensive rebound rate
- Good team defender, plays with sound positioning, can struggle on the ball against quicker players due to a lack of mobility

Newcomers

Moritz Wagner

	Height	Weight	Cap #	Years Left
	6'11"	245	$1.762M	1 + 2 TO

Baseline Basic Stats

MPG	PTS	AST	REB	BLK	STL
19.5	8.4	1.1	3.8	0.5	0.6

Advanced Metrics

USG%	3PTA/FGA	FTA/FGA	TS%	eFG%	3PT%
21.5	0.144	0.277	0.500	0.464	0.300

AST%	TOV%	OREB%	DREB%	STL%	BLK%
9.3	12.4	7.0	15.1	1.5	1.7

PER	ORTG	DRTG	WS/48	VOL
13.16	100.8	108.6	0.052	N/A

- Drafted by the Lakers in the first round with the 25th pick
- Very good showing at both the Las Vegas and Sacramento Summer Leagues
- Highly energetic on defense, got steals, blocks and defensive rebounds at a high rate
- Generally played with solid positioning, but racked up fouls at an extremely high rate
- Still unpolished offensively, played with high effort by crashing the offensive boards, running the floor in transition and drawing fouls inside
- Struggled to shoot efficiently from the field, shot below 40% on field goals overall and below 30% on threes

Svi Mykhailiuk

	Height	Weight	Cap #	Years Left
	6'8"	205	$1.488M	1

Baseline Basic Stats

MPG	PTS	AST	REB	BLK	STL
19.9	6.6	1.4	2.9	0.2	0.5

Advanced Metrics

USG%	3PTA/FGA	FTA/FGA	TS%	eFG%	3PT%
17.7	0.353	0.177	0.485	0.460	0.345

AST%	TOV%	OREB%	DREB%	STL%	BLK%
11.8	12.0	4.0	12.7	1.4	0.6

PER	ORTG	DRTG	WS/48	VOL
10.67	99.1	109.2	0.027	N/A

- Drafted by the Lakers in the second round with the 47th overall pick
- Excellent showing in the Las Vegas Summer League, named to the All-Tournament second team
- Shot the ball very well over the course of seven games, made 40.8% of his threes in almost 50 attempts
- Showed solid passing skills and rarely turned the ball over
- Better than average as an on-ball position defender, solid on the defensive glass

Isaac Bonga

		Height	Weight	Cap #	Years Left
		6'8"	179	$1.000M	2

Baseline Basic Stats

MPG	PTS	AST	REB	BLK	STL
22.3	8.2	2.1	3.1	0.4	0.8

Advanced Metrics

USG%	3PTA/FGA	FTA/FGA	TS%	eFG%	3PT%
16.2	0.267	0.362	0.501	0.438	0.274

AST%	TOV%	OREB%	DREB%	STL%	BLK%
18.1	19.4	2.9	11.8	1.8	1.3

PER	ORTG	DRTG	WS/48	VOL	
11.08	93.5	100.0	0.073	0.725	

- Drafted by Philadelphia with the 39th overall pick, then traded to the Lakers
- Played last season with the Fraport Skyliners in the German Bundesliga, projection uses translated German BBL stats
- Struggled mightily at Summer League, right now is a project, needs to develop his skills in the G-League
- Had difficulties on offense, extremely turnover prone, didn't shoot efficiently from the field
- Got the free throw line at a high rate, but only made 50% of his free throws
- Has tools defensively, but tends to be out of position, not especially polished as an on-ball defender
- Active help defender that gets steals and blocks

DENVER NUGGETS

<u>Last Season</u>: 46 – 36, Missed the Playoffs

<u>Offensive Rating</u>: 112.5, 6th in NBA   <u>Defensive Rating</u>: 111.0, 25th in NBA

<u>Primary Executive</u>: Tim Connelly, President of Basketball Operations

<u>Head Coach</u>: Mike Malone

Key Roster Changes

Subtractions
Wilson Chandler, trade
Kenneth Faried, trade
Darrell Arthur, trade
Devin Harris, free agency
Richard Jefferson, free agency

Additions
Michael Porter, Jr., draft
Jarred Vanderbilt, draft
Isaiah Thomas, free agency

RAFER Projected Win Total: 43.7

Projected Best Five-Man Unit
1. Jamal Murray
2. Gary Harris
3. Will Barton
4. Paul Millsap
5. Nikola Jokic

Other Rotation Players
Mason Plumlee
Isaiah Thomas
Trey Lyles
Juan Hernangomez
Malik Beasley

Remaining Roster

- Torrey Craig
- Tyler Lydon
- Monte Morris
- Jarred Vanderbilt
- Michael Porter, Jr.
- Thomas Welsh, 22, 7'0", 255, UCLA (Two-Way)
- DeVaughn Akoon-Purcell, 25, 6'5", 200, Illinois State (Two-Way)
- Emanuel Terry, 22, 6'9", 220, Lincoln Memorial University (Exhibit 10)

Season Forecast

The Denver Nuggets have fallen short of the playoffs by a single game in each of the last two seasons. Rather than make a major move to change their fortunes, Denver took a quieter approach by simply re-signing core players like Nikola Jokic and Will Barton to long-term deals and banking on some internal growth from younger players like Trey Lyles, Juan Hernangomez and Malik Beasley. They also took a flyer on former All-Star Isaiah Thomas to possibly add some scoring off the bench. As it stands now, the Western Conference is still as competitive as it has been over the last few years, so it might be tough for them to sneak into playoffs with this current roster. However, if their primary players play up to their capabilities and they catch a lucky break or two, they could get a lower playoff seed this season.

Otherwise, the results from this season are likely to be similar to the previous two seasons and the Nuggets could finish just outside of the playoffs for the third straight year.

Denver has been one of the best offensive teams in the league for the last two seasons, ranking in the top ten in Offensive Rating each year. Most of the key personnel is intact, so the team should be highly effective on offense once again. Stylistically, they'll mainly rely on a unit that will really space the floor with four or five three-point threats. Then, they will utilize the passing skills of Jokic, Barton and Jamal Murray to consistently find open looks and easier shot opportunities. The only real concern is that head coach, Mike Malone tends to use a very short rotation that leans heavily on his starters. This doesn't give the team much room for error because the depth behind their starters is relatively untested. Because of this, the team's main core has to stay healthy or their offensive performance will drop off to the point where they could definitely miss the playoffs. Isaiah Thomas is a wild card in this equation because it's uncertain as to which version of him will show up in Denver. If Thomas played like he did last season, then his only real positive value may be that he could allow Malone to stagger the minutes of his guards to better maintain their offense for a full 48 minutes. On the other hand, if Thomas plays anything like he did in Boston prior to last season, Denver could have an excellent sixth man that gives them more offensive firepower.

No matter which Thomas shows up on offense, his presence could make an already bad defense even worse. Over the last two seasons, Denver has finished in the bottom third in Defensive Rating and switching out a solid defender in Wilson Chandler for a traditionally below average defender like Thomas is likely to make them worse defensively. In addition to this switch, Denver didn't really add anyone to the rotation to shore up any part of their defense. Also, the team's rotation now is lacking wing players and there may be too many small guards. Therefore, the Nuggets won't have the versatility to handle different lineups. If the team makes no more changes, any gains on offense are likely to be negated by some struggles on defense. Overall, Denver is going to be a competitive team this season because their highly efficient offense will allow them to score with anyone. However, their defense will hold them back to the point where they will likely miss the playoffs once again this season.

Veterans

Nikola Jokic

	Height	Weight	Cap #	Years Left
	6'10"	250	$25.467M	4

Similar at Age 22

		Season	SIMsc
1	Julius Randle	2016-17	901.6
2	Greg Monroe	2012-13	891.6
3	Derrick Favors	2013-14	885.7
4	Carlos Boozer	2003-04	882.4
5	Blake Griffin	2011-12	880.6
6	Al Horford	2008-09	876.0
7	Willy Hernangomez	2016-17	873.1
8	Karl Malone*	1985-86	871.9
9	Al Jefferson	2006-07	871.2
10	J.J. Hickson	2010-11	870.9

Baseline Basic Stats

MPG	PTS	AST	REB	BLK	STL
31.3	16.7	2.6	9.1	0.8	1.0

Advanced Metrics

USG%	3PTA/FGA	FTA/FGA	TS%	eFG%	3PT%
24.1	0.146	0.313	0.595	0.554	0.403

AST%	TOV%	OREB%	DREB%	STL%	BLK%
21.5	13.1	9.4	24.2	1.7	1.9

PER	ORTG	DRTG	WS/48	VOL
23.50	118.9	106.3	0.203	0.362

- Entering his age-23 season, has been producing at an All-Star level for the last two seasons
- One of the best passing big men in the league
- Has been effective as a pick-and-roll ball handler in a limited amount of possessions
- Very good post-up player, excellent in spot-up situations, made almost 40% of his threes last season
- Limited mobility, not as effective as roll man on offense, struggles to defend in space against quicker players
- Very good overall rebounder, not effective as a rim protector, middling shot blocker

Gary Harris

	Height	Weight	Cap #	Years Left
	6'4"	210	$16.518M	3

Similar at Age 23

		Season	SIMsc
1	O.J. Mayo	2010-11	942.8
2	Dion Waiters	2014-15	935.3
3	Kentavious Caldwell-Pope	2016-17	934.1
4	Voshon Lenard	1996-97	928.4
5	C.J. McCollum	2014-15	923.5
6	Buddy Hield	2016-17	919.7
7	Courtney Lee	2008-09	918.5
8	Austin Rivers	2015-16	917.0
9	Michael Redd	2002-03	916.3
10	Allen Crabbe	2015-16	915.2

Baseline Basic Stats

MPG	PTS	AST	REB	BLK	STL
29.2	13.6	2.4	3.2	0.2	1.0

Advanced Metrics

USG%	3PTA/FGA	FTA/FGA	TS%	eFG%	3PT%
21.2	0.427	0.207	0.575	0.542	0.394

AST%	TOV%	OREB%	DREB%	STL%	BLK%
14.1	10.6	2.3	8.9	2.0	0.5

PER	ORTG	DRTG	WS/48	VOL
16.00	112.8	110.9	0.109	0.267

- Entering his age-24 season, maintained his production level from the previous season
- Very effective complementary scorer, excelled as a spot-up shooter and cutter
- Above average at running off screens, below average in isolation situations
- Very good three-point shooter, made almost 40% of his threes last season
- Decent playmaking skills, was effective as a pick-and-roll ball handler in a small sample of possessions last season
- Fairly decent on-ball defender, good at contesting shots on the perimeter
- Can struggle to contain the drive, middling rebounder, but will get steals

Jamal Murray

	Height	Weight	Cap #	Years Left
	6'4"	207	$3.500M	Team Option

Similar at Age 20

		Season	SIMsc
1	Bradley Beal	2013-14	936.5
2	Eric Gordon	2008-09	916.8
3	Zach LaVine	2015-16	913.3
4	Ben McLemore	2013-14	903.9
5	Emmanuel Mudiay	2016-17	903.9
6	Brandon Knight	2011-12	903.7
7	Devin Booker	2016-17	897.7
8	Daequan Cook	2007-08	894.0
9	James Harden	2009-10	892.2
10	D'Angelo Russell	2016-17	890.9

Baseline Basic Stats

MPG	PTS	AST	REB	BLK	STL
31.1	15.1	3.0	3.2	0.2	1.0

Advanced Metrics

USG%	3PTA/FGA	FTA/FGA	TS%	eFG%	3PT%
23.1	0.423	0.211	0.551	0.512	0.377

AST%	TOV%	OREB%	DREB%	STL%	BLK%
16.0	12.2	2.7	9.2	1.6	0.7

PER	ORTG	DRTG	WS/48	VOL	
14.79	108.2	112.0	0.090	0.297	

- Significantly improved in his second season, very durable over the last two seasons, has only missed one game

- Good playmaker and shooter, effective as a pick-and-roll ball handler, good spot-up shooter that can also run off screens

- Above average three-point shooter overall, excellent in the corners throughout his career with a percentage of 43.1%

- Not quite a primary scoring option, struggled in isolation situations

- Below average on-ball defender, has difficulty containing quicker guards, middling defensive rebounder

Will Barton

	Height	Weight	Cap #	Years Left
	6'6"	174	$11.830M	2 + PO

Similar at Age 27

		Season	SIMsc
1	Brent Barry	1998-99	915.2
2	Vernon Maxwell	1992-93	913.6
3	Ricky Davis	2006-07	910.3
4	Kerry Kittles	2001-02	905.2
5	Justin Holiday	2016-17	905.1
6	Todd Day	1996-97	903.3
7	Gerald Wilkins	1990-91	901.1
8	Marco Belinelli	2013-14	898.6
9	Jamal Crawford	2007-08	897.6
10	Wesley Person	1998-99	897.2

Baseline Basic Stats

MPG	PTS	AST	REB	BLK	STL
32.6	14.0	3.5	3.5	0.3	1.1

Advanced Metrics

USG%	3PTA/FGA	FTA/FGA	TS%	eFG%	3PT%
20.4	0.400	0.220	0.539	0.504	0.364

AST%	TOV%	OREB%	DREB%	STL%	BLK%
18.1	11.8	2.6	12.2	1.6	1.1

PER	ORTG	DRTG	WS/48	VOL	
14.63	108.4	109.6	0.095	0.274	

- Had a career best season in his sixth year at age 27
- Greatly improved his playmaking skills, posted the highest Assist Percentage of his career
- Good as a pick-and-roll ball handler last season
- Excelled as a complementary scorer by being effective as a spot-up shooter, cutter and finisher in transition
- Made 37% of his threes for the second consecutive season
- Solid on-ball wing defender, could use length to contest shots, good defensive rebounding wing

Paul Millsap

	Height	Weight	Cap #	Years Left
	6'8"	245	$29.231M	Team Option

Similar at Age **32**

		Season	SIMsc
1	David West	2012-13	910.1
2	Bob Lanier*	1980-81	909.2
3	Luis Scola	2012-13	901.4
4	Frank Brickowski	1991-92	895.5
5	Rodney Rogers	2003-04	894.8
6	Amar'e Stoudemire	2014-15	889.7
7	Sam Perkins	1993-94	888.5
8	Danny Manning	1998-99	885.5
9	Herb Williams	1990-91	880.3
10	Chris Webber	2005-06	878.2

Baseline Basic Stats

MPG	PTS	AST	REB	BLK	STL
25.7	11.6	2.3	5.6	0.7	0.9

Advanced Metrics

USG%	3PTA/FGA	FTA/FGA	TS%	eFG%	3PT%
21.2	0.240	0.319	0.545	0.505	0.307

AST%	TOV%	OREB%	DREB%	STL%	BLK%
15.0	13.5	5.8	18.8	1.8	2.5

PER	ORTG	DRTG	WS/48	VOL
16.19	106.8	104.3	0.115	0.379

- Missed most of the first half of last season due to a sprained left wrist that required surgery
- Production was slightly down from the year before
- Efficient scorer overall, good on post-ups, middling in other situations, decent passing four man
- Shot a break-even percentage on threes last season, has historically been better in the corners
- Posted the lowest Defensive Rebound Percentage of his career last season, increased his blocks rate
- Solid on-ball defender in previous seasons, but slipped a bit last season

Mason Plumlee

	Height	Weight	Cap #	Years Left
	6'10"	235	$12.918M	1

Similar at Age 27

		Season	SIMsc
1	Mark West	1987-88	940.2
2	John Salley	1991-92	914.4
3	Steve Johnson	1984-85	913.4
4	Joakim Noah	2012-13	911.7
5	Tiago Splitter	2011-12	911.5
6	Alton Lister	1985-86	909.2
7	Ronny Turiaf	2009-10	902.3
8	John Shumate	1979-80	901.0
9	Anderson Varejao	2009-10	900.6
10	Will Perdue	1992-93	899.8

Baseline Basic Stats

MPG	PTS	AST	REB	BLK	STL
23.6	8.4	1.6	6.5	1.2	0.7

Advanced Metrics

USG%	3PTA/FGA	FTA/FGA	TS%	eFG%	3PT%
15.9	0.005	0.478	0.574	0.555	0.069

AST%	TOV%	OREB%	DREB%	STL%	BLK%
13.7	17.4	9.8	20.9	1.5	3.4

PER	ORTG	DRTG	WS/48	VOL	
15.97	112.8	106.0	0.122	0.263	

- Solid in a rotational role with Denver last season, production slightly down from his career averages
- Primarily a low volume rim runner that scored from close range, drew fouls and crashed the offensive boards
- Most effective at running the floor in transition, solid passing big man
- Solid rim protector, good shot blocker and defensive rebounder
- Struggles to defend on the ball, lacks lateral mobility to defend quicker players, a bit foul prone

Isaiah Thomas

	Height	Weight	Cap #	Years Left
	5'9"	185	$1.513M	0

Similar at Age 28

	Player	Season	SIMsc
1	Nate Robinson	2012-13	897.3
2	J.J. Barea	2012-13	886.7
3	Mo Williams	2010-11	876.7
4	Michael Adams	1990-91	873.7
5	Tyronn Lue	2005-06	866.3
6	D.J. Augustin	2015-16	864.9
7	Tim Hardaway	1994-95	863.4
8	Mike Bibby	2006-07	862.4
9	Brian Roberts	2013-14	862.4
10	Damon Stoudamire	2001-02	859.1

Baseline Basic Stats

MPG	PTS	AST	REB	BLK	STL
25.5	12.9	4.5	2.3	0.1	0.8

Advanced Metrics

USG%	3PTA/FGA	FTA/FGA	TS%	eFG%	3PT%
26.4	0.446	0.312	0.544	0.483	0.346

AST%	TOV%	OREB%	DREB%	STL%	BLK%
29.1	14.1	1.9	7.5	1.4	0.3

PER	ORTG	DRTG	WS/48	VOL	
16.76	107.9	110.6	0.104	0.410	

- Missed the first half of last season recovering from a right hip injury
- Production fell off dramatically, went from 12.5 Win Shares in 2016-17 with Boston to 0.2 Win Shares last season with Cleveland and the Lakers
- Struggled to get to the rim and make outside shots, still an above average mid-range shooter
- Effective as a playmaker, but much more turnover prone
- Posted the highest Turnover Percentage of his career last season
- Has always been a defensive liability due to his small stature
- Posted his lowest Steal Percentage last season

Trey Lyles

	Height	Weight	Cap #	Years Left
	6'10"	234	$3.364M	0

Similar at Age 22

		Season	SIMsc
1	Vladimir Radmanovic	2002-03	924.0
2	Ersan Ilyasova	2009-10	923.1
3	Ryan Anderson	2010-11	921.5
4	Frank Kaminsky	2015-16	916.5
5	Charlie Villanueva	2006-07	915.7
6	Markieff Morris	2011-12	911.9
7	Ryan Kelly	2013-14	911.3
8	Tim Thomas	1999-00	911.3
9	Dario Saric	2016-17	909.9
10	Donte Greene	2010-11	908.0

Baseline Basic Stats

MPG	PTS	AST	REB	BLK	STL
23.4	10.1	1.3	4.6	0.4	0.7

Advanced Metrics

USG%	3PTA/FGA	FTA/FGA	TS%	eFG%	3PT%
20.8	0.372	0.220	0.542	0.512	0.365

AST%	TOV%	OREB%	DREB%	STL%	BLK%
9.9	10.3	5.1	18.9	1.3	1.5

PER	ORTG	DRTG	WS/48	VOL	
15.16	107.9	107.7	0.094	0.295	

- Had his best season in the NBA as a regular rotation player for Denver in his age-22 season
- Greatly improved on offense, very effective as a spot-up shooter, made 38.1% of his threes
- Also good as the roll man in pick-and-roll situations, effective as a post-up player
- Improved as a passer, has consistently cut his Turnover Percentage in each of his three seasons
- Played solid on-ball defense, good defensive rebounder, occasionally blocked shots
- Had some lapses when making defensive rotations, team was slightly worse on defense with him on the floor

Juan Hernangomez

	Height	Weight	Cap #	Years Left
	6'9"	230	$2.166M	Team Option

Similar at Age 22

		Season	SIMsc
1	Luke Babbitt	2011-12	935.1
2	Sam Dekker	2016-17	923.6
3	Omri Casspi	2010-11	916.1
4	Paul Zipser	2016-17	901.5
5	Solomon Hill	2013-14	900.2
6	Sergei Monia	2005-06	899.0
7	Perry Jones	2013-14	897.5
8	Sasha Pavlovic	2005-06	896.8
9	Justin Anderson	2015-16	890.8
10	Jason Kapono	2003-04	890.3

Baseline Basic Stats

MPG	PTS	AST	REB	BLK	STL
20.3	7.4	1.0	3.2	0.3	0.5

Advanced Metrics

USG%	3PTA/FGA	FTA/FGA	TS%	eFG%	3PT%
16.3	0.496	0.250	0.533	0.494	0.338

AST%	TOV%	OREB%	DREB%	STL%	BLK%
7.0	9.2	4.6	14.6	1.4	1.1

PER	ORTG	DRTG	WS/48	VOL	
11.97	109.0	111.3	0.079	0.464	

- Not a regular part of Denver's rotation, only played 277 minutes last season
- Mostly a low volume spot-up shooter in his two seasons
- Shot well in his rookie year, percentages were down last season
- League average three-point shooter for his career
- Good off ball player in motion that is effective at cutting at the rim and coming off screens
- Frequently used in this role as a rookie, not as much last season
- Decent on-ball defender that is capable of guarding both forward spots, solid defensive rebounder

Malik Beasley

	Height	Weight	Cap #	Years Left
	6'5"	196	$1.774M	1

Similar at Age 21

		Season	SIMsc
1	Marco Belinelli	2007-08	946.0
2	Terrence Ross	2012-13	938.4
3	Malachi Richardson	2016-17	927.0
4	Ben McLemore	2014-15	916.1
5	Kentavious Caldwell-Pope	2014-15	915.4
6	Allen Crabbe	2013-14	913.3
7	Shannon Brown	2006-07	911.9
8	Manny Harris	2010-11	911.2
9	Delonte West	2004-05	909.3
10	Jeremy Lamb	2013-14	906.9

Baseline Basic Stats

MPG	PTS	AST	REB	BLK	STL
22.7	9.3	1.7	2.4	0.2	0.7

Advanced Metrics

USG%	3PTA/FGA	FTA/FGA	TS%	eFG%	3PT%
18.5	0.294	0.200	0.527	0.497	0.338

AST%	TOV%	OREB%	DREB%	STL%	BLK%
10.9	11.6	2.6	9.2	1.7	0.6

PER	ORTG	DRTG	WS/48	VOL
11.39	104.5	111.9	0.069	0.440

- Received increased playing time for Denver last season, per-minute production decreased
- Mainly used as a low usage spot-up shooter, roughly average in those situations, shot above break-even on threes
- Below average in every other offensive situation last season
- Solid on-ball defender with the capability of guarding multiple positions
- Rebounded well on the defensive glass last season

Torrey Craig

	Height	Weight	Cap #	Years Left
	6'6"	215	$2.000M	1

Similar at Age 27

		Season	SIMsc
1	Sam Young	2012-13	925.5
2	Stephen Graham	2009-10	923.4
3	Sasha Pavlovic	2010-11	906.2
4	Chase Budinger	2015-16	902.1
5	Michael Curry	1995-96	898.6
6	Mickael Pietrus	2009-10	895.1
7	Thabo Sefolosha	2011-12	893.9
8	Matt Carroll	2007-08	893.7
9	Kyle Singler	2015-16	890.7
10	Jud Buechler	1995-96	889.7

Baseline Basic Stats

MPG	PTS	AST	REB	BLK	STL
16.9	5.2	0.8	2.4	0.3	0.5

Advanced Metrics

USG%	3PTA/FGA	FTA/FGA	TS%	eFG%	3PT%
13.5	0.449	0.202	0.526	0.503	0.308

AST%	TOV%	OREB%	DREB%	STL%	BLK%
6.4	11.3	5.2	13.4	1.2	1.5

PER	ORTG	DRTG	WS/48	VOL
10.05	107.3	109.2	0.074	0.534

- Played last season on a two-way contract
- Got playing time with Denver after a strong performance in the G-League with Sioux Falls
- Effective in a low usage role as a spot-up shooter and cutter, shot fairly efficiently
- Shot below break-even on threes overall, but shot fairly well on corner threes and mid-range shots
- Played solid on-ball defense in limited minutes, active to contest shots
- Good defensive rebounding wing that posted a good blocks rate

Tyler Lydon

	Height	Weight	Cap #	Years Left
	6'10"	215	$1.875M	2 Team Options

Similar at Age 21

		Season	SIMsc
1	Sam Dekker	2015-16	788.7
2	Ben Bentil	2016-17	764.4
3	Hassan Whiteside	2010-11	752.2
4	Pete Williams	1986-87	714.5
5	Slavko Vranes	2003-04	712.6
6	Antoine Wright	2005-06	694.7
7	Von Wafer	2006-07	685.1

Baseline Basic Stats

MPG	PTS	AST	REB	BLK	STL
20.7	7.8	0.7	2.9	0.4	0.4

Advanced Metrics

USG%	3PTA/FGA	FTA/FGA	TS%	eFG%	3PT%
12.8	0.019	0.245	0.531	0.489	0.350

AST%	TOV%	OREB%	DREB%	STL%	BLK%
5.2	8.2	3.1	13.2	1.2	1.3

PER	ORTG	DRTG	WS/48	VOL
15.12	108.7	111.2	0.185	0.094

- Only played two minutes for Denver in his rookie season
- Projection may be somewhat fluky due to the small sample of minutes
- Spent most of the season with Rio Grande Valley in the G-League
- Also missed the second half of last season due to a left knee injury that required surgery
- Very effective as a low volume spot-up shooter, made almost 38% of his threes and posted a 64.4% True Shooting Percentage
- More of a help defender in the G-League, good on the defensive boards, occasionally got blocks and steals, still struggles a bit as an on-ball defender

Monte Morris

	Height	Weight	Cap #	Years Left
	6'3"	175	$1.349M	2

Similar at Age 22

		Season	SIMsc
1	Jeremy Lin	2010-11	808.7
2	Rod Strickland	1988-89	795.8
3	Milt Palacio	2000-01	788.3
4	Fat Lever	1982-83	787.4
5	Ricky Rubio	2012-13	784.6
6	Armon Johnson	2011-12	784.5
7	Eric Maynor	2009-10	784.0
8	Cory Joseph	2013-14	782.6
9	Eric Snow	1995-96	780.9
10	Ennis Whatley	1984-85	780.4

Baseline Basic Stats

MPG	PTS	AST	REB	BLK	STL
20.6	8.0	3.7	1.9	0.1	1.0

Advanced Metrics

USG%	3PTA/FGA	FTA/FGA	TS%	eFG%	3PT%
16.3	0.166	0.345	0.636	0.575	0.192

AST%	TOV%	OREB%	DREB%	STL%	BLK%
33.1	13.3	1.3	8.1	3.9	0.3

PER	ORTG	DRTG	WS/48	VOL	
21.00	131.7	106.9	0.218	0.678	

- Played on a two-way contract, only played 25 minutes with Denver
- Spent most of the season in the G-League with Rio Grande Valley
- Good playmaker that excelled at avoiding turnovers, shot efficiently overall
- Better at making two-point shots, could penetrate to draw fouls, shot just below break-even on threes
- Active help defender that got steals and rebounded well for his size, had struggles defending on the ball, tended to gamble a bit too much

Michael Porter Jr.

	Height	Weight	Cap #	Years Left
	6'10"	215	$2.894M	1 + 2 TO

Baseline Basic Stats

MPG	PTS	AST	REB	BLK	STL
10.3	4.0	0.4	1.7	0.2	0.3

Advanced Metrics

USG%	3PTA/FGA	FTA/FGA	TS%	eFG%	3PT%
20.5	0.260	0.237	0.482	0.449	0.303

AST%	TOV%	OREB%	DREB%	STL%	BLK%
6.5	12.3	6.2	12.6	1.4	1.4

PER	ORTG	DRTG	WS/48	VOL
10.13	95.6	105.3	0.039	N/A

- Drafted by Denver in the first round with the 14th overall pick
- Did not play at Summer League, recovering from a second surgery on his back
- Timetable to recover is still uncertain, may not play much next season, if at all
- Potential three-and-D combo forward if he's healthy
- Good in catch-and-shoot situations, possibly can guard multiple positions

Jarred Vanderbilt

	Height	Weight	Cap #	Years Left
	6'9"	214	$0.838M	2

Baseline Basic Stats

MPG	PTS	AST	REB	BLK	STL
9.2	2.9	0.4	2.2	0.2	0.3

Advanced Metrics

USG%	3PTA/FGA	FTA/FGA	TS%	eFG%	3PT%
15.8	0.025	0.367	0.501	0.467	0.128

AST%	TOV%	OREB%	DREB%	STL%	BLK%
7.4	16.5	9.5	17.5	1.9	1.9

PER	ORTG	DRTG	WS/48	VOL
10.77	100.1	105.9	0.056	N/A

- Drafted by Orlando with the 41st overall pick, then traded to Denver
- Missed Summer League due to a foot injury, expected to recover in time for training camp
- Skills very raw, could use additional seasoning in the G-League
- Mainly a rim runner on offense, athleticism gives him great potential on defense
- Excellent rebounder and shot blocker, can potentially defend multiple positions, but lacks discipline

LOS ANGELES CLIPPERS

Last Season: 42 – 40, Missed the Playoffs

Offensive Rating: 110.3, 8th in NBA   Defensive Rating: 110.2, 20th in NBA

Primary Executive: Lawrence Frank, Executive Vice President of Basketball Operations

Head Coach: Doc Rivers

Key Roster Changes

Subtractions
Austin Rivers, trade
Sam Dekker, trade
DeAndre Jordan, free agency
C.J. Williams, waived

Additions
Shai Gilgeous-Alexander, draft
Jerome Robinson, draft
Marcin Gortat, trade
Luc Mbah a Moute, free agency
Mike Scott, free agency

RAFER Projected Win Total: 41.3

Projected Best Five-Man Unit
1. Patrick Beverley
2. Lou Williams
3. Danilo Gallinari
4. Tobias Harris
5. Montrezl Harrell

Other Rotation Players
Avery Bradley
Marcin Gortat
Milos Teodosic
Luc Mbah a Moute
Wesley Johnson

Remaining Roster

- Boban Marjanovic
- Mike Scott
- Sindarius Thornwell
- Jawun Evans
- Tyrone Wallace
- Shai Gilgeous-Alexander
- Jerome Robinson
- Johnathan Motley, 23, 6'9", 238, Baylor (Two-Way)
- Angel Delgado, 24, 6'10", 245, Seton Hall (Two-Way)
- Desi Rodriguez, 22, 6'6", 240, Seton Hall (Exhibit 10)

Season Forecast

The Los Angeles Clippers are officially a team in transition, as they let the last part of the Lob City era depart when they allowed DeAndre Jordan to sign with the Dallas Mavericks in free agency. They didn't make any major moves for the short-term in order to preserve their cap space for next summer when many big names are expected to hit the open market. For this season, they made smaller moves like bringing Luc Mbah a Moute back and adding a couple of young guards in the draft in Shai Gilgeous-Alexander and Jerome Robinson. To fill the void left by Jordan, the Clippers decided to re-sign Montrezl Harrell and trade for Marcin Gortat, giving them a couple of options to replace his production. The Clippers have a roster with a lot of useful players, so they should be competitive throughout the season.

However, they simply may not have enough top-end talent to compete with the playoff level teams in the Western Conference, so they will most likely miss the playoffs and spend another season in the lottery.

The Clippers were one of the best offensive teams in the league despite the fact they traded Blake Griffin in the middle of last season. They mainly were effective on offense because they played at a fast pace and aggressively attacked the rim either on pick-and-rolls or on the offensive glass. Much of the team's success at the rim was due to Jordan, but Gortat and Harrell can make back some of Jordan's rim running and foul drawing strengths to a lesser extent. If they get a relatively healthy season from Danilo Gallinari, they could improve as a shooting team because he historically has been a very good three-point shooter. Also, they have a lot of solid ball movers and Lou Williams is coming off an All-Star caliber season, so they do have a reliable shot creator that they count on. With all of this in mind, the Clippers could be a solid offensive team once again this upcoming season. Their defense could be another story because they were below average last year with Jordan. The team actually defended a little better with Harrell on the floor last season, so they may not be as affected by the loss of Jordan as it would seem on paper. Also, the addition of Mbah a Moute and the return of Patrick Beverley from injury could improve the defense incrementally. However, the rest of the rotation is still relatively intact and that may cause some issues at the defensive end. In particular, their backcourt is going to skew smaller with Williams, Beverley and Avery Bradley in their regular rotation and they don't have many reliable on-ball defending wing players. Therefore, their defense doesn't really have the versatility to handle different kinds of lineups and opponents will have an easier time finding mismatches to pick on. As a result, the Clippers' defense will probably be just below average at best or somewhere in the bottom third of the league. Generally speaking, the Clippers' offense will allow them to score enough to keep them in games, but they may not be able to get enough stops to pull out wins against the better teams in the West. Because of this, they will most likely miss the playoffs, but they did maintain enough cap flexibility to make a major move to improve their fortunes in the summer of 2019.

Lou Williams

	Height	Weight	Cap #	Years Left
	6'2"	175	$8.000M	2

Similar at Age **31**

		Season	SIMsc
1	Jason Terry	2008-09	935.4
2	World B. Free	1984-85	922.1
3	Luke Ridnour	2012-13	914.7
4	Rafer Alston	2007-08	904.1
5	Joe Dumars*	1994-95	903.3
6	Tony Parker	2013-14	901.6
7	John Starks	1996-97	901.5
8	Nick Van Exel	2002-03	900.1
9	James Silas	1980-81	899.9
10	Mike James	2006-07	898.5

Baseline Basic Stats

MPG	PTS	AST	REB	BLK	STL
29.6	14.4	3.7	2.4	0.2	1.0

Advanced Metrics

USG%	3PTA/FGA	FTA/FGA	TS%	eFG%	3PT%
25.2	0.383	0.343	0.556	0.495	0.367

AST%	TOV%	OREB%	DREB%	STL%	BLK%
21.6	12.2	1.6	7.2	1.7	0.6

PER	ORTG	DRTG	WS/48	VOL	
17.38	110.1	111.4	0.109	0.399	

- Had one of the best seasons of his career at age 31, set a career high in Win Shares last season
- Named 2017-18 Sixth Man of the Year
- Excellent all-around high volume scorer, great with the ball in his hands in isolations and as a pick-and-roll ball handler
- Displayed very good playmaking skills and he kept his turnover rate down
- Very effective off the ball in spot-up situations and running off screens, made almost a league average percentage on threes
- Below average overall defender, needs to be hidden in favorable matchups

Tobias Harris

	Height	Weight	Cap #	Years Left
	6'8"	226	$14.800M	0

Similar at Age 25

		Season	SIMsc
1	Peja Stojakovic	2002-03	941.0
2	Luol Deng	2010-11	937.6
3	Dennis Scott	1993-94	932.0
4	Chuck Person	1989-90	929.2
5	Mike Miller	2005-06	928.0
6	Glen Rice	1992-93	927.8
7	Antawn Jamison	2001-02	920.9
8	Mike Scott	2013-14	919.5
9	Desmond Mason	2002-03	919.5
10	Tim Thomas	2002-03	917.4

Baseline Basic Stats

MPG	PTS	AST	REB	BLK	STL
32.6	16.0	2.5	5.0	0.4	0.9

Advanced Metrics

USG%	3PTA/FGA	FTA/FGA	TS%	eFG%	3PT%
21.9	0.348	0.227	0.563	0.525	0.379

AST%	TOV%	OREB%	DREB%	STL%	BLK%
12.3	9.2	3.1	14.5	1.4	0.9

PER	ORTG	DRTG	WS/48	VOL
16.68	112.3	108.8	0.127	0.354

- Had a career best season with two teams, played better in the second half after being traded from Detroit to the Clippers
- Improved as a passer, was even effective in a limited number of possessions as a pick-and-roll ball handler
- Scored efficiently because he excelled as a roll man and in isolations, also very good in spot-up situations
- Shot a career 41.1% on threes last season, historically better in the corners, shot 44.6% on corner threes in 2017-18
- Decent on-ball defending combo forward that can guard multiple positions
- Better at handling perimeter wing players, solid defensive rebounder

Danilo Gallinari

	Height	Weight	Cap #	Years Left
	6'10"	225	$21.588M	1

Similar at Age 29

		Season	SIMsc
1	Mike Dunleavy, Jr.	2009-10	938.8
2	Keith Van Horn	2004-05	913.1
3	Peja Stojakovic	2006-07	902.6
4	Terry Mills	1996-97	897.4
5	Walter Herrmann	2008-09	893.6
6	Tim Thomas	2006-07	892.4
7	Dennis Scott	1997-98	891.8
8	Danny Ferry	1995-96	891.2
9	Hedo Turkoglu	2008-09	890.3
10	Andres Nocioni	2008-09	888.8

Baseline Basic Stats

MPG	PTS	AST	REB	BLK	STL
26.5	12.2	1.4	3.8	0.3	0.6

Advanced Metrics

USG%	3PTA/FGA	FTA/FGA	TS%	eFG%	3PT%
19.3	0.417	0.362	0.582	0.515	0.379

AST%	TOV%	OREB%	DREB%	STL%	BLK%
8.3	8.6	2.5	13.9	1.0	0.9

PER	ORTG	DRTG	WS/48	VOL	
14.96	117.1	112.0	0.117	0.474	

- Missed most of last season due to a strained left gluteus muscle and a fractured right hand
- Production last season dipped significantly as a result of the injuries
- Posted the lowest PER and Win Share total since his rookie season
- Still excellent in spot-up situations despite a career low three-point percentage
- Made up for the low percentage by attacking aggressive closeouts to draw shooting fouls at a high rate
- Scored efficiently overall by being above average on post-ups and isolations, good cutter off the ball
- Fairly good defensive rebounder, solid on-ball defender that guards both forward spots despite some limitations in mobility

Marcin Gortat

	Height	Weight	Cap #	Years Left
	6'11"	240	$13.565M	0

Similar at Age 33

		Season	SIMsc
1	Dale Davis	2002-03	931.5
2	Robert Parish*	1986-87	923.1
3	P.J. Brown	2002-03	922.6
4	Bill Laimbeer	1990-91	919.1
5	David Lee	2016-17	913.5
6	Bill Cartwright	1990-91	913.2
7	Christian Laettner	2002-03	909.2
8	Herb Williams	1991-92	903.0
9	Antonio McDyess	2007-08	902.8
10	Kurt Thomas	2005-06	899.8

Baseline Basic Stats

MPG	PTS	AST	REB	BLK	STL
27.7	9.6	1.5	7.4	0.9	0.6

Advanced Metrics

USG%	3PTA/FGA	FTA/FGA	TS%	eFG%	3PT%
15.6	0.014	0.269	0.544	0.516	0.140

AST%	TOV%	OREB%	DREB%	STL%	BLK%
8.6	13.0	9.6	22.8	1.1	2.3

PER	ORTG	DRTG	WS/48	VOL
14.41	110.7	105.7	0.115	0.414

- Extremely durable center that has only missed eight games in the last five seasons
- Production has been in decline for the last two seasons
- Has now become a low volume rim runner, still efficient
- Less effective as a roll man due to diminishing athleticism
- Shoots a solid percentage on shots between 3 and 16 feet
- Posted the highest Assist Percentage of his career last season
- Fairly good rim protector, but not the shot blocker that he once was, good overall rebounder
- Has some struggles on the ball against quicker players due to mobility limitations

Avery Bradley

	Height	Weight	Cap #	Years Left
	6'2"	180	$12.000M	1

Similar at Age **27**

		Season	SIMsc
1	James Robinson	1997-98	936.9
2	Jannero Pargo	2006-07	934.4
3	C.J. Watson	2011-12	930.2
4	Eddie House	2005-06	929.6
5	Craig Hodges	1987-88	922.2
6	Luther Head	2009-10	920.6
7	Brian Roberts	2012-13	919.6
8	Jordan Farmar	2013-14	919.5
9	Mike Conley	2014-15	918.1
10	Vernon Maxwell	1992-93	917.2

Baseline Basic Stats

MPG	PTS	AST	REB	BLK	STL
25.1	11.1	3.0	2.5	0.2	0.9

Advanced Metrics

USG%	3PTA/FGA	FTA/FGA	TS%	eFG%	3PT%
21.3	0.412	0.160	0.528	0.502	0.383

AST%	TOV%	OREB%	DREB%	STL%	BLK%
16.0	12.2	2.2	9.7	1.8	0.5

PER	ORTG	DRTG	WS/48	VOL	
12.95	102.8	108.6	0.061	0.324	

- Missed portions of last season due to a sore groin and surgery to repair a sports hernia
- Production severely declined last season, struggled to find his role in Detroit and with the Clippers
- Very effective at cutting and running off screens in Boston prior to last season
- Possibly misused by playing exclusively in a stationary role last season with two teams
- Scoring efficiency decreased dramatically due to a change in his role
- Took more inefficient shots as a result, mid-range shot attempts increased while threes and shots at the rim decreased
- Still made threes at an above league average rate last season
- Solid stay-at-home on-ball defender that guards multiple positions

Montrezl Harrell

	Height	Weight	Cap #	Years Left
	6'8"	240	$6.000M	1

Similar at Age 24

		Season	SIMsc
1	Brandon Bass	2009-10	927.4
2	Paul Millsap	2009-10	919.2
3	Craig Smith	2007-08	907.2
4	Kris Humphries	2009-10	905.7
5	Samaki Walker	2000-01	903.3
6	David West	2004-05	900.7
7	Joe Courtney	1993-94	899.8
8	Bison Dele	1993-94	899.8
9	Randy White	1991-92	898.0
10	Terrence Jones	2015-16	897.2

Baseline Basic Stats

MPG	PTS	AST	REB	BLK	STL
25.4	11.9	1.2	6.2	0.8	0.6

Advanced Metrics

USG%	3PTA/FGA	FTA/FGA	TS%	eFG%	3PT%
21.9	0.038	0.353	0.620	0.594	0.248

AST%	TOV%	OREB%	DREB%	STL%	BLK%
9.9	9.4	8.3	18.1	1.2	2.6

PER	ORTG	DRTG	WS/48	VOL	
22.12	122.4	108.3	0.183	0.211	

- Has continued to improve in each of his three seasons in the NBA, thrived as a rotation player for the Clippers last season

- Showed great improvement on the offensive end, excellent at running the floor in transition and rolling to the rim on pick-and-rolls

- Very effective on post-ups used his strength and athleticism to score inside

- Drew shooting fouls at a high rate, has become a solid passing big man

- Good rim protector that can contest and block shots, good rebounder on both ends

- Has the mobility to defend in space, but is a bit too foul prone

- Undersized to play center, has difficulty playing on-ball defense against skilled interior players

Patrick Beverley

	Height	Weight	Cap #	Years Left
	6'1"	180	$5.027M	0

Similar at Age 29

		Season	SIMsc
1	Eddie House	2007-08	932.1
2	C.J. Watson	2013-14	930.7
3	Tony Delk	2002-03	919.4
4	Dee K. Brown	1997-98	916.9
5	Toney Douglas	2015-16	915.4
6	Jordan Farmar	2015-16	910.9
7	Jaren Jackson	1996-97	908.4
8	Pooh Richardson	1995-96	905.4
9	Brian Roberts	2014-15	902.0
10	Haywoode Workman	1994-95	901.5

Baseline Basic Stats

MPG	PTS	AST	REB	BLK	STL
23.3	8.4	2.9	2.5	0.2	1.0

Advanced Metrics

USG%	3PTA/FGA	FTA/FGA	TS%	eFG%	3PT%
18.0	0.436	0.184	0.520	0.488	0.370

AST%	TOV%	OREB%	DREB%	STL%	BLK%
18.7	14.5	3.7	10.8	2.2	0.8

PER	ORTG	DRTG	WS/48	VOL
12.68	105.6	108.1	0.079	0.328

- Missed most of last season due to surgery to repair the meniscus in his right knee
- Predominantly a low volume spot-up shooter in Houston, used in a similar role last season with the Clippers before the injury
- Solid three-point shooter throughout his career, made 40% of his threes last season
- Very good transition player last season, got more shots inside of three feet as a result
- Aggressive on-ball defender against point guards, gets steals at a fairly high rate

Luc Mbah a Moute

	Height	Weight	Cap #	Years Left
	6'8"	230	$4.321M	0

Similar at Age **31**

		Season	SIMsc
1	Eduardo Najera	2007-08	936.6
2	Anthony Tolliver	2016-17	909.4
3	Thabo Sefolosha	2015-16	906.8
4	James Posey	2007-08	900.1
5	Luol Deng	2016-17	899.8
6	Jared Dudley	2016-17	898.1
7	Devean George	2008-09	894.9
8	Dennis Scott	1999-00	893.8
9	Andre Iguodala	2014-15	893.2
10	Shane Battier	2009-10	890.9

Baseline Basic Stats

MPG	PTS	AST	REB	BLK	STL
23.7	7.1	1.1	3.6	0.3	0.8

Advanced Metrics

USG%	3PTA/FGA	FTA/FGA	TS%	eFG%	3PT%
12.9	0.481	0.241	0.590	0.566	0.391

AST%	TOV%	OREB%	DREB%	STL%	BLK%
5.5	12.4	2.6	12.2	1.9	1.4

PER	ORTG	DRTG	WS/48	VOL	
10.73	110.2	108.6	0.088	0.310	

- Missed about a month last season due to a dislocated right shoulder
- Extremely low usage offensive player that was mainly used as a spot-up shooter, shot just over league average on threes
- More effective as a cutter and screener in pick-and-roll situations
- Solid on-ball defender that can defend multiple positions, better at handling perimeter wing players
- Decent defensive rebounder, Steal Percentage has been higher than his career average for the last two seasons

Milos Teodosic

	Height	Weight	Cap #	Years Left
	6'5"	196	$6.300M	0

Similar at Age 30

		Season	SIMsc
1	Derek Anderson	2004-05	912.9
2	Sarunas Jasikevicius	2006-07	909.1
3	Nick Young	2015-16	896.6
4	Marco Belinelli	2016-17	896.5
5	Keyon Dooling	2010-11	893.8
6	Willie Green	2011-12	893.3
7	Mario Elie	1993-94	890.5
8	Anthony Morrow	2015-16	888.4
9	Hubert Davis	2000-01	887.9
10	Trent Tucker	1989-90	885.2

Baseline Basic Stats

MPG	PTS	AST	REB	BLK	STL
19.7	7.2	1.8	1.8	0.1	0.6

Advanced Metrics

USG%	3PTA/FGA	FTA/FGA	TS%	eFG%	3PT%
16.9	0.567	0.157	0.557	0.530	0.373

AST%	TOV%	OREB%	DREB%	STL%	BLK%
19.4	16.7	1.7	9.8	1.3	0.5

PER	ORTG	DRTG	WS/48	VOL
11.18	107.1	111.7	0.075	0.422

- Missed a portion of his rookie season last year due to plantar fasciitis in his left foot
- Lower volume, pass-first big point guard that showed good playmaking skills as a pick-and-roll ball handler, a little turnover prone
- Excellent in spot-up situations, ranked by the NBA in the 96th percentile
- Made 37.9% of his threes overall, shot 42.1% on corner threes
- Fairly decent position defender that can guard multiple positions, solid defensive rebounder

Wesley Johnson

	Height	Weight	Cap #	Years Left
	6'7"	205	$6.135M	0

Similar at Age 30

		Season	SIMsc
1	Francisco Garcia	2011-12	947.2
2	Jamario Moon	2010-11	919.9
3	George McCloud	1997-98	914.3
4	Ime Udoka	2007-08	911.5
5	DeMarre Carroll	2016-17	901.1
6	Brandon Rush	2015-16	896.7
7	James Posey	2006-07	892.7
8	Keith Askins	1997-98	889.3
9	Garrett Temple	2016-17	886.2
10	James White	2012-13	885.0

Baseline Basic Stats

MPG	PTS	AST	REB	BLK	STL
19.3	6.1	1.0	3.1	0.5	0.7

Advanced Metrics

USG%	3PTA/FGA	FTA/FGA	TS%	eFG%	3PT%
13.9	0.519	0.164	0.507	0.484	0.334

AST%	TOV%	OREB%	DREB%	STL%	BLK%
7.1	10.9	2.8	15.7	1.9	2.7

PER	ORTG	DRTG	WS/48	VOL	
10.04	100.1	107.4	0.054	0.198	

- Regular rotation player for the Clippers for the last three seasons, production still consistent with his career averages
- Low volume, middling efficiency offensive player that mainly plays a spot-up role
- Historically a slightly above break-even three-point shooter, better in the corners throughout his career
- Effective help defender, good shot blocking wing player, plays passing lanes to get steals, good defensive rebounder
- Fairly solid as an on ball defender, sometimes guards multiple positions, better at handling wing players

Boban Marjanovic

	Height	Weight	Cap #	Years Left
	7'3"	290	$7.000M	0

	Similar at Age	29	
		Season	SIMsc
1	Petur Gudmundsson	1987-88	813.1
2	Rik Smits	1995-96	806.1
3	Zeljko Rebraca	2001-02	800.3
4	Aron Baynes	2015-16	794.8
5	Luc Longley	1997-98	793.7
6	Zydrunas Ilgauskas	2004-05	792.0
7	Dwight Howard	2014-15	787.2
8	Nene Hilario	2011-12	787.0
9	Marc Gasol	2013-14	786.9
10	Vitaly Potapenko	2004-05	786.1

Baseline Basic Stats

MPG	PTS	AST	REB	BLK	STL
22.9	11.4	1.4	6.3	1.0	0.4

Advanced Metrics

USG%	3PTA/FGA	FTA/FGA	TS%	eFG%	3PT%
25.5	0.013	0.448	0.576	0.516	0.189

AST%	TOV%	OREB%	DREB%	STL%	BLK%
10.1	14.1	12.3	27.0	1.1	3.1

PER	ORTG	DRTG	WS/48	VOL	
21.93	111.3	101.4	0.184	0.829	

- Has struggled to land a regular rotational role in three seasons despite being a per-minute production warrior
- Severe mobility limitations make him unable to play for extended stretches, needs to be matched up against other big body centers
- Very good rim protector in limited minutes, massive size and height allows him to clog the lane and contest shots
- Fairly good shot blocker, excellent rebounder on both ends
- Very efficient scorer that does most of his damage inside of three feet, draws fouls at a high rate, career 78.4% free throw shooter

Mike Scott

	Height	Weight	Cap #	Years Left
	6'8"	237	$4.321M	0

Similar at Age **29**

		Season	SIMsc
1	Mirza Teletovic	2014-15	939.0
2	Pat Garrity	2005-06	927.5
3	Anthony Tolliver	2014-15	920.8
4	LaPhonso Ellis	1999-00	918.2
5	Wilson Chandler	2016-17	917.4
6	Richard Anderson	1989-90	916.7
7	Matt Barnes	2009-10	913.4
8	Dennis Scott	1997-98	913.0
9	Ersan Ilyasova	2016-17	912.0
10	Tracy Murray	2000-01	911.5

Baseline Basic Stats

MPG	PTS	AST	REB	BLK	STL
19.3	7.3	1.1	3.5	0.3	0.5

Advanced Metrics

USG%	3PTA/FGA	FTA/FGA	TS%	eFG%	3PT%
17.4	0.410	0.191	0.534	0.506	0.341

AST%	TOV%	OREB%	DREB%	STL%	BLK%
9.0	11.4	4.9	15.2	1.1	1.1

PER	ORTG	DRTG	WS/48	VOL
11.66	105.4	108.0	0.079	0.363

- Had a bounce back season in Washington after falling out of Atlanta's rotation and being waived by Phoenix in 2016-17
- Had his most efficient offensive season last year
- Excelled as a spot-up shooter and screener in pick-and-roll situations
- Shot a career best 40.5% on threes overall and 45.2% on corner threes
- Decent on-ball position defender against fours, solid defensive rebounder

Sindarius Thornwell

	Height	Weight	Cap #	Years Left
	6'5"	212	$1.378M	1

Similar at Age 23

		Season	SIMsc
1	Alonzo Gee	2010-11	922.6
2	Thabo Sefolosha	2007-08	921.4
3	Arron Afflalo	2008-09	919.1
4	Greg Buckner	1999-00	914.6
5	John Salmons	2002-03	914.3
6	Mickael Gelabale	2006-07	911.5
7	Dan Majerle	1988-89	910.6
8	Antoine Wright	2007-08	908.8
9	Mitchell Butler	1993-94	908.4
10	Jeryl Sasser	2002-03	907.2

Baseline Basic Stats

MPG	PTS	AST	REB	BLK	STL
22.7	7.0	1.5	3.2	0.3	0.9

Advanced Metrics

USG%	3PTA/FGA	FTA/FGA	TS%	eFG%	3PT%
14.4	0.312	0.314	0.526	0.485	0.365

AST%	TOV%	OREB%	DREB%	STL%	BLK%
9.1	13.8	3.4	10.7	2.0	1.3

PER	ORTG	DRTG	WS/48	VOL	
10.18	104.9	108.9	0.065	0.380	

- Cracked the Clippers' regular rotation as a rookie last season
- Primarily a defensive specialist, solid on-ball wing defender, active help defender
- Will rotate to block shots, fairly good at getting steals, solid defensive rebounder
- Played a low volume role, played mostly as a spot-up shooter
- Shot 37.7% overall on threes, drew fouls at a high rate when attacking closeouts
- Settles for too many mid-range shots, shoots a below average percentage on them
- Struggles to finish at the rim, only shot 50.5% on shots inside of three feet last season

Jawun Evans

	Height	Weight	Cap #	Years Left
	6'0"	185	$1.378M	Team Option

Similar at Age 21

		Season	SIMsc
1	Mo Williams	2003-04	938.0
2	Jeff Teague	2009-10	922.0
3	Tyler Ennis	2015-16	915.4
4	Shane Larkin	2013-14	909.9
5	Jonny Flynn	2010-11	907.7
6	Sebastian Telfair	2006-07	904.0
7	Cory Joseph	2012-13	903.5
8	Cameron Payne	2015-16	902.4
9	Khalid El-Amin	2000-01	897.1
10	Kenny Satterfield	2002-03	893.6

Baseline Basic Stats

MPG	PTS	AST	REB	BLK	STL
19.2	6.9	3.2	1.9	0.1	0.7

Advanced Metrics

USG%	3PTA/FGA	FTA/FGA	TS%	eFG%	3PT%
17.4	0.172	0.235	0.485	0.442	0.323

AST%	TOV%	OREB%	DREB%	STL%	BLK%
24.4	15.1	1.6	9.3	2.1	0.6

PER	ORTG	DRTG	WS/48	VOL	
11.05	101.0	111.6	0.046	0.457	

- Fringe rotation player for the Clippers in his rookie season, played 778 minutes
- Struggled overall on the offensive end in a low volume role
- Rarely committed turnovers, had greater than a 2-to-1 assist to turnover ratio
- Could not score efficiently, didn't finish shots at the rim, below break-even three-point shooter
- Flashed some potential on defense, aggressive to pressure his man, but struggles to contest shots due to his small stature
- Gets steals at a fairly high rate, good rebounder for his size

Tyrone Wallace

	Height	Weight	2018 Cap #	Years Left
	6'5"	205	$1.349M	1

Similar at Age **23**

		Season	SIMsc
1	Greg Minor	1994-95	935.7
2	Kevin Loder	1982-83	935.3
3	Harold Miner	1994-95	934.0
4	Shandon Anderson	1996-97	926.1
5	Todd Lichti	1989-90	926.0
6	Tracy Jackson	1982-83	924.7
7	Aaron McKie	1995-96	924.1
8	Chris Carr	1997-98	923.8
9	Sonny Weems	2009-10	922.4
10	Gerald Henderson	2010-11	922.4

Baseline Basic Stats

MPG	PTS	AST	REB	BLK	STL
21.9	8.2	1.8	2.8	0.3	0.8

Advanced Metrics

USG%	3PTA/FGA	FTA/FGA	TS%	eFG%	3PT%
17.3	0.181	0.279	0.530	0.484	0.315

AST%	TOV%	OREB%	DREB%	STL%	BLK%
12.6	13.2	3.3	10.3	1.7	1.0

PER	ORTG	DRTG	WS/48	VOL	
12.03	105.8	110.4	0.075	0.399	

- Spent the early part of last season in the G-League with the Agua Caliente Clippers
- Started a majority of his games after being called up to the Clippers in the second half of the season
- Slashing guard that mainly looked to drive to the rim to either finish from close range or draw fouls
- Got favorable matchups on offense because he shared the backcourt with Lou Williams in almost 58% of his minutes
- Effective at attacking weaker defensive guards in isolation situations
- Playmaking guard in the G-League, but mainly a low volume, off-ball guard in the NBA
- Not an efficient shooter from beyond three feet, below average mid-range shooter and made only 25% of his threes last season
- Good on-ball defender that can defend both guard spots, can use length to actively contest shots, solid defensive rebounding guard

Newcomers

Shai Gilgeous-Alexander	Height	Weight	Cap #	Years Left
	6'6"	180	$3.375M	1 + 2 TO

Baseline Basic Stats

MPG	PTS	AST	REB	BLK	STL
22.6	8.3	3.6	2.5	0.2	0.8

Advanced Metrics

USG%	3PTA/FGA	FTA/FGA	TS%	eFG%	3PT%
21.4	0.196	0.289	0.461	0.412	0.310

AST%	TOV%	OREB%	DREB%	STL%	BLK%
25.5	17.1	2.9	9.8	1.9	0.6

PER	ORTG	DRTG	WS/48	VOL
12.80	98.5	110.4	0.032	N/A

- Drafted by Charlotte with the 11th overall pick, then traded to the Clippers
- Strong showing at the Las Vegas Summer League
- Displayed good playmaking and ball control skills
- Scored at a high volume, but not with efficiency
- Made 50% of his two-point shots, but was 3-for-12 on threes
- Aggressive defender that can defend both guard spots, got rebounds, blocks and steals at a high rate

Jerome Robinson

	Height	Weight	Cap #	Years Left
	6'6"	191	$3.046M	1 + 2 TO

Baseline Basic Stats

MPG	PTS	AST	REB	BLK	STL
22.0	10.0	2.6	2.1	0.1	0.7

Advanced Metrics

USG%	3PTA/FGA	FTA/FGA	TS%	eFG%	3PT%
23.3	0.333	0.215	0.512	0.473	0.366

AST%	TOV%	OREB%	DREB%	STL%	BLK%
20.0	14.5	2.5	8.7	1.6	0.5

PER	ORTG	DRTG	WS/48	VOL
13.03	100.6	110.4	0.021	N/A

- Drafted by the Clippers in the first round with the 13th overall pick
- Strong showing at Summer League in July
- Shot very efficiently in a moderate volume role, was 7-for-19 on threes, posted a True Shooting Percentage of 55.6%
- Solid as a passer, limited turnovers
- Didn't really stand out either way on defense, more of a stay-at-home position defender, decent defensive rebounder

PORTLAND TRAIL BLAZERS

Last Season: 49 – 33, Lost 1st Round to New Orleans (0 – 4)

Offensive Rating: 109.1, 15th in NBA   Defensive Rating: 106.4, 8th in NBA

Primary Executive: Neil Olshey, President of Basketball Operations

Head Coach: Terry Stotts

Key Roster Changes

Subtractions
Ed Davis, free agency
Shabazz Napier, free agency
Pat Connaughton, free agency
Georgios Papagiannis, waived

Additions
Anfernee Simons, draft
Gary Trent, Jr., draft
Nik Stauskas, free agency
Seth Curry, free agency

RAFER Projected Win Total: 41.0

Projected Best Five-Man Unit
1. Damian Lillard
2. C.J. McCollum
3. Maurice Harkless
4. Al-Farouq Aminu
5. Jusuf Nurkic

Other Rotation Players
Evan Turner
Zach Collins
Seth Curry
Meyers Leonard
Nik Stauskas

Remaining Roster

- Caleb Swanigan
- Jake Layman
- Wade Baldwin
- Anfernee Simons
- Gary Trent, Jr.
- Chinanu Onuaku, 22, 6'10", 245, Louisville (Exhibit 10)
- Gary Payton II, 26, 6'3", 190, Oregon State (Exhibit 10)
- Cameron Oliver, 22, 6'8", 239, Nevada (Exhibit 10)

Season Forecast

In recent years, the Portland Trail Blazers have been a team that has overperformed analytical projections. Coming into the past few seasons, they haven't had a whole lot of depth from top to bottom and their role players have either been inexperienced or have a history of inconsistency. However, they've been able to beat projections models, including this one by getting stellar performances from their All-Star level backcourt of Damian Lillard and C.J. McCollum. Then, they typically get some improvement from either an untested young player or a veteran coming off a down year. Last season, they got some unexpected production in their rotation from players like Shabazz Napier, Ed Davis and Pat Connaughton. However, all three of those players left for other teams in free agency. Therefore, the Blazers will have to replace them, but the existing replacements on the roster do not have solid historical track records. There is a possibility that Portland could drop in the standings if no one steps up to provide complementary production around their stars. If they find production from unlikely sources once again, they could be a playoff team in the West, but not to the extent that they were last season because the rest of the conference got better. Most likely, if the Blazers play to their talent level, they will probably miss the playoffs this season.

Portland hasn't really established a true strength on either side of the ball over the course of the last three or four seasons. Some years they play better on offense, other years they excel on defense. Last season, they ranked as one of the league's ten best defenses, even though they don't really have any elite individual defenders. They got stops last year mainly by steering opponents into the inefficient parts of the floor. This worked well in the regular season, but their defensive flaws were exposed in their series against New Orleans in the playoffs. Specifically, they don't have the versatility to switch screens due to the fact that they often are playing two small guards and a lumbering big man in Jusuf Nurkic. Therefore, the better offensive teams in the league have an easier time of finding exploitable mismatches. The Blazers really didn't address this concern with any of their personnel moves because they only really have two true wing players on the roster and the players that they brought in haven't been known as great individual defenders in their past, so their issues with defensive versatility may still persist. With this in mind, there's a distinct possibility that Portland could be worse on the defensive end this coming season. On offense, the Blazers have been either good or above average in each of the last three seasons. However, their offensive efficiency rankings have steadily declined each season because they've gradually lost depth due to their salary cap situations. They once again were strapped against the luxury tax line, so they weren't able to make any notable additions to offset their personnel losses. As a result, more responsibility is going to fall on the shoulders of Lillard and McCollum to generate quality offense, but the workload might be too great for them to overcome any potential decrease in performance from the supporting players. Aside from Nurkic and maybe Al-Farouq Aminu, none of the other players on the roster have established themselves as reliable players capable of playing critical minutes. With this in mind, Portland probably will be about average at best on offense. This team has had a history of playing better than its true talent level in the past, so it wouldn't be much of a surprise if they did this once again and made the playoffs. On the other hand, if the team's performance falls more in line with its actual talent level, then Portland will be competitive on a night-to-night basis, but they will probably fall short of the playoffs this season.

Veterans

Damian Lillard

	Height	Weight	Cap #	Years Left
	6'3"	195	$27.978M	2

Similar at Age **27**

		Season	SIMsc
1	Chauncey Billups	2003-04	913.0
2	Steve Nash*	2001-02	909.1
3	Deron Williams	2011-12	905.0
4	Mike Bibby	2005-06	900.9
5	Ray Allen*	2002-03	900.6
6	Steve Francis	2004-05	899.3
7	Stephen Curry	2015-16	896.9
8	Eric Bledsoe	2016-17	893.4
9	Derrick Rose	2015-16	890.9
10	John Starks	1992-93	890.7

Baseline Basic Stats

MPG	PTS	AST	REB	BLK	STL
34.8	20.0	6.4	3.7	0.2	1.1

Advanced Metrics

USG%	3PTA/FGA	FTA/FGA	TS%	eFG%	3PT%
27.8	0.439	0.356	0.583	0.514	0.379

AST%	TOV%	OREB%	DREB%	STL%	BLK%
31.7	12.1	2.1	10.7	1.5	0.5

PER	ORTG	DRTG	WS/48	VOL
22.82	118.1	109.6	0.189	0.129

- Had the best season of his six year career, named to the All-NBA first team
- Excellent with the ball in his hands, very good isolation scorer that can make outside shots or drive the lane to finish at the rim or draw fouls
- One of the best pick-and-roll ball handlers in the league, great playmaker that limits turnovers
- Effective off the ball by running off screens and cutting to the rim, above league average three-point shooter
- Middling on-ball position defender, doesn't do much on help defense

C.J. McCollum

	Height	Weight	Cap #	Years Left
	6'4"	200	$25.760M	2

Similar at Age 26

		Season	SIMsc
1	Cuttino Mobley	2001-02	938.3
2	Allan Houston	1997-98	936.2
3	Willie Green	2007-08	935.1
4	Isaiah Rider	1997-98	931.2
5	Ray Allen*	2001-02	924.6
6	Jeff Malone	1987-88	922.0
7	Shannon Brown	2011-12	920.1
8	Darrell Griffith	1984-85	916.7
9	Mitch Richmond*	1991-92	914.8
10	Nick Young	2011-12	913.7

Baseline Basic Stats

MPG	PTS	AST	REB	BLK	STL
33.1	17.4	3.2	3.4	0.3	1.0

Advanced Metrics

USG%	3PTA/FGA	FTA/FGA	TS%	eFG%	3PT%
25.1	0.308	0.207	0.548	0.509	0.403

AST%	TOV%	OREB%	DREB%	STL%	BLK%
17.0	10.5	2.2	9.4	1.4	0.8

PER	ORTG	DRTG	WS/48	VOL	
16.81	108.8	109.7	0.106	0.419	

- Production has been consistent with his career averages, durable guard that has only missed five games in the last three seasons
- Effective high volume scorer, excellent shooter that knock down pull-up jumpers or run off screens, made almost 40% of his threes last season
- Good with the ball in his hands, has enough playmaking skills to be a solid pick-and-roll ball handler, good as a one-on-one isolation player
- Very jump shot dependent, rarely gets to the rim
- Less than 18% of his shots for his career are inside of three feet
- Decent position defender if hidden in favorable matchups
- Posted the best Defensive Rebound Percentage of his career last season

Jusuf Nurkic

	Height	Weight	Cap #	Years Left
	6'11"	280	$11.111M	3

Similar at Age 23

		Season	SIMsc
1	Vitaly Potapenko	1998-99	894.3
2	Elton Brand	2002-03	891.0
3	Roy Hibbert	2009-10	887.5
4	DeMarcus Cousins	2013-14	884.2
5	Jared Sullinger	2015-16	884.0
6	Patrick Ewing*	1985-86	881.3
7	Sharone Wright	1995-96	878.9
8	Michael Olowokandi	1998-99	877.7
9	Samuel Dalembert	2004-05	875.9
10	Derrick Favors	2014-15	875.7

Baseline Basic Stats

MPG	PTS	AST	REB	BLK	STL
28.7	14.0	1.5	8.1	1.4	0.7

Advanced Metrics

USG%	3PTA/FGA	FTA/FGA	TS%	eFG%	3PT%
25.1	0.006	0.369	0.540	0.503	0.001

AST%	TOV%	OREB%	DREB%	STL%	BLK%
11.2	15.3	10.0	24.4	1.5	3.9

PER	ORTG	DRTG	WS/48	VOL
19.01	103.6	104.1	0.101	0.519

- Had his best season in the NBA in his fourth year, was a full-time starter for the first time in his career

- Fairly good passing big man, very good finisher inside that made 64.3% of his shots inside of three feet, good offensive rebounder

- Used as a screener in pick-and-roll situations and on post-ups, but was not especially efficient on a per-possession basis

- Pretty good rim protector, bulk allows him to clog the lane, good shot blocker, excellent defensive rebounder

- Can be exploited by quicker players due to a lack of mobility, struggles at on-ball defense as a result

Al-Farouq Aminu

	Height	Weight	Cap #	Years Left
	6'9"	215	$6.957M	0

Similar at Age 27

		Season	SIMsc
1	David Benoit	1995-96	924.9
2	Marvin Williams	2013-14	923.0
3	Omri Casspi	2015-16	915.6
4	DeMarre Carroll	2013-14	913.7
5	Mindaugas Kuzminskas	2016-17	903.9
6	Patrick Patterson	2016-17	900.5
7	Kyle Korver	2008-09	897.7
8	Darrell Arthur	2015-16	897.4
9	Jamario Moon	2007-08	897.1
10	Mickael Pietrus	2009-10	896.7

Baseline Basic Stats

MPG	PTS	AST	REB	BLK	STL
25.5	9.1	1.2	5.1	0.5	0.9

Advanced Metrics

USG%	3PTA/FGA	FTA/FGA	TS%	eFG%	3PT%
15.8	0.595	0.183	0.539	0.515	0.380

AST%	TOV%	OREB%	DREB%	STL%	BLK%
7.1	11.1	4.7	20.7	1.7	1.5

PER	ORTG	DRTG	WS/48	VOL	
12.74	107.4	105.4	0.093	0.545	

- Solid starter for Portland, production still consistent with his career averages

- Strictly a low volume spot-up shooter, almost two-thirds of his shots last season were open ones

- Shot a career high 36.9% on threes over last season, historically has been better in the corners

- Below average on a per-possession basis in every offensive situation except spot-up shooting

- Good defensive rebounder, more of a position defender in Portland, fairly decent on-ball defender

Evan Turner

	Height	Weight	Cap #	Years Left
	6'7"	205	$17.869M	1

Similar at Age 29

		Season	SIMsc
1	Robert Reid	1984-85	930.5
2	Rod Higgins	1988-89	930.1
3	Sean Elliott	1997-98	929.0
4	Chris Mills	1998-99	927.4
5	Marko Jaric	2007-08	925.2
6	Anthony Bowie	1992-93	925.2
7	Willie Anderson	1995-96	922.5
8	Vincent Askew	1995-96	921.9
9	Eric Piatkowski	1999-00	918.7
10	Mario Elie	1992-93	913.3

Baseline Basic Stats

MPG	PTS	AST	REB	BLK	STL
23.7	8.7	1.9	3.2	0.3	0.7

Advanced Metrics

USG%	3PTA/FGA	FTA/FGA	TS%	eFG%	3PT%
17.1	0.243	0.214	0.511	0.472	0.322

AST%	TOV%	OREB%	DREB%	STL%	BLK%
13.2	13.1	2.5	11.7	1.4	1.0

PER	ORTG	DRTG	WS/48	VOL	
11.12	102.7	107.5	0.070	0.310	

- Played starter-level minutes last season for Portland
- Production over the last two seasons is down from his career averages
- Improved his efficiency in a lower usage role, mainly a spot-up shooter, 56.8% of his shots were open looks
- Below break-even as a three-point shooter, good mid-range shooter
- Solid enough playmaker to have some effectiveness as a pick-and-roll ball handler
- Fairly good on-ball defender, has become more of a stay-at-home position defender
- Posted the lowest Defensive Rebound and Steal Percentages of his career last season

Maurice Harkless

	Height	Weight	Cap #	Years Left
	6'8"	208	$10.837M	1

Similar at Age 24

		Season	SIMsc
1	Andre Roberson	2015-16	945.7
2	Shane Battier	2002-03	936.5
3	Antoine Wright	2008-09	922.3
4	Devean George	2001-02	922.2
5	Dorell Wright	2009-10	920.5
6	Wesley Johnson	2011-12	919.8
7	Danny Green	2011-12	916.4
8	Scott Burrell	1994-95	909.7
9	DerMarr Johnson	2004-05	909.5
10	Bill Willoughby	1981-82	909.5

Baseline Basic Stats

MPG	PTS	AST	REB	BLK	STL
25.9	9.2	1.5	3.9	0.6	0.9

Advanced Metrics

USG%	3PTA/FGA	FTA/FGA	TS%	eFG%	3PT%
15.8	0.398	0.224	0.563	0.535	0.374

AST%	TOV%	OREB%	DREB%	STL%	BLK%
8.4	10.9	4.5	11.8	1.7	2.1

PER	ORTG	DRTG	WS/48	VOL	
13.32	111.7	108.2	0.107	0.394	

- Missed a portion of last season due to a knee injury that required surgery
- Increased his offensive efficiency in a lower volume role, excelled as a spot-up shooter
- Made 41.5% of his threes, was ranked in the 94th percentile in spot-up situations by the NBA
- Solid on-ball defending wing that will actively contest shots
- Posted the highest Block Percentage of his career last season
- Can occasionally defend fours, much better at guarding wing players

Zach Collins

	Height	Weight	Cap #	Years Left
	7'0"	232	$3.629M	2 Team Options

	Similar at Age	**20**	
		Season	**SIMsc**
1	Domantas Sabonis	2016-17	932.2
2	Trey Lyles	2015-16	904.6
3	Donte Greene	2008-09	896.7
4	Noah Vonleh	2015-16	893.9
5	Andray Blatche	2006-07	890.8
6	Bobby Portis	2015-16	887.2
7	Yi Jianlian	2007-08	886.4
8	Shawne Williams	2006-07	885.3
9	Dirk Nowitzki	1998-99	881.9
10	Johan Petro	2005-06	881.8

Baseline Basic Stats

MPG	PTS	AST	REB	BLK	STL
21.3	8.4	1.2	4.7	0.6	0.5

Advanced Metrics

USG%	3PTA/FGA	FTA/FGA	TS%	eFG%	3PT%
18.5	0.349	0.193	0.509	0.483	0.353

AST%	TOV%	OREB%	DREB%	STL%	BLK%
9.0	13.5	5.4	18.1	1.0	1.9

PER	ORTG	DRTG	WS/48	VOL
11.36	100.1	108.4	0.048	0.380

- Cracked Portland's rotation as a rookie, played better in the playoffs than he did in the regular season
- Fairly effective as a rim protector, used length to contest shots, decent defensive rebounder
- Needs to improve his position defense, struggles to defend interior players on the ball, fouls at a high rate
- Used as a low volume stretch big, shot below break-even on threes overall, shot much better on corner threes at 39.4%
- Has the athleticism to be a good roll man on pick-and-rolls, but doesn't set solid screens

Seth Curry

	Height	Weight	Cap #	Years Left
	6'2"	185	$2.795M	0

Similar at Age **27**

		Season	SIMsc
1	Craig Hodges	1987-88	951.5
2	Patty Mills	2015-16	942.6
3	Jerryd Bayless	2015-16	930.7
4	Derek Fisher	2001-02	927.1
5	Lou Williams	2013-14	926.2
6	Bryce Drew	2001-02	924.1
7	George Hill	2013-14	922.0
8	B.J. Armstrong	1994-95	921.4
9	Marco Belinelli	2013-14	921.3
10	James Robinson	1997-98	917.6

Baseline Basic Stats

MPG	PTS	AST	REB	BLK	STL
23.2	9.5	2.8	2.1	0.1	0.8

Advanced Metrics

USG%	3PTA/FGA	FTA/FGA	TS%	eFG%	3PT%
19.0	0.478	0.196	0.572	0.540	0.412

AST%	TOV%	OREB%	DREB%	STL%	BLK%
18.8	12.3	1.5	8.8	1.7	0.3

PER	ORTG	DRTG	WS/48	VOL	
14.42	111.2	110.0	0.101	0.375	

- Missed all of last season due to a stress reaction in the tibia of his left leg
- When healthy, excellent three-point shooter in a low volume role
- Great in spot-up situations, excels at running off screens
- Shot 42.5% on threes in 2016-17 for Dallas
- Solid enough playmaker to be effective as a pick-and-roll ball handler
- Decent position defender if hidden in favorable matchups

Meyers Leonard

	Height	Weight	Cap #	Years Left
	7'1"	245	$10.596M	1

Similar at Age 25

		Season	SIMsc
1	Kelly Olynyk	2016-17	894.0
2	Joffrey Lauvergne	2016-17	877.4
3	Mike Muscala	2016-17	870.7
4	Channing Frye	2008-09	868.8
5	Matt Bonner	2005-06	867.3
6	Hanno Mottola	2001-02	859.8
7	Spencer Hawes	2013-14	859.4
8	Danny Ferry	1991-92	856.5
9	Matt Freije	2006-07	856.2
10	Donald Hodge	1994-95	854.5

Baseline Basic Stats

MPG	PTS	AST	REB	BLK	STL
20.3	7.7	1.3	4.6	0.4	0.5

Advanced Metrics

USG%	3PTA/FGA	FTA/FGA	TS%	eFG%	3PT%
16.1	0.489	0.158	0.601	0.579	0.396

AST%	TOV%	OREB%	DREB%	STL%	BLK%
10.4	10.6	4.7	21.8	1.2	1.0

PER	ORTG	DRTG	WS/48	VOL
14.64	117.8	107.5	0.142	0.365

- Fell out of the rotation in Portland last season, only played 254 minutes, has been inconsistent throughout his career
- Has been a low usage stretch big throughout his career
- Solid overall three-point shooter for his career, excellent in the corners
- Mainly takes open shots with no dribbles, 64.1% of his shots last season were open, took a shot with no dribbles almost 81% of the time
- Below average defender, struggles on the ball due to a lack of quickness
- Limited as a rim protector because he doesn't really block shots, solid defensive rebounder

Nik Stauskas

	Height	Weight	Cap #	Years Left
	6'6"	205	$1.513M	0

Similar at Age 24

		Season	SIMsc
1	J.J. Redick	2008-09	922.1
2	Reggie Williams	2010-11	921.0
3	Hollis Thompson	2015-16	919.8
4	Daequan Cook	2011-12	917.3
5	James Anderson	2013-14	916.7
6	Martell Webster	2010-11	912.0
7	Kyle Korver	2005-06	911.4
8	Bill Walker	2011-12	911.0
9	Tim Hardaway, Jr.	2016-17	909.3
10	Rudy Fernandez	2009-10	908.9

Baseline Basic Stats

MPG	PTS	AST	REB	BLK	STL
23.1	8.8	1.5	2.9	0.3	0.6

Advanced Metrics

USG%	3PTA/FGA	FTA/FGA	TS%	eFG%	3PT%
17.2	0.586	0.199	0.550	0.519	0.380

AST%	TOV%	OREB%	DREB%	STL%	BLK%
12.0	12.1	1.6	12.0	1.2	0.9

PER	ORTG	DRTG	WS/48	VOL	
11.20	105.2	111.4	0.058	0.474	

- Played sparingly for Philadelphia and Brooklyn, production still consistent with his career averages
- Primarily a low volume spot-up shooter with some ability to run off screens
- Break-even three-point shooter for his career, better in the corners
- Below average effectiveness in every other offensive situation
- Decent position defender if he's hidden in favorable matchups

Caleb Swanigan

	Height	Weight	Cap #	Years Left
	6'8"	250	$1.740M	2 Team Options

Similar at Age 20

		Season	SIMsc
1	Anthony Bennett	2013-14	916.2
2	Samaki Walker	1996-97	888.4
3	Zach Randolph	2001-02	887.3
4	Jackie Butler	2005-06	879.6
5	Damien Inglis	2015-16	876.6
6	Brandon Bass	2005-06	876.0
7	Kris Humphries	2005-06	875.0
8	Wilson Chandler	2007-08	866.1
9	J.J. Hickson	2008-09	864.3
10	Jeremy Tyler	2011-12	864.1

Baseline Basic Stats

MPG	PTS	AST	REB	BLK	STL
16.6	6.7	0.7	3.9	0.3	0.4

Advanced Metrics

USG%	3PTA/FGA	FTA/FGA	TS%	eFG%	3PT%
19.9	0.145	0.302	0.527	0.487	0.260

AST%	TOV%	OREB%	DREB%	STL%	BLK%
9.0	16.3	8.8	19.0	1.2	1.3

PER	ORTG	DRTG	WS/48	VOL	
12.58	102.8	105.7	0.082	0.634	

- Played sparingly in his rookie season, split time between Portland and Canton in the G-League
- Flashed decent passing skills, but was turnover prone in both leagues
- Had difficulties making outside shots in both leagues, shot just below 31% on threes in the G-League
- Had more success inside with Canton, struggled to effectively score in the post against NBA interior players
- Solid rebounder overall, played effective below-the-rim interior defense in limited minutes in the NBA

Jake Layman

	Height	Weight	Cap #	Years Left
	6'9"	210	$1.545M	0

	Similar at Age	**23**	
		Season	**SIMsc**
1	James Nunnally	2013-14	917.2
2	Bostjan Nachbar	2003-04	911.0
3	Cleanthony Early	2014-15	904.6
4	Hollis Thompson	2014-15	904.5
5	DerMarr Johnson	2003-04	892.2
6	Matt Freije	2004-05	892.1
7	Anthony Brown	2015-16	888.6
8	Devin Ebanks	2012-13	887.8
9	Antoine Wright	2007-08	886.1
10	Jordan Hamilton	2013-14	884.0

Baseline Basic Stats

MPG	PTS	AST	REB	BLK	STL
19.6	7.0	1.0	2.9	0.3	0.5

Advanced Metrics

USG%	3PTA/FGA	FTA/FGA	TS%	eFG%	3PT%
16.9	0.487	0.147	0.475	0.450	0.302

AST%	TOV%	OREB%	DREB%	STL%	BLK%
8.7	9.2	3.3	11.5	1.4	1.2

PER	ORTG	DRTG	WS/48	VOL
9.46	98.6	109.2	0.055	0.758

- Has played very little in two NBA seasons, only 409 minutes total
- Mainly used as a low usage spot-up shooter, has really struggled to shoot efficiently
- Career True Shooting Percentage is below 40%
- Hasn't established any other offensive strengths
- Defensive ability is unclear, only plays garbage time minutes, not enough data to detect any strengths or weaknesses

Wade Baldwin

	Height	Weight	Cap #	Years Left
	6'4"	202	$1.545M	0

Similar at Age 21

		Season	SIMsc
1	Shannon Brown	2006-07	909.7
2	Malcolm Lee	2011-12	904.2
3	Austin Rivers	2013-14	900.8
4	Rashad McCants	2005-06	889.7
5	Delonte West	2004-05	888.9
6	Keyon Dooling	2001-02	888.8
7	Archie Goodwin	2015-16	888.0
8	Alec Burks	2012-13	886.7
9	Willie Warren	2010-11	886.7
10	Zoran Planinic	2003-04	885.4

Baseline Basic Stats

MPG	PTS	AST	REB	BLK	STL
19.8	7.9	1.8	2.2	0.2	0.6

Advanced Metrics

USG%	3PTA/FGA	FTA/FGA	TS%	eFG%	3PT%
17.7	0.202	0.337	0.558	0.527	0.414

AST%	TOV%	OREB%	DREB%	STL%	BLK%
15.0	14.4	2.2	9.2	1.7	1.0

PER	ORTG	DRTG	WS/48	VOL	
11.97	108.1	109.1	0.084	0.560	

- Played on a two-way contract last season, only played 80 minutes for Portland

- Spent most of the year with Texas in the G-League

- Solid as a higher volume scoring guard, relied on slashing to the rim to get layups or draw fouls

- Decent as a playmaker, cut his turnover rate significantly, still a below break-even three-point shooter

- Active in help defense, good rebounding guard that gets steals at a high rate

- Needs to work his overall position defense, middling on the ball, also tends to gamble a bit too much

Anfernee Simons

		Height	Weight	Cap #	Years Left
		6'4"	180	$1.836M	1 + 2 TO

Baseline Basic Stats

MPG	PTS	AST	REB	BLK	STL
16.3	6.3	1.6	1.9	0.2	0.5

Advanced Metrics

USG%	3PTA/FGA	FTA/FGA	TS%	eFG%	3PT%
17.9	0.475	0.172	0.550	0.518	0.316

AST%	TOV%	OREB%	DREB%	STL%	BLK%
12.0	11.0	1.7	11.1	1.7	0.4

PER	ORTG	DRTG	WS/48	VOL	
12.70	105.2	101.1	0.093	0.515	

- Drafted by Portland in the first round with the 24th overall pick
- Did not play in college or in an overseas league, projection uses translated Summer League stats
- Solid performance at the Las Vegas Summer League in July
- Scored efficiently in a moderate volume role, posted a True Shooting Percentage of 56.6%
- Effective at driving to the basket, making pull-up mid-range jumpers and occasionally making threes at an above break-even percentage
- Rarely looked to pass, only had three assists in 120 minutes
- Could benefit by spending some time in the G-League to develop his playmaking skills
- Energetic defensively, grabbed defensive rebounds and got steals at a high rate, solid as an on-ball defender

Gary Trent, Jr.

	Height	Weight	Cap #	Years Left
	6'6"	209	$0.838M	2

Baseline Basic Stats

MPG	PTS	AST	REB	BLK	STL
10.2	3.7	0.8	1.4	0.1	0.3

Advanced Metrics

USG%	3PTA/FGA	FTA/FGA	TS%	eFG%	3PT%
18.2	0.352	0.190	0.470	0.437	0.324

AST%	TOV%	OREB%	DREB%	STL%	BLK%
9.2	10.0	3.5	12.2	1.4	0.4

PER	ORTG	DRTG	WS/48	VOL
9.32	96.9	110.7	0.024	N/A

- Drafted by Sacramento with the 37th overall pick, then traded to Portland
- Played well at Summer League
- Better on the defensive end, active in help defense by getting rebounds, steals and blocks at a high rate
- Played solid on-ball defense against opposing wings
- Was used in a catch-and-shoot role, scored in volume, but struggled to make shots efficiently
- Only made 30% of his threes and shot under 40% on two-pointers, did make all of his free throws
- Could use some additional seasoning in the G-League to adapt to the NBA three-point line

DALLAS MAVERICKS

Last Season: 24 – 58, Missed the Playoffs

Offensive Rating: 106.3, 24th in NBA   Defensive Rating: 109.5, 17th in NBA

Primary Executive: Donnie Nelson, General Manager and President of Basketball Operations

Head Coach: Rick Carlisle

Key Roster Changes

Subtractions	Additions
Doug McDermott, free agency	Luka Doncic, draft
Nerlens Noel, free agency	Jalen Brunson, draft
Seth Curry, free agency	Ray Spalding, draft
Aaron Harrison, free agency	DeAndre Jordan, free agency
Yogi Ferrell, free agency	Devin Harris, free agency
Kyle Collinsworth, waived	Ryan Broekhoff, free agency

RAFER Projected Win Total: 40.7

Projected Best Five-Man Unit	Other Rotation Players
1. Devin Harris	Dennis Smith, Jr.
2. Luka Doncic	Dirk Nowitzki
3. Harrison Barnes	Wesley Matthews
4. Dwight Powell	Maxi Kleber
5. DeAndre Jordan	Salah Mejri

Remaining Roster

- J.J. Barea
- Dorian Finney-Smith
- Ryan Broekhoff
- Jalen Brunson
- Ray Spalding
- Kostas Antetkounmpo, 21, 6'10", 197, Dayton (Two-Way)
- Daryl Macon, 23, 6'3", 185, Arkansas (Two-Way)
- Ding Yanyuhang, 25, 6'7", 205, China (Exhibit 10)
- Jalen Jones, 25, 6'7", 223, Texas A&M (Exhibit 10)
- Codi Miller-McIntyre, 24, 6'3", 205, Wake Forest (Exhibit 10)

Season Forecast

After missing the playoffs for the previous two seasons, the Dallas Mavericks made a push this summer to become more competitive in the Western Conference and secure a part of their future. They made a move to do the latter on draft day by trading with the Atlanta Hawks to land Luka Doncic, arguably the draft's best prospect, to serve as one of the franchise's building blocks for the foreseeable future. Then, they used their cap space to finally land the big man in DeAndre Jordan that they thought they had landed three years earlier, but this time without needing to participate in a hostage free agency or a social media emoji war to acquire his services. These two major additions should make the Mavericks a more improved unit on both sides of the ball. However, the level of competition in the West may be too high for them for them to land a playoff spot with their existing talent level. As a result, they still might be at least a year away from competing for the playoffs and they will probably wind up as a lottery team once again this coming season.

Dallas was in the bottom half of the league on both sides of the ball last season, so the team's new acquisitions should help to improve their offense and defense. On the surface, it would seem like the defense would get the biggest boost because of Jordan's reputation as a rim protector. However, the NBA game has shifted to the point where having a valued rim protector isn't as impactful as it once was. After all, NBA offenses have become more pick-and-roll heavy and they use more screen action to create exploitable mismatches. As a result, team-wide defensive versatility has become more important in building a successful defense. While Jordan will allow the Mavericks to finish a few more possessions off with a defensive rebound and force a few more misses with his shot blocking presence, the best acquisition that Dallas made to improve its defense may have actually been Doncic. The reason for this is that he addresses one of the team's primary issues, which has been its lack of versatility on defense. In the previous few seasons, head coach, Rick Carlisle has favored playing lineups with two smaller guards and a traditional big man. These lineups have worked to generate ball movement on offense, but they also give some of those points back by giving opponents more mismatches to consistently exploit. By essentially giving the departed Yogi Ferrell's minutes to Doncic, the team trades a potential size mismatch for a ball handler with wing size that is capable of defending multiple positions, which gives opponents one fewer matchup to pick on to help Dallas' defense. From there, Dallas' offense should improve simply because Doncic and Jordan are more talented and effective than the outgoing players that they are replacing. Also, their skill sets easily fit into Carlisle's established system with Doncic being either the primary and secondary ball handler in a two ball handler system and Jordan being the rim running big man. Finally, the infusion of additional talent will help to reduce the workload of Dennis Smith, Jr., which may help him to be more efficient on offense to help the team. Overall, the Mavericks should see a significant increase in their win total this coming season, but it might not be enough for them to firmly make the playoffs in a very tough Western Conference. If they stay close to playoff contention in the second half of the season, the season could be considered a mild success. Otherwise, if the results stay close to what they were last season, then serious changes may be needed to improve their fortunes.

Veterans

DeAndre Jordan

	Height	Weight	Cap #	Years Left
	6'11"	250	$22.897M	0

Similar at Age 29

		Season	SIMsc
1	Joel Przybilla	2008-09	891.1
2	Erick Dampier	2004-05	881.1
3	Dale Davis	1998-99	880.2
4	Dwight Howard	2014-15	879.1
5	Tyson Chandler	2011-12	876.2
6	Samuel Dalembert	2010-11	873.2
7	Marcin Gortat	2013-14	872.8
8	Mark West	1989-90	870.8
9	Ian Mahinmi	2015-16	866.1
10	Omer Asik	2015-16	861.1

Baseline Basic Stats

MPG	PTS	AST	REB	BLK	STL
27.3	9.7	0.9	9.9	1.3	0.6

Advanced Metrics

USG%	3PTA/FGA	FTA/FGA	TS%	eFG%	3PT%
15.5	0.003	0.633	0.614	0.616	0.033

AST%	TOV%	OREB%	DREB%	STL%	BLK%
5.8	15.9	13.5	32.6	1.0	3.5

PER	ORTG	DRTG	WS/48	VOL
18.52	118.4	103.0	0.161	0.384

- Entering his age-30 season, still producing at a near All-Star level
- Extremely durable big man, has only missed 13 games in the last eight seasons
- One of the best rebounders in the NBA, led the league in Defensive Rebound and Overall Rebound Percentage last season
- Solid rim protector, historically has been one of the league's best shot blockers, Block Percentage decreased significantly last season
- Opposing teams are putting him in space more often, has difficulty keeping opposing players in front of him
- Strictly a low volume rim runner, excels as a roll man and as an offensive rebounder that scores on put-backs
- Shot a career high of 58% at the free throw line, below 45% on free throws for his career

Harrison Barnes

	Height	Weight	Cap #	Years Left
	6'8"	210	$24.107M	Player Option

Similar at Age 25

		Season	SIMsc
1	Chuck Person	1989-90	943.1
2	Glen Rice	1992-93	937.7
3	Tayshaun Prince	2005-06	924.3
4	Kyle Korver	2006-07	922.5
5	Peja Stojakovic	2002-03	920.6
6	Gordon Hayward	2015-16	920.5
7	Luol Deng	2010-11	920.0
8	Antawn Jamison	2001-02	919.9
9	Nick Young	2010-11	919.1
10	Evan Turner	2013-14	917.8

Baseline Basic Stats

MPG	PTS	AST	REB	BLK	STL
34.8	18.1	2.7	4.9	0.4	0.9

Advanced Metrics

USG%	3PTA/FGA	FTA/FGA	TS%	eFG%	3PT%
23.5	0.255	0.253	0.549	0.506	0.368

AST%	TOV%	OREB%	DREB%	STL%	BLK%
11.6	8.8	3.6	13.7	1.2	0.6

PER	ORTG	DRTG	WS/48	VOL
16.40	109.2	109.3	0.104	0.288

- In his prime, consistently productive in his two seasons with Dallas
- Maintained his effectiveness as a high volume scorer
- Excelled in one-on-one situations, pretty good on isolations and post-ups
- Showed some abilities as a pick-and-roll ball handler by making pull-up mid-range shots and getting to the rim to draw fouls
- Solid off-the-ball, good cutter and spot-up shooter
- Shot almost a league average on threes, historically better in the corners
- Good on-ball defending combo forward, posted the highest Defensive Rebound Percentage of his career last season

Dennis Smith, Jr.

	Height	Weight	Cap #	Years Left
	6'3"	195	$3.820M	2 Team Options

Similar at Age 20

		Season	SIMsc
1	D'Angelo Russell	2016-17	925.1
2	Kyrie Irving	2012-13	913.7
3	Brandon Knight	2011-12	908.0
4	Bradley Beal	2013-14	901.4
5	Emmanuel Mudiay	2016-17	896.3
6	Tony Wroten	2013-14	894.5
7	Jrue Holiday	2010-11	891.5
8	Russell Westbrook	2008-09	888.6
9	Keyon Dooling	2000-01	888.3
10	Brandon Jennings	2009-10	886.9

Baseline Basic Stats

MPG	PTS	AST	REB	BLK	STL
31.3	16.7	4.4	3.6	0.2	1.1

Advanced Metrics

USG%	3PTA/FGA	FTA/FGA	TS%	eFG%	3PT%
27.7	0.362	0.229	0.512	0.474	0.351

AST%	TOV%	OREB%	DREB%	STL%	BLK%
26.7	13.9	2.5	10.5	1.8	0.6

PER	ORTG	DRTG	WS/48	VOL	
15.17	100.9	109.8	0.052	0.375	

- Regular starter for Dallas, made the All-Rookie second team last season
- Scored in volume, but struggled to make shots efficiently, shot below 30% from mid-range, below break-even on threes
- Quick enough to get to the rim, shot a solid percentage inside of three feet
- Did not draw fouls at a high rate, solid as a playmaker
- Defended both guard spots at a below average level, slightly better at defending two guards last season, good defensive rebounder for his size

Dwight Powell

	Height	Weight	Cap #	Years Left
	6'11"	240	$9.631M	Player Option

Similar at Age 26

		Season	SIMsc
1	Troy Murphy	2006-07	918.6
2	Gorgui Dieng	2015-16	915.5
3	Steve Stipanovich	1986-87	912.8
4	Marcin Gortat	2010-11	906.3
5	Clemon Johnson	1982-83	904.2
6	Greg Foster	1994-95	901.8
7	Nenad Krstic	2009-10	900.2
8	Raef LaFrentz	2002-03	899.9
9	Anderson Varejao	2008-09	899.8
10	Jason Thompson	2012-13	895.3

Baseline Basic Stats

MPG	PTS	AST	REB	BLK	STL
24.4	9.1	1.2	6.2	0.7	0.7

Advanced Metrics

USG%	3PTA/FGA	FTA/FGA	TS%	eFG%	3PT%
16.7	0.144	0.353	0.590	0.551	0.324

AST%	TOV%	OREB%	DREB%	STL%	BLK%
7.2	10.7	8.1	20.4	1.6	1.9

PER	ORTG	DRTG	WS/48	VOL
16.32	118.1	106.9	0.154	0.411

- Had a career best season in his fourth year, posted career highs in PER and Win Shares
- Very efficient in a low usage role, excelled as a roll man, ranked in the 95th percentile according to the NBA
- Effective in a small sample of post-ups
- Added some stretch ability, shot a break-even percentage on threes last season
- Below average on-ball interior defender with some mobility to defend on the perimeter for a few dribbles
- Limited rim protection skills, not really a shot blocker, solid overall rebounder

Dirk Nowitzki

	Height	Weight	Cap #	Years Left
	7'0"	237	$5.000M	0

Similar at Age 39

		Season	SIMsc
1	Clifford Robinson	2005-06	862.5
2	Robert Parish*	1992-93	861.3
3	Patrick Ewing*	2001-02	844.4
4	Sam Perkins	2000-01	836.4
5	Kareem Abdul-Jabbar*	1986-87	835.8
6	Grant Hill*	2011-12	827.0
7	Tim Duncan	2015-16	825.5
8	Kevin Willis	2001-02	818.7
9	James Edwards	1994-95	798.2
10	Vince Carter	2015-16	791.6

Baseline Basic Stats

MPG	PTS	AST	REB	BLK	STL
24.1	10.8	1.4	5.6	0.8	0.6

Advanced Metrics

USG%	3PTA/FGA	FTA/FGA	TS%	eFG%	3PT%
19.3	0.147	0.219	0.549	0.514	0.400

AST%	TOV%	OREB%	DREB%	STL%	BLK%
10.4	9.2	3.6	24.4	1.0	2.6

PER	ORTG	DRTG	WS/48	VOL	
15.21	107.9	106.1	0.093	0.535	

- Entering his age-40 season, still effective but in the decline stage of his career
- Most effective player in the league at avoiding turnovers, had the lowest Turnover Percentage in the NBA
- Usage has decreased, still an efficient scorer that can post up and knock down spot-up jumpers
- Took more threes, shot 40.9% on threes last season
- Limited defensively due to a decline in mobility, has to be hidden defensively
- Good defensive rebounder, can occasionally block shots

Wesley Matthews

	Height	Weight	Cap #	Years Left
	6'5"	220	$18.623M	0

Similar at Age 31

		Season	SIMsc
1	Jason Richardson	2011-12	931.4
2	Alan Anderson	2013-14	931.2
3	Anthony Parker	2006-07	923.9
4	Devin Brown	2009-10	923.9
5	Richard Jefferson	2011-12	921.9
6	Caron Butler	2011-12	919.6
7	Anthony Peeler	2000-01	917.0
8	Courtney Lee	2016-17	917.0
9	Raja Bell	2007-08	916.7
10	Michael Finley	2004-05	915.2

Baseline Basic Stats

MPG	PTS	AST	REB	BLK	STL
26.7	9.6	1.9	3.0	0.2	0.8

Advanced Metrics

USG%	3PTA/FGA	FTA/FGA	TS%	eFG%	3PT%
16.8	0.531	0.164	0.540	0.510	0.383

AST%	TOV%	OREB%	DREB%	STL%	BLK%
11.8	10.2	1.6	10.3	1.6	0.6

PER	ORTG	DRTG	WS/48	VOL
11.39	106.7	109.8	0.068	0.324

- Missed the last month of the season due to a fractured right fibula
- Production over the last three seasons has been down from his career averages
- Mainly used as a low usage spot-up shooter
- Shot over 38% on threes overall and almost 43% on corner threes for his career
- Has shown enough playmaking abilities to be effective as a pick-and-roll ball handler in a small sample of possessions
- Solid on-ball defending wing player in previous seasons, may be losing a step due to his age

Devin Harris

	Height	Weight	Cap #	Years Left
	6'3"	185	$2.394M	0

Similar at Age 34

		Season	SIMsc
1	Terry Porter	1997-98	924.6
2	Bobby Jackson	2007-08	922.5
3	Danny Ainge	1993-94	921.3
4	Byron Scott	1995-96	918.5
5	Brad Davis	1989-90	913.0
6	Leandro Barbosa	2016-17	911.4
7	Randy Smith	1982-83	908.3
8	Anthony Johnson	2008-09	906.3
9	John Starks	1999-00	905.5
10	Jon Barry	2003-04	904.1

Baseline Basic Stats

MPG	PTS	AST	REB	BLK	STL
19.7	7.3	2.3	2.0	0.1	0.7

Advanced Metrics

USG%	3PTA/FGA	FTA/FGA	TS%	eFG%	3PT%
17.6	0.463	0.334	0.555	0.500	0.354

AST%	TOV%	OREB%	DREB%	STL%	BLK%
16.9	12.5	1.6	10.6	1.8	0.7

PER	ORTG	DRTG	WS/48	VOL	
13.03	110.5	109.0	0.099	0.337	

- Entering his age-35 season, in a slight decline stage, has maintained his current level of production for the last three seasons
- Effective as a pick-and-roll ball handler, solid playmaking skills, can still get to the rim to finish inside
- Good in spot-up situations, will attack closeouts to draw shooting fouls
- A slightly below break-even three-point shooter for his career
- Decent on-ball position defender, better against bigger guards because he lacks the quickness to stay in front of point guards

Maxi Kleber

	Height	Weight	Cap #	Years Left
	6'10"	220	$1.378M	0

Similar at Age 26

		Season	SIMsc
1	Pete Chilcutt	1994-95	918.3
2	Earl Clark	2013-14	914.1
3	Robert Horry	1996-97	907.1
4	Serge Ibaka	2015-16	906.1
5	Marvin Williams	2012-13	902.9
6	Vladimir Radmanovic	2006-07	898.3
7	Jawad Williams	2009-10	897.2
8	Willie Reed	2016-17	894.9
9	Jonas Jerebko	2013-14	892.3
10	Luke Babbitt	2015-16	892.0

Baseline Basic Stats

MPG	PTS	AST	REB	BLK	STL
21.8	8.0	1.0	4.5	0.6	0.7

Advanced Metrics

USG%	3PTA/FGA	FTA/FGA	TS%	eFG%	3PT%
16.0	0.447	0.186	0.551	0.525	0.324

AST%	TOV%	OREB%	DREB%	STL%	BLK%
6.7	8.8	6.2	17.1	1.4	2.7

PER	ORTG	DRTG	WS/48	VOL	
13.72	111.8	107.9	0.106	0.400	

- Regular part of Dallas' rotation last season, started half of the games that he appeared in
- Played in a lower volume role, scored efficiently as a roll man and spot-up shooter
- Shot a below break-even percentage on threes, but very good from mid-range
- Effective in a small sample of post-ups, ranked by the NBA in the 95th percentile on a per-possession basis
- Active help defender that can block shots, below average as a position defender
- Sacrifices position to go for blocks, middling rebounder, lacks lateral quickness to defend on the ball

Salah Mejri

	Height	Weight	Cap #	Years Left
	7'1"	245	$1.513M	0

Similar at Age 31

		Season	SIMsc
1	Andrew Bogut	2015-16	891.4
2	Adonal Foyle	2006-07	880.6
3	Tyson Chandler	2013-14	879.3
4	Ronny Turiaf	2013-14	879.1
5	Ervin Johnson	1998-99	878.5
6	Marvin Webster	1983-84	878.5
7	Ryan Hollins	2015-16	868.5
8	Will Perdue	1996-97	859.0
9	Samuel Dalembert	2012-13	852.7
10	Tree Rollins	1986-87	851.4

Baseline Basic Stats

MPG	PTS	AST	REB	BLK	STL
20.1	5.0	0.9	6.5	1.3	0.5

Advanced Metrics

USG%	3PTA/FGA	FTA/FGA	TS%	eFG%	3PT%
11.8	0.011	0.447	0.595	0.579	0.120

AST%	TOV%	OREB%	DREB%	STL%	BLK%
6.3	19.6	11.9	25.3	1.3	6.0

PER	ORTG	DRTG	WS/48	VOL
15.19	115.3	102.9	0.136	0.573

- Fringe rotation player for Dallas for the last three seasons, was most productive last season
- Very good rim protector, excellent shot blocker and rebounder on both ends
- Struggles to stay on the floor due to his limited mobility, below average defender on the ball as a result
- Almost strictly a low volume rim runner on offense, above average as a roll man, will score on put-backs
- Draws fouls at a high rate, but shoots under 60% from the free throw line

J.J. Barea

	Height	Weight	Cap #	Years Left
	6'0"	175	$3.711M	0

Similar at Age **33**

		Season	SIMsc
1	Tim Hardaway	1999-00	937.9
2	Mark Price	1997-98	917.7
3	Nick Van Exel	2004-05	899.0
4	Mo Williams	2015-16	892.1
5	Damon Stoudamire	2006-07	883.8
6	Jameer Nelson	2015-16	877.1
7	Mark Jackson	1998-99	874.3
8	Jason Terry	2010-11	870.1
9	Dana Barros	2000-01	869.7
10	Jannero Pargo	2012-13	868.7

Baseline Basic Stats

MPG	PTS	AST	REB	BLK	STL
24.4	10.3	4.8	2.5	0.1	0.7

Advanced Metrics

USG%	3PTA/FGA	FTA/FGA	TS%	eFG%	3PT%
23.4	0.451	0.137	0.514	0.491	0.354

AST%	TOV%	OREB%	DREB%	STL%	BLK%
35.6	15.4	1.3	11.2	1.3	0.2

PER	ORTG	DRTG	WS/48	VOL
15.30	103.8	108.8	0.076	0.378

- Still effective in a bench role entering his age-34 season, had a career year last season

- Posted the highest Assist Percentage of his career, excelled with the ball in his hands

- Good as a pick-and-roll ball handler and in isolation situations, shot 66.4% on shots inside of three feet

- Pretty good mid-range shooter and shot above the league average on threes last season

- Limited as an on-ball defender due to his small size, very good defensive rebounding point guard

Dorian Finney-Smith

	Height	Weight	Cap #	Years Left
	6'8"	220	$1.545M	0

Similar at Age **24**

		Season	SIMsc
1	James Jones	2004-05	951.3
2	Victor Claver	2012-13	938.2
3	Kostas Papanikolaou	2014-15	935.6
4	Yakhouba Diawara	2006-07	931.0
5	Robbie Hummel	2013-14	930.1
6	Solomon Hill	2015-16	928.1
7	James Ennis	2014-15	920.4
8	Brian Evans	1997-98	920.2
9	Johnny Taylor	1998-99	918.9
10	Quincy Pondexter	2012-13	916.5

Baseline Basic Stats

MPG	PTS	AST	REB	BLK	STL
19.4	6.4	1.0	2.8	0.3	0.5

Advanced Metrics

USG%	3PTA/FGA	FTA/FGA	TS%	eFG%	3PT%
15.0	0.526	0.179	0.507	0.477	0.332

AST%	TOV%	OREB%	DREB%	STL%	BLK%
8.2	11.7	4.0	13.0	1.3	1.0

PER	ORTG	DRTG	WS/48	VOL
9.38	101.6	110.0	0.050	0.412

- Missed most of last season due to tendinitis in his left knee and left quadriceps

- Has mostly been used as a low usage spot-up shooter, has struggled to make shots

- More than half of his shots are threes, has made less than 30% of them

- Effective as a cutter when healthy, ranked in the 93rd percentile on cuts by the NBA on a per-possession basis in 2016-17

- Solid on-ball defending combo forward, decent defensive rebounder

Newcomers

Luka Doncic

		Height	Weight	Cap #	Years Left
		6'7"	218	$6.561M	1 + 2 TO

Baseline Basic Stats

MPG	PTS	AST	REB	BLK	STL
23.9	10.9	1.9	3.5	0.3	0.9

Advanced Metrics

USG%	3PTA/FGA	FTA/FGA	TS%	eFG%	3PT%
23.2	0.457	0.340	0.578	0.525	0.291

AST%	TOV%	OREB%	DREB%	STL%	BLK%
25.3	13.8	3.1	15.8	1.9	1.0

PER	ORTG	DRTG	WS/48	VOL	
15.39	113.4	116.2	0.097	0.483	

- Drafted by Atlanta with the 3rd overall pick, then traded to Dallas
- Played with Real Madrid last season, projection uses translated EuroLeague stats
- Named EuroLeague MVP in 2017-18
- Excellent playmaking big guard that limits turnovers
- Scores efficiently mainly by driving to the rim to finish inside or draw fouls
- Can make threes but can be streaky, percentages fluctuate from year-to-year
- Not overly quick, but can competently defend multiple positions, better suited to handling wings
- Good rebounder that can get steals and occasionally block shots

Jalen Brunson

	Height	Weight	Cap #	Years Left
	6'3"	190	$0.838M	3

Baseline Basic Stats

MPG	PTS	AST	REB	BLK	STL
12.2	4.3	1.5	1.3	0.1	0.4

Advanced Metrics

USG%	3PTA/FGA	FTA/FGA	TS%	eFG%	3PT%
19.3	0.287	0.238	0.466	0.430	0.329

AST%	TOV%	OREB%	DREB%	STL%	BLK%
17.9	11.1	2.6	8.4	1.5	0.5

PER	ORTG	DRTG	WS/48	VOL
10.44	99.3	111.5	0.030	N/A

- Drafted by Dallas in the second round with the 33rd overall pick
- Had his struggles at Summer League
- Showed some playmaking ability, but was quite turnover prone
- Really had difficulties in shooting efficiently in a high volume role, could benefit from additional seasoning in the G-League
- Shot selection wasn't especially great, shot less than 25% from the field and made 30% of his threes
- Got steals at a high rate, but was middling at best as an on-ball defender

Ray Spalding

	Height	Weight	Cap #	Years Left
	6'10"	215	$0.838M	3

Baseline Basic Stats

MPG	PTS	AST	REB	BLK	STL
10.5	3.4	0.4	2.5	0.3	0.4

Advanced Metrics

USG%	3PTA/FGA	FTA/FGA	TS%	eFG%	3PT%
14.9	0.019	0.355	0.506	0.477	0.124

AST%	TOV%	OREB%	DREB%	STL%	BLK%
5.5	16.0	9.7	19.6	1.7	3.3

PER	ORTG	DRTG	WS/48	VOL
11.22	100.8	104.6	0.063	N/A

- Drafted by Philadelphia with the 56th overall pick, then traded to Dallas
- Very effective at Summer League
- Played with great energy by blocking shots, getting steals and crashing the boards at both ends
- Flashed some potential as an on-ball defender with decent positioning
- Mainly a rim runner on offense, shot a high percentage from the field
- Showed a little bit of stretch potential by shooting 2-for-6 on threes
- Could use some additional seasoning in the G-League to develop some more skill offensively

Ryan Broekhoff

		Height	Weight	Cap #	Years Left
		6'7"	215	$0.838M	1

Baseline Basic Stats

MPG	PTS	AST	REB	BLK	STL
17.8	5.7	0.8	2.4	0.2	0.5

Advanced Metrics

USG%	3PTA/FGA	FTA/FGA	TS%	eFG%	3PT%
13.0	0.755	0.197	0.621	0.600	0.394

AST%	TOV%	OREB%	DREB%	STL%	BLK%
6.8	7.1	5.2	14.4	1.6	1.4

PER	ORTG	DRTG	WS/48	VOL	
12.20	120.1	99.0	0.112	0.515	

- Played last season with Lokomotiv Kuban in Russia, projection uses translated Eurocup stats
- Enters the NBA as a rookie in his age-28 season
- Very effective as a low volume, three-point specialist, made 48.9% of his threes last season
- Rarely turns the ball over, has made over 88% of his free throws over the last two seasons
- Uncertain if he can guard NBA wings, not overwhelmingly athletic
- Effective position defender overseas that also got steals and rebounded at a fairly high rate

MEMPHIS GRIZZLIES

Last Season: 22 – 60, Missed the Playoffs

Offensive Rating: 104.5, 27th in NBA

Defensive Rating: 111.0, 26th in NBA

Primary Executive: Chris Wallace, General Manager

Head Coach: J.B. Bickerstaff

Key Roster Changes

Subtractions
Ben McLemore, trade
Deyonta Davis, trade
Jarell Martin, trade
Tyreke Evans, free agency
Mario Chalmers, free agency
Omari Johnson, waived

Additions
Jaren Jackson, Jr., draft
Jevon Carter, draft
Garrett Temple, trade
Kyle Anderson, free agency
Omri Casspi, free agency
Shelvin Mack, free agency

RAFER Projected Win Total: 40.4

Projected Best Five-Man Unit
1. Mike Conley
2. Garrett Temple
3. Kyle Anderson
4. Jaren Jackson, Jr.
5. Marc Gasol

Other Rotation Players
Chandler Parsons
JaMychal Green
Dillon Brooks
Omri Casspi
Shelvin Mack

Remaining Roster

- Andrew Harrison
- Wayne Selden
- Ivan Rabb
- MarShon Brooks
- Jevon Carter
- Yuta Watanabe, 24, 6'9", 205, George Washington (Two-Way)
- Markel Crawford, 24, 6'4", 210, Mississippi (Exhibit 10)
- Brandon Goodwin, 23, 6'2", 180, Florida Gulf Coast (Exhibit 10)
- Doral Moore, 22, 7'1", 265, Wake Forest (Exhibit 10)

Season Forecast

The Memphis Grizzlies finished with one of the league's worst records last season after being a playoff team in each of the previous seven seasons. Most of this was personnel related, as they were without Mike Conley for the bulk of the season due to a foot injury and some of their long-term veterans had left for other teams. This summer, Memphis shook up its roster to recapture some its defensive identity from the past with slight adaptations for the modern game. As a result, they drafted Jaren Jackson, Jr. with the fourth overall pick in this past draft to serve as a modern style rim protector and they also brought in Kyle Anderson and Garrett Temple to provide some additional defensive versatility. However, this infusion of defensive talent may not be enough for Memphis to return to the playoffs because they may be a bit overmatched when it comes to offensive firepower. Also, Conley and Marc Gasol are both in their 30s and have shown some signs of decline, so the team may not be able to rely on them as much as they have in the past. In all likelihood, Memphis will be a bit more competitive this coming season, but they will probably miss the playoffs for the second straight year.

The Grizzlies will stand to improve the most on the defensive end. In the "Grit and Grind" era, Memphis played a more traditional style of defense that looked to funnel the action inside to the big men, who were looking to protect the rim and clog the paint. However, the team's effectiveness on defense got gradually worse as the rest of the league started embracing a faster paced, modern style of offense that relied on floor spacing, skill and versatility. As it was mentioned earlier, Memphis in the summer brought in several players like Jackson, Anderson, Temple and Shelvin Mack to help modernize the defense. Specifically, these four players are rangier, more athletic defenders that are capable of defending multiple positions. The addition of these players into the rotation gives Memphis an ability to switch screens and keep themselves out of bad matchups. If they stay relatively healthy, they could be a much better defensive team this season. On offense, they have never really been an efficient unit, even in their good years, so Conley and Gasol will continue to carry the brunt of the responsibility. They both are getting older and Conley is coming off a pretty serious injury, which makes it uncertain if the both of them can sustain the necessary offensive workload. They will need someone else to take on some offensive responsibility to ease the burden, but no one else on their roster has proven that they can do this over the course of an entire season. Of their available options, Jackson has the most potential. However, he's still in a developmental stage and he's only shown that he can be effective in short stretches. Chandler Parsons was productive in his early years, but he has broken down and has been pretty ineffective in his two seasons in Memphis. With this in mind, the Grizzlies will probably once again be a bottom third offensive team this coming season. Generally speaking, the moves that Memphis made this offseason were a step in the right direction because they will help to re-establish themselves as a defensive minded team. However, they still won't be able to contend for the playoffs because they still haven't found a way to mesh their defensive identity with an efficient offensive structure. It may take them some time to do that, so they may be in the lottery for the next few seasons.

Veterans

Mike Conley

	Height	Weight	Cap #	Years Left
	6'1"	180	$30.521M	1 + PO

Similar at Age **30**

		Season	SIMsc
1	George Hill	2016-17	934.3
2	Bobby Jackson	2003-04	917.2
3	C.J. Watson	2014-15	916.2
4	Lou Williams	2016-17	915.5
5	Jannero Pargo	2009-10	914.2
6	Kyle Lowry	2016-17	908.0
7	Mo Williams	2012-13	907.2
8	Stephon Marbury	2007-08	904.5
9	J.J. Barea	2014-15	903.6
10	Brian Roberts	2015-16	901.4

Baseline Basic Stats

MPG	PTS	AST	REB	BLK	STL
25.1	11.6	3.5	2.6	0.1	0.8

Advanced Metrics

USG%	3PTA/FGA	FTA/FGA	TS%	eFG%	3PT%
22.7	0.440	0.279	0.539	0.490	0.364

AST%	TOV%	OREB%	DREB%	STL%	BLK%
22.8	10.9	1.3	9.5	1.7	0.6

PER	ORTG	DRTG	WS/48	VOL
15.48	109.9	110.2	0.106	0.545

- Missed most of last season due to a sore Achilles and surgery to smooth a bone in his left heel
- When healthy, excellent playmaking point guard that rarely turns the ball over
- Good at using his quickness to beat defenders off the dribble in isolation situations when at full strength
- Effective pick-and-roll ball handler that can penetrate to draw fouls or knock down outside shots
- Has been a good three-point shooter overall for his career, has shot 42.4% on corner threes over his career
- Moves well off the ball, very good at cutting to the rim and running off screens
- Fairly solid on-ball defender, has some difficulty contesting shots due to his size, decent defensive rebounding point guard

Marc Gasol

	Height	Weight	Cap #	Years Left
	7'1"	265	$24.119M	Player Option

Similar at Age 33

		Season	SIMsc
1	Tim Duncan	2009-10	875.8
2	Arvydas Sabonis*	1997-98	865.1
3	Dirk Nowitzki	2011-12	863.0
4	Pau Gasol	2013-14	860.9
5	Hakeem Olajuwon*	1995-96	858.2
6	Patrick Ewing*	1995-96	849.2
7	Vlade Divac	2001-02	847.8
8	Brad Miller	2009-10	843.4
9	Kareem Abdul-Jabbar*	1980-81	842.5
10	Zydrunas Ilgauskas	2008-09	839.9

Baseline Basic Stats

MPG	PTS	AST	REB	BLK	STL
30.9	16.5	2.7	8.1	1.5	0.8

Advanced Metrics

USG%	3PTA/FGA	FTA/FGA	TS%	eFG%	3PT%
24.7	0.191	0.307	0.539	0.488	0.387

AST%	TOV%	OREB%	DREB%	STL%	BLK%
17.6	12.4	4.7	23.2	1.3	3.8

PER	ORTG	DRTG	WS/48	VOL	
18.79	106.7	103.5	0.131	0.231	

- Entering his age-34 season, productivity decreased last season, possibly entering a decline stage
- Excellent passing big man, shooting threes with greater frequency, above break-even three-point shooter for his career
- Overall scoring efficiency dropped, post-up effectiveness has decreased, missing more shots inside of 16 feet
- Good interior defender, very good rim protector that blocks shots, clogs the lane and grabs defensive rebounds
- Seems to have lost step in terms of lateral quickness due to his age and size

Kyle Anderson

	Height	Weight	Cap #	Years Left
	6'9"	230	$8.641M	3

Similar at Age 24

		Season	SIMsc
1	Larry Nance Jr.	2016-17	951.3
2	Robert Horry	1994-95	909.1
3	Dante Cunningham	2011-12	905.0
4	Rudy Gay	2010-11	900.4
5	Ronnie Brewer	2009-10	896.8
6	Patrick Patterson	2013-14	895.4
7	Marvin Williams	2010-11	894.7
8	Andrew DeClercq	1997-98	887.7
9	Rick Fox	1993-94	887.6
10	Danny Manning	1990-91	887.1

Baseline Basic Stats

MPG	PTS	AST	REB	BLK	STL
25.6	8.8	2.0	5.2	0.7	1.1

Advanced Metrics

USG%	3PTA/FGA	FTA/FGA	TS%	eFG%	3PT%
14.9	0.213	0.303	0.554	0.516	0.343

AST%	TOV%	OREB%	DREB%	STL%	BLK%
13.9	13.4	5.6	17.0	2.4	2.2

PER	ORTG	DRTG	WS/48	VOL
15.44	112.6	101.6	0.148	0.421

- Had his best season in his fourth year in the NBA, first time as a regular starter for San Antonio
- Excelled as a defender that could guard multiple positions, solid as an on-ball defender
- Active help defender that posted career high Steal and Block Percentages, solid defensive rebounder
- Effective as a low volume, secondary ball handler
- Solid playmaking skills allowed him to be a good pick-and-roll ball handler
- Could slash to the rim to either draw fouls or make shots inside of three feet at almost 69%
- Good mid-range shooter that can occasionally hit a three
- Slightly above break-even as a three-point shooter for his career, historically much better in the corners

JaMychal Green

	Height	Weight	Cap #	Years Left
	6'8"	228	$7.8667M	0

Similar at Age 27

		Season	SIMsc
1	Udonis Haslem	2007-08	936.4
2	Kurt Thomas	1999-00	932.3
3	David Benoit	1995-96	929.4
4	Kenny Gattison	1991-92	924.6
5	Trevor Booker	2014-15	919.0
6	Marvin Williams	2013-14	918.1
7	Jon Leuer	2016-17	915.2
8	Darrell Arthur	2015-16	913.1
9	Pat Cummings	1983-84	910.4
10	Lance Thomas	2015-16	910.4

Baseline Basic Stats

MPG	PTS	AST	REB	BLK	STL
23.7	8.7	1.2	5.8	0.4	0.6

Advanced Metrics

USG%	3PTA/FGA	FTA/FGA	TS%	eFG%	3PT%
16.7	0.251	0.276	0.546	0.509	0.359

AST%	TOV%	OREB%	DREB%	STL%	BLK%
7.8	12.9	8.9	21.5	1.1	1.3

PER	ORTG	DRTG	WS/48	VOL	
13.45	109.6	107.7	0.093	0.411	

- Missed games last season due to injuries to both of his ankles and knees

- Low volume offensive player that's most effective as an offensive rebounder

- Can draw fouls inside and finish shots around the rim

- Good at running the floor to finish plays in transition

- Has increased his three-attempt attempt rate in the last two seasons, shoots above break-even on threes

- Decent stay-at-home on-ball defender against interior players, very good defensive rebounder

Dillon Brooks

	Height	Weight	Cap #	Years Left
	6'6"	220	$1.378M	1

Similar at Age 22

		Season	SIMsc
1	Khris Middleton	2013-14	954.3
2	Jason Richardson	2002-03	943.3
3	Jarvis Hayes	2003-04	937.7
4	C.J. Miles	2009-10	927.8
5	Corey Maggette	2001-02	924.3
6	Kirk Snyder	2005-06	923.3
7	Mike Miller	2002-03	923.0
8	Lance Stephenson	2012-13	922.5
9	Chase Budinger	2010-11	921.6
10	Mickael Pietrus	2004-05	920.3

Baseline Basic Stats

MPG	PTS	AST	REB	BLK	STL
28.3	12.1	2.2	4.0	0.3	0.9

Advanced Metrics

USG%	3PTA/FGA	FTA/FGA	TS%	eFG%	3PT%
19.8	0.342	0.235	0.538	0.503	0.364

AST%	TOV%	OREB%	DREB%	STL%	BLK%
11.6	12.1	2.8	11.9	1.7	0.8

PER	ORTG	DRTG	WS/48	VOL
12.56	103.8	109.9	0.061	0.396

- Played in all 82 games for Memphis last season as a rookie, was a regular starter

- Effective in a low volume, complementary role

- Mainly used as a spot-up shooter and cutter, shot almost a league average percentage on threes last season

- Flashed some ability to run off screens, good in a small sample of possessions

- Fairly good on-ball wing defender, more of a stay-at-home guy, decent defensive rebounder

Garrett Temple

	Height	Weight	Cap #	Years Left
	6'6"	190	$8.000M	0

Similar at Age 31

		Season	SIMsc
1	George McCloud	1998-99	928.9
2	Chris Ford	1979-80	921.3
3	Wesley Person	2002-03	921.0
4	Sasha Vujacic	2015-16	920.3
5	Kirk Hinrich	2011-12	919.5
6	Eddie Jones	2002-03	919.3
7	Jaren Jackson	1998-99	918.2
8	Andre Iguodala	2014-15	914.7
9	Johnny Newman	1994-95	914.1
10	Anthony Bowie	1994-95	913.6

Baseline Basic Stats

MPG	PTS	AST	REB	BLK	STL
24.0	8.2	2.1	2.7	0.3	0.9

Advanced Metrics

USG%	3PTA/FGA	FTA/FGA	TS%	eFG%	3PT%
15.5	0.457	0.190	0.543	0.514	0.387

AST%	TOV%	OREB%	DREB%	STL%	BLK%
13.2	13.0	2.1	9.6	1.9	1.1

PER	ORTG	DRTG	WS/48	VOL	
11.37	106.9	109.0	0.077	0.326	

- Steady rotation player for Sacramento, production is still consistent with his career averages
- Mainly a defensive specialist, still a good on-ball wing defender
- Blocks rate is still consistent with his career averages, decent defensive rebounder
- Primarily a low volume spot-up shooter, has been a good three-point shooter in his two seasons in Sacramento
- Shot just over 38% on threes over the last two seasons, historically has been slightly better above the break than in the corners

Chandler Parsons

	Height	Weight	Cap #	Years Left
	6'9"	200	$24.107M	1

Similar at Age 29

		Season	SIMsc
1	Sean Elliott	1997-98	924.3
2	Dorell Wright	2014-15	915.2
3	Matt Bullard	1996-97	912.7
4	Travis Outlaw	2013-14	910.5
5	Ricky Davis	2008-09	906.9
6	Wesley Person	2000-01	904.6
7	Gerald Green	2014-15	904.1
8	Mike Dunleavy, Jr.	2009-10	902.5
9	Tayshaun Prince	2009-10	900.8
10	Kyle Korver	2010-11	899.6

Baseline Basic Stats

MPG	PTS	AST	REB	BLK	STL
22.5	9.2	1.5	2.9	0.3	0.5

Advanced Metrics

USG%	3PTA/FGA	FTA/FGA	TS%	eFG%	3PT%
18.5	0.437	0.155	0.539	0.517	0.373

AST%	TOV%	OREB%	DREB%	STL%	BLK%
12.3	9.1	2.1	12.4	1.2	1.2

PER	ORTG	DRTG	WS/48	VOL
12.87	108.1	110.0	0.095	0.576

- Has missed most of the last two seasons due to knee injuries
- Solid playmaking forward that has been effective as a pick-and-roll ball handler
- Knee injuries have limited his ability to go to the rim, taking fewer shots inside of three feet and drawing fewer fouls
- Has now become almost strictly a jump shooter, shot much better last season than he did in 2016-17
- Shot 37.7% on threes overall and 44.0% from the corner for his career
- Decent on-ball position defender when healthy, injuries may have limited his lateral mobility, still a solid defensive rebounder

Shelvin Mack

	Height	Weight	Cap #	Years Left
	6'3"	215	$1.513M	0

Similar at Age 27

		Season	SIMsc
1	Donald Sloan	2014-15	938.0
2	Beno Udrih	2009-10	918.2
3	Malcolm Delaney	2016-17	915.8
4	O.J. Mayo	2014-15	912.8
5	Fred Jones	2006-07	912.6
6	Kirk Hinrich	2007-08	908.1
7	Shammond Williams	2002-03	907.9
8	Bob Sura	2000-01	906.8
9	Randy Foye	2010-11	906.2
10	Jerryd Bayless	2015-16	906.1

Baseline Basic Stats

MPG	PTS	AST	REB	BLK	STL
25.1	9.3	3.9	2.5	0.1	0.9

Advanced Metrics

USG%	3PTA/FGA	FTA/FGA	TS%	eFG%	3PT%
18.3	0.363	0.218	0.524	0.491	0.351

AST%	TOV%	OREB%	DREB%	STL%	BLK%
25.9	15.5	1.9	10.4	1.8	0.4

PER	ORTG	DRTG	WS/48	VOL
13.21	106.2	109.9	0.076	0.377

- Bounced back to have a solid season with Orlando as their backup point guard after a down year with Utah

- Played a low usage, pass-first role last season, good playmaker, a little turnover prone

- Most effective in spot-up role, shot just above break-even on threes, attacked closeouts by driving hard to the rim to draw shooting fouls

- Can defend both guard spots, aggressive on-ball defender that can occasionally get steals, good defensive rebounding guard

Omri Casspi

	Height	Weight	Cap #	Years Left
	6'9"	225	$2.176M	0

Similar at Age 29

		Season	SIMsc
1	Kevin Restani	1980-81	910.6
2	Chris Wilcox	2011-12	907.5
3	Lawrence Funderburke	1999-00	903.7
4	Alan Henderson	2001-02	903.2
5	Vladimir Radmanovic	2009-10	902.9
6	Antonio McDyess	2003-04	902.7
7	Pete Chilcutt	1997-98	901.9
8	Kenny Gattison	1993-94	901.7
9	David Wood	1993-94	901.6
10	Major Jones	1982-83	901.3

Baseline Basic Stats

MPG	PTS	AST	REB	BLK	STL
16.4	5.8	0.8	3.9	0.4	0.4

Advanced Metrics

USG%	3PTA/FGA	FTA/FGA	TS%	eFG%	3PT%
16.2	0.159	0.302	0.563	0.529	0.338

AST%	TOV%	OREB%	DREB%	STL%	BLK%
8.2	13.7	7.0	19.4	1.3	1.6

PER	ORTG	DRTG	WS/48	VOL
13.20	109.0	107.5	0.101	0.253

- Fringe rotation player for Golden State before he was waived at the end of the season to make room for Quinn Cook
- Played a low volume role, mainly used as a spot-up shooter and cutter
- Over 80% of his shots last season were inside of ten feet, drew fouls at a high rate
- Made 45.5% of his threes last season, but did not take threes with any kind of frequency
- Played with great energy on defense, posted the highest Defensive Rebound and Block Percentages of his career last season
- Decent as a position defender, but was hidden in favorable matchups

Andrew Harrison

	Height	Weight	Cap #	Years Left
	6'6"	213	$1.545M	0

Similar at Age 23

		Season	SIMsc
1	Spencer Dinwiddie	2016-17	933.1
2	George McCloud	1990-91	924.7
3	Mickael Pietrus	2005-06	914.8
4	Bernard Thompson	1985-86	910.2
5	Darrun Hilliard	2016-17	909.8
6	Antoine Wright	2007-08	907.3
7	Kareem Rush	2003-04	907.2
8	Josh Richardson	2016-17	906.8
9	Thabo Sefolosha	2007-08	905.9
10	Casey Jacobsen	2004-05	903.4

Baseline Basic Stats

MPG	PTS	AST	REB	BLK	STL
21.8	8.6	1.9	2.9	0.3	0.7

Advanced Metrics

USG%	3PTA/FGA	FTA/FGA	TS%	eFG%	3PT%
19.2	0.411	0.330	0.528	0.475	0.332

AST%	TOV%	OREB%	DREB%	STL%	BLK%
18.0	13.2	2.7	11.3	1.7	1.4

PER	ORTG	DRTG	WS/48	VOL
12.95	106.1	109.5	0.072	0.379

- Was a starter in more than half of Memphis' games last season, missed the last month due to a wrist injury
- Excelled as a pick-and-roll ball handler, displayed solid playmaking skills, cut his turnover rate
- Good at slashing to the rim to finish shots inside of three feet or draw fouls
- Improved his outside shot, but still shoots threes at just below a break-even percentage
- Has defended both guard spots, but below average at defending either position on the ball
- Lacking in lateral quickness, better at using length to contest shots, solid defensive rebounder

Wayne Selden

	Height	Weight	Cap #	Years Left
	6'5"	230	$1.545M	0

Similar at Age 23

		Season	SIMsc
1	Kelenna Azubuike	2006-07	921.9
2	Orlando Johnson	2012-13	921.4
3	Alan Anderson	2005-06	918.4
4	Carlos Delfino	2005-06	906.9
5	Darrun Hilliard	2016-17	903.0
6	Dion Glover	2001-02	902.2
7	James Anderson	2012-13	901.6
8	Justin Anderson	2016-17	900.8
9	Bubba Wells	1997-98	898.8
10	Kirk Snyder	2006-07	898.0

Baseline Basic Stats

MPG	PTS	AST	REB	BLK	STL
19.3	6.9	1.2	2.8	0.2	0.5

Advanced Metrics

USG%	3PTA/FGA	FTA/FGA	TS%	eFG%	3PT%
17.6	0.482	0.231	0.540	0.513	0.342

AST%	TOV%	OREB%	DREB%	STL%	BLK%
10.8	12.1	2.8	9.7	1.3	0.7

PER	ORTG	DRTG	WS/48	VOL	
10.81	104.1	111.8	0.046	0.468	

- Missed portions of last season due to knee and quadriceps injuries
- Took on a higher usage role when he was healthy
- Improved his playmaking to the point where he was pretty effective as a pick-and-roll ball handler
- Effective in a spot-up role, made 40.2% of his threes last season, flashed some ability to run off screens
- Below average on-ball defender, not too active from a help defense standpoint, may need to be hidden in favorable matchups

Ivan Rabb

	Height	Weight	Cap #	Years Left
	6'10"	220	$1.378M	Team Option

Similar at Age 20

		Season	SIMsc
1	Skal Labissiere	2016-17	920.1
2	Chris Wilcox	2002-03	918.5
3	Cheick Diallo	2016-17	908.6
4	Kevon Looney	2016-17	905.8
5	Serge Ibaka	2009-10	898.3
6	Antonis Fotsis	2001-02	891.7
7	Jackie Butler	2005-06	890.7
8	J.J. Hickson	2008-09	890.7
9	Andray Blatche	2006-07	890.5
10	Samaki Walker	1996-97	881.5

Baseline Basic Stats

MPG	PTS	AST	REB	BLK	STL
19.0	7.2	0.8	4.9	0.8	0.5

Advanced Metrics

USG%	3PTA/FGA	FTA/FGA	TS%	eFG%	3PT%
18.6	0.003	0.251	0.570	0.536	0.074

AST%	TOV%	OREB%	DREB%	STL%	BLK%
8.4	14.8	10.3	19.9	1.3	2.5

PER	ORTG	DRTG	WS/48	VOL	
15.89	110.2	108.0	0.111	0.446	

- Fringe rotation player for Memphis in his rookie season
- Split time between the Grizzlies and the Memphis Hustle of the G-League
- Excelled in limited minutes as low volume rim runner
- Most effective at running the floor in transition and being the screener in pick-and-roll situations
- Flashed some passing skills, but was still a bit turnover prone
- Good rebounder on both ends, can occasionally block shots
- Below average overall defender, not quite strong enough to defend interior players on the ball, can be out of position to make rotations

MarShon Brooks

	Height	Weight	Cap #	Years Left
	6'5"	200	$1.656M	0

Similar at Age 29

	Player	Season	SIMsc
1	Freeman Williams	1985-86	866.2
2	Manu Ginobili	2006-07	862.1
3	Chris Mullin*	1992-93	857.9
4	Aaron McKie	2001-02	851.1
5	Dell Curry	1993-94	851.0
6	Kobe Bryant	2007-08	844.9
7	Ben Gordon	2012-13	844.7
8	Doug Christie	1999-00	844.2
9	David Thompson*	1983-84	843.8
10	Eddie Jones	2000-01	843.8

Baseline Basic Stats

MPG	PTS	AST	REB	BLK	STL
30.3	16.5	3.4	3.7	0.3	1.2

Advanced Metrics

USG%	3PTA/FGA	FTA/FGA	TS%	eFG%	3PT%
26.3	0.299	0.248	0.589	0.547	0.476

AST%	TOV%	OREB%	DREB%	STL%	BLK%
21.4	12.2	4.0	9.2	2.5	1.1

PER	ORTG	DRTG	WS/48	VOL
21.37	113.6	108.1	0.161	0.867

- Joined Memphis for the last month of last season, only played 193 minutes
- Spent the previous three seasons in China
- Extremely effective as a high volume isolation scorer in his short stint with Memphis last season
- Was mainly a jump shooter, above average from mid-range, went 19-for-32 on threes in his seven games last season
- Showed dramatically improved playmaking ability, posted an Assist Percentage well above his career average last season
- Got steals at a much higher rate, still below average as an on-ball wing defender, tended to gamble a bit too much

Newcomers

Jaren Jackson, Jr.

	Height	Weight	Cap #	Years Left
	6'11"	242	$5.915M	1 + 2 TO

Baseline Basic Stats

MPG	PTS	AST	REB	BLK	STL
20.2	7.6	0.7	5.1	1.0	0.5

Advanced Metrics

USG%	3PTA/FGA	FTA/FGA	TS%	eFG%	3PT%
18.0	0.092	0.355	0.544	0.505	0.319

AST%	TOV%	OREB%	DREB%	STL%	BLK%
5.7	13.3	9.4	19.5	1.2	3.9

PER	ORTG	DRTG	WS/48	VOL
14.75	107.0	105.1	0.105	N/A

- Drafted by Memphis in the first round with the 4th overall pick
- Great overall showing in both the Salt Lake City and Las Vegas Summer League
- Effective on offense as a rim runner and stretch big
- Was more of a shooter in Utah, played inside more in Vegas
- Drew fouls at a high rate overall, went 14-for-28 on threes over both Summer Leagues
- Went to the offensive boards much more in Vegas
- Solid defensively throughout, blocked shots at a high rate, decent defensive rebounder, generally displayed sound positioning

Jevon Carter

	Height	Weight	Cap #	Years Left
	6'2"	205	$0.838M	1

Baseline Basic Stats

MPG	PTS	AST	REB	BLK	STL
13.0	4.4	1.8	1.2	0.1	0.5

Advanced Metrics

USG%	3PTA/FGA	FTA/FGA	TS%	eFG%	3PT%
18.6	0.246	0.248	0.475	0.434	0.319

AST%	TOV%	OREB%	DREB%	STL%	BLK%
23.1	16.4	2.6	8.2	2.0	0.4

PER	ORTG	DRTG	WS/48	VOL	
10.49	97.1	110.8	0.020	N/A	

- Drafted by Memphis in the second round with the 32nd overall pick
- Mixed showing in Summer League overall, better in Vegas than he was in Salt Lake City
- Solid as a defender in both Summer Leagues, aggressive on the ball
- Got steals at a high rate, good defensive rebounding point guard
- Good playmaker that rarely turned the ball over
- Scored in volume in Vegas, but didn't shoot efficiently in either Summer League
- Shot below 25% on threes, did not draw many fouls, had difficulties getting to the rim
- Could use some additional seasoning in the G-League to improve his shooting

PHOENIX SUNS

Last Season: 21 – 61, Missed the Playoffs

Offensive Rating: 103.5, 30th in NBA   Defensive Rating: 112.8, 30th in NBA

Primary Executive: Ryan McDonough, General Manager   Head Coach: Igor Kokoskov

Key Roster Changes

Subtractions
Marquese Chriss, trade
Brandon Knight, trade
Jared Dudley, trade
Elfrid Payton, free agency
Alex Len, free agency
Alan Williams, waived

Additions
DeAndre Ayton, draft
Mikal Bridges, draft
Elie Okobo, draft
Ryan Anderson, trade
Richaun Holmes, trade
Trevor Ariza, free agency
Isaiah Canaan, free agency

RAFER Projected Win Total: 28.3

Projected Best Five-Man Unit
1. Devin Booker
2. Trevor Ariza
3. T.J. Warren
4. Ryan Anderson
5. DeAndre Ayton

Other Rotation Players
Josh Jackson
Mikal Bridges
Tyson Chandler
Richaun Holmes

Remaining Roster

- Dragan Bender
- Troy Daniels
- Davon Reed
- Shaquille Harrison
- Isaiah Canaan
- Elie Okobo
- George King, 25, 6'6", 225, Colorado (Two-Way)

Note: Darrell Arthur was acquired in a trade for Jared Dudley, it's been rumored for months that he will be waived, but it still has not happened yet.

Season Forecast

The offseason for the Phoenix Suns got off to a pretty good start when they came away with DeAndre Ayton, Mikal Bridges and Elie Okobo on draft day. From there, the rest of Phoenix's summer got interesting, as they began to push some of the chips in the middle. They re-signed Devin Booker to a five-year maximum extension and then they committed significant cap dollars to bring in veterans like Trevor Ariza and Ryan Anderson to potentially help them improve in the short-term. With the current strength of the Western Conference, it's doubtful that the additions of these veterans will help them enough to make the playoffs. Therefore, it's likely that the Suns will miss the playoffs once again and spend another season as a lottery team.

Last season, the Suns were the worst team in the league on both sides of the ball. The team will take a sizeable hit early on because Booker is recovering from surgery on his right hand. When he comes back, the Suns could improve the most on offense. This is mainly because Anderson and Ariza will give them a couple of additional shooters to spread the floor and give their scorers additional space to operate. Then, the Suns are possibly receiving a talent upgrade and a valuable source of inside scoring if Ayton plays close to his potential. As this book is being written, Phoenix doesn't have an established point guard on the roster, so if the team stays as is, the Suns might have some trouble getting into its offense and generating open looks. However, Devin Booker has flashed enough playmaking skills to suggest that he could be moved to the point, which could give the Suns a more dynamic option than they would have otherwise. On the other hand, if the team keeps Booker as a two-guard, then may very well end up dealing for a veteran point guard if the various online rumors are true. With all of this in mind, Phoenix is getting some upgrades on the offensive end, but the team's improvement will only be incremental because most of the roster is still in a developmental stage and there are a lot of new pieces to integrate at once. Therefore, they aren't going to be a cohesive unit right away, but they could get better as the season goes on. Defensively, it's uncertain if the Suns will be much better than they have been in recent years. After all, Phoenix is still relying on a lot of younger players that are still figuring out NBA rotation schemes and their veterans are either in advanced stages of their career or haven't historically been effective defenders in the past. As a result, the team's defense is probably going to still be in the bottom third of the league, but they might not be as bad as they were last season. This is primarily because there will be some more defensive structure installed under new head coach and former Utah Jazz assistant, Igor Kokoskov. Therefore, they could get a few more stops by steering opponents to the inefficient parts of the floor, but they will still be a bottom third defensive team because their main rotation players haven't established themselves on defense. Despite making a push to be more competitive, the Phoenix Suns will likely be a lottery team once again this season. If their young players show significant improvement as individuals and flash signs of becoming a cohesive unit, then their season could be considered a mild success. Otherwise, if they continue to languish at the bottom of the standings with no direction, then they may need to take a hard look at changing its course as a franchise.

Veterans

Devin Booker

	Height	Weight	Cap #	Years Left
	6'6"	206	$3.314	5

Similar at Age 21

		Season	SIMsc
1	Ben Gordon	2004-05	923.0
2	Klay Thompson	2011-12	918.9
3	Ray Allen*	1996-97	913.4
4	Kobe Bryant	1999-00	905.7
5	Dion Waiters	2012-13	902.4
6	Tyreke Evans	2010-11	898.2
7	O.J. Mayo	2008-09	894.5
8	Gerald Green	2006-07	893.1
9	Timothe Luwawu-Cabarrot	2016-17	889.1
10	Bradley Beal	2014-15	889.0

Baseline Basic Stats

MPG	PTS	AST	REB	BLK	STL
34.8	19.7	3.7	3.9	0.3	1.1

Advanced Metrics

USG%	3PTA/FGA	FTA/FGA	TS%	eFG%	3PT%
27.1	0.220	0.295	0.535	0.482	0.355

AST%	TOV%	OREB%	DREB%	STL%	BLK%
20.7	12.9	2.2	9.9	1.4	0.5

PER	ORTG	DRTG	WS/48	VOL
15.75	104.9	112.7	0.073	0.273

- In and out of the lineup due to injuries to his groin, hip, ribs, triceps and hand

- Had his best season in his third year in the NBA

- Had surgery on his right hand in September, could miss the early part of this coming season

- Excellent outside shooter that moves well without the ball

- Very effective at running off screens, cutting to the basket and spotting up

- Three-Point Percentage has continued to increase, shot 38.3% on threes last season

- Improved with the ball, better playmaker

- Assist Percentage increased significantly, solid pick-and-roll ball handler

- Below average on-ball wing defender, not especially active help defender, does not get steals, solid defensive rebounder

Trevor Ariza

	Height	Weight	Cap #	Years Left
	6'8"	200	$15.000M	0

Similar at Age 32

		Season	SIMsc
1	Kyle Korver	2013-14	910.9
2	James Posey	2008-09	907.4
3	Dan Majerle	1997-98	903.1
4	Nick Anderson	1999-00	890.6
5	Anthony Parker	2007-08	890.6
6	Steve Smith	2001-02	884.4
7	Devean George	2009-10	882.5
8	Raja Bell	2008-09	881.7
9	Shane Battier	2010-11	881.0
10	Dale Ellis	1992-93	879.4

Baseline Basic Stats

MPG	PTS	AST	REB	BLK	STL
29.3	9.9	2.1	4.0	0.3	1.0

Advanced Metrics

USG%	3PTA/FGA	FTA/FGA	TS%	eFG%	3PT%
14.5	0.667	0.165	0.556	0.529	0.361

AST%	TOV%	OREB%	DREB%	STL%	BLK%
9.8	10.0	1.8	13.9	1.9	0.6

PER	ORTG	DRTG	WS/48	VOL	
11.51	110.6	107.8	0.087	0.334	

- Entering his age-33 season, production has been slightly declining for the last three seasons
- Almost strictly a low usage spot-up shooter in Houston last season
- Shot just over the league average last season, historically has been better in the corners
- Excellent transition player that can either spot up for threes or finish plays at the rim
- Solid on-ball wing defender, may be losing a step
- Steal Percentage was at a career low last season, above average defensive rebounder

T.J. Warren

	Height	Weight	Cap #	Years Left
	6'8"	215	$11.750M	3

Similar at Age 24

		Season	SIMsc
1	Al Thornton	2007-08	934.4
2	Luol Deng	2009-10	929.4
3	James Worthy*	1985-86	924.3
4	Travis Outlaw	2008-09	923.8
5	Orlando Woolridge	1983-84	923.6
6	Calbert Cheaney	1995-96	923.4
7	Mike Mitchell	1979-80	922.5
8	Ken Norman	1988-89	921.8
9	Morris Peterson	2001-02	919.7
10	Toby Knight	1979-80	918.6

Baseline Basic Stats

MPG	PTS	AST	REB	BLK	STL
31.0	15.0	1.8	5.1	0.6	1.0

Advanced Metrics

USG%	3PTA/FGA	FTA/FGA	TS%	eFG%	3PT%
22.4	0.149	0.238	0.537	0.501	0.296

AST%	TOV%	OREB%	DREB%	STL%	BLK%
8.6	8.0	5.6	12.1	1.6	1.4

PER	ORTG	DRTG	WS/48	VOL	
16.55	110.1	110.4	0.101	0.344	

- Had a career best season in his fourth year with Phoenix
- Efficient high volume scorer despite not being a three-point shooter or an efficient isolation player
- Good post-up wing that also excels at cutting to the rim
- Good overall mid-range shooter, draws fouls at an increasingly higher rate
- Solid on-ball defending combo forward, better at guarding threes than fours, decent defensive rebounder

Ryan Anderson

	Height	Weight	Cap #	Years Left
	6'10"	240	$20.422M	1

Similar at Age 29

		Season	SIMsc
1	Matt Bonner	2009-10	932.1
2	Anthony Tolliver	2014-15	929.2
3	Terry Mills	1996-97	921.9
4	Pat Garrity	2005-06	911.1
5	Walter McCarty	2003-04	908.6
6	Marvin Williams	2015-16	908.1
7	Walter Herrmann	2008-09	903.0
8	Raef LaFrentz	2005-06	900.8
9	Richard Anderson	1989-90	891.9
10	Jonas Jerebko	2016-17	891.7

Baseline Basic Stats

MPG	PTS	AST	REB	BLK	STL
19.7	7.0	0.9	3.4	0.3	0.4

Advanced Metrics

USG%	3PTA/FGA	FTA/FGA	TS%	eFG%	3PT%
15.5	0.608	0.198	0.570	0.539	0.377

AST%	TOV%	OREB%	DREB%	STL%	BLK%
5.6	8.0	5.1	14.9	0.9	1.0

PER	ORTG	DRTG	WS/48	VOL	
12.29	115.5	109.1	0.109	0.288	

- Production has declined as his role was decreased in his second season with Houston
- Mostly a low volume spot-up shooter at this stage, still consistently good at shooting threes
- Excellent at coming off screens, very good at knocking down trail threes in transition
- Limited defensive value, needs to be hidden in favorable matchups
- Not a rim protector, lacks lateral mobility, decent defensive rebounder

Josh Jackson

	Height	Weight	Cap #	Years Left
	6'8"	207	$6.042M	2 Team Options

Similar at Age 20

		Season	SIMsc
1	Harrison Barnes	2012-13	911.4
2	Rudy Gay	2006-07	908.7
3	Antoine Walker	1996-97	903.2
4	Tony Wroten	2013-14	900.2
5	Sasha Pavlovic	2003-04	900.0
6	Andrew Wiggins	2015-16	899.9
7	Maurice Harkless	2013-14	899.9
8	Paul George	2010-11	898.9
9	Rashard Lewis	1999-00	897.5
10	Tracy McGrady*	1999-00	896.4

Baseline Basic Stats

MPG	PTS	AST	REB	BLK	STL
29.9	14.6	2.1	5.4	0.6	1.1

Advanced Metrics

USG%	3PTA/FGA	FTA/FGA	TS%	eFG%	3PT%
25.7	0.257	0.278	0.499	0.464	0.289

AST%	TOV%	OREB%	DREB%	STL%	BLK%
11.4	11.3	4.8	14.0	2.0	1.1

PER	ORTG	DRTG	WS/48	VOL	
13.98	99.4	109.4	0.050	0.452	

- Almost played starter level minutes in his rookie season with Phoenix, named to the All-Rookie second team
- Scored in volume, but struggled to shoot efficiently, shot below average on all shots outside of three feet
- Effective cutter that could draw fouls, made less than two-thirds of his free throw attempts
- Has the athleticism to be great in transition, plays too wildly, prone to commit turnovers or force bad shots
- Capable of defending multiple positions, undisciplined as on-ball defender right now, foul rate is a bit high
- Active help defender that got steals, can occasionally block shots, solid defensive rebounder

Tyson Chandler

	Height	Weight	Cap #	Years Left
	7'1"	235	$13.585M	0

Similar at Age 35

		Season	SIMsc
1	Dale Davis	2004-05	876.5
2	Billy Paultz	1983-84	867.1
3	Jermaine O'Neal	2013-14	855.3
4	Chris Andersen	2013-14	852.3
5	Caldwell Jones	1985-86	851.7
6	Artis Gilmore*	1984-85	849.5
7	Chris Dudley	2000-01	848.3
8	Bill Cartwright	1992-93	847.8
9	Robert Parish*	1988-89	846.5
10	Hot Rod Williams	1997-98	846.5

Baseline Basic Stats

MPG	PTS	AST	REB	BLK	STL
22.3	7.9	0.9	7.0	0.9	0.4

Advanced Metrics

USG%	3PTA/FGA	FTA/FGA	TS%	eFG%	3PT%
12.3	0.002	0.573	0.639	0.609	0.071

AST%	TOV%	OREB%	DREB%	STL%	BLK%
5.6	20.0	12.3	26.7	0.9	2.4

PER	ORTG	DRTG	WS/48	VOL
14.70	118.4	108.0	0.126	0.525

- Missed most of last season due to a neck injury
- In a decline stage, production down from his career averages
- Decent rim protector, uses length to contest shots, not the shot blocker he once was
- Block rates are significantly lower than his career averages
- Very good rebounder at both ends, struggles to defend on the ball due to limitations in his mobility
- Strictly a low volume rim runner on offense, still good as a roll man and will run the floor in transition

Richaun Holmes

	Height	Weight	Cap #	Years Left
	6'10"	245	$1.601M	0

Similar at Age 24

		Season	SIMsc
1	Kyle O'Quinn	2014-15	940.6
2	Mike Muscala	2015-16	918.1
3	Jordan Hill	2011-12	915.4
4	Henry Sims	2014-15	913.7
5	Terrence Jones	2015-16	909.6
6	D.J. White	2010-11	908.7
7	Jerome Moiso	2002-03	908.2
8	Ed Davis	2013-14	907.5
9	Dwight Powell	2015-16	906.4
10	Paul Millsap	2009-10	906.1

Baseline Basic Stats

MPG	PTS	AST	REB	BLK	STL
21.3	8.4	1.2	5.2	0.8	0.6

Advanced Metrics

USG%	3PTA/FGA	FTA/FGA	TS%	eFG%	3PT%
18.2	0.135	0.256	0.575	0.550	0.310

AST%	TOV%	OREB%	DREB%	STL%	BLK%
10.9	10.6	8.1	20.0	1.5	3.1

PER	ORTG	DRTG	WS/48	VOL	
17.50	115.3	105.1	0.159	0.432	

- Fringe rotation player in each of the last three seasons for Philadelphia
- Most effective as a low volume rim runner that cuts to the rim, shoots almost 75% on shots inside of three feet for his career
- Passing has improved, cut his turnover rate
- Tries to shoot threes, but is very inconsistent, career three-point percentage is well below break-even
- Has some rim protection skills, solid shot blocker, good rebounder on both ends
- Undisciplined position defender, highly foul prone, below average on-ball defender

Dragan Bender

	Height	Weight	Cap #	Years Left
	7'1"	225	$4.661M	Team Option

Similar at Age 20

		Season	SIMsc
1	Domantas Sabonis	2016-17	879.0
2	Donte Greene	2008-09	856.3
3	Trey Lyles	2015-16	849.0
4	Shawne Williams	2006-07	845.6
5	Meyers Leonard	2012-13	843.1
6	Bruno Sundov	2000-01	839.7
7	Yi Jianlian	2007-08	831.9
8	Mario Hezonja	2015-16	831.3
9	Johan Petro	2005-06	828.4
10	Noah Vonleh	2015-16	827.4

Baseline Basic Stats

MPG	PTS	AST	REB	BLK	STL
21.7	8.4	1.1	4.3	0.6	0.5

Advanced Metrics

USG%	3PTA/FGA	FTA/FGA	TS%	eFG%	3PT%
17.1	0.491	0.177	0.515	0.491	0.338

AST%	TOV%	OREB%	DREB%	STL%	BLK%
8.5	13.8	4.2	16.6	0.9	2.0

PER	ORTG	DRTG	WS/48	VOL	
10.53	99.3	111.0	0.029	0.516	

- Improved slightly in his second year, over-extended in a role playing starter level minutes
- Primarily used as a low volume spot-up shooter
- Made threes at just above a league average rate, shot better on corner threes in his two-year career
- Effective as a screener in the pick-and-roll, can roll to the rim or pop out on the perimeter
- No other offensive strengths at this point
- Somewhat able to use his length to protect the rim, blocks shots occasionally
- Middling rebounder, below average on-ball defender, has lapses when making defensive rotations

Troy Daniels

	Height	Weight	Cap #	Years Left
	6'4"	200	$3.259M	0

Similar at Age 26

		Season	SIMsc
1	Gary Neal	2010-11	928.5
2	J.J. Redick	2010-11	916.6
3	Marcus Thornton	2013-14	913.2
4	Anthony Peeler	1995-96	906.6
5	Wayne Ellington	2013-14	904.2
6	Roger Mason	2006-07	895.5
7	Rex Walters	1996-97	895.1
8	Sasha Danilovic	1996-97	895.0
9	O.J. Mayo	2013-14	892.5
10	Sean Kilpatrick	2015-16	892.1

Baseline Basic Stats

MPG	PTS	AST	REB	BLK	STL
23.3	9.7	1.5	2.3	0.1	0.6

Advanced Metrics

USG%	3PTA/FGA	FTA/FGA	TS%	eFG%	3PT%
19.2	0.654	0.128	0.558	0.534	0.404

AST%	TOV%	OREB%	DREB%	STL%	BLK%
8.5	8.8	1.1	9.3	1.1	0.3

PER	ORTG	DRTG	WS/48	VOL	
11.58	106.6	112.5	0.058	0.341	

- Regular rotation player for Phoenix last season, overall production down from his career averages
- Used as a low usage three-point shooter, almost 80% of his shots were threes
- Good at running off screens and making spot-up jumpers, shot 40% on threes last season
- Played decent position defense, was hidden in favorable matchups against opposing second units

Davon Reed

	Height	Weight	Cap #	Years Left
	6'5"	208	$1.378M	2

Similar at Age 22

		Season	SIMsc
1	Iman Shumpert	2012-13	920.9
2	Jodie Meeks	2009-10	917.9
3	Daequan Cook	2009-10	916.6
4	Devyn Marble	2014-15	907.7
5	Charles O'Bannon	1997-98	907.4
6	Adam Harrington	2002-03	906.9
7	Chris Robinson	1996-97	903.8
8	Malcolm Lee	2012-13	903.4
9	Norman Powell	2015-16	902.2
10	Joe Crawford	2008-09	900.5

Baseline Basic Stats

MPG	PTS	AST	REB	BLK	STL
21.8	8.2	1.4	3.9	0.2	0.7

Advanced Metrics

USG%	3PTA/FGA	FTA/FGA	TS%	eFG%	3PT%
17.3	0.430	0.237	0.494	0.461	0.393

AST%	TOV%	OREB%	DREB%	STL%	BLK%
8.7	12.7	3.3	17.7	1.9	0.6

PER	ORTG	DRTG	WS/48	VOL
10.04	96.8	109.3	0.037	0.795

- Missed the first half of his rookie season while recovering from surgery to repair a torn meniscus in his left knee
- Split time between Phoenix and Northern Arizona in the G-League
- Mainly a low volume spot-up shooter in the NBA
- Struggled to shoot efficiently, made less than 30% of his threes
- Flashed potential as an on-ball defending wing
- Solid on-ball defender in a small sample of minutes
- Active help defender that got steals at a solid rate, good defensive rebounder

Shaquille Harrison

	Height	Weight	Cap #	Years Left
	6'4"	190	$1.378M	0

Similar at Age 24

		Season	SIMsc
1	Delon Wright	2016-17	923.3
2	Jon Barry	1993-94	914.8
3	Antonio Daniels	1999-00	913.0
4	Antonio Burks	2004-05	910.2
5	Lance Blanks	1990-91	909.2
6	Morlon Wiley	1990-91	906.5
7	Markel Brown	2015-16	906.4
8	Lorenzo Brown	2014-15	902.7
9	Ronnie Price	2007-08	901.5
10	Jeff McInnis	1998-99	901.5

Baseline Basic Stats

MPG	PTS	AST	REB	BLK	STL
16.4	5.3	2.2	1.7	0.2	0.7

Advanced Metrics

USG%	3PTA/FGA	FTA/FGA	TS%	eFG%	3PT%
16.5	0.270	0.262	0.534	0.496	0.306

AST%	TOV%	OREB%	DREB%	STL%	BLK%
21.9	14.8	2.7	12.3	2.4	1.1

PER	ORTG	DRTG	WS/48	VOL
13.84	108.4	109.0	0.093	0.365

- Started the season with Northern Arizona in the G-League
- Cracked Phoenix's rotation after being called up in the second half of last season
- Penetrating combo guard, effective at driving to finish around the rim or draw fouls
- Effective in a small sample of isolation possessions
- Decent playmaker that avoids turnovers
- Not an effective outside shooter, struggled to make shots outside of three feet
- Aggressive on-ball defender that can defend both guard spots
- Active help defender that got steals, blocked shots and grabbed defensive rebounds at a high rate

Isaiah Canaan

	Height	Weight	Cap #	Years Left
	6'0"	188	$1.513M	0

Similar at Age 26

		Season	SIMsc
1	Patty Mills	2014-15	937.5
2	Shammond Williams	2001-02	923.5
3	Luther Head	2008-09	920.9
4	Chris Whitney	1997-98	920.4
5	Eddie Gill	2004-05	916.0
6	Chris Quinn	2009-10	910.4
7	Brandon Jennings	2015-16	908.7
8	Derek Fisher	2000-01	908.2
9	A.J. Price	2012-13	907.3
10	D.J. Augustin	2013-14	907.1

Baseline Basic Stats

MPG	PTS	AST	REB	BLK	STL
20.5	7.9	2.8	1.8	0.1	0.7

Advanced Metrics

USG%	3PTA/FGA	FTA/FGA	TS%	eFG%	3PT%
18.3	0.496	0.254	0.535	0.482	0.353

AST%	TOV%	OREB%	DREB%	STL%	BLK%
20.5	12.9	1.3	9.0	1.7	0.2

PER	ORTG	DRTG	WS/48	VOL
12.58	107.2	111.5	0.078	0.516

- Spent most of the first half of last season with Phoenix before being waived in February
- Improved his playmaking skills, posted the highest Assist Percentage of his career
- Decent penetrator that could get high percentage shots at the rim and draw fouls
- Limited effectiveness as a spot-up shooter, took a lot of threes, but only made them at a break-even rate
- Decent position defender if hidden in favorable matchups, solid defensive rebounder for his size

Newcomers

DeAndre Ayton

	Height	Weight	Cap #	Years Left
	7'1"	250	$8.165M	1 + 2 TO

Baseline Basic Stats

MPG	PTS	AST	REB	BLK	STL
29.5	13.5	1.5	8.1	1.1	0.6

Advanced Metrics

USG%	3PTA/FGA	FTA/FGA	TS%	eFG%	3PT%
21.8	0.088	0.322	0.553	0.515	0.344

AST%	TOV%	OREB%	DREB%	STL%	BLK%
9.1	13.2	9.8	22.1	1.0	2.9

PER	ORTG	DRTG	WS/48	VOL
17.55	108.2	106.4	0.114	N/A

- Drafted by Phoenix in the first round with the 1st overall pick
- Strong performance at Summer League
- Efficient post-up player that shot a high percentage from inside, shot almost 60% from the field
- Drew fouls at a high rate, very active on the offensive glass
- Highly turnover prone, did not get an assist at Summer League
- Effective interior defender that ate up space inside, very good rebounder
- Provided solid rim protection by using his length to block shots
- Mobility may be a concern, may not have enough lateral quickness to be effective as an on-ball defender

Mikal Bridges

	Height	Weight	Cap #	Years Left
	6'7"	210	$3.553M	1 + 2 TO

Baseline Basic Stats

MPG	PTS	AST	REB	BLK	STL
23.8	9.9	1.7	3.1	0.4	0.9

Advanced Metrics

USG%	3PTA/FGA	FTA/FGA	TS%	eFG%	3PT%
20.6	0.251	0.242	0.516	0.478	0.339

AST%	TOV%	OREB%	DREB%	STL%	BLK%
12.3	12.4	4.2	10.7	1.9	1.2

PER	ORTG	DRTG	WS/48	VOL
13.33	102.3	107.8	0.053	N/A

- Drafted by Philadelphia with the 10th overall pick, then traded to Phoenix
- Solid showing in Summer League
- Played a lower volume role, used mainly as a spot-up shooter, was 7-for-16 on threes
- Didn't do much else besides catch and shoot, turned the ball over at a fairly high rate
- Displayed great defensive potential, solid as an on-ball wing defender
- Very active in help defense, got steals and blocks at a high rate, was solid on the defensive boards

Elie Okobo

		Height	Weight	Cap #	Years Left
		6'2"	180	$1.238M	2 + TO

Baseline Basic Stats

MPG	PTS	AST	REB	BLK	STL
19.9	7.9	2.7	1.9	0.1	0.7

Advanced Metrics

USG%	3PTA/FGA	FTA/FGA	TS%	eFG%	3PT%
19.3	0.484	0.219	0.540	0.508	0.358

AST%	TOV%	OREB%	DREB%	STL%	BLK%
22.8	15.6	1.6	8.6	1.7	0.5

PER	ORTG	DRTG	WS/48	VOL	
13.11	100.5	104.1	0.086	0.513	

- Drafted by Phoenix in the second round with the 31st overall pick
- Played last season for Pau-Orthez in France, projection uses translated LNB Pro A stats
- Struggled in Summer League, playing time was limited
- Displayed good passing skills, but turned the ball over at a high rate
- Really had difficulty shooting efficiently in a low volume role, shot less than 25% from the field, only 1-for-6 on threes
- Solid on-ball defender, played more of a stay-at-home style, good defensive rebounding point guard

SACRAMENTO KINGS

Last Season: 27 – 55, Missed the Playoffs

Offensive Rating: 103.7, 29th in NBA   Defensive Rating: 111.1, 28th in NBA

Primary Executive: Vlade Divac, Vice President of Basketball Operations and General Manager

Head Coach: Dave Joerger

Key Roster Changes

Subtractions	Additions
Garrett Temple, trade	Marvin Bagley III, draft
Vince Carter, free agency	Ben McLemore, trade
Bruno Caboclo, free agency	Deyonta Davis, trade
Nigel Hayes, waived	Nemanja Bjelica, free agency
	Yogi Ferrell, free agency

RAFER Projected Win Total: 20.0

Projected Best Five-Man Unit	Other Rotation Players
1. Yogi Ferrell	De'Aaron Fox
2. Bogdan Bogdanovic	Buddy Hield
3. Justin Jackson	Marvin Bagley III
4. Nemanja Bjelica	Zach Randolph
5. Willie Cauley-Stein	

Remaining Roster

- Ben McLemore
- Frank Mason
- Kosta Koufos
- Skal Labissiere
- Deyonta Davis
- Harry Giles
- Iman Shumpert
- Wenyen Gabriel, 21, 6'9", 205, Kentucky (Two-Way)
- Jamel Artis, 26, 6'7", 213, Pittsburgh (Exhibit 10)

Season Forecast

The Sacramento Kings appear to be fully committed to the rebuilding process because they didn't make any major moves this summer. Instead, they have stuck with their core of young players like Bogdan Bogdanovic, Buddy Hield and De'Aaron Fox and the Kings seem to be content with giving them ample opportunity to develop. They did take Marvin Bagley III with the second overall pick in this past draft to give them another young player to possibly build around. From there, they filled the remaining holes in their roster by signing Nemanja Bjelica and Yogi Ferrell to fairly reasonable contracts. Even so, Sacramento will likely finish as one of the worst teams in the league, but not due to a lack of talent. It is mainly because of the strength of the Western Conference gives them a much tougher schedule than a similarly talented team in the East like Orlando or Atlanta. Therefore, the Kings will probably end up with more losses than their actual talent level as a result.

The Kings finished near the bottom of the league on both sides of the ball last season. With the roster that they currently have now, they may not be much better on either side, but they might be incrementally improved on offense. This is mainly because Sacramento brought a couple of extra shooters in Bjelica and Ferrell to give their offense some additional spacing. Additionally, their main young players like Fox, Hield and Justin Jackson are still in the developmental stages of their careers, so the Kings could get some internal growth. However, Zach Randolph's presence is holding Sacramento back because head coach, Dave Joerger is employing a slow-down, post-oriented attack to accommodate an aging Randolph rather than using a faster, more wide-open offense to play to the strengths of the team's young core. The team's best hope is that Randolph plays well enough in the first half of the season to entice a contender to deal for him around the trade deadline. Otherwise, they may just have to buy him out to allow some of their younger big men like Bagley, Skal Labissiere and Harry Giles to get more playing time to further their development. Defensively, they are still very far away from being at least average because most of the roster consists of still developing young players that haven't quite figured out NBA rotation schemes. Additionally, a lot of the team's primary young players didn't come into the league with great defensive reputations, so the learning curve on defense for the Kings is going to be much steeper than it will be on offense. Finally, the veteran players that they have right now are more offensive minded, so they aren't likely to help matters very much on the defensive side of the ball. Overall, Sacramento is going through its seemingly perpetual rebuild and they will most likely finish near the bottom of the standings once again this coming season. There is still some hope for the Kings because they do have some interesting young players on their roster like Bogdanovic, Hield, Fox, Jackson and Bagley. If those players continue to improve throughout the season and show signs of becoming a coherent unit, then the season could be considered a mild success. On the other hand, if there are signs of stunted growth, Sacramento should look into making changes to either the front office or the coaching staff to find a system that maximizes the existing talent on the roster in a more optimal way.

Veterans

Bogdan Bogdanovic

	Height	Weight	Cap #	Years Left
	6'6"	205	$9.000M	1

<u>Similar at Age</u> **25**

		Season	SIMsc
1	George McCloud	1992-93	939.8
2	Gordan Giricek	2002-03	939.2
3	Wesley Person	1996-97	933.2
4	Kyle Korver	2006-07	928.7
5	Fred Jones	2004-05	928.0
6	Bobby Simmons	2005-06	926.8
7	Lewis Lloyd	1984-85	924.7
8	Allan Houston	1996-97	924.3
9	O.J. Mayo	2012-13	923.5
10	Terrence Ross	2016-17	923.1

Baseline Basic Stats

MPG	PTS	AST	REB	BLK	STL
29.5	13.0	2.7	3.4	0.3	0.9

Advanced Metrics

USG%	3PTA/FGA	FTA/FGA	TS%	eFG%	3PT%
20.1	0.419	0.194	0.551	0.518	0.381

AST%	TOV%	OREB%	DREB%	STL%	BLK%
16.9	12.5	2.0	10.9	1.7	0.8

PER	ORTG	DRTG	WS/48	VOL
14.01	107.4	110.7	0.078	0.372

- Made the All-Rookie second team last season after spending the previous three seasons with Fenerbahce in Turkey
- Mainly a lower volume spot-up shooter, made 39.2% of his threes overall and 47.5% of his corner threes last season
- Solid playmaking skills made him effective with the ball in his hands
- Above average in isolations and as a pick-and-roll ball handler
- Decent on-ball wing defender if hidden in favorable matchups, solid on the defensive boards

Willie Cauley-Stein

	Height	Weight	Cap #	Years Left
	7'0"	240	$4.697M	0

Similar at Age 24

		Season	SIMsc
1	Cody Zeller	2016-17	945.2
2	Patrick Ewing*	1986-87	924.0
3	Derrick Favors	2015-16	919.6
4	James Edwards	1979-80	915.1
5	Dwight Powell	2015-16	913.4
6	Steve Stipanovich	1984-85	912.0
7	Kelly Olynyk	2015-16	910.6
8	Spencer Hawes	2012-13	909.4
9	Dave Corzine	1980-81	908.6
10	Melvin Turpin	1984-85	908.2

Baseline Basic Stats

MPG	PTS	AST	REB	BLK	STL
27.0	12.1	1.7	7.0	1.1	0.8

Advanced Metrics

USG%	3PTA/FGA	FTA/FGA	TS%	eFG%	3PT%
20.2	0.029	0.330	0.553	0.518	0.230

AST%	TOV%	OREB%	DREB%	STL%	BLK%
11.5	12.1	7.8	20.9	1.6	2.9

PER	ORTG	DRTG	WS/48	VOL	
17.35	110.0	106.8	0.119	0.418	

- First full season as a starter for Sacramento, had the best season of his three-year career
- Usage has increased because he's being used more as a post-up player, not especially effective in these situations, scoring efficiency hurt as a result
- More effective at running the floor to score in transition, passing skills have continued to improve
- Decent rim protector that can block shots, Defensive Rebound Percentage has increased in each of his three seasons
- Struggles to defend on the ball, not disciplined enough to defend in space on the perimeter, not strong enough to handle interior players

De'Aaron Fox

	Height	Weight	Cap #	Years Left
	6'3"	170	$5.471M	2 Team Options

Similar at Age	**20**		
	Season	SIMsc	
1 Monta Ellis	2005-06	920.8	
2 Jrue Holiday	2010-11	919.4	
3 Tony Parker	2002-03	911.4	
4 Mike Conley	2007-08	908.9	
5 Brandon Jennings	2009-10	908.5	
6 Zach LaVine	2015-16	908.3	
7 Sebastian Telfair	2005-06	905.6	
8 Brandon Knight	2011-12	904.7	
9 Dejounte Murray	2016-17	902.3	
10 Stephon Marbury	1997-98	901.3	

Baseline Basic Stats

MPG	PTS	AST	REB	BLK	STL
29.9	14.1	4.7	3.2	0.2	1.2

Advanced Metrics

USG%	3PTA/FGA	FTA/FGA	TS%	eFG%	3PT%
24.2	0.216	0.250	0.513	0.473	0.323

AST%	TOV%	OREB%	DREB%	STL%	BLK%
25.5	14.5	2.2	9.4	1.9	0.6

PER	ORTG	DRTG	WS/48	VOL
14.61	102.1	110.9	0.051	0.216

- Played starter level minutes in his rookie season with Sacramento
- Good at using his speed to get to the rim in isolation situations
- Made almost 65% of his shots inside of three feet and drew fouls at a solid rate
- Showed decent playmaking skills, but was a little turnover prone
- Struggled to shoot efficiently, shot just below 35% from mid-range, below 31% on threes
- Below average on-ball defender, can get overpowered to the rim on drives
- Gambles a bit too much and can be out of position, good defensive rebounding point guard

Buddy Hield

	Height	Weight	Cap #	Years Left
	6'4"	214	$3.834M	Team Option

Similar at Age **24**

		Season	SIMsc
1	Victor Oladipo	2016-17	948.7
2	O.J. Mayo	2011-12	929.7
3	Marcus Thornton	2011-12	929.3
4	Anthony Morrow	2009-10	929.0
5	Tim Hardaway, Jr.	2016-17	915.2
6	Shannon Brown	2009-10	913.9
7	James Anderson	2013-14	913.6
8	Voshon Lenard	1997-98	912.5
9	Randy Foye	2007-08	910.7
10	Wesley Matthews	2010-11	910.6

Baseline Basic Stats

MPG	PTS	AST	REB	BLK	STL
26.5	12.6	2.3	2.8	0.2	0.9

Advanced Metrics

USG%	3PTA/FGA	FTA/FGA	TS%	eFG%	3PT%
22.9	0.440	0.152	0.543	0.514	0.397

AST%	TOV%	OREB%	DREB%	STL%	BLK%
13.8	10.9	2.4	12.2	1.7	0.7

PER	ORTG	DRTG	WS/48	VOL	
14.69	104.5	110.4	0.073	0.305	

- Greatly improved in his second season, very durable guard that has only missed two games in the last two seasons
- Effective in a sixth man role for Sacramento, excelled off the ball by running off screens and making spot-up jumpers
- Made 43.1% of his threes overall and 53.7% of his corner threes last season
- Ball handling and passing have improved, Assist Percentage increased slightly
- Was above average in limited isolation possessions
- Active help defender that increased his Defensive Rebound, Steal and Block Percentages
- Below average as an on-ball defender, not quite quick enough to contain smaller guards, a little undersized to handle taller wing players

Zach Randolph

	Height	Weight	Cap #	Years Left
	6'9"	253	$11.692M	0

Similar at Age 36

		Season	SIMsc
1	Karl Malone*	1999-00	884.9
2	Dan Issel*	1984-85	877.1
3	Charles Barkley*	1999-00	869.6
4	Juwan Howard	2009-10	867.4
5	Luis Scola	2016-17	858.3
6	Tim Duncan	2012-13	857.8
7	Kevin Garnett	2012-13	849.5
8	Bill Laimbeer	1993-94	848.6
9	Dirk Nowitzki	2014-15	847.1
10	Terry Cummings	1997-98	845.1

Baseline Basic Stats

MPG	PTS	AST	REB	BLK	STL
26.1	13.8	2.0	7.1	0.5	0.8

Advanced Metrics

USG%	3PTA/FGA	FTA/FGA	TS%	eFG%	3PT%
26.4	0.100	0.222	0.517	0.480	0.323

AST%	TOV%	OREB%	DREB%	STL%	BLK%
13.1	11.4	7.8	24.3	1.4	1.1

PER	ORTG	DRTG	WS/48	VOL
17.54	102.2	105.9	0.086	0.587

- Entering his age-37 season, production down from his career averages
- Starting to play further away from the basket, getting to the rim less often and drawing fewer fouls
- Shooting threes in greater frequency, shot an above break-even percentage on threes last season, good mid-range shooter
- Less effective on post-ups, has improved his passing
- Posted the highest Assist Percentage of his career last season
- Limited defensively due to his age and lack of mobility, has difficulty defending on the ball
- Not a rim protector, does not block shots, still a good defensive rebounder

Justin Jackson

	Height	Weight	Cap #	Years Left
	6'8"	200	$2.808M	2 Team Options

Similar at Age 22

		Season	SIMsc
1	Tony Snell	2013-14	940.4
2	Hollis Thompson	2013-14	925.6
3	Paul Zipser	2016-17	919.8
4	Harrison Barnes	2014-15	917.1
5	Nicolas Batum	2010-11	914.3
6	Caris LeVert	2016-17	910.9
7	Reggie Bullock	2013-14	906.6
8	Otto Porter	2015-16	904.2
9	Maurice Harkless	2015-16	903.3
10	Josh Richardson	2015-16	902.3

Baseline Basic Stats

MPG	PTS	AST	REB	BLK	STL
26.2	10.0	1.4	3.8	0.4	0.8

Advanced Metrics

USG%	3PTA/FGA	FTA/FGA	TS%	eFG%	3PT%
16.4	0.432	0.129	0.544	0.524	0.354

AST%	TOV%	OREB%	DREB%	STL%	BLK%
8.3	8.4	2.3	12.7	1.2	1.0

PER	ORTG	DRTG	WS/48	VOL	
11.59	107.0	111.9	0.066	0.452	

- Regular part of Sacramento's rotation, started a majority of the games that he played
- Primarily used as a low usage spot-up shooter, good from mid-range
- Below break-even on threes, better in the corners, effective as a cutter
- Solid in transition by either finishing plays at the rim or spotting up for trail threes
- Solid on-ball defending combo forward, more of a stay-at-home position defender, good defensive rebounder

Yogi Ferrell

	Height	Weight	Cap #	Years Left
	6'0"	180	$3.023M	1

Similar at Age **24**

		Season	SIMsc
1	Isaiah Canaan	2015-16	936.7
2	Daniel Gibson	2010-11	931.4
3	Chris Duhon	2006-07	927.0
4	George Hill	2010-11	926.7
5	J.J. Barea	2008-09	925.4
6	Chris Quinn	2007-08	923.4
7	Kyle Lowry	2010-11	920.3
8	Jordan Farmar	2010-11	917.2
9	Toney Douglas	2010-11	916.3
10	Avery Bradley	2014-15	915.2

Baseline Basic Stats

MPG	PTS	AST	REB	BLK	STL
23.5	9.1	3.1	2.1	0.1	0.7

Advanced Metrics

USG%	3PTA/FGA	FTA/FGA	TS%	eFG%	3PT%
18.2	0.460	0.198	0.539	0.503	0.370

AST%	TOV%	OREB%	DREB%	STL%	BLK%
20.3	11.5	1.6	9.7	1.6	0.5

PER	ORTG	DRTG	WS/48	VOL	
13.11	109.0	110.8	0.084	0.367	

- Played a starter's workload in Dallas, production down from the season before
- Effective in a lower volume role, often shared the court with Dennis Smith, Jr.
- Did not have as many touches as much as he did in 2016-17
- Assist Percentage dropped significantly as a result, cut his turnover rate
- Still good in isolation situations and as a pick-and-roll ball handler, did not get to the rim as frequently
- Solid spot-up shooter that made over 37% of his threes, could also run off screens
- Fairly good at defending both guard spots, better against point guards due to his small size
- More of a position defender, good rebounder for his size

Nemanja Bjelica

	Height	Weight	Cap #	Years Left
	6'10"	240	$6.508M	2

Similar at Age **29**

		Season	SIMsc
1	Matt Bonner	2009-10	948.4
2	Richard Anderson	1989-90	947.0
3	Jonas Jerebko	2016-17	944.3
4	Pete Chilcutt	1997-98	938.0
5	Pat Garrity	2005-06	928.1
6	Scott Padgett	2005-06	924.3
7	Raef LaFrentz	2005-06	920.5
8	Vladimir Radmanovic	2009-10	919.1
9	Tim Thomas	2006-07	918.7
10	Anthony Tolliver	2014-15	916.0

Baseline Basic Stats

MPG	PTS	AST	REB	BLK	STL
17.5	5.6	1.0	3.3	0.3	0.5

Advanced Metrics

USG%	3PTA/FGA	FTA/FGA	TS%	eFG%	3PT%
14.8	0.478	0.147	0.542	0.520	0.379

AST%	TOV%	OREB%	DREB%	STL%	BLK%
8.8	11.7	5.1	17.5	1.5	1.2

PER	ORTG	DRTG	WS/48	VOL	
11.53	108.4	107.9	0.082	0.255	

- Regular rotation player for Minnesota for the last three seasons, had his best season in his third year
- Effective in a low usage role, Turnover Percentage has decreased for the third straight year
- Good in spot-up situations, made 41.5% of his threes last season
- Also solid as a cutter and screener in pick-and-roll situations
- Decent position defending combo forward, somewhat lacking in quickness, solid defensive rebounder

Ben McLemore

	Height	Weight	Cap #	Years Left
	6'5"	195	$5.460M	0

Similar at Age 24

		Season	SIMsc
1	Elliot Williams	2013-14	927.4
2	Marco Belinelli	2010-11	926.4
3	Rex Walters	1994-95	926.4
4	Trajan Langdon	2000-01	926.4
5	Jeff Martin	1990-91	924.4
6	Markel Brown	2015-16	924.0
7	Terrence Ross	2015-16	922.9
8	Shannon Brown	2009-10	922.7
9	Eric Washington	1998-99	922.4
10	Lucious Harris	1994-95	922.2

Baseline Basic Stats

MPG	PTS	AST	REB	BLK	STL
22.3	9.2	1.6	2.4	0.2	0.7

Advanced Metrics

USG%	3PTA/FGA	FTA/FGA	TS%	eFG%	3PT%
19.5	0.411	0.205	0.536	0.501	0.363

AST%	TOV%	OREB%	DREB%	STL%	BLK%
10.4	11.7	2.7	10.8	1.5	0.8

PER	ORTG	DRTG	WS/48	VOL	
11.64	103.8	111.4	0.049	0.411	

- Missed the first month of last season while recovering from surgery to repair a fractured right foot
- Mainly utilized as a stationary low volume spot-up shooter
- Career 35.1% three-point shooter overall, much better in the corners
- Hasn't shown many other offensive skills
- Decent on-ball defending wing, posted the highest Steal Percentage of his career, solid defensive rebounder

Frank Mason III

	Height	Weight	Cap #	Years Left
	6'0"	189	$1.378M	1

Similar at Age 23

		Season	SIMsc
1	Yogi Ferrell	2016-17	922.6
2	Mo Williams	2005-06	919.0
3	J.J. Barea	2007-08	913.6
4	Trey Burke	2015-16	913.6
5	Jameer Nelson	2005-06	912.2
6	Eddie House	2001-02	911.2
7	Leon Wood	1985-86	910.9
8	Isaiah Canaan	2014-15	909.6
9	John Bagley	1983-84	908.0
10	Gerald Fitch	2005-06	906.6

Baseline Basic Stats

MPG	PTS	AST	REB	BLK	STL
24.8	10.4	4.1	2.4	0.1	0.9

Advanced Metrics

USG%	3PTA/FGA	FTA/FGA	TS%	eFG%	3PT%
21.4	0.271	0.286	0.524	0.472	0.382

AST%	TOV%	OREB%	DREB%	STL%	BLK%
26.3	14.2	2.6	10.9	1.8	0.7

PER	ORTG	DRTG	WS/48	VOL
15.12	106.8	111.0	0.080	0.486

- Missed a month of his rookie season due to a bruised right heel
- Decent playmaker that could avoid turnovers, struggled to shoot efficiently inside the three-point arc
- Limited effectiveness as a pick-and-roll ball handler, could not finish at the rim, shot below 50% on shots inside of three feet
- Good in spot-up situations, made threes at a league average rate
- Fairly decent on-ball defender, will aggressively pressure his man and contest shots
- Can occasionally get steals, good rebounder for his size
- Bigger guards can shoot over him due to his small size

Kosta Koufos

	Height	Weight	Cap #	Years Left
	7'0"	265	$8.740M	0

Similar at Age 28

		Season	SIMsc
1	Kwame Brown	2010-11	894.1
2	Nick Collison	2008-09	887.6
3	Kelvin Cato	2002-03	887.1
4	Blair Rasmussen	1990-91	886.0
5	Felton Spencer	1995-96	885.8
6	Paul Mokeski	1984-85	884.3
7	Omer Asik	2014-15	884.3
8	Scot Pollard	2003-04	883.8
9	Rasho Nesterovic	2004-05	883.2
10	Andrew Bogut	2012-13	882.7

Baseline Basic Stats

MPG	PTS	AST	REB	BLK	STL
20.1	6.4	0.8	5.4	0.7	0.4

Advanced Metrics

USG%	3PTA/FGA	FTA/FGA	TS%	eFG%	3PT%
15.3	0.025	0.209	0.542	0.529	0.182

AST%	TOV%	OREB%	DREB%	STL%	BLK%
7.5	12.2	10.3	22.4	1.3	2.5

PER	ORTG	DRTG	WS/48	VOL
14.31	110.0	107.4	0.097	0.536

- Regular part of Sacramento's rotation for the last three years, had a career best season in 2017-18
- Effective on offense due to above average post-up skills, decent as a rim runner
- Consistently grabs offensive rebounds at a high rate
- Improved as a passer, posted the highest Assist Percentage of his career last season
- Uses his size to clog the lane, good defensive rebounder
- Lacks the necessary mobility to effectively defend on the ball, shot blocking rates have declined for the last five seasons

Skal Labissiere

	Height	Weight	Cap #	Years Left
	6'11"	225	$1.545M	Team Option

Similar at Age 21

		Season	SIMsc
1	Tony Battie	1997-98	923.1
2	Chris Wilcox	2003-04	914.0
3	Shawne Williams	2007-08	913.0
4	Rasheed Wallace	1995-96	911.3
5	Donte Greene	2009-10	911.2
6	Lorenzen Wright	1996-97	910.5
7	Al Harrington	2001-02	909.7
8	Drew Gooden	2002-03	906.1
9	Marreese Speights	2008-09	905.7
10	Jason Smith	2007-08	905.2

Baseline Basic Stats

MPG	PTS	AST	REB	BLK	STL
23.9	10.5	1.2	5.7	0.9	0.6

Advanced Metrics

USG%	3PTA/FGA	FTA/FGA	TS%	eFG%	3PT%
20.4	0.070	0.291	0.524	0.484	0.324

AST%	TOV%	OREB%	DREB%	STL%	BLK%
9.1	12.6	8.3	18.8	1.3	2.4

PER	ORTG	DRTG	WS/48	VOL	
14.72	104.8	108.3	0.080	0.317	

- Cracked Sacramento's regular rotation for the first time in his two-year career
- Missed a month due to a strained left shoulder
- Used more as a post-up player, post-up skills still unpolished, less efficient on offense as a result
- Better as a rim runner, flashed some stretch potential by making 35.3% of his threes in a small sample of attempts
- Decent rim protector due to his solid shot blocking skills, still a work-in-progress as a position defender
- Sacrifices position to go for blocks, decent defensive rebounder but could be better, below average as an on-ball defender

Deyonta Davis

	Height	Weight	Cap #	Years Left
	6'11"	237	$1.545M	0

Similar at Age 21

		Season	SIMsc
1	Jermaine O'Neal	1999-00	914.5
2	Sean Williams	2007-08	914.1
3	Jason Smith	2007-08	907.6
4	Cedric Simmons	2006-07	905.0
5	LaMarcus Aldridge	2006-07	904.5
6	Andris Biedrins	2007-08	902.3
7	Steven Hunter	2002-03	901.6
8	JaVale McGee	2008-09	899.6
9	Alex Len	2014-15	894.4
10	Ed Davis	2010-11	894.2

Baseline Basic Stats

MPG	PTS	AST	REB	BLK	STL
21.0	7.4	0.8	5.8	1.2	0.5

Advanced Metrics

USG%	3PTA/FGA	FTA/FGA	TS%	eFG%	3PT%
15.7	0.007	0.317	0.551	0.529	0.100

AST%	TOV%	OREB%	DREB%	STL%	BLK%
7.1	12.9	9.3	20.0	1.1	3.8

PER	ORTG	DRTG	WS/48	VOL
14.28	110.4	106.3	0.111	0.500

- Fringe rotation player for Memphis last season, played 943 minutes, had the best season of his two-year career
- Mainly a low usage, high efficiency, rim runner that excelled as a roll man, could also run the floor in transition
- Showed solid post-up skills in a limited sample of possessions
- Improved as a decision maker, assist rate increased, turnovers decreased
- Decent rim protection skills, uses length and athleticism to contest shots, good rebounder and shot blocker
- Below average position defender, still undisciplined, highly foul prone, has lapses when making defensive rotations

Iman Shumpert

	Height	Weight	Cap #	Years Left
	6'5"	212	$11.011	0

Similar at Age 27

		Season	SIMsc
1	Thabo Sefolosha	2011-12	943.3
2	Chase Budinger	2015-16	928.7
3	Richie Frahm	2004-05	927.0
4	Sam Young	2012-13	921.4
5	Michael Curry	1995-96	920.9
6	Greg Buckner	2003-04	920.0
7	Greg Minor	1998-99	914.4
8	Quinton Ross	2008-09	911.6
9	Fred Jones	2006-07	910.9
10	Royal Ivey	2008-09	908.6

Baseline Basic Stats

MPG	PTS	AST	REB	BLK	STL
19.3	5.9	1.2	2.3	0.2	0.6

Advanced Metrics

USG%	3PTA/FGA	FTA/FGA	TS%	eFG%	3PT%
14.2	0.517	0.231	0.530	0.496	0.341

AST%	TOV%	OREB%	DREB%	STL%	BLK%
9.1	14.2	2.7	11.6	1.6	0.9

PER	ORTG	DRTG	WS/48	VOL	
9.48	103.4	110.2	0.059	0.495	

- Missed most of last season due to left knee surgery and plantar fasciitis in his left foot
- Mainly a low volume spot-up shooter when healthy
- Around a break-even three-point shooter for his career, a little better in the corners, percentages tend to fluctuate from year-to-year
- Solid on-ball wing defender when healthy, good defensive rebounder
- Steal Percentage has been declining for the last four seasons

Newcomers

Marvin Bagley III

	Height	Weight	Cap #	Years Left
	6'11"	234	$7.306M	1 + 2 TO

Baseline Basic Stats

MPG	PTS	AST	REB	BLK	STL
26.8	11.7	1.4	5.5	0.7	0.7

Advanced Metrics

USG%	3PTA/FGA	FTA/FGA	TS%	eFG%	3PT%
21.4	0.140	0.326	0.525	0.482	0.327

AST%	TOV%	OREB%	DREB%	STL%	BLK%
9.1	12.9	7.2	16.3	1.4	1.9

PER	ORTG	DRTG	WS/48	VOL
14.87	103.6	107.4	0.077	N/A

- Drafted by Sacramento in the first round with the 2nd overall pick
- Inconsistent in Summer League before being pulled due to a pelvic bone bruise, should be ready for training camp
- Forced up too many outside shots in Sacramento, shot below 32% from the field, did not go to the offensive glass in either Summer League
- Better in Vegas, played inside more, scored in volume but not efficiently, shot under 40% from the field, drew fouls at a high rate
- Good shot blocker and defensive rebounder, position defense still needs work
- Struggled to defend on the ball, prone to lapses when making defensive rotations

Harry Giles

	Height	Weight	Cap #	Years Left
	6'10"	240	$2.207M	2 Team Options

Baseline Basic Stats

MPG	PTS	AST	REB	BLK	STL
15.3	5.9	0.6	3.7	0.6	0.4

Advanced Metrics

USG%	3PTA/FGA	FTA/FGA	TS%	eFG%	3PT%
18.3	0.100	0.299	0.533	0.502	0.312

AST%	TOV%	OREB%	DREB%	STL%	BLK%
5.9	13.1	9.5	18.2	1.2	2.9

PER	ORTG	DRTG	WS/48	VOL
13.64	106.0	107.8	0.085	N/A

- Drafted by Portland with the 20th overall pick in 2017, then traded to Sacramento
- Missed all of last season while recovering from his past knee injuries
- Got increasingly more effective as Summer League went on
- Active as help defender, solid rebounder on both ends, good at getting deflections and steals
- Below the rim interior defender as a result of the injuries, played decent position defense
- Scored in volume but not efficiently, played more as a mid-range shooter, rarely drew fouls or got to the rim
- Flashed some decent passing skills, but was highly turnover prone

My 2018-19 NBA Predictions

If you have gotten this far, you have seen how my RAFER projection system has forecasted every player and team in the NBA. For the most part, my personal evaluations are in line with the system, but I have some disagreements based on my own eye test. As a result, I will go through and give you my adjustments to provide the best estimation as to how this upcoming NBA season might play out.

Eastern Conference

	RAFER Rankings		My Rankings
1	Toronto	1	Toronto
2	Boston	2	Boston
3	Philadelphia	3	Philadelphia
4	Washington	4	**Milwaukee**
5	Milwaukee	5	**Miami**
6	Miami	6	**Indiana**
7	Charlotte	7	**Washington**
8	Detroit	8	**Charlotte**
9	Indiana	9	**Detroit**
10	Cleveland	10	Cleveland
11	Brooklyn	11	Brooklyn
12	New York	12	New York
13	Orlando	13	Orlando
14	Atlanta	14	**Chicago**
15	Chicago	15	**Atlanta**

Based on the eye test, I moved Milwaukee up to the fourth seed because the combination of the talent of Giannis Antetokounmpo and the coaching system of Mike Budenholzer could cause the Bucks to outperform the projections a bit. Also, I think Indiana has a better chance to make the playoffs than my system is giving it because they probably have more talent than either Charlotte or Detroit. I moved Washington down because historically, Dwight Howard has been something of a chemistry disruption in recent years and there has been no evidence to suggest that he has changed his ways, so the Wizards' record could take a hit. I then had Charlotte beating out Detroit for the eighth seed because the Hornets are simply a much deeper team than the Pistons. Finally, Atlanta may be more likely to have the East's worst record because their roster is probably not going to be same at the end of the season. They will probably sell off a few of their veterans like Kent Bazemore and Jeremy Lin at the deadline to get assets and bump up their lottery odds.

Western Conference

	RAFER Rankings		My Rankings
1	Golden State	1	Golden State
2	Houston	2	Houston
3	Oklahoma City	3	Oklahoma City
4	Minnesota	4	**Utah**
5	Utah	5	**San Antonio**
6	San Antonio	6	**L.A. Lakers**
7	New Orleans	7	**Minnesota**
8	L.A. Lakers	8	**New Orleans**
9	Denver	9	Denver
10	L.A. Clippers	10	L.A. Clippers
11	Portland	11	Portland
12	Dallas	12	Dallas
13	Memphis	13	Memphis
14	Phoenix	14	Phoenix
15	Sacramento	15	Sacramento

I project the same eight teams to make the playoffs but just in a different order. I moved Minnesota down because though they have talent, their pieces don't quite fit together like they do in Utah or San Antonio. As a result, Utah and San Antonio were moved up because not only do they have talent, they each have a well-organized team structure that helps to maximize talent. Then, the Lakers were bumped up because the system may be underestimating the potential impact of their acquisition of LeBron James. Finally, New Orleans may drop off a bit because they are incorporating weaker defenders into their rotation and their defense will take a hit as a result. However, they still should make the playoffs because they simply may have enough complementary talent around Anthony Davis to consistently win games in the Western Conference.

Playoffs

First Round

- (E) 1. Toronto over 8. Charlotte (4 - 1)
- (E) 2. Boston over 7. Washington (4 - 1)
- (E) 3. Philadelphia over 6. Indiana (4 - 3)
- (E) 4. Milwaukee over 5. Miami (4 - 2)
- (W) 1. Golden State over 8. New Orleans (4 - 0)
- (W) 2. Houston over 7. Minnesota (4 - 1)
- (W) 6. L.A. Lakers over 3. Oklahoma City (4 - 3)
- (W) 4. Utah over 5. San Antonio (4 - 3)

Second Round

- (E) 4. Milwaukee over 1. Toronto (4 - 3)
- (E) 2. Boston over 3. Philadelphia (4 - 1)
- (W) 1. Golden State over 4. Utah (4 - 1)
- (W) 2. Houston over 6. L.A. Lakers (4 - 3)

Conference Finals

- (E) 2. Boston over 4. Milwaukee (4 - 2)
- (W) 1. Golden State over 2. Houston (4 - 2)

NBA Finals

- (W) Golden State over (E) Boston (4 - 1)

THANK YOU

Thank you to everybody responsible for putting this preview almanac together. For anyone that made the request for me to put this book out after reading any of my two previous books, thank you very much for supporting my work and I hope you enjoy this one. If you are reading my work for the first time, thank you for reading this and hopefully you will pick up the next one set to come out in June of 2019. If you have any questions or comments, please feel free to contact me through the information I provided in the credits section. Thanks once again, I hope you continue to support my work and I look forward to putting out more books in the future for all of you to enjoy.

Player Index

Made in the USA
Las Vegas, NV
20 July 2021